F. P. Stephanoff. L. Stocks.

Portrait of Her Majesty.

London Published by Longman & Co. Feby 1840.

THE
BOOK OF ARCHERY

GEORGE AGAR HANSARD

The Naval & Military Press Ltd

published in association with

ROYAL
ARMOURIES

Published by
The Naval & Military Press Ltd
Unit 10 Ridgewood Industrial Park,
Uckfield, East Sussex,
TN22 5QE England
Tel: +44 (0) 1825 749494
Fax: +44 (0) 1825 765701
www.naval-military-press.com

in association with

ROYAL
ARMOURIES

In reprinting in facsimile from the original, any imperfections are inevitably reproduced and the quality may fall short of modern type and cartographic standards.

THE BOOK OF ARCHERY

BY

GEORGE AGAR HANSARD, ESQ:

GWENT BOWMAN.

Robin Hood and Maid Marian.

LONDON.
LONGMAN, ORME, BROWN, GREEN, AND LONGMANS
1840.

INTRODUCTION.

READER; the wisdom of our ancestors has said,—

"Speak well of archers, for your father shot in a bow,"—

a time-honoured proverb, originating in that martial age, when her sons deemed

"England not worth a fling,
But for the crooked yew and grey goose wing."

Yet is there a hold upon your sympathies far more powerful than a thousand wise saws or modern instances, such as these;— I mean the strong propensity of youth and age for recreations which unbend the mental faculties, while the body enjoys the exhilarating influence of sun and summer breeze, which tempt us to climb the upland lawn, plunge into the deep rocky glyn, wander over fern-clad heaths, and wend our way through the shadowy, pathless woods. These advantages are the archer's; his are the glories of sea, earth, and sky, with all the pleasures of the young and opening year; for his pastime belongs to that fair season only, when, as the old forest glee has it,—

"Summer is coming in,
Merry sing cuckoo!
Groweth seed,
And bloweth mead,
And springeth the wood anew;
Ewe bleateth after lamb.
Loweth after calf, cow;
Bullock starteth,
Buck verteth,
Merry sing cuckoo;
Well sing'st thou cuckoo,
Nor cease to sing now."

For the body, archery provides a wholesome and graceful exercise: to the mind it proves a source of a thousand romantic speculations, since its history is a brief chronicle of England's martial daring, for at least six centuries. "I am no stranger unto you," says a curious treatise, by an old writer, entitled *The Lament of the Bow;* "but by birth your countrywoman, by dwelling your neighbour, by education your familiar; neither is my company shameful, for I haunt the light and open fields; nor my conversation dangerous — nay, it shields you from dangers, and those not the least, the dangers of warre. And as in fight I give you protection, so in peace I supply you pastime; to your limbs I yield active plyantnesse, and to your bodies healthful exercise; yea, I provide you food when you are hungry, and help digestion when you are full. Whence then proceedeth this unkinde and unusual strangenesse? Am I heavy for burden? Forsooth, a few stickes of light wood. Am I cumbrous for carriage? I couch a part of me close under your girdle, and the other part serveth for a walking stick in your hand. Am I unhandsome in your sight? Every piece of me is comely, and the whole keepeth an harmonious proportion. I appeale to your valiant princes, Edwards and Henries; to the battles of Cressy, Poictiers, Agincourt, and Flodden; to the regions of Scotland, France, Spain, Italy, Cyprus, yea and Jury, to be umpires of the controversie: all of which, I doubt not, will with their evidence plainly prove, that when my adverse party * was yet scarcely born, or lay in her swathling clouts, through me only your ancestors defended their country, vanquished their enemies, succoured their friends, enlarged their dominions, advanced their religion, and made their names fearful to the present age, and their fame everlasting to those that ensue. Wherefore, my dear friends, seeing I have so substantially evicted the right of my cause, conform your wills to reason, confirm your reason by practice, and convert your practice to the good of your countrie. If I be praiseworthy,

---

* Fire-arms.

esteem mee; if necessary, admit mee; if profitable, employ mee: so shall you revoke my death to life, and shew yourself no degenerate issue of such honourable progenitors. And thus much for archery, whose tale, if it be disordered, you must bear withall, for she is a woman, and her minde is passionate."

There is an energetic spirit in this passage, sufficient to rouse the sympathies of even the most apathetic. And, indeed, whether the " mead of the green archer be battled for in the target ground," accompanied with all the pomp and circumstance of banners, pavilions, and strains of martial music; or whether, in our lonely rambles, we seek to strike the cushat from the tall pine's topmost spray, or transfix the dusky cormorant, as with outstretched neck and flagging wings, she rises from the shingled beach, to seek her rocky home in some far off islet of the sea,—there are few of us, I believe, who, at such moments, do not in imagination ante-date existence a century or two, identifying ourselves with those greenwood rovers, as we see them on the title-page; and whose vocation and feelings are thus shadowed forth:—

> " For my profession then, and for the life I lead,
> All others to excel, thus for myself I plead.
> I am the prince of sports—the forest is my fee!
> He's not upon the earth for pleasure lives like me.
> The morn no sooner puts her rosy mantle on,
> But from my quiet lodge I instantly am gone,
> When the melodious birds, from every bush and briar
> Of the wide spacious wastes, make a continual choir.
> The mottled meadows there, new varnished by the sun,
> Shoot up their spicy sweets upon the winds that run
> In every ambling gale; and softly seem to pace,
> That too the longer night their richness may embrace.
> As princes and great lords have palaces, so I
> Have in the forest here my hall and gallery;
> The tall and stately woods, which underneath are plain;
> The groves my gardens are; the heath and downs again
> My wide and spacious walks: then say all what ye can,
> The forester is still your only gallant man."

Having thus thrust our dashing woodsman upon the stage, to deliver his own prologue, as I hope before a prepossessed and admiring audience, allow him further to illustrate the universal popularity of his art, by a few of those picturesque proverbial expressions having reference to the bow, by which, in the lapse of ages, our own, as well as every other European language, has been enriched. And though most of our early poets indulge in this favourite species of illustration, none have so happily applied the technicalities of his craft as Shakspeare, himself a practised bowman. Of this, a hundred quotations scattered over the following pages shall bear ample testimony, in addition to what we know touching his midnight visitations to Sir Thomas Lucy's deer park. Thus :—

" At the Duke's Oak we meet;
Hold, or cut bowstrings."

The tardy forester, who lingered behind his fellows, already assembled at the place of tryst, had his bowstring divided by those who were more punctual in their arrival ; and the penalty, though trifling, was probably sufficient to hold him regular to his duty, at least for a considerable period. The phrase, however, naturally escaping beyond the purlieus of vert and venison, became engrafted, with a multitude besides, now completely obsolete, on the colloquial style of Shakspeare's age.

" He hath twice or thrice cut Cupid's bowstring," says Don Pedro in the Comedy of *Much Ado about Nothing ;* " and the little hangman dare not shoot at him."

" Alas, poor Romeo! the very pin of his heart
Cleft with Cupid's buttshaft."

" Buttshaft," a blunt arrow ; the pin is a wooden peg, thrust through the centre of the white paper, fixed as a mark upon the butt.

" You are better at proverbs, by how much a fool's bolt is soon shot."

" Indeed he must shoot nearer, or he'll ne'er hit the white."

" He shoots wide of the mark," says the Clown Costard, in reference to a vague foolish guess.

In their figurative application, the following will be considered extremely terse and significant:—

" An archer is known by his aim, not by his arrows;"

" But you," says Euphues in his *England*, " aim so ill, that if you knew how far from the white your shaft lighteth, you would rather break your bow than bend it."

" Every man will shoot at the foe, but few will gather up the shafts."

" He will shoot higher that shoots at the moon, than he who shoots at a dunghill, though he miss the mark."

" Draw not thy bow before thy arrow be fixed."

" A word spoken, is an arrow let fly."

" Swift as an arrow," " Upright as a bolt "* —

are phrases still familiar to every one. Even at the present day, we—" Kill two birds with one shaft;" and,—" Get the shaft hand of our adversaries."

Like Sir Abel Handy in the play, your unready Englishman of ancient days had always —

" A famous bow, but 't was up at the Castle."

---

* Wincing she was, as is a jolly colt,
Tall as a lance, and upright as a bolt."

Our ancestors expressed liberality of sentiment, and their opinion that merit belonged exclusively to no particular class or locality, by the following pithy adage : —

" Many a good bow besides one in Chester."*

When familiar with the foibles of friend or foe, they had —

" Found the measure of his shaft."

The triumph of making an enemy's machinations recoil upon himself, was, —

" To outshoot a man in his own bow."

Of silly unprofitable conversation, they said, —

" A fool's bolt, soon shot."

The maiden who kept a lover in reserve, lest her first admirer should prove faithless, was said to have —

" Two strings to her bow."†

And of vain-glorious gasconade, they satirically remarked, that,—

" Many talked of Robin Hood, who never shot in his bow."

" Debander l'arc ne guérit pas la playe."

" A wound is not healed by the unbending of the bow," —

is an elegant French proverb, implying that mere sorrow is an insufficient atonement for serious wrong.

They say likewise, —

" Ceste flêche n'est pas sortie de mon carquois."
" That arrow came not out of my quiver."

---

* Anciently famous for manufacturing implements of archery.
† The military archers used a double string in the field, to prevent delay in refitting the bow in case of accident.

INTRODUCTION.

"Faire de tous bois flêches."

"To make a shaft of any wood"

"Even the holy man of God will be better with his bow and arrows about him."*

"Nid hyder ond bwa." †

"No dependence like the bow."

"Mal y saith err llynin." ‡

"He that shoots always straight, forfeits his arrow."

In the body of this work, the bow is considered merely in reference to itself, no comparison being attempted with what Carew quaintly calls the " hell-born murderer," to which in modern days it has given place. Men, in general, look upon the arrow as a good enough means of offence whilst no better missile existed, but treat as mere absurdity the attempt to place it upon an equality with the bullet. Let us see, and cite before us to this intent Sir John Smyth§, a gallant veteran, who wielded sword and pen in the days of Queen Bess, and had been long accustomed to view the effects of archers and musketeers in the battle field. The change effected in the military weapons of this kingdom, says he, " was owing to the youth, inexperience, and vanity of some men, who were unable to offer any solid reason, and, in fact, were averse to offer any reason at all, for a conduct opposite to the opinion of soldiers, both English and foreign ; and therefore for the experience, I, and many others, both noblemen, gentlemen, and great captains

---

* Irish. † Welsh. ‡ Ibid.
§ Discourse on Weapons, MSS. Lansd. Collection.

of many nations, whom I have served amongst, have had of the small effects of weapons of fire in the field, with the reasons before alleged; for my part, I will never doubt to adventure my life, or many lives, if I had them, amongst eight thousand archers complete, well chosen and appointed, and therewithal provided with great store of sheaves of arrows, as also with a good overplus of bows and bowstrings, against twenty thousand of the best arquebusseers that are in Christendom. Now I, and divers other gentlemen of our nation, yet living, that were in France in King Edward the Sixth's time, and also many times since, have frequently heard French captains and gentlemen attribute all former victories of the English, against themselves and their ancestors the French, more to the effect of our archers than to any extraordinary valliance of our nation; and therewithal further report, that they did think the English archers used to poison their arrow-heads, because that of great numbers of the French nation, that many times had been wounded or hurt with arrows, very few had escaped with their lives, by reason that their wounds did so imposthume, they could not be cured. In which conceits, they did greatly err; because, in truth, these imposthumations proceeded of nothing else but of the rust of the arrow-heads remaining rankling in their wounds; and, therefore, by the experience of our ancient enemies, not only the great, but the small wounds of our arrows have been always found more dangerous and hard to be cured, than the fire of any shot unpoisoned. Besides all which, it is to be noted that horses in the field, being wounded or but slightly hurt with arrows, do presently fall yerking, flinging, and leaping as if they were mad, through the great pain that upon every motion they do feel in their flesh, veins, and sinews, by the shaking of the arrows with their barbed heads hanging in them. In such sort, as be it in squadron or in troop, they do disorder one another, and never leave until they have cast their masters. Whereas, contrariwise, horses that are in their vital parts hurt with bullets, they, after the first shrink at the entering of the bullet, do pass their carriere as though they had very little or no hurt. And this of the hurting of horses with bullets, both I myself, and all others do know, that have seen any actions performed in the field.

"In one time, King Henry the Eighth, being at the siege of Terouenne, a convoy of provisions was coming from Guines towards Terouenne; the French captains of Picardy and Vermandois having intelligence of it, assembled all the men-at-arms, arquebusseers, and crossbowmen, and lay in ambush; which being perceived by the English, they so placed their archers, that after a long fight, and many charges by the French men-at-arms and their shot given, they far exceeding the English in number, the French having a number of horses wounded and slain, were completely repulsed and overthrown by the excellence of the archers."

The mean opinion entertained of fire-arms by Sir John Smyth and other military writers of the same period, has been erroneously accounted for, by presuming that the guns of the sixteenth and seventeenth centuries were excessively unmanageable, and the powder coarse and deficient in strength. There is, however, little difficulty in showing this opinion to be entirely without foundation. Two centuries ago, at all events, they were not so badly off. A well-supported tradition exists among the Worcester folk, that the day before old Noll's "second crowning mercy,"* Prince Rupert and his staff amused themselves with ball practice, at the weathercock of Pershore church. We may hence infer, that both pistols and ammunition were somewhat after the rate; but we have better evidences than mere oral testimony.

"The Pilhaunan," says Josseleyn, " is the king of birds of prey in New England.† Some take him for a kind of eagle,

---
* So he used to term his victory at Worcester.
† Voyage to New England, 1644.

others for the Indian rock, the biggest bird that is, except the ostrich. Mr. Hilton, residing at Pascatawny, had the hap to kill one of them. Being by the sea side, he perceived a great shadowe over his head, the sun shining out clear. Casting up his eyes, he saw a monstrous bird soaring aloft in the air; and of a sudden, all the ducks and geese (there being a great many) diving under water, nothing of them appearing but their heads. Mr. Hilton having made ready his piece, shot and brought her down to the earth. How he disposed of her I know not; but had he taken her alive and sent her over to England, neither Bartholomewe nor Greenwich fair could have produced such another sighte."* Here we have a sportsman of Charles the First's time, who *shoots flying with single ball;* for as well might he have pelted a bird of that size with peas, as with small shot.

There is an old tract, entitled " The Arrival and Entertainment of the Embassador Olkaid Jaura Ben Abdallah, from Morocco," A. D. 1637. Speaking of this illustrious Moor, the author says: " He is so good a marksman with his piece, that he will shoot *eight score* at a mark as big as an English sixpence, and hit it with a round bullet." My next evidence is taken from the French traveller Thevenot, not a very modern authority either. " I remember," says he, " a janissary belonging to the French consul at Cairo, having on a time charged his piece with a bullet of size, shot at two turtles on a tree; he struck off the head of one, and pierced the other through the body." †

" We came to Namaschet," says the account of a journey to

---

* " Were I in England now as once I was, and had but this fish painted, not a holiday fool but would give a piece of silver; there would this monster make a man — any strange beast there makes a man; when they will not give a doit to relieve a lame beggar, they will lay down ten to see a dead Indian." — *Tempest.*

† Travels in the Levant, p. 72.

Packanock, the habitation of the great king Massassoye, written in 1620, " about three in the afternoon. The inhabitants entertained us with joy in the best manner they could, giving us a kind of bread by them called maizian, and the spawn of shads, which then they got in abundance, but we had no spoones to eat them. With these, they boiled musty acorns; yet of the shads we eat heartily. After this, they desired one of our men to shoot at a crow, complaining what damage they sustained in their corn by them; who shooting one some *four score yards off*, and killing, they much admired it, as they did our shots on other occasions."

" After dinner, Massassowal desired me to get him a goose or a duck, and make him some pottage therewith, as speedily as I could. So I took a man with me, and made a shot at a couple of ducks some six score off, and killed one; at which he wondered." *

After perusing these anecdotes, I think no one can hesitate to admit that at the period when mere handsful of our yeomen archers engaged successfully with large bodies of musketeers, guns and ammunition, as well as the skill of those who handled them, were, for all practical purposes, almost as near perfection as could be desired. And still, as we approach our own time, it will be found that the same results invariably followed every attempt to bring into comparison the merits of the two weapons. During the month of August, 1792, a match was decided at Pacton Green, Cumberland, between the gun and the bow, at one hundred yards. Victory fell to the latter, which put sixteen arrows into the target; the former only twelve balls. During, the same year, a similar contest took place at Chalk Farm between Mr. Glynn of the Toxophilite Society, and Dr. Higgins of Greek Street, Soho; distance also one hundred yards. The result was, that out of twenty-one shots each at a four-foot target, the former gentleman scored fifteen, the latter only twelve.

* Good News from New England, 1621.

And now let me wind up a somewhat tedious exordium, with one or two observations respecting the nature and execution of this volume. Many years of my life have been devoted to its arrangement, for, like Rome, the work contemplated was not to be finished in a day. Those public stores of history, accessible to all who have patience and industry to consult them; traditionary anecdotes, never heard beyond the locality which was the scene of the events they commemorate; and those almost unknown, faded or fading archives, which lie mouldering within the muniment chests of many an honourable family, have been rifled of their treasures to illustrate the history of a weapon, by which Britons secured their freedom, while many a bloody field was lost and won.

But labor ipse voluptas; the labour we delight in physics pain; yet, if, in the general execution of his task, to borrow the congenial phraseology of the shooting ground, the author should have failed to deliver himself " right yeomanlie and well," he alone is to blame, the subject being not deficient either in interest or materials; neither can he plead want of familiarity with the grey goose quill — truly, he

" Claims kindred there, and has his claim allow'd ;"

for during years past, *that* has been his constant associate, more, however, as the wing of many a goodly buttshaft than as tenant of the author's inkhorn. Let those who form the public taste decide; but after whatever shape they may handle me, whether mercifully forbearing their shafts, or making me the butt whereon to empty their quivers' " iron sleet of arrowy shower," one thing is more than probable; from the days when a congenial spirit, I mean Tom Shawn Catti, the Robin Hood of Wales, here first drew his unerring bowstring, even to the present hour, no mortal except myself has sojourned within these wild and lonesome glyns, to whom criticism was a source of anxiety either in its smiles or frowns.

I cannot close these pages, without offering my grateful acknowledgments to the artists whose labours have embellished the *Book of Archery*. For the imaginative portion of these illustrations, I am indebted to the pencil of F. P. Stephanoff, Esq.; and to the burins of Messrs. Portbury, Engleheart, Stocks, Staines, Bull, and Smith. The historical plates are designed and executed by W. H. Brooke, Esq., F.S.A., whose indefatigable researches, during a space of upwards of two years, merit my warmest thanks, since they have produced a series of upwards of one hundred subjects, which, for classical truth and correctness of detail, leave nothing to be desired.

Machynlleth, South Wales,
Dec. 1839.

TABLE OF CONTENTS.

Section I.—JUVENILE BOWMEN.

	Page
State of archery before the Conquest	1
After that event: Shakspeare: Anecdote	3
Adroitness of English bowmen	4
Dreaded by the French: Proverbial expressions	5
Harry V.: Sir N. H. Nicholas's Battle of Agincourt: Wars of the Roses	6
Drayton: Battle of Towton	7
Paston letter	8
Old English foresters	9
Robin Hood: Anecdote of Bishop Latimer	10
Life and death of Robin Hood	11
Goths and Persians: Caribbee Indians	13
Anecdotes	14
Scandinavian boys: Bashkir archers	17
Margravine of Anspach: Young Indians of Demerara: Catabuwa warriors at Sadler's Wells	18
Bows of Indian children: Tupinamba archers	20
Floridan archers	21
Anecdotes	22
Remarkable instance of skilful shooting	25
Manilla archers	26
Oriental book of archery	26
Soldier and snake	27
Anecdotes of young Tartar bowmen	31
Chinese arrows	33
Mameluke archers	35
Bow and arrow symbolical	36
Henry VIII. at Field of Cloth of Gold	37
Privy-purse expenses	40
Henry VII.	41
Edward VI.: Princes Henry and Charles	42
Lord de Vesci	44
Feud of Elland	45
Wages of old English archer	51
Martin Expence	53
John Pearson: Wat Tinlinn: Richard Arundel	54
Robert Bone, of Antony: The archer Coles: Left-handed bowman: Death of Lord de Lisle: Barons of Berkeley	56
Archers and knights	58
Kynge and Hermyt	59
Friar Tuck	60
King John	61
Eton and Harrow: Roger Ascham	62
Archery at Harrow school	65

Section II.—EQUIPMENTS OF YOUNG ARCHER.

	Page
Stringing the bow	73
Battle of Cressy: An archer's day	75
Shakspearian rules: Standing	76
John de Rous: Poetical sketch of ancient archer	77

TABLE OF CONTENTS.

	Page
Nocking arrow	78
Handling arrow: Shakspeare's directions for recovering lost shaft	79
Crescentius de Re Rustica	81
Holding: Drawing: Loosing	82
Handling: Bowstring: Drawing: Drawing fingers respected among cannibals	83
Rules for straight shooting	84
Anecdote	85
Point blanc shooting	86
Rules for modern bow meetings	87
Awkward squad of archers	98
Shakspeare	99
Belt: Bracer: Shooting glove	101
Description of ancient bracer	102
Gloves	103
Ancient prices	104
Bowstrings	105
Female patriotism ; Indian suicide	106
Cutting bowstring	107
Archer's marks: Dr. Nott	108
Butt fields	109
Modern butts	110
Laughable anecdote	112
Targets	113
Target card	115
Flight shooting: Roman targets: Fire shafts	116
Oriental target: Confucius: Chinese archery	117
Archery at Constantinople	119
Equestrian archery: Anecdote	121

Section III.—FEMALE ARCHERY.

	Page
Star of the archers	126
Bow meetings in harem of the Shah: Penthesilea: Bow meetings; their effect on fate and fortunes of the fair	129
Earl of Arran, character of	130
Oriental shooting grounds	131
Persian bowyers: Death by bowstring	134
Oriental mode of bracing bow	135
Persian arrows: Sefin or thumb rings	136
Bracer: Flight shooting	137
Female archer guard	138
Tartar archeress	139
Anecdote of Eastern Queen	141
Tasso's Clorinda	142
Black Agnes	143
Anecdotes of female archers	145
Anna Boleyn	146
Queen Bess and Cadenham oak	147
Advantages of the bow as a female pastime	150
Her Majesty Queen Victoria	151
Marchioness of Salisbury's archery: Diploma	152
Archery fêtes at Grove House: Hon. Mrs. Crespigny	153
Miss Littledale	156
Ladies' archery dresses	157
Catalogue of skilful bow-women	158

Section IV.—WELSH ARCHERY.

	Page
Antiquity of bow: Flint arrow heads: Sir R. C. Hoare	162
Declarations of peace and war: Howel Dha	163
Bow of war and peace	164
Anecdotes	165
Price of Welsh bow and arrows	167
Twenty-four Welsh games: Hunting	168
Anecdote of Rhys Wyn	169
Welsh improvisatori: Gwinddelw, Homer of Welsh Bards	169
Sheriff's breakfast	171
Davyth ap Gwilym, the Archer Bard	173
Gilded bows	177
Gwilym's frequent allusions to archery	178

	Page		Page
Beautiful address to skylark	179	Davyth ap Gwilym and "Hunchback," his rival	190
Recapitulation of youthful accomplishments; address to the Wind	179	Sir Howell of the Pole Axe	191
Shooting matches	180	Anecdote of Welsh cross-bowman	192
Jevan ap Robert, archer and bishop's cook	181	Howel Sele, or the Goblin's Hollow Oak	194
Admirable portrait of a Welsh archer	182	Archers of Gwentland	199
Curious domestic habits: Squire's Yeoman	186	Harry of Monmouth: David Gam and his brave comrades in arms	201
Remarkable shot	187	Cambro-Britons to their harp	203
Anecdote	188	Society of Royal British Bowmen	206
Cross-bow unpopular in Wales	189		

Section V. — FRENCH ARCHERY.

Ineffectual attempts to cultivate archery in France	208	Modern bowmen of Paris and Chantilly	222
Book of King Modus, an ancient treatise on the bow	211	Flemish archery	224

Section VI. — THE CROSSBOW.

French and Spanish crossbow	226	The prodd	238
Companies for practice of this weapon	227	Curious wager	239
Description of French and Flemish crossbow	228	Death of Richard Cœur-de-Lion	240
Bolt-in-Tun	229	Rufus Oak: Sir Walter Tyrrel	244
Description of a perfect crossbow	231	Scene from Shakspeare	249
Extreme range of ditto	232	Fatal accident of Archbishop Abbot	250
Spanish hunter's crossbow	233	Baron de Chantal	252
Crossbowmen highly esteemed in Spain: Bolts and quarrils	236	Suicide of Sir William Hankford	253
Stone-bow	237	Killing poachers: Singular duel with crossbow	255
		Battle with Indian chief	257
		Anecdotes	258

Section VII. — SOCIETIES OF MODERN ARCHERS.

Latest appearance of archers in battle-field	260	Battle of Blore Heath	265
Prince Arthur's knights	262	Long Jamie	266
Richmond archers: Sir Walter Raleigh	263	Revival of archery: George IV.	267
Anecdote: Queen Elizabeth's body guard	264	List of modern societies	268
		Royal Toxophilites	270

	Page
Toxophilite mania: Anecdotes of Roger Ascham	273
Thomson the poet	274
Prince George and Littlejohn	276
Grand meeting of archers	277
Anderson	279
Sir W. Wood, Marshal of Finsbury archers	280
Anecdotes of skilful modern bowmen	283
Royal Toxophilite shooting grounds	285
Woodmen of Forest of Arden	286
Trysting tree	288
Bow-bearer: Tenures by archery	289
Meetings of woodmen of Arden	291
List of original members	292
Winners of prizes	293
Herefordshire bowmen, &c.	297
ROYAL EDINBURGH ARCHERS: QUEEN'S BODY GUARD FOR SCOTLAND	301
Early history	302
Present state	303
Verses to the Duke of Hamilton	304
Royal charter: Costume: Public processions	305
Chief prizes	306
Anecdotes: Goose shooting	310
Poems addressed to Royal Company of Archers	311
Gift of colours to body guard by George IV.: Perth archers	315
Anecdote: Grenadiers of Highland regiments	316
Church militant: Calum Dhu	317

SECTION VIII.—YEW TREES, YEW BOWS, &c.

	Page
Growth of yew	325
Its ancient value	326
Yew trees in village churchyards	327
Longevity of the yew: Mr. Jesse	328
Motives for planting yews around the church: Welsh cemeteries	331
Yew: where found plentifully	333
The oak: King Richard in Sherwood Forest	335
Foresters' oaks	337
Forest laws	338
Self and backed bows	340
Observations on the Toxophilus	345
Bows of bamboo	346
Powerful shooting	347
Anecdotes in refutation of Humphrey Barwick: Return of killed and wounded	348
Description of ancient yew bow	351
Peculiar formation of old English bow	352
Rules for bowmaking	353
Modern bowyers: Foreign bow woods	358
Polishing bows	359
An Ascham	360

SECTION IX.—POWER OF MODERN BOWS.

	Page
Shooting short lengths: Ancient statutes	362
Anecdote	363
Enchanted arrows	366
Shooting in public: Sketch of perfect bowman	367
Choice of bows	368

SECTION X.—THE SHAFT.

	Page
Toxophilus, a meagre production compared with "Contemplative Man's Recreation"	371
Droll anecdote	372
Length of ancient arrows	375
Chevy Chase	376

	Page		Page
Cornish archers	377	Peacock's feathers	390
Kempe on ancient arrows at Cothele	378	Eagle's ditto: Old English archers	391
Sir S. R. Meyrick: List of arrow woods	382	Art of winging arrows	393
		War, butt, and roving piles	394
Droll contest between fletchers and patten makers	384	Arrow marks	394
		Barbed and poisoned arrows	394
Piecing arrows	386	Zisca: Death of Harold	397
Guiana Indian shafts: Anecdote: Specimen of old English arrow at Goodrich Court	387	Edith of the Swan's Neck: Indian breastplate	398
		Ludicrous anecdote of a friar	399
Turkish and English arrow nocks: Feathering	388	Indian suicide	400
		Messire Ambroise Paré: Mode of treating arrow wounds	402
Unfledged arrows: Lieut. Gore and Tabourai Tamaide: Consumption of goose feathers: Anecdote	389	Anecdotes: Indian arrows for bleeding	405

Section XI. — ROVING OR RURAL ARCHERY.

The somnambulist archer: Necessity of constant practice out of shooting ground	406	Fauna gooma, or rat-shooting in South Sea Islands	412
Heron shooting	408	Popinjay shooting: Fine poetical description: Anderson's archery ground	416
Rabbit ditto: Britton Ferry	409		
Birding bows	410	"Ayme for Finsbury archers:" A. Kempe, F.S.A.	417
Archer's decoy birds	411		

Section XII. — GREEK AND ROMAN ARCHERY.

Symmetry of Grecian bow	423	Ulysses: His position whilst shooting	434
Of what materials composed: Homer's description	424	Piercing oaken portals	436
Goat horns: Pashley's Crete	425	Athenian archer guard: St. John's Athens and Sparta	437
Archery of Teshoo Lama: Anecdote of horn bow	427	Anecdote of Scythian bowmen: Julius Africanus: Calculation of arrow's flight	438
Ancient figures from island of Egina	428		
Drawing bowstring to the breast	429	Smyrnus the Scythian: Bardisanes the Parthian	439
Gibbon: Odyssey	430	Roman archer's dicipline	440
Penelope mourning over the bow of Ulysses: Oriental bow-cases	431	Gratian: Commodus: Domitian	441
		Cambyses and Prexaspes	442
Grecian marks	432	Aster and King Philip	446
Anecdote	433	Conclusion: Song	447

POSITION OF THE PLATES.

PORTRAIT OF HER MAJESTY, IN AN ARCHERY COSTUME.
Engraved by L. STOCKS - - - - FRONTISPIECE.
ROBIN HOOD AND MAID MARIAN. Engraved by L. STOCKS   TITLEPAGE.
DEATH OF ROBIN HOOD. Engraved by R. STAINES   *to face Page* 12
HENRY VIII. AT THE FIELD OF THE CLOTH OF GOLD.
Engraved by CHARLES FOX - - - - ... 38
FEUD OF ELLAND. Engraved by R. STAINES - - ... 49
ORIENTAL FEMALE ARCHERY. Engraved by E. PORTBURY ... 130
PERSIAN ARCHERS. Engraved by F. ENGLEHEART - ... 135
THE TARTAR MAID. Engraved by F. ENGLEHEART - ... 140
QUEEN ELIZABETH SHOOTING A BUCK IN COWDERAY
PARK. Engraved by E. PORTBURY - - - ... 148
THE BOW OF PEACE AND WAR. Engraved by J. HOLLIS ... 164
Y PAUN BACH. Engraved by R. STAINES - - ... 183
DEATH OF WILLIAM RUFUS. Engraved by C. FOX - ... 247
CALLUM DHU. Engraved by E. BULL - - - ... 324
EDITH OF THE SWAN NECK DISCOVERING THE BODY OF
HAROLD, AFTER THE BATTLE OF HASTINGS. Engraved
by E. SMITH - - - - - ... 398
ULYSSES DESTROYING HIS WIFE'S SUITORS. Engraved by
L. STOCKS - - - - - - ... 434

OUTLINES OF ILLUSTRATIONS, with DESCRIPTIONS prefixed, to be placed at the end of the Volume.

THE BOOK OF ARCHERY.

SECTION I.

JUVENILE BOWMEN.*

Sir boy, now let us see your archery,
Look you *draw home enough*, and 'tis there straight.
Titus Andronicus.

Ye children of Englande, for the honor of the same,
Take bowe and shafts in hande, learn shootinge to frame,
That ye another day may soe playe your partes,
As to serve your prince as well with handes as heartes.
  Sing up hearte, sing up hearte, be never caste downe,
  But joye in Kinge Edward that weareth the crowne.
Archers' Chorus at Coronation of Edward the Sixth.

———— Delightful task,
To teach the young idea how to *shoot!*

For ages anterior to the Conquest, the inhabitants of Britain held archery in little estimation, except as an appliance of sylvan sport, when her chieftains sought relief from the tedium of domestic tranquillity, by warring upon the antlered denizens of the waste. Besides a preference for other weapons,

* Three words of the motto from Shakspeare, printed in italics, are worth a whole chapter of Ascham.

  Fight, gentlemen of England — fight, bold yeomen;
  Draw, archers — draw your arrows *to the head!*

is merely a repetition of the same important element of good shooting. Failing in that, the archer shall fail of his mark, ten arrows out of twelve,

the sportsman, necessarily habituated to a bow of feeble range*, grew mistrustful of its powers in more serious contests, those mightier huntings, where the game was man.

But " Norman William came," and on the blood-stained field of Hastings† our Saxon forefathers first learned to appreciate rightly the merit of yew bow and bearded cloth-yard shaft. A general disarming followed that event; but the haughty victor, with sound military policy, threw back these simple weapons to the vanquished of every grade. Whilst smarting under a sense of national degradation, the privilege to bear arms of any sort was regarded by the Saxon freeholder

---

whether at one, or ten score paces. Elsewhere, Shakspeare represents Richard as a consummate general; here we have him a perfect master of weapons in detail. Another drama assigned to our bard contains some pithy counsel on this subject, as, indeed, which of them does not? It is a right merry conceit; since " mine host of the George," already plenus Bacchi et pinguis ferinæ, is wholly incapable of illustrating the maxim he lays down.

" Hush, tush! the knaves keepers are my bonas socias and my pensioners. Nine o'clock!— Be valiant, my little Gog Magogs. I'll fence with all the justices in Hertfordshire. I'll have a buck till I die; I'll slay a doe whilst I live. HOLD YOUR BOW STRAIGHT AND STEADY." — *Merry Devil of Edmonton.*

* See 𝕷𝖊 𝕽𝖔𝖞 𝕸𝖔𝖉𝖚𝖘.

† When addressing his troops previous to that battle, the Duke of Normandy endeavoured to excite their contempt for the Saxons, by telling them they were come to fight with a people who " knew not the use of the bow." — Sir J. HEYWARD. " Among all the English artillery," says Camden, " archerie challenges the pre-eminence; as peculiar to our nation, as the Sarissa was to the Macedonians, the Gesa to the old Gauls, the Framea to the Germans, the Machara generally to the Greeks. First showed to the English by the Danes, brought in by the Normans, and continued by their successors, to the great glory of England in achieving honourable victories; but now dispossessed by gunnery, how justly let others judge" Pontoppidan, the scientific traveller, alludes to the skilful archery of that race from whom the Conqueror and his followers were originally descended: " I was born," says he, " in the uplands of Norway, where the inhabitants handle so well the bow."

as a most grateful boon. It formed the line of distinction between him and the weaponless serf*, who, like the soil and cattle he tilled and fed, was transferred to the highest bidder, whenever the demands of necessity or improvidence induced their owner to seek a market. The once neglected bow, therefore, now became an object of more than ordinary affection, stimulated, perhaps, by jealous rivalry of the skill with which they saw it wielded in stranger hands. At home, whether in hall or cottage, it occupied the place of honour above the blazing hearth; abroad, it was borne like the modern fowling-piece by country gentlemen, whilst strolling over their estates, with a bolt for the pheasant whirring from the brake, and a broad arrow for the dun deer that sprang from the bracken around his path.† Indeed, from the prince down to his meanest subject, the love of archery was the ruling passion

---

* Within the purlieus of a royal forest the peasants were restricted the use of a bow and bolts, to prevent their killing the venison. Elsewhere, they might carry bow and broad arrow. — CHAUNCEY.

The bolt being blunt-headed was feeble, and destructive to birds and small animals only, which will illustrate a very beautiful allusion of Shakspeare: — "To be generous, guiltless, and of free disposition, is to take those things for bird-bolts which you deem cannon bullets."

"I saw a little devil flye out of her eye like a bird-bolt, which at this hour is up to the feathers in my heart." — *Witch of Edmonton.*

"Shot, by Jove! proceed Cupid; thou hast thumpt him with thy bird-bolt under the left pap." — *Love's Labour Lost.*

† The practice of carrying about implements of archery is illustrated by a story in a MS. Common Place Book which once belonged to a son of George Fox, the historian, A.D. 1608: — "A gentleman, very prodigal of his speeche, which made his mouth often to run over, recounted that having one daye strolled out into the forest with his bowe, he at one shot cutte awaye a deare's ear and his foote together, and killed a foxe. The company saying it was impossible, his man, which stood bye, accustomed to smooth his master's lies, sayd that the deare *cratching* his eare with his hinder foot, lost bothe, and the arrowe glancing, killed the foxe; yet with this hint in his master's ear, that he should next time lye within compasse, "for," quoth he, "I had never so much ado as to bring the eare and foote together."

of every class of society. It is, I believe, not very generally known, that, previous to the Spanish Armada embarking for our shores, the Pope had despatched his emissaries into England to report upon the character and resources of its people. Their observations, which were committed to writing, still remain in MS. in the Vatican Library; and one of them affords a passage so illustrative of English habits, during the sixteenth century, that I shall present its substance to my readers. The author states, the weapon in which our ancestors then most excelled as the bow and arrow; and such delight took they in its exercise, that there was no rank or profession but pursued it with enthusiasm. As the hopes of a country rest principally upon the valour of the rising generation, boys, from the age of ten years, were taught to draw the bow, and all possible means practised to make the love of it supersede every other juvenile diversion. The success attendant on this diligent application, he asserts, would be incredible to those who had not been witnesses of their proficiency. Of such as were but moderately skilled, whether they took aim in an horizontal or other direction, there were few who could not lodge the arrow within a palm of their mark. In the more experienced, force was so united with dexterity, that they pierced not only corslets*, but a complete suit of armour.† Other foreigners who visited the island at various early periods remark that its populace, in town and country, followed archery to the neglect of almost every other recreation. Hentzner, a German traveller, says he saw the husbandmen going forth to their daily toil with bow and arrows, which they laid either on the plough, or in a corner of the field under cultivation.

* A military garment formed of small steel plates sewn upon leather, but flexible, so as not to impede the wearer's motions. Patricius says that an arrow, with a little wax upon the point, will penetrate the stoutest breastplate.

† " Relation of the most noble Giovanni Michele, at his return to Venice, A. D. 1557."—*Library of the Vatican,* No. 3432. p. 33.

But those great achievements which shed lustre upon our annals, making an Englishman's heart throb with triumph as he reads, belong to a much earlier period in the history of our archers. The nation, grown wise by that terrific lesson inflicted at Hastings, in a single generation had organised its bands of martial yeomen, whose exploits, to use the expressive phraseology of an old chronicler*, "made all France afraid," at once the terror and the admiration of their foes. "Milice redoubtable," exclaimed a chivalrous old Gaul, on witnessing the good-humoured, ruddy, embrowned visages, muscular forms, and characteristic equipment, of a knot of tall English bowmen; "Milice redoubtable! la fleur des archiers du monde." † Yet as France experienced the evils of their scourging visitations more frequently than any other European country, terror rather than admiration predominated in the popular mind. Like the Italians when assailed by the fierce hordes of the north, they made their chapels and abbeys, during the fourteenth and fifteenth centuries, resound with litanies and prayers to avert the calamitous descent of English bowmen upon their shores. ‡ "These were the men," continues the old English writer above quoted, "amongst whom the kings of England in foughten battles, were wont to remain (who were their footmen), as the French kings did among their knights, the prince thereby showing where his chief strength did exist." § His statement receives

* Holinshed, p. 275.
† Philip de Comines.
‡ One of these Italian compositions still extant commences thus: — " A sagittis Hunnorum, nos defenda Domine!" From the arrows of the Huns defend us O Lord. — " J'ai payé tous mes Anglois"— I have paid off all my Englishmen — is an ancient proverbial expression still current in France when a man finds himself out of debt, which originated in the ruinous contributions our countrymen levied there.

§ Certain ancient military ordinances, still extant, show the high estimation our sovereigns entertained for their yeomen archers. " And in special," says one of them " at the first moustre, every archere shall have his bowe and arrowes hole, that is to wytte, in arrowes xxx. or xxiv. at the least, headed

confirmation from circumstances connected with the battle of Agincourt, that great triumph of English archery. Owing to the nature of the combats, in which the hero of the day was personally engaged, it is evident he quitted his mounted chivalry at the battle's commencement, to fight on foot among the ranks of his meanest soldiers. *

During five centuries and a half subsequent to the Conquest, every male inhabitant of the island was engaged in the practice of this noble recreation. England, therefore, at all times possessed a national militia, ready for the field at an hour's warning; and hence sprang the large bodies of efficient troops, which, in an almost incredibly short time, were seen marching under the blood-stained banners of the Red and White Rose. That the result of a single engagement, like Towton or St. Albans†, should have proved the temporary anni-

---

and in a sheaf. And furthermore, that every archere do sweare that his bowe and arrowes be his own, or his mastyr's or captyne's. And also that no man, ones moustered and admitted as an archere, alter or change himself to any other condition, without the kinge's special leave, upon payne of imprisonment."

* Sir Harris Nicolas's Battle of Agincourt. This interesting work should be upon the shelves of every archer's library, and I am aware it is already extensively known to the craft. Indeed, so minutely accurate are the details, that, whilst perusing it, time, place, the very cunning of the scene, present themselves as a terrible dream to our excited imaginations. Like the ancient chronicler, whose curious narrative the author introduces in his work, we almost fancy ourselves " seated among the baggage," viewing the combat. These impressions are in some degree assisted by its curious antique typography.

† It appears that the Earl of Warwick broke into the town by the gardens, between the sign of the Key and the Exchequer, in Holliwell Street. No sooner had his soldiers entered, than they raised a tremendous shout of " A Warwick! A Warwick!" and rushed to the onslaught. The King was shot into the neck at the onset; Humphrey Duke of Buckingham, and the Lord Sandys, in their faces, and the Earl of Strafford in his right hand, with arrows. The Marquis of Dorset also received many similar hurts, so that, being able neither to ride on horseback nor to walk, he was carried away in a cart. When the King perceived his men had deserted him, he retired from the field, taking refuge in a poor man's cottage from the shot

hilation of both factions, will excite no surprise when we reflect they came to the field armed with, and equally skilled in,

---

of arrows which flew like snow about him. This affair was entirely with the archers, for the men-at-arms never joined.

> Now followeth that black scene, borne up so wondrous high,
> That but a poor dumb show before a tragedy
> The former battles fought have seemed to this to be.
> O Towton! let the blood Palm Sunday pour'd on thee
> Affright the future times, when they the muse shall hear
> Deliver'd so to them; and let the ashes there
> Of forty thousand men, in that long quarrel slain,
> Arise out of the earth, as they would live again
> To tell the manly deeds that bloody day were wrought.
>   DRAYTON.

The battle of Towton occurred on the 29th of March, being Palm Sunday. It commenced with a discharge from Henry's archers, but, owing to a snow-storm which drove into their faces as they shot, and prevented their seeing the foe, the arrows were of no execution, having all dropped short of the enemy. Lord Falconbridge, who commanded the Yorkists, like an able general, took instant advantage of this circumstance: he ordered his men, after shooting one flight, instantly to retire several paces backwards and stand, which they did until the enemy had vainly emptied their quivers; for, as an old writer observes, not one arrow came nearer than " forty tailors' yards." The Yorkists then advanced upon them, and not only discharged their own shafts with full advantage of the wind, but also in their march picked up all those which had fallen short, and returned them to their masters. Then the Lancastrians gave way and fled towards York, but seeking in a tumultuous manner to gain the bridge at Tadcaster, so many of them fell into the river Cock that it was quite filled up, and the Yorkists went over their backs in pursuit of their brethren. This rivulet, and the river Wharfe, into which it empties itself hereabouts, are said to have been dyed with blood. Indeed, the tradition is more than probable, if, as historians assert, 36,000, out of the 100,000 Englishmen that were in the field on that day, "paid the penalty of their fathers' transgressions"— the dethronement and murder of Richard II.; and the wounds, being caused by arrows and battle-axes, bled plentifully. "The blood of the slain," says an old writer, "became caked with the snow, which at that time lay plentifully on the ground, and, afterwards dissolving, ran down in a most horrible manner through the furrows and ditches of the fields

the same destructive weapon. That when thus destroyed, their armies should be re-organised so rapidly, that, like the teeth sown by Cadmus, they appeared to have sprung out of the ground, is also natural, because wherever there were men, there were disciplined soldiers. In the equally sanguinary, but more justifiable struggles for national freedom, which stain the pages of our annals at various other periods, the bow played its part.

On the very first summons, in accordance with the prevailing martial spirit,

>Up rose the land at the sound of war.

The ploughman left his team motionless in the furrow, the woodman abandoned his axe, the artisan his loom, the brawny smith his iron to cool upon the anvil, and snatching up the ever ready bow and shaft, hastened to the place of tryst. They met there then, not an ill-armed, undisciplined rabble, but as men

>With hearts resolved, and hands prepared,
>The blessings they enjoy'd to guard;

every one sufficiently master of his weapon to riddle a steel corslet at five score paces, and act with terrific effect against masses of cavalry; while the majority could bring down the falcon

>Hovering in her pride of place;

or with a broad arrow, strong and unerring as rifle shot, transfix

---

for two or three miles together. ' Occisorum nempe cruor cum nive jam commixus,'" &c. &c.

One of the Paston letters was written to calm a parent's anxiety respecting the fate of a beloved son, who fought in this disastrous conflict. "Mother," says the writer, "I commend me to you, letting you weet (know) that, blessed be God, my brother John is alive and fareth well, and in no peril of death. Nevertheless he is hurt with an arrow on his right arm, beneath the elbow, and I sent him a surgeon, which hath dressed him, and he telleth me he trusteth he shall be whole within right short time." April 18. 1471.

the wild deer in its fleetest course. Such men could be neither oppressed nor enslaved.*

Thus it is that the perusal of our national annals awakens in the minds of youth and eld, a thousand glowing, grateful recollections of " England's famous archerie." The romantic, perhaps not less veracious legends of the ballad maker, appeal to our sympathies under a different, and even more seductive, form. All our ideas of the blythe vocation of the forester,—

Merrie, and free,

lord of dale and down, who maketh his couch beneath the woodland bough,—are associated with bow and shafts, the village green, and crowds of jovial rustics congregated at summer's eve

---

* The author trusts he will not himself be mistaken for a " hardy and notorious rebel," because he quotes the following anecdotes to illustrate that gallantry and skill which formed the birthright of our old English peasantry : — " That noble gentleman Ambrose, Earl of Warwick, accompanied the Duke of Northumberland, his father, who in the year 1548 was sent with an army of horsemen and footmen to suppress the rebellion of Ket, in Norfolk, who at that time lay encamped with a great power of hardy and notorious rebels by the city of Norwich, upon a high hill, called Mount Surry. Having entered the city, the Duke brought four and twenty field-pieces, to the chief charge whereof he appointed Colonel Compenick, an Alman and a valiant leader, with his regiment of Almans, all of them old soldiers. But before they could well entrench themselves, those furious rebels, contrary to all expectations, descended their hill with such fury of shot of arrows, that they gave such a terror to our people, both strangers and English, as they were fain to run away with the loss of ordnance and slaughter of soldiers; and before the Duke could make head against them, they had captured eighteen field-pieces and carried them up their hill." After some further particulars, the writer goes on to say, that " whereas the Duke, on the first assembly of his army, changed many archers into arquebusiers, because he had no opinion of the long bow, he, after this victory and suppression of the rebels, upon the experience which he had of the danger and terror of the arrows, (his own horse being wounded under him with three or four, whereof he died,) did many times after openly protest his error before Count Malatista Baglion, an ancient and honourable soldier, an Italian, and other great captains, saying, from that time forwards he would hold the bow to be the only weapon in the world."— Sir J. SMITH's *Discourse on Weapons. MS. Lansdown.*

around its archer butts. Thence, by a natural, pleasing transition, we pass to the records of that bold Saxon outlaw, whose still cherished memory exhibits some faint traces of an animosity, once universal, amongst the native English, towards all of Norman race. Our venerable Bishop Latimer has recorded an amusing instance of this popular enthusiasm. During one of his pastoral journeys, he arrived towards evening at a small town near London, and gave notice of his intention to preach on the morrow, that being a holiday. "When I came there," he says, "the church door was fast locked. I tarried an hour or more, and at last the key was found, and one of the parishioners came to me, and says, — 'Syr, this is a busy day with us; we cannot hear you: it is Robin Hoode's daye; the parish are gone abroad to gather for Robin Hoode.'" The good bishop had clothed himself *in pontificalibus;* but he was obliged to unfrock, and go forwards on his way, leaving the place to the archers, who, beneath an avenue of old oak trees, were rehearsing the parts of Robin Hood, Little John, and all the band. The placid meekness which formed one distinguished characteristic of the most illustrious of England's martyrs need not be enlarged upon here. Yet this unceremonious preference of an outlaw's bow to the pastoral crook entirely overset the bishop's equanimity. He therefore rates the offenders soundly; but, owing to the changes which time has made in colloquial expressions, his reproof reminds us of the grumblings of some offended overgrown schoolboy; at once quaint and ludicrous. Yet, had the pursuits of these May-day revellers been "in season," could they have failed of sympathy with one, who informs us elsewhere, in a sermon, that his father "taught him to shoot like a true Englishman; and bought him bows bigger and bigger as he increased in years; and of whom the author of the MS. defence of Archbishop Abbot * writes thus: — "Non

---

* His fatal accident with a crossbow is noticed elsewhere under that particular head.

fuerat quisquam, qui in generosum equum salire, aut tractare elegantior potuit?"—No one could vault upon a high-mettled steed, or launch his arrows at the mark, with a more noble and becoming grace.

Perhaps there lives not throughout the whole realm of merry England a single educated youth who has not dreamed through the pages of that little volume, elegantly entitled "The Garland," which contains a poetic chronicle of the exploits of Sherwood's famous Robber Chief. Stout of heart and ready of hand, we see him reign lord paramount over its finest glades, in defiance of lion-hearted Richard, and his still more inveterate enemy, the "Sheriffe of Nottingham," to boot. With a manly dexterity, which few could rival in that age of stalwart archery, he launches the grey goose wing,

> To cleave the willow wand;

or

> Hit the mark a hundred rod,
> And cause a hart to die.

At the close of life, influenced by that chivalrous bravery which had formed its guiding star, he forbids retaliation upon the treacherous woman who drained the life's blood from his heart.

> I never hurt fair maid in all my time,
> Nor at my end will I now. *

And, finally, how natural and impressive appears the ruling passion, strong in death, exhibited in this expiring forester's attachment to the trusty yew which had extricated him from a

---

* Local tradition asserts that, being taken ill, Robin Hood applied for surgical assistance at Sopwell Abbey, where a nun purposely bled him to death. No doubt the lancet was thrust through the vein upon the artery, which produces aneurism, generally followed by mortification and death; that such a man should have submitted literally to be "bled to death" seems improbable. In the latter case, I believe, a swelling of the limb ensues, with other symptoms, especially fatal to an archer.

hundred dangers, and the green woodlands and sunny hills where he had run his race.

> Give me my bent bow in my hand,
> And a broad arrow I'll let flee;
> And where that arrow lighteth,
> There shall my grave digged be.

Deep and lasting are the impressions produced by this sort of reading. They outlive the results of graver studies, and to them we may attribute much of the daily increasing fondness for archery which prevails among our English youth.* The obvious practical advantages resulting from the pursuit of an elegant amusement have of course lent their aid to the Good Cause, for such, my fellow-countrymen, you will esteem it, so long as it seems desirable to enlarge the number of our home-bred exercises, tending, in these days of foreign estrangement, to revive the dear domestic hospitalities, once so characteristic of English rural life. Could we promote among the gentlemen,— and on the present occasion it is most important to add, the ladies of England,—an enthusiasm for recreations especially congenial to the beautiful domains which surround their ancestral homes, our object would be attained, and archery reign triumphant; since who amongst us is ignorant of the alliance claimed by Britain's time-honoured pastime with lawn and woodland glade, heath-clad hill, and ancient trysting oak?

Amidst such congenial scenes, as I rambled near the source of "Towy's foaming flood," the present chapter suggested itself. Thus to address all primary instructions to the juveniles of either sex; to appear ambitious only of "teaching the *young* idea how to shoot," cancels the impertinence of an attempt

---

* Twelve years ago London possessed but two establishments for vending archery tackle, Waring's and another; at present, they amount to a score at least.

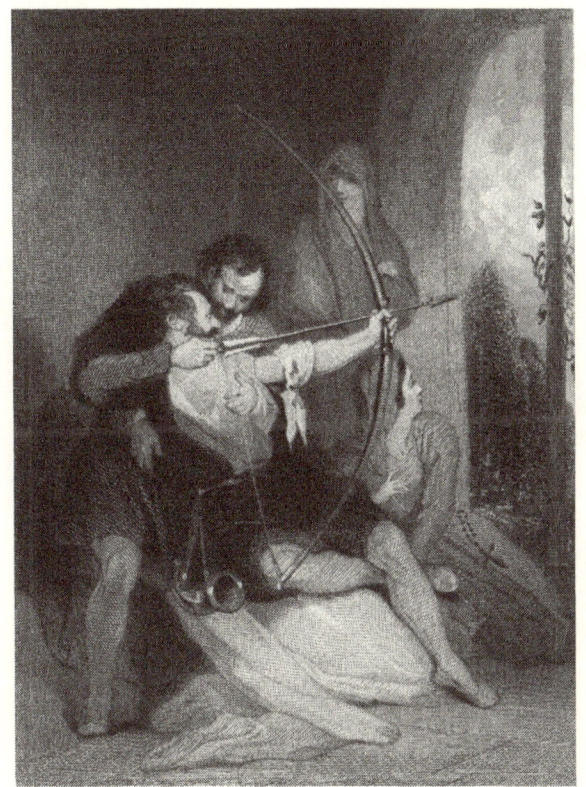

Death of Robin Hood.

to lecture full-grown ladies and gentlemen into a knowledge of our right prince-like pastime.

Remember, then, boys, that in youth only we readily acquire every accomplishment, and for none is early initiation more requisite than for archery. All nations famed for their adroitness with the bow seem to have been aware of this. The Goths, like the ancient Persians, esteemed an inviolable attachment to truth, and skilful shooting, to be the most desirable attainments a young man could possess. They suspended implements of archery over a male infant's cradle, at once to indicate its sex, and the profession to which, thereafter, it was to be devoted. Traces of a somewhat similar custom are also discernible in the East. "When a son is born in a family," says a Chinese proverb, "the bow and quiver are hung up at the gate."* Other remarkable usages, connected with this almost universal weapon, prevail in St. Vincent and Tobago, the only islands of the West Indies whence the aboriginal inhabitants have not been extirpated. The Rev. Thomas Davies, of Llanelly, in South Wales, about the year 1606, wrote an amusing account of the Caribbees. He thus explains, by reference to archery, an extraordinary receding of the forehead observable in the male inhabitants of that race. " As soon," says he, " as the children are born, the mothers make their foreheads flat, and press them so, that there is a descent backwards; for besides that this form is accounted one of the principal pieces of beauty amongst them, they affirm it facilitates their shooting up to the top of a tree, standing at the foot, whereat they are extremely expert, as being brought up to it from their childhood. At a hundred paces, they will hardly fail striking a half-crown piece.† Among every celebrated

* Han Kiou Koan.

† Caribbee Indians of the present day excel in shooting, and use a very tall bow, with arrows little inferior in length. I possess many of both, and well remember a captain of a vessel who visited one of their villages, and was so delighted with his reception, that he accompanied them into the woods, on their favourite expedition of shooting monkeys, which they

nation of archers a fondness for the bow has been imbibed as it were with the mother's milk; and the little rogues readily

---

strike with fatal certainty from the tallest trees by a perpendicular shot. On bidding adieu to his hospitable, kind-hearted entertainers, one of the white men imprudently took more notice of a young Indian girl than was agreeable to Indian notions of propriety. All instantly retired, leaving him and his party alone; upon which his knowledge of the habits of these savages induced him to warn them that instant flight could alone preserve them from "being treated as they had seen the monkeys." Already had they got about eighty paces, and were just about to turn an angle of rock which would have effectually screened them from every kind of missile, when the captain was observed to spring some four feet from the ground, and with a groan fall dead upon the sands, with one arrow sticking in his head, and another between his shoulders, which had come out at his breast. No pursuit was attempted; the outraged Caribs having been to all appearance appeased by this sacrifice of the offending Englishman. The fate of a number of his countrymen, who attempted to settle among these Indians about two centuries and a half since, also furnishes us with a very lively description of the terrors of their archery.

"Then came the arrows so thick out of the wood," says one of the survivors, "that we could not get our match in" (they were armed with matchlocks) "for pulling them out of our bodies; so amongst the band there were but five or six pieces discharged, which, when the Indians saw give fire, they did fall flat on the ground, shouting and crying with a most hellish noise, naming us by our names when their arrows pierced us.

"So, when they saw we could not hit them with our pieces, they would come so near us as though they purposed to make choice in what place to hit us. Some they shot in the faces, others through the shoulders, and of others they would nail the feet and the ground together.

"Master Budge and Robert Shaw ran both into the sea, and were there drowned or killed with arrows. Master Finch had a little buckler, with which he did save himself a long time, but at the last an arrow passed through both legs, that he could not go, and, stooping to pull it out, they killed him; and if any of us offered to run at one or two savages, straightway they fled a little distance, but suddenly twenty or thirty would enclose us, and still shooting arrows into them until they were down, with a great Brazil sword they beat them to death. Master Kettlebye did behave himself very gallantly, for he did not respect what arrows he received in his body so he could reach one stroke at a Caribbee; but they were too nimble for us, in regard they were naked. Yet, nevertheless, we ran through them all,

exercise themselves in shooting from the moment they are able to clutch a bow and arrows.

---

thinking if we could escape that ambush there had been no more to trouble us; but as I was pulling arrows out of his body, to the number of twenty at the least, a third ambush burst out of the woods, from whence came an arrow and hit him in the breast, which he perceived would be his death, for he could not stand but as I held him; and I was forced to let him go and shift for myself.

"Then I overtook young St. John, his body almost full of arrows, of which I pulled out a number; but what for the blood that ran from him, and the extreme heat he was in from his flight, he failed to overtake the rest of our company that was before.

"And still the Caribbees did gather ground upon us, and arrows came thick on every side.

"And then the poor youth willed me to entreat his men to stay; and so, having overtaken one, I caused him to stay, which he was not willing to do; for he told me his sword would not come forth of the scabbard, so I took hold of the hilt, and betwixt us both pulled it out: but before we had made an end, these cruel and bloody Caribbees had encompassed young St. John; yet to my grief I did stand and behold his end, who, before he fell, did make them give back like so many curs from a lion, for which way soever he ran they all fled before him. His body was so loaded with arrows that he fell to the ground; and upon one hand and knee he did keep them from him with his sword, so much he scorned basely to die at their hands.

"Myself and the man whose sword I had helped to set free, were now the only marks they aimed at; for having rifled young St. John they pursued very hotly, which caused us to make haste to four of our fellows who were entered into a narrow path leading through the woods from the sands, to the houses where we dwelt. But there was in the path another ambush, which drove us back to the sands; and when they saw us so hardly chased they entered the path with us again.

"On one side thereof was a high mountain, the other went down a low valley. The first four of our friends took up the mountain, by which means they offered too fair a mark for them to hit, who dropped down one after another.

"All this time neither Harry, Peter Stokesley's man (a merchant now in Bucklersbury), nor myself, was shot; but as we thought desperately to burst through them into the narrow path, there came an arrow and pierced quite through his head, of which he fell suddenly, and I ran to lift him up, but he was dead without speaking one word to me at all.

"Then came there two arrows and hit me in the back, the one directly

An intelligent writer*, who passed much of his time in studying Scandinavian habits and customs, asserts that he had seen boys of eleven and twelve years, " so cunning in shooting, that, at the option of a spectator they unerringly struck the head, breast, or feet, of the smallest birds, with an arrow." He adds, " So will old men that have their sight." Saxo, the Danish historian, cites a monstrous example of skill in these senile archers. He asserts that he knew an old man whose crossbow had such a huge nut †, that he could set ten arrows to the string, and these being shot vigorously against the enemy, made as many wounds in his body.

Many Scandinavian youths became archers by profession, and subsisted altogether on the produce of their bows. The large black bear, with which northern Europe is infested, was the special object of their pursuit. In autumn, the animal feeds on a species of ripe red fruit, growing in clusters, like

---

against my heart the other through my shoulder blade; so sword in hand ran I upon them desperately, thinking before I had died to have been the death of some of them: and in my running I saw Captain Anthony, with an arrow in his bow drawn against me, who stood until I came very near him, for he purposed to have sped me with that shot, which, when I espied coming, I thought to have put it by with my sword, but, lighting upon my hand, it passed through the handle of my weapon, and nailed both together. Nevertheless I continued running at him still, and before he could nock another, made him and all the rest turn their backs and flee unto the sands again; which opportunity when I espied I leaped into the wood, down to the valley, where I found a salt lake; and hearing them with loud shouts and cry, which they use in sign of triumph and victory, pursue me still, I leaped into the water, with my sword nailed to my hand, and two arrows in my back, and, by the help of God, swam over, but with much ado, for the further side was shallow, and I waded in mud up to the waist, which had almost spent me." — *Another Class of Indian News; or a true and tragical Discourse, showing the lamentable Miseries endured by Sixty-seven Englishmen, &c. By John Nichol, one of the aforesaid Company.* A. D. 1608.

* Aldrovandus Magnus. See also Olaus Magnus, &c.

† That part of a crossbow which holds the string, when the weapon is charged, is called the nut.

grapes. To procure this, the bear either ascends the trees, which he can do with the agility of a cat, or, standing on his two hind legs, pulls down the branches within his reach. The cunning hunter, who lies concealed behind a tree or fragment of rock, now pierces his distended body with a broad-headed arrow, and maddened by pain, the enraged animal immediately rushes upon a rude image of a man, purposely placed to attract his attention. Whilst engaged in tearing and rending it, a second arrow, discharged by the hunter from his hiding-place, generally laid the shaggy monster prostrate in death.

Many boys also gained their entire support by shooting crows in the fields. They reserved the backs only, strung upon a small osier twig; and on exhibiting these to the elders of their village, they received a small gratuity in money, with arrows, in proportion to the number of birds.

But young gentlemen and young ladies, likewise, are sometimes fickle and capricious even in their sports, the toy or pursuit which has amused them at one moment being often thrown aside in the next: the parents were aware of this, for human nature changes not with time or place; and knowing, moreover, that the lives and freedom, as well as the daily subsistence of their offspring, depended upon their adroitness, they adopted some judicious expedients to secure that constant application so essential to the acquirement of excellence in every art. Besides daily instruction from professors who taught the proper method of holding the weapon when aiming aloft, or at an object beneath them, their mothers never permitted them to breakfast until they had repeatedly struck a very small mark. Thus it is with the Bashkirs, a modern nation of archers subject to Russia, who inhabit the shores of Lake Aral. A large squadron of these Tartar warriors hung upon and harassed the French, during their memorable retreat from Moscow, and entered Paris with the allied army in 1816. They were greatly esteemed by the Emperor, since, with no other weapons than their bow and quiver, they had rendered him most important services. Now, bread and vegetables being unknown to these uncultivated sons of the desert, they subsist entirely upon flesh procured in hunting; and when the reader is aware that, from the age of seven years, their children receive no food except what they strike down with their arrows, he will not be surprised that the Russians should esteem a Bashkir archer equal to the best rifleman in their service. The Margravine of Anspach describes the exploits of a neighbouring horde of Tartars, several of whose young men had assembled one morning beneath her chamber window; at fifty paces they broke an egg, and killed a goose at one hundred.

In the same manner the little Indian of Demerara gets no breakfast until his arrows reach the maize cake and dried venison which his mother has placed in the fork of some lofty tree.

You may be disposed, my little friends, to consider these as hard conditions. Be resolute, however, in abstaining from yours every morning, for one twelvemonth, until half a dozen arrows have hit the target, and I'll stake my best yew bow against a hazel wand, your proficiency shall equal that of the Catabuwa warriors, who, about forty years ago, delighted the archery world by an exhibition of their skill at one of the London theatres.* Some of your parents probably witnessed these extraordinary performances: they can inform you the mark was scarcely bigger than a shilling; yet, for many evenings, they hit it at every shot; and, on an average, never missed oftener than two out of five.

In all operations dependent on manual dexterity, how great are the advantages possessed by the child over the grown man! A youth shall become a far better archer in one than the other in three years' practice, and must infallibly prove victorious over his full-grown competitor in every contest. It is down-

* Sadler's Wells. *Times*, July 25. 1795.

right impiety, says Xenophon, for such as have never learned to ride, to supplicate the gods for victory in a charge of horse; or for such as never learned the use of the bow, to ask the superiority over those who in childhood have laboured to acquire dexterity therein.

We esteem it the peculiar excellence of archery, that neither satiety nor fatigue attend it. At the close of the livelong summer's day, I believe no archer ever heard the upshot given * without regret; without wishing his pastime was then but to commence. From the first initiatory lesson of stringing the bow, to the attainment of that excellence which enables the archer to " clap into the clout at twelve score," all is pleasurable excitement. Assiduity and exertion are indispensable; but

The labour we delight in physics pain.

The first bows used by Indian children are nothing more than a bent stick, their arrows a stout straw or small reed found abundantly in the savannahs. With this simple contrivance they will hit a small piece of tobacco-pipe twenty times successively, at the distance of a dozen yards. They have a favourite game practised with a bow and two shafts; one of which, short and unfledged, being cast into the air, the archer aims to strike it with the other in its descent. As the youths approach manhood, their weapons are gradually strengthened, and more carefully constructed. Patient and laborious, the tawny hunter works at his bow from day to day, scraping it into form with a flint stone, or the sharp edge of some sea-shell; he next manufactures a string, tough and strong, from the entrails of deer, or a thong of hide carefully twisted. His task being thus complete, he lays it aside to acquire a little seasoning, and in the meantime sets about his arrows;

---

* The final target round, which puts an end to the day's sport.

" Then will she get the upshot by the cleaving of the pin."—*Old Comedy.*

for which he picks out a number of straight young sprigs, pointing them with a sharp bone, two inches in length. The great wood squirrel, wild turkeys, and other winged game are killed with these. Another kind of arrow he forms of a fine yellow reed, pierced with hard wood; the spur or bill of a wild turkey-cock, or a splinter of crystal, serves for the head; and in winging them the Indian exhibits similar ingenuity. With a knife made from a bit of reed, sharpened like a surgeon's scalpel, the feathers are cut to their proper form, and then neatly sewn on with cotton thread of his own spinning. The nock he forms with a beaver's tooth, set in a small stick; rubbing patiently until it is deep enough. Such is the slow, and often laborious process, by which the little North American savage equips himself for war or the chase.

Of all the archers of the New World, those nations who inhabit the vast interior of its southern continent seem at this day to exhibit the greatest strength, adroitness, and accuracy of aim. Their ancestors bore a similar reputation, especially the Tupinambas, whose weapons De Lery has so accurately described: their bows were made of iron-wood, either red or black, longer and thicker than what are used in Europe; nor could any European bend them. A plant called tocon formed the string, which, though slender, was so strong that a horse could not by fair pulling break it. Their arrows were a full cloth yard in length, and curiously constructed in three parts — the middle being of reed, the two others of heavy hard wood; the feathers were fastened on with cotton; and the head was either of bone, or a blade of dry reed, cut into the form of an old lancet, or the sting of a certain species of fish. They were incomparable archers. "With leave of the English," says De Lery, "who are so excellent in this art, I must say that a Tupinamba would shoot twelve arrows before an Englishman could let fly six." The Fidalgo of Elvas adds, that an Indian would shoot five arrows before the Spanish cross-bowman could make one discharge. " Well might they speak of the bows of the mighty," exclaims Dr. Southey, " for an arrow sent by a Tomoyo would fasten the shield to the arm that held it; and sometimes it has passed through the body, and continued its way with such force as to pierce a tree and hang quivering in the trunk."*

Among the bowmen of the far West, hardihood, strength, and address distinguish the natives of the Floridas. The exercise of archery forms the first sport of childhood; and their young and agile warriors consider its implements confer a peculiar grace on all who bear them. No sooner does the infant walk, than, actuated by the spirit of imitation peculiar to that age, he watches his father as he arms himself for the chase, and following his footsteps beneath the tall forest trees, earnestly begs from him a mimic bow and arrows. Should his request be denied or neglected — which, it may be presumed, is rarely the case — the little urchin himself forms a rude imitation with the branch of some small tree growing around the wigwam, and wages war upon mice and vermin which infest his native hut. When these are entirely driven away or destroyed, he sallies forth to hunt lizards and other reptiles concealed in the tall grass, or watches patiently for hours around their holes, until the want of food obliges them to come out, and affords their persecutor an opportunity of getting a shot. With muscles thus hardened by daily exercise, ere the Indian has attained his eighteenth summer he is master of a bow, such as even in the prime of manhood the most skilful modern Toxophilite is seldom found competent to manage. It is repeatedly asserted by the Spanish historians, that none of their countrymen could ever draw the string of a Floridan's bow to his face, while the young natives did so with ease even behind the ear.

In common with other parts of the New World, this country

* De Lery. — Dr. Southey's History of Brazil (Notes).

was exposed to the desolating visits of the Spaniards, who, under pretence of settling a colony, wasted it with fire and sword, about the close of the fifteenth century. Among the troops composing the expedition was a body of 400 cavalry, all equipped in the completest manner, as they considered their coats of mail musket-proof, and used bucklers, for the admirable tempering of which their native armourers have always enjoyed a deserved reputation. How far these defences availed them against the arrows of a people unacquainted with the use of iron, I now proceed to show. In one of their earliest skirmishes with the Apalachites, a Spanish general called Moscoso received an arrow in his right side, which pierced his buff jerkin and coat of mail, but did not prove mortal, because it entered in a slanting direction. The officers of his staff, wondering that a piece of armour valued at more than 150 ducats should be unable to resist a reed arrow headed merely with a sharp flint, resolved to prove the temper of their own, in order to ascertain how far they might be depended on. Whilst, therefore, they were quartered in the town of Apalachia, several who wore that species of defence procured a wicker basket, very strong and closely woven, and hung around it a coat of mail which was judged to be about the heaviest and most impregnable in the whole army. Then ordering a youthful Indian captive to be introduced, they promised him freedom in case he pierced the mark at the distance of 150 paces. Immediately the barbarian clenched his fists, shook himself violently, and contracted and extended his arms as if to awaken all his force; then stringing a bow which had been previously delivered to him, he elevated it at the mark; and loosing his arrow, it drove through both armour and basket, and came out at the opposite side with violence sufficient to have slain a man. The Spaniards, finding a single piece of armour was ineffectual to resist the arrow, threw a second upon the basket, and ordered the Indian to repeat his shot; when he immediately pierced that likewise. Nevertheless, as the shaft did not pass entirely through, but remained sticking half in front and half behind, because, as the barbarian asserted, he had failed this time to put forth his utmost strength, he begged to be allowed to shoot a third time, on condition that if he failed to drive the arrow through and through, he should immediately suffer death.

The Spaniards, satisfied with what they had already witnessed, refused to comply with his request, but ever afterwards held their coats of mail in little esteem, and contemptuously styled them "Dutch Holland." However, as a more effectual protection for the horses, they invented a sort of body clothes made of strong thick felt, doubled and trebled until about four fingers thick, which covered the animal's breast and croup, and was found to repel the arrow better than any thing besides.*

* Of upwards of three hundred beautiful war steeds which they brought with them from Cuba, thirty alone escaped the arrows of the Floridans; and these also would have perished in a similar manner, had not their owners bled them to death, and cured their flesh as provisions for the camp. Of those which were killed in battle was a gallant steed called Ageituno, ridden by the Spanish general; he fell pierced with eight arrows, for at him the Indians principally directed their aim. Indeed, in all battles with the Christians, they aimed at the horses rather than at their riders, knowing if the former were destroyed their distant shooting and swiftness of foot would render them a match for the Spaniards; and many instances of their success occurred during this invasion. On one occasion, twelve cavaliers and as many foot soldiers, desirous of furnishing themselves with slaves, placed themselves in ambush to intercept the natives, who usually came to pick up such trifles as the Christians left behind on breaking up their encampments. Having posted themselves beneath the shelter of a group of trees, with a centinel among the branches of one of the loftiest, their plan succeeded so well that a number of Indians were surrounded and taken; of these the Spaniards made an equal distribution; and then the party agreed to return to their quarters, one trooper excepted, who, dissatisfied that two captives only had fallen to his share, insisted on remaining until he procured another, and as his comrades found him obstinately resolved neither to defer his intentions to a better opportunity, nor to accept one of theirs instead, they unwillingly consented.

These examples will serve to illustrate the force and vigour with which early discipline enabled the Indian youth to ply their bows. I will but detain my little readers with an additional anecdote to show the minute accuracy of their aim. A poor mariner named Alexander Cockburn, about a century since, suffered shipwreck upon the shores of the Isthmus of Darien, and being desirous of reaching some Christian settlement, penetrated into the interior of the country for several hundred miles on foot. During this long and painful expedition, his sole dependence was upon the hospitality of the tawny inhabitants of the forest; and as each declining sun successively admonished him to seek food and shelter for the night, he

---

Whilst they were thus disputing, their centinel gave notice that he saw a young Indian in the neighbourhood; and Paez, whose previous mishaps should have rendered him more prudent, instantly spurred straight towards the barbarian, who, as usual, sought refuge beneath a tree. The branches being low, the Spaniard was unable to ride beneath them, but, wheeling his charger upon the gallop, made a sidelong thrust over the bridle-arm with his lance. He missed his aim, however; and then the Indian, who held his bow-arm extended, and his arrow ready nocked, drew up to the head, and wounded the horse in his flank: the shot proved a mortal one, for the animal, after stumbling forwards about twenty paces, fell dead. Bolanos, who had closely followed his comrade, was similarly treated, his steed being slain outright. Juan de Vega now came, up at a hand gallop, and enraged to see his companions thus dismounted by a naked savage, spurred towards him with the utmost fury. The latter, however, advanced without the slightest symptom of fear, evidently intending to slay the horse, and then seek shelter in the forest. But the cavalier, warned by the accident that occurred a short time previously to Paez, had provided his with a threefold breastplate of cow's hide, like the other horsemen of his band. No sooner, however, did the Indian get within bowshot, than he aimed at De Vega's horse; and the shaft, driven completely through the leathern protection, entered three fingers deep within its breast. Having thus effected his purpose, the barbarian fled towards the forest, but was quickly surrounded and slain. The crest-fallen Spaniards then steered homewards, admiring the courage and adroitness of their enemy, whilst they blamed the folly of him who had been the cause of such irreparable losses.

boldly entered the first reed-thatched dwelling which presented itself, and was ever welcomed to both. "One day about noon," says he, "I came to a great river, where, after I had allayed my thirst, I sought about for wood to make a fire; and whilst busied about this, I espied a wigwam on the other side of the river; then, instead of minding my fire any longer, I ran, catched up my nets, swam across to it, and then had the mortification to find nobody near. Looking about withoutside the wigwam, I saw an arrow sticking in the sand at one end of it, and within there hung a net containing two ripe plantains, which I made bold to eat." He then visits another dwelling, "where I found," says he, "a fire, and an earthen crock full of plantains and wild hog boiling. Without so much as considering what I was about to do, I presently took the victuals off the fire, and ate so heartily that I thought I should never be satisfied. Never had I met with such delicious fare as this seemed to me at the time, not having tasted anything for above forty days but cocoa-nuts and such like food." At length he is joined by the owner of the wigwam and his two sons, who provide him with a second supper, with a couch of warm skins, and on the following morning proffer their services as guides. After describing how these hospitable Indians detained him several days in order that he might recruit his strength, and heal with the juice of herbs the wounds he had received in "fencing with the rocks," he adds, that the two boys grew extremely attached to him, and were curious to know whether he could use a bow and arrows. Having made them understand, in broken Spanish, that he was entirely unacquainted with them, because in his own country guns only were used, they often displayed astonishing feats of dexterity by striking down the smallest bird flying. He says that he has seen them stand perhaps a hundred yards from a bird feeding upon the ground, and, by shooting directly upwards, cause the arrow to pin it to the earth; and mentions, as a further instance of their skill, that they would stick a shaft upright, and, retiring a great way off, shoot perpendicularly as before, when the arrow so shot descended exactly upon the other which was fixed in the ground, and split it in two.

Beltroni describes how dexterously some Indian children hit a five sous piece, in size equal to our sixpence, which he fixed up at twenty-five paces as a mark, often at the second trial. By-and-bye he was fain to remove it ten paces further, or very soon they would have emptied the little purse prepared for his visit to their encampment.

The Indians of Manilla, especially those called Zambales, who live in the mountains, are dexterous archers. They have, in fact, no other weapon, offensive or defensive, than the bow and arrow. M. Navaretti, a French gentleman, who landed there during his voyage to China, witnessed a remarkable feat performed by these savages. "I had heard," says he, "ancient men narrate such marvels of their skill as I could not but consider mere fables. Experience, however, soon taught me that if it becomes us to be cautious in implicitly receiving all we hear, neither ought we to be so incredulous as I was. In rambling through some mountains in the interior of the island, a party of natives overtook me. Among them were four boys about seven or eight years of age, all equipped as archers. Considering this a fair opportunity to witness a specimen of their skill, I took an orange from my pocket and threw it high into the air, saying, 'Shoot that, my lads.' All four struck it in its descent, and beat it to pieces. This occurred in the little town they call Albucanamtas."

Let us next draw a few illustrations from the "Oriental Book of Archery."

Busjady, one of the youthful descendants of Kajan, was renowned for his expertness; and having on a certain occasion quarrelled with his brother, they met on horseback to decide their mutual differences with the bow; but fear entered into the heart of Cabuscheira at the moment they were about to commence the duel. He therefore leaned his body quite on one side, and held his bow directly before him, trusting to the proudly arched neck of his steed as a protection from Busjady's shaft. This pusillanimous manœuvre saved his life, for pity succeeded to rage within the brother's breast; he resolved not to kill him, as he could easily have done, but merely to exhibit some memorable token of his skill. With this view, he aimed at Cabuscheira's cheek, and struck from his ear the pendant of pearls, leaving behind the gold ring to which it had been attached.*

I will next present my little disciples with a few flowers plucked from an Eastern parterre; or, to speak less figuratively, the history of a young Indian archer, written with that amusing extravagance of language for which Oriental people have always been remarkable. Should the reader chance to light upon a scarce work called Inatulli, or the Garden of Delhi, he may there peruse the original.

Let it not be concealed that from this period, about twenty years, your atom-like slave lived as a soldier. One day, in company with some faithful friends and similarly minded companions, I went to visit a fruit garden. In it was a tree taller than all the rest, its dates hanging in clusters, like moist confections, delicious, full of juice, sweet, and full-flavoured; but, from the great height, the hand of no one's power could pluck the fruit. No person having yet had the boldness to climb the tree, its produce was free from the devastation of man.

> It was a date tree of tallest growth,
> From whose size the garden received honour;
> Every cluster of its fruits was a storehouse of sweets,
> From which the crow and paroquet seized a treasure.

As your slave, in the exercise of climbing trees, especially the date, the cocoa-nut, and the palmyra, had attained the utmost

---

* Vie de Bayadur Khan, p. 131.

agility, and my friends esteemed me famous in this art, all of them at once laying the hand of avidity on my skirt, said, 'Under the auspices of your kindness, we hope that we shall taste the rare and richly flavoured dates of this tree, and also have the pleasure of beholding how you can ascend so lofty a stem, whose head reached the battlements of the sky, and of whose fruit none hath yet eaten but the soarers of the air. It must be by miracle, for what power has humanity to scale the turrets of the heavens?' Though I turned myself aside from this request, begging in every mode to be excused, and evaded the trial, my friends, out of extreme longing for the dates, would not withdraw their hold from my poor person. At length, in spite of disinclination, I tucked up my skirts like a running footman, and drawing in my sleeves in the manner of a magic acting rope-dancer, climbed up this heaven-touching tree, which you might have styled the ladder of the sky; while a vast crowd below formed a circle round the trunk to admire my agility.

When I got to the top, the tallest and lustiest men seemed from its towering height to my eye as little children, and sometimes my sight was lost halfway. The crowd began to form alarming conjectures in their minds concerning my safety. In short, having gathered some clusters of great beauty, richness, and fragrance, I put them in the skirts of my vest, and threw others to my friends below, when suddenly a black snake, with a white hood tinged with yellow, of great thickness and length, from whose life-destroying glance the gall would melt to water, and the stoutest heart dissolve like salt, appeared among the leaves, and darted towards me, devoted to death. A trembling seized my whole frame at the sight; and, from dread at his monstrous figure, my joints and members seemed as if they would separate from each other, and the bird of life would quit the nest of my body. Should I throw myself down, reasoned I to myself, the spiritual soarer will, half-way in the descent, break her elemental cage; and if I stop here, this heart-melting serpent, which resembles a divine judgment or sudden calamity will devour me in an instant at one morsel. Both these are grievous; but what is still more afflicting is my becoming a mark for the tongue of mankind, who will say, 'This foolish wretch, a slave to gluttony, sacrificed his life for a few dates.' While I was thus meditating, the blood-devouring serpent reached me, and folding himself around me, hung from my neck like a wreath, distending his jaws, full of wind and venom, close to my mouth; and fixing his dark poisonous eyes upon my face, began to dart out his tongue.

From affright my senses now deserted me, so that to describe my alarm and despair is out of the power of relation. My hair even now stands erect at the remembrance. Such a dryness seized my joints and members from terror, that not the least moisture remained in my body, and the blood became stagnant in my veins. My nails clung so closely to the trunk, that you would have said they were the fingers of the Chinar* growing from the tree. A vast concourse of people stood around below, who beat together their hands in distress, and from despair uttered cries and shrieks, which reached my ears in horrible sound; while my kinsmen and friends in despondency scattered dust upon their heads.

At this crisis, a well-looking young man, of tall stature, mounted on a horse without a saddle, and accompanied by a servant carrying a bow and two or three arrows, came to the place, and inquired the reason for the assemblage of so great a concourse, and their outcries. Some of them informed him, pointing me out with their fingers. The youth having examined my situation, and the folds of the serpent around my neck, said, 'Are there here any of the nearest kin to this death-devoted person?' Upon which my brethren and relations present, who

* I believe the Oriental plane. — *Translator.*

were shedding the tears of regret at my condition, replied, 'Yes; what would you say to us?' The youth continued, 'It must be evident to all that death already sits upon the forehead of yonder unfortunate, whose escape from calamity by means of human wisdom seems improbable, if not impossible; yet if, laying hold on the strong cord of resignation, you will give me leave, trusting in Him who is all-powerful to deliver, I will shoot an arrow through the body of the blood-devouring snake, and try the predestination of this death-seized youth. I am a perfect judge of distance, and in the skill of archery a professor. I can hit the foot of an ant in a dark night; and should they hang a grain of mustard seed by a single hair, I should not miss it a hair's breadth. My skill in this art is such as I cannot express; for the direction point of the arrow is the bent of my power. As an instance—at present I shall not miss, and at the first aim so bring down the head of yonder serpent, that even the wind of the arrow will not reach the face of the young man, or an injury happen to a single hair. Thus far I confide in myself;—yet as Divine decree rules all things, and Providence acts for itself, it is possible that the matter may turn out contrary to my wishes, and you in that case, fixing your hands on my skirts, may accuse me of shedding his blood.'

The whole concourse now, with one voice, exclaimed and said, 'For the delivery of the young man there can be no remedy but this; if he has a predestination of longer life, the arrow of prayer will reach the mark of acceptance; if not, he is already placed in the jaws of fate.' My kinsmen, also, resigned themselves to destiny, and consented to the young man's shot.

The youth—may the mercy of God attend his soul!—took his auspicious omened bow in his grasp, and placing an arrow on the string, prayed the Almighty to direct his aim for my sake. Then, like a magician practised in sorcery—not magic-like, but altogether miraculously drew the shaft, and aiming at the eye of the serpent, let fly.

The heavens exclaimed Well! and the world Bravo!

The point of the arrow reaching its mark, brought down the monster's head to the ground; and this exclamation from the crowd ascended to the skies, 'Praise be to the Giver of life! He cannot die whom he destines to live, though he seemeth dead. God is potent over all things.'*

The weapon remained in the jaws, and the young archer laying his arrows aside, advancing, took up the head of the serpent, which suddenly moving, and as if the cup of the hero's age was become flowing over, seized his lip with its mouth, and closed its envenomed teeth. The noble youth, angel like, fleeted to Paradise in the twinkling of an eye; and the head of the snake, like a paper-catching fish†, remained fastened on his lip.

The Persians assert that Aresh, the best archer of his day, shot an arrow previously marked, in order that it might be recognised, from the top of the mountain Damovend to the banks of the river Gihon. Agoutha, a Tartar prince, long before his tenth year, displayed the greatest fondness for the bow, and even at that early age was an unrivalled archer. One day, certain ambassadors being in the court yard of his father's palace, and espying Agoutha, who stood holding his bow in one hand and an arrow in the other, they requested him to shoot at some birds then passing over their heads; Agoutha complied, and with three arrows brought down an equal quantity of game. One of the ambassadors, delighted with this proof of juvenile adroitness, exclaimed,—"Behold an extraordinary child, worthy to reign over the great empire of the Manchons!" an opinion amply justified by the transactions of his future years. On another occasion Agoutha, assisting at a banquet in the house of Ono Li Han of the He che Lie tribe, went out with several

---

* A verse of the Koran, much quoted by the Mussulmans as a proof of predestination.

† What this means I cannot explain; perhaps a bait made of coloured paper.

of the guests to stroll over a neighbouring plain. Perceiving a hillock at some distance, he requested all present to loose their arrows at it, but none fell within even a reasonable space of the mark; then Agoutha, with his first arrow, shot beyond the bank, and on measuring, the distance was found to be 320 paces. The arrow of Manthou, a boy of the same race as Agoutha, and previously accounted the cleverest bowman of his age, fell 100 yards short of that of his kinsman. In the year 1151, a monument was erected where the successful shaft had alighted, with an inscription commemorative of such extraordinary distant shooting in a child.

"When I was in Tartary," says the Baron de Tott, "they made me particularly notice Khrim Gouray's second son, whose youthful courage burned for an opportunity to distinguish itself, and who, by the constantly exercising his arms, was enabled to bend two bows at once. This prince had occupied himself with archery almost from the cradle, and when not more than nine years of age, the Khan, wishing to mortify his self-love, observed, contemptuously, that 'a distaff would better become the hand of such a poltron, than the manly weapon with which he was then exercising.' — 'Poltron!' cried the child, and his countenance became of an ashy paleness, 'I fear no man, not even you,' at the same time furiously loosing an arrow, which happily missed the Khan, but buried itself in the wainscoting of the apartment two fingers deep.

Teon Man, Khan of the Tartars, wishing to disinherit and destroy his eldest son Mothé, in order to give the kingdom to a child by his second empress, sent him as hostage to the king of the Yuetchi, whose dominions he immediately afterwards ravaged with fire and sword, in the hope this outrage might be avenged by the death of his obnoxious son. The unnatural desire would have been gratified, had not Mothé mounted a swift horse taken from the stables of his enemy, and fled with the utmost speed homewards. On the boy being thus suddenly restored to his presence, nature resumed her sway, and Teon Man, admiring such courage and address in one of tender years, appointed him over 10,000 horse, whose devotion and attachment Mothé used every art to secure, being desirous of retaliating upon his father the fate to which he had been recently consigned. To this end, he caused a number of whistling arrows* to be prepared for his own use, but ordered his men to ride with quivers filled with those having sharp steel heads. He next published a general order, that such of his squadron as hesitated to loose the latter at any object, to which he directed attention by first shooting at it him-

---

* Chinese Tartar arrows are made of a light wood, resembling beech, and vary considerably in length, weight, and size. The largest, used for butt practice only, instead of the iron pile, have a button of horn or hard wood at the point, pierced with several holes. When discharged from the bow, these arrows make a shrill whistling noise, caused by the rush of air through the apertures, and in war are useful for night signals. Letters, also, secured in these holes, are often shot into the enemy's camp; though, as a Chinese author remarks, these missiles sometimes fall into the hands of persons for whom they were never intended, but who, nevertheless, do not fail to turn them to good account. The arrow next in size has usually a steel spear-shaped head; and a third sort is armed with a formidable trident of the same metal.

The fletcher's art seems to be carried to a high degree of perfection in China. Besides those already described, most of their quivers contain a certain number, classed as follows; viz., the eyebrow (*i.e.* half moon) shape; the scissors' shape; those for piercing breast-plates; those for dividing the arm at the shoulder.

They use also a remarkable description of arrow, styled by the French *esprits cachés*, having a triple head rivetted upon a small steel plate. With these they can strike a very minute object from one hundred yards' distance; and for all of them the archer has distinct compartments in his leathern quiver. In the first are the largest or butt shafts; the second has a triple partition, each space holding four, smaller than the preceding, and with sharp steel piles; the third compartment has also three divisions, each containing an arrow with the trident-shaped head.

Whistling arrows were well known in England at least as early as the time of Henry VIII.

self, were to suffer instant death. Being at the chase soon afterwards, he aimed a whistling arrow at an antelope: through forgetfulness, some disobeyed the order, and these he ordered to be beheaded upon the spot. A few days subsequent to this transaction, he shot at one of the noblest Arab horses in his stud; again many cavaliers, influenced by fear, hesitated to obey, and instantly underwent the fate of their companions. His next victim was a very beautiful female slave, for whom he had manifested the extreme of tenderness. The death signal, whistling through the air, struck her full upon the breast: pity and terror again binding up the hands of many, with savage sternness he ordered their companions to hew them in pieces with their sabres. As he rode forth soon afterwards he espied one of the finest of his father's horses grazing in a meadow; instantly he struck him with a fatal shaft. Then, his whole suite following the example, rained a storm of arrows upon the poor beast, which fell absolutely larded therewith. Apparently now secure of their devotion, Mothé one day persuaded his father to take part in a grand hunting match, and, loosing at him the death signal, in an instant he sunk from his horse pierced by a thousand arrows. The wretched parricide immediately returned to the palace, where he was soon declared Schen Yu, that is, emperor, in the room of his murdered parent.*

Some years previous to the treacherous massacre of the Mamelukes by Mohammed Ali Pasha, that splendid barbaric chivalry, as they are happily styled by Sir Walter Scott, held frequent archery parades. One of these magnificent spectacles, which took place about two centuries ago, has been graphically described by an eye-witness, and I shall here give the substance of his very accurate narrative.

On one side of the castle of Cairo there was a large plain

---

* D'Herbelot, Bibliothèque Orientale, iv. 49.

field, which had been prepared for a review of the Mameluke horsemen in manner following. About its middle, and on one side, were three artificial hillocks of sand, about fifty paces distant one from the other, and on the summit of each stood a spear and banner, being marks destined for the archers. Similar preparations had been made on the opposite side, so that the intermediate space barely allowed six horses to run abreast. Here was drawn up a body of youths selected to exhibit their address in mimic warfare, who, accoutred in their usual light harness, and mounted on sprightly steeds, awaited the signal to begin. The Sultan himself, a " swart and lusty companion," viewed the spectacle from an elevated kiosk, having latticed windows. He wore a pointed diadem, a black thick curling beard, and was arrayed in the purest white, as were the whole sixty thousand Mamelukes who stood before him, with an air of the most respectful submissive devotion.

He waved his hand, and immediately the sports commenced by several of these youths running at full career between the first two hillocks, dexterously shooting at the marks right and left, until they were absolutely covered with arrows. They next passed at equal speed throughout the other vacant spaces, not one missing his aim, but, galloping with reins loose, each discharged sometimes two, sometimes three arrows. Again they cantered back towards the goal, and, spurring their foaming horses, leaped on and off, six or seven times successively, and discharged arrows at intervals, without once missing their aim. Whilst the horses absolutely seemed to fly over the sand, three Mamelukes unstrung their bows, whirled them around their heads by means of the string; restrung them, nocked their arrows, and failed not to transfix the butt. A fresh party now advanced, who, after throwing themselves off their horses thrice backwards, again vaulted into the saddle, and drove into the mark without a single miss. Three times also did they saddle and unsaddle their galloping horses without dismounting, and used their bows at intervals with the same unrivalled adroitness. Some lay backward on the horse's croup, and, taking his tail between their teeth, raised themselves upright, and shot as well as at first. Others sat between sharp-pointed drawn swords, three before and three behind, whilst the riders were protected only by a light silken dress, so that the smallest inclination of their body could not fail of wounding them. Yet so adroitly did they manage themselves that there was, in reality, no danger, and, surrounded thus, they were still successful with their arrows. Of all these youths, however, one only was seen to stand barefooted and erect upon the backs of two of the swiftest horses, and, putting them to the utmost speed, to plant in the butt three arrows discharged in front, and also backwards like a Parthian. Another also performed several feats of dexterity peculiar to himself: galloping without a saddle, no sooner did he come between the marks, than, laying his back close to that of his horse, with feet elevated for an instant into the air, he sprang upright, and drove his shafts thrice into the object of his aim. At length, when the marks appeared quite loaded with arrows, the master of these youths, a venerable grey-bearded man, advanced, and seizing the banners, first held them aloft, and then cast them on the earth, whereupon his scholars showered down their lances and arrows, as if about to end the lives of ten thousand wounded adversaries, and then rode away, making their horses curvet triumphantly up and down the arena.

So much for the ancient Mameluke archer. I shall only add, in reference to these Oriental matters, that, among the Monguls, a bow is symbolical of a king, an arrow of an ambassador or viceroy; the one sending, the other being sent. Common arrows made of reeds are called Schem in Arabic, and those of the Persians, formed of hard wood, they style Neschab. The latter nation possesses a very curious treatise, entitled "Ahkan al remi u besaif," or instructions for the use of the bow and the sword.* E Kūs is the Arab word for the former weapon; and a particularly smooth well made arrow they style Azlam.

I have already remarked how solicitous our own brave forefathers were to train up a race of expert archers in defence of their own and their prince's rights. Their feelings on this important subject are well expressed in the spirited lines selected as a motto to the present chapter. My little toxophilites, however, may be tolerable historians, without knowing how many English monarchs and nobles excelled in the art which they admire, such information belonging rather to the private than the public annals of a people. Yet they must have heard of that gorgeous interview between our Henry the Eighth and Francis of France, styled, by way of pre-eminence, "The Field of the Cloth of Gold." Their sports were all of martial character, in accordance with the habits and practice of the age; and in these it is asserted that the crafty Frenchmen allowed our bluff King Hal a petty pre-eminence, since to effect the political objects of the conference was of far greater moment than splintering a lance, or the surrender of courser and corslet.* To a certain extent this may be true. France reckoned among her chivalry many noble and accomplished knights; and, in the sports of the tournament, policy perhaps dictated the surrender of a triumph where victory would have been easy. But when, after a morning passed in exercises of mimic warfare, Henry, at the particular request of the French monarch, undertook to exhibit the skill and vigour with which Englishmen wielded the long bow and cloth-yard arrow, he owed nothing to the concessions of his adversaries. Having retired to his tent,

* Bibliothèque Orientale.
† By the laws of the tournay, the victorious knight was entitled to the horse and arms of his adversary.

and divested himself of the heavy tilting armour, he re-appeared habited in the forest garb of merry England. The bugle horn of gold, suspended from his shoulder, was sustained by a baldric richly embossed with the same precious metal, a number of arrows couched beneath his embroidered girdle, and in his hand he carried a long bow of the finest Venetian yew. The crowd of nobles who waited on their monarch were equipped in a corresponding style of magnificence; and the gallant bearing of this hunter band, as they stationed themselves around the butt, called forth a spontaneous burst of admiration from the whole French court. Henry was then in the bloom of youth: to a handsome countenance he added a figure of the most perfect symmetry, and his height was considerably above six feet. The plumed bonnet and sylvan dress, assumed for the present occasion, served to enhance these personal advantages not a little, and, in truth, he appeared a noble personification of the tall English archer.* When, therefore, he stepped forth from among the group of attendant foresters, and, with a manly vigorous air, was seen to brace his trusty bow, expectation rose on tiptoe. As he drew the first arrow from his belt, the French, delighted with the novelty of this spectacle, suffered not a whisper to escape them; the English, forgetful that the fame of their archery resounded throughout all Europe, felt as though it depended solely upon their royal champion's success. And right well did Henry on that day maintain the reputation of his countrymen. He repeatedly shot into the centre of the white, though the marks were erected at the extraordinary distance of twelve score yards apart. A simultaneous burst of admiration marked the delight and astonishment of the vast assembly who witnessed this fine display of skill and personal strength;

* Nemo enim ipso rege (Henry VIII.) Britannicum ingentem arcum contentius flexit; nemo certius atque validius sagittavit. — " No man in his dominions drew the great English bow more vigorously than Henry himself; no man shot further, or with a more unerring aim." — *Paulus Jovius.*

Henry the Eighth at the Field of the Cloth of Gold.

London Published by Longman & C? Feb? 1840.

applause, no doubt, as sincere as it was well deserved: for the attempts of some cross-bowmen belonging to the French king's body-guard, who tried their quarrels* at the same dutts, served but to betray their own inexpertness, and the inferiority of that weapon. A contemporary writer, whilst briefly alluding to this gorgeous pageant, paints Henry's dexterity in the following quaint terms:—" Après allèrent tirer à l'arc, et le Roy d'Angleterre luy même, qui est merveilleusement bon archer et fort; et le fesoit bon à voir." Afterwards they went to practise archery with the king of England, who is a marvellous good archer and a strong; and it was right pleasant to behold.

In after years, our bluff Hal lost none of the relish for this exercise which had distinguished his boyhood. When a gentleman named Cavendish waited on him at Hampton Court, in obedience to his majesty's commands, he found him engaged with a party, shooting rounds, or butts, in a portion of the park situated behind the garden. " Perceiving him so occupied," says he, " I thought it not my duty to trouble him, but leaned to a tree, intending to stand there, and await his gracious pleasure. Being in a great study, at the last the King came suddenly behind me where I stood, and clapped his hands upon my shoulders; and when I perceived him I fell upon my knee, to whom he said, calling me by name, ' I will,' quoth he, ' make an end of my game, and then I will talk with you;' and so departed to his mark, whereat the game was ended. Then the King delivered his bowe unto the yeoman of his bowes, and went his way towards the palace."

In the privy-purse expences of this monarch† we find numerous memorandums connected with archery. Of these, some relate to losses at shooting matches, others to presents of archery gear, dear ones, indeed, but with which the courtiers aimed to bespeak their prince's gracious favour by ministering to a dominant taste.

* Bolts for the crossbow. † Edited by Sir N. H. Nicolas.

" *Item*, 2*d August*, 1530. Paid to a servant of my Lord of Suffolk, in reward for bringing bowes and arrowes to the King's grace, xl*s.*

" *Item*, 18*th August.* Paid to the French fletcher*, in reward towards his surgery, xl*s.*

" *Item*, 28*th October.* Paid to a servant of Maister Bryan's, in reward for bringing of a cross-bowe, a quyver with arrowes, and a hawk glove, xx*s.*

" *Item*, 20*th March*, 1531. Paid to George Coton, for vii shott lost by the King's grace unto him at Totthill, at 6*s.* 8*d.* the shotte, xlvj*s.* viij*d.*

" *Item*, 15*th March.* Paid in rewarde to a fletcher, that gave the King a cane staff and a stone bowe, xl*s.*

" *Item*, 29*th March.* Paid to George Clifford, for soe much money as he won of the King's grace at Totehill at shooting, xij*s.* vi*d.*

" *Item*, 8*th May.* Paid to George Coton, for that he wonne of the King's grace at the roundes, the laste daye of Aprill, iii*l.*

" *Item*, ——— Paid to one of the guarde, for shooting at Greenwiche, ij*s.*

" *Item*, 30*th June.* Paid to the iij Cotons iij setts, the which the King's grace lost to them at Greenwiche Parke, xx livres.

" *Item*, ——— To the same Coton, for one upshott that he wonne of the King's grace, vj*s.* viij*d.*

" *Item*, 8*th July*, 1531. Paid to my Lord of Rocheford, for shooting with the King's grace at Hampton Court, lviij*l.*

" *Item*, 10*th July.* Paid to Thomas Carey, for shooting money, xx*d.*

" *Item*, 26*th July.* Paid to my Lord of Rocheford, for shooting money, vi ryalles, iii livres, vii*s.* vi*d.*

" *Item*, ——— Paid to Gwillim, for pellets for the stone bowe, viii*s.*

---

* Fletcher, an arrow-maker; from *flèche,* an arrow.

"*Item*, 20*th July*, 1532. Paid to Gwillim, the French fletcher, in rewarde, xx *s*.

"*Item*, 7*th October*, 1532. Paid to Henry Birds, for divers bowes and shaftes for the King's grace, for one year, xvj*l*."

The attachment which Henry felt for the bow induced him to confer rewards and honours on all who exhibited any extraordinary dexterity. At the close of a grand shooting match held in Windsor Park, the upshot being given, he observed a guardsman, named Barlow, preparing to discharge his last arrow; upon which the king exclaimed, "Beat them all, Barlow, and thou shalt be Duke of Archers." He shot, and placed his arrow in the centre of the butt; whereupon the king immediately redeemed his promise, by conferring on this archer the title of Duke of Shoreditch, the place of his birth.

Henry the Seventh, his father, showed an equal love for archers, who principally composed the army by which he triumphed over the tyrant Richard. After disembarking at Milford Haven, the Earl of Richmond marched northward, and rested a night at Wern Newydd*, near Aberaeron, the seat of David Llwyd, Esq., still inhabited by a lineal descendant of that family. His son, Einon Llwyd, was one of those formidable Welsh archers, whose prowess excited as much terror among their English neighbours, as theirs had done among French and Spaniards; and, Richmond being a countryman†, he readily joined his standard with a party of hardy mountain warriors, brave and skilful like himself.

On his departure, as a testimony of grateful friendship, the Earl presented his hospitable entertainer with a silver flagon, still possessed by the Llwyd family. The apartments and bed

---

* New Alders, the seat of Evan Pryce Llwyd, Esq., also of Llanseven, Carmarthenshire.

† Catharine of France, widow of Agincourt's hero, married Owen Tudor, a Welsh gentleman of ancient family. Richmond was the issue of this union.

in which Henry slept also remain in their original condition; and the following inscription, painted on the wall in old English characters, commemorates that remarkable visit: —

"Hon yw'r Ystafell lle cysgodd Harry Iarll Richmond y VII. yn y flwyddyn 1485, gyda a Inon ap Dafydd Llwyd, Esquire, ar ei daith o Aberdangleddan ir fruydr enwog ar faes Bosworth, yor yr hony lladdwyd Richard y III. a Harry a ærth oddynno i Lundain ac agafodd ei goroniyn frenin Lloegr."—"This is the apartment in which the Earl of Richmond, afterwards Henry VII., slept with Einon, son of David Llwyd, Esquire, when marching to the memorable battle on Bosworth Field, where Richard the Third was slain. Henry went thence to London, and was crowned king of England."

Among the festivities which crowned the union of the two roses, on Henry's marriage with the Princess Elizabeth, archery was not omitted. The king himself took an active part in these shooting matches; a fact thus alluded to in a very ancient ballad: —

> Look where he shooteth at the buttes,
> And with him lords three;
> He weareth a gown of velvet black,
> And 't is coted above the knee.*

Edward the Sixth is also entitled to notice among the list of England's royal archers. Whilst quite a youth he kept a journal, still preserved among the manuscripts in the British Museum. It contains many allusions to archery, particularly some curious memoranda of the amiable young prince's successes and disappointments at matches in which he took a part.

Prince Henry, and his brother Charles the First, were great admirers of the bow. An engraving of the latter, in archer's costume, forms the frontispiece of Markham's Treatise. As a

---

* Harleian Lib. 365.

work of art it is vilely executed, and his majesty is represented drawing his shaft villanously low at the breast.

Charles the Second, on his restoration, did much towards the revival of archery. It is not generally known that the merry monarch, endowed with facile manners, which readily accommodated themselves to the tastes and habits of all with whom he associated, was a member of an archery society during his exile in the Low Countries. I really forget whether Ghent or Bruges, but his majesty's statue occupies the *salon* belonging to an ancient fraternity of bowmen in one or the other.

George the Fourth was, in his youth, a magnificent patron of archery*, but as the interest he manifested for this, the favourite pastime of his illustrious ancestors, has been fully detailed elsewhere, I merely allude to it here.

And now, my little friends, having done our devoir as regards the achievements of princes and potentates, we will next take a hasty survey of archery as it flourished in a less exalted sphere of life. The famous Earl Pembroke, surnamed Strongbow, would have acquired among the Romans the cognomen of Longæ manus †, just as the poet Ovid was nicknamed Naso, from the extraordinary dimensions of his nose. This preternatural length of arm gave him an immense advantage over ordinary archers. We may, therefore, conclude contemporary writers have not exaggerated, when they assert that, at the age of eighteen, he was master of a bow in which no other man could draw an arrow to the head. During his expedition for the conquest of Ireland, he frequently resigned sword and lance, the ordinary weapons of knighthood, to fight among his archers, armed with this redoubtable bow.

The young Lord Henry Vesci was remarkable for skill in archery, and his untimely fate. Being indicted by the sheriff of Yorkshire for some trivial offences against the forest laws, a warrant was issued to Henry de Clydnau for his apprehension.

* See " Modern Archery." † Long arms.

To this the refractory noble refused to submit. Catching up his bow and shafts, he fled through a wood, pursued by the deputy-sheriff and his men, and would certainly have escaped, had not revenge induced him to slacken his pace, that he might bring his adversaries within bowshot. Then, discharging his cloth-yard shafts with fatal aim, three of the foremost quickly bit the dust.

> The outlaw's shot it was so strong,
> That no man might him drive,
> And the proud sheriff's men,
> They fled away full blythe,—

dreading the fate of their comrades; and, after retreating some distance, halted to hold a council of war. Naturally suspicious that Vesci would still track and keep them in sight, they resolved to quit the wood altogether, in the hope of lulling their victim into security. And their stratagem had the desired effect; for the young lord, really believing pursuit at an end, for the present, unstrung his bow, and, throwing it on the turf beside him, soon fell asleep beneath the shade of a large tree. In the mean time the sheriff and his followers made a large circuit, and, creeping separately through the thick underwood, they stole upon the defenceless youth, and killed him where he lay.*

My next illustration of youthful archery is also taken from England's domestic annals, and exhibits so revolting a picture of society in the fourteenth century, that we might be disposed to question its authenticity, did not our public records furnish many equally atrocious.†

Sir John Elland, high sheriff of York, had inherited with his

---

* Hale's " Placit. Coron."

† See " Murder of the Hartgills by Lord Stourton," a domestic tragedy, thus alluded to by Heywood: — "——— Great dearthe in Englande; For base murder, died, at Salisburie, Lord Stourton."

patrimony a fierce family feud against Sir Robert Beaumont, of Crosland Hall, in the same county. Unwilling to expose his schemes of revenge to the hazard of disappointment, he declined engaging in his quarrel those public forces which were at his command by virtue of the shrievalty, but contented himself with a band of trusty neighbours and tenants, whose hearts and hands lay wholly devoted to his pleasure. Possessing the lordship of Elland town, all its inhabitants were his homagers, and, as such, had sworn themselves his doomed servants, according to the ancient phraseology of law.

With this knot of desperadoes, he, "most illegally, being himself but a private gentleman," marched, in the middle of the night, to Quarmby Hall, the dwelling of Quarmby of Quarmby, Sir Robert Beaumont's nearest relative; and, having broken into the house, incontinently slew its worthy proprietor, whilst wrapt in the arms of sleep.

Unsatiated with blood, the high sheriff and his followers passed on to the house of Lockwood of Lockwood, a gentleman universally esteemed as the darling and oracle of his county. Him also they murdered, in the midst of his domestic retirement, having no power of armed men to protect him, because neither fearing nor expecting such an assault.

Sir Robert Beaumont being thus deprived of his most trusty friends, the ferocious Elland, ere day had dawned, bent his steps towards Crosland Hall. But that house was deeply moated, and, the drawbridge being up, they were compelled to halt. Evil fortune, however, favoured his designs, for, after an ambush of three hours, a girl, who had occasion to be early stirring, approached and let down the bridge. Rushing from their concealment, the Ellanders seized the terrified maid, whom they dragged with them into the house. But her screams had roused the family, and they found Sir Robert in his bedchamber, with as many servants about him as could be assembled upon so sudden an emergency. Resistance, however, availed not against their more numerous and better armed assailants, who seized the poor old knight, and haled him down stairs into the hall, where the murderous Elland, nothing moved by the piteous shrieks of his terrified lady, stood by, whilst they severed his head from his body with the stroke of a sword. He then commanded all the bread and wine in the house to be brought forth, and the party sat down to regale after their bloody tragedy. As he sat, Elland espied the two sons of his victim, and ordered them to approach and eat. The younger complied, but his brother refusing, he furiously exclaimed, " See ye yon lad ! how heinously he doth take his father's death, and looketh as if meditative of revenge: but fear not ye; Elland's watch and ward shall keep the young spawn of a traitor from being ever able to work us any mischance."

When at sunrise they departed, and were out of sight, the widowed mother, pale but tearless, justly fearing a recurrence of these sanguinary enormities, immediately interred, with decent funeral, the remains of her beloved husband. Then, leaving mansion and property to its fate, she took refuge with her boys at the house of Townley of Brereton, her near kinsman, who gave a kind reception, with free and generous entertainment. Having associated themselves with young Lacy of Crumble Bottom, Lockwood of Lockwood, and Quarmby of Quarmby, both whose fathers, as I have already said, perished by Elland's hand, the young Beaumonts spent their time in devising schemes of retaliation. With this view, they laboured to acquire dexterity in such martial exercises as were calculated to render them dexterous in the anticipated game of death; namely, riding, tilting, the sword, and shooting in the long bow, then England's most famous and redoubtable artillery.

Whilst halting between hope and fear, and daily busied with uncertain rumours, Dawson and Haigh, two faithful dependants of their family, suddenly visited them. They brought news that the sheriff-turn would shortly be held at Brigg House, where Elland never failed to appear in person. For many reasons it was unanimously decided that a better opportunity of avenging their slaughtered parents could not be selected. The roads, too, at such periods, were usually crowded with uncouth and strange persons, so that none would be likely to question whence they came or whither they went.

Accordingly, taking Dawson and Haigh as guides, and accompanied by a body of picked archers, these adventurous youths commenced their hazardous expedition. They passed unobserved through bye-ways or forest paths, and with vengeful punctuality reached Crumble Bottom Wood, true to the day of the sheriff-turn. Here they placed themselves in ambush, Sir John Elland little dreaming, amidst the pride and gallantry of his shrievalty, and whilst assisting at the execution of meaner criminals, that, in a few short hours, his life would be devoted to expiate his own dark catalogue of crime.

And now the spies placed in Brigg House arrived breathless, to tell that Elland was mounted, and on his journey homewards. Then the Beaumonts arrayed their men upon the hill tops leading from Brookfoot to Brigg House; and then, with countenances changed to fearful ghastliness, compressed lips, and eyes gleaming like those of the vengeful adder, they paced to and fro upon its narrow brow, intently looking towards that distant point which concealed or brought to view all who journeyed along the road. At length, three horsemen abreast rounded it suddenly, followed by a numerous cavalcade, two and two; and, after sweeping quickly along the valley's sinuosities, continued to ascend the narrow hill path at a sharp trot. The appearance of an armed company thus loitering in the road might naturally have excited alarm; but the sheriff evidently suspected nothing, for, riding briskly up at the head of his party, he courteously vailed to them his bonnet. Adam Beaumont fiercely returned his salute. "Thy courtesy, Sir Knight," he exclaimed, "shall avail thee little; I am Adam Beaumont. My father's noble blood staineth thy hands, and to recompense his inhuman death presently shalt thou also be slain."

Thus saying, this little band discharged their arrows against the Ellanders, who for some time made stout resistance, until Beaumont managed to separate the sheriff from his company at the lane's end, and there incontinently slew him.

Their main object being thus accomplished, the young leaders fled away that very night to Furness Fells, a place between forty and fifty miles from the scene of their revenge. In this wild and remote district they took up their winter quarters, to plot new schemes for extirpating the whole male line of Elland. With this view they surrounded the Hall with constant spies, by whose advice, at the opening of spring, the Beaumonts returned to Crumble Bottom, and on Palm Sunday eve, in the silence of midnight, took forcible possession of Elland mill; for, being near the hall, it was well adapted for assaulting the young knight and his family, the following morning, on their way to church. Still the conspirators' arrival was not managed so secretly as to prevent its being observed by the neighbouring cottagers. From them several dark hints reached Sir John, warning him to be on his guard that he was not surprised in his bed. A consciousness of his father's crimes, and his recent expiation of them, tended to strengthen these suspicions. He was unwilling to trust himself abroad, and mentioned to his wife that armed men were reported to have been seen lurking in the vicinity. However, she made light of his fears, and merely answered, "This day is Palm Sunday: we must certainly go to church and serve God on his holy festival."

It so happened that the miller, being in want of some meal, sent his wife to the mill, early on that morning, to fetch it. On her approach she found the door open, and the conspirators in possession, by whom she was straightway seized, bound hand and foot, and laid in a secure place. The woman not returning so soon as her husband expected, he began to be wroth, threaten-

The Feud of Elland.

ing sharply and severely to chastise her. On repairing to the mill, in great haste, he finds his wife a captive, and the gentlemen present ready to explain the delay, by binding and laying him in a similar posture close by her side.

In the mean while Sir John Elland and his family were preparing for church. The warning he had received lay heavy upon his spirit, and he secretly clad himself in a breastplate of proof. Their usual path was by the mill-pool side, but, during low water, a shorter passage lay over the dam stones; and from their hiding-place Beaumont and his associates had a full view of the party, as cautiously and one behind the other they began to cross the stream. Elland came first: no sooner had he reached the centre stone, than the mill door flew open, and Beaumont rushed forth, holding his weapon bent and an arrow ready nocked, which he sped with furious aim, and the knight received it full upon his breast. Repelled, however, by the armour, it glanced away and dropt harmless. Seeing this, Wilkin of Lockwood ran forward, and exclaiming fiercely, "Cousin, you shoot wide!" drew his shaft to the head, which, though admirably directed, was unsuccessful from the same cause. Thus, for a moment, it seemed destined their victims should escape; but Beaumont, grown wise by experience, fully comprehended the reason of their failure; and, discharging a second arrow, pierced his victim through the brain. He fell headlong into the mill-stream, whose waters were crimsoned with his gore, and, at the same instant, Lockwood's second arrow mortally wounded his only boy. The affrighted domestics carried him and his swooning mother back to the house, where he almost immediately expired; and so perished the last male branch of Elland of Elland Hall.*

The crimes of the father being thus visited upon his children with more than Arab retribution, Lockwood and Quarmby

* Now, or recently, in possession of the noble family of Halifax.

made a precipitate retreat; but the Ellanders were already in arms, breathing vengeance and slaughter for the death of their lord. Scarcely, therefore, had they gained Aneley Wood ere they distinctly heard the shouts of their pursuers as the foremost viewed their chase. Seeing no hope of escape, the whole party resolutely faced about, and, ranged in a hollow square, made brave resistance, until their arrows were spent: then Quarmby, the strongest and most resolute man of the band, refusing to flee one foot from his ground, fell covered with wounds; and the Ellanders fiercely pursued Lockwood through the wood; but he outstripped them, and, after encountering many hardships and hair-breadth escapes, arrived at Camel Hall, a solitary mansion near Cawthorpe, inhabited by a peasant. It appears he there became deeply enamoured of his host's daughter, a young woman possessing great beauty, united with apparent artlessness. Their place of assignation was the park, for Camel Hall once belonged to a family of distinction. It unfortunately happened that the keeper, in going his evening rounds, observed Lockwood in earnest conversation with this damsel: he recognised him, and quickly conveyed intelligence to Boswell, the under-sheriff, and landlord of Camel Hall. Boswell immediately rode over to his tenant, to contrive some mode of seizing the youth at his next visit. Overawed by threats of being expelled from his farm, and tempted by the offer of a considerable reward, the farmer promised his assistance: accordingly, no sooner did Lockwood again enter into Camel Hall than it was surrounded by his foes. The bold archer, however, who never stirred abroad without his trusty bow, quickly ascended the stairs to an upper room, and appeared at the open window, breathing defiance against his enemies: equally regardless of threats and offers of mercy, he replied to both by launching a deadly arrow, whenever any one of their number ventured within bowshot. Again, his escape was more than probable, had it not been for an act of treachery, which, if rare among the sex, is also unexampled in its atrocity. The woman on whom the heroic Lockwood had placed his affections, far from making suitable return, actually sold herself, as her father had done, to his destroyers. Stealing cautiously behind him, with a sharp knife, as he was in the act of drawing his bow, she suddenly cut the string, and left him defenceless. The rest is soon told. No longer kept at bay by the terror of his archery Boswell rushed in, and quickly seized and bound the unfortunate Lockwood. He was then led forth, and instantly put to death.

Having so far furnished an abstract and brief chronicle of exploits, where princes, nobles, or knights, alone figure as the chief performers, let us next glance at an inferior, but highly important class—I mean our yeomen archers, who drew their bowstrings at sixpence daily pay. Here, however, much patient research has been ill rewarded; and, where the amplest information was anticipated, nothing exists beyond a few meagre details. "In my time," says Ascham, "men that were learned, did not understand archery; and those who shot well, were unlearned." Indeed, a profound ignorance of even the commonest elementary knowledge, distinguished the lower grades of society from the eleventh to the close of the fifteenth century. Oral traditions unquestionably abounded among the populace; but those qualified by education to collect and record them, unconscious of their value to the men of other generations, felt no interest in the task: and each romantic tale perished almost with him who was its hero.

The wages above cited were given to our archers at least five centuries ago. They seem disproportionate when we reflect on the relative value of money then and at present; but the Veel Manuscript expressly states that Sir Maurice Berkeley had the king's[*] warrant to receive, out of the customs of wool, at 6*l.* per sack, his own pay and that of twenty men at arms; viz.

[*] Edward III.

4s. per diem to himself as a banneret; 2s. each to his knights; 12d. for an esquire; and 6d. per diem for an archer. How highly, therefore, must the services of this force have been estimated, when a poor peasant was rewarded with an eighth of the stipend given to one of Edward the Third's most powerful feudal lords. And in cases of pressing emergency, some additional bounty seems to have been added: for instance, so much blood had been shed during the wars of the roses, that, on the termination of their fatal quarrel, the few persons of distinction who survived found themselves almost tenantless*, and, in consequence, often greatly embarrassed to complete their stipulated number of followers when summoned on foreign service. Some dilemma of this nature gave rise to correspondence between Sir Roger L'Estraunge who had fought on King Edward's side, and his brother in arms Sir John Paston, in the reign of Henry the Seventh. "Master Paston," says he, "I commend me to you; so it is, that I am not yet purveyed of men to my number of archers, such as should go over sea with me. Wherefore, sir, I beseech you to do so much, as to have purveyed for me two or three such as ye think shall be for me. Sir, I understand that Sir Terry Robsart lieth but little from you, where, as I trow, he might help me of one by your means; and as for their wages, say they shall have the king's

---

* Civil warfare has been attended with similar results at every period of our history. An aged woman of Dorsetshire once told me, as a tradition received from her grandmother, how, during the height of the quarrel between King Charles and his Parliament, the unusual event of a wayfarer passing through her village excited so much curiosity, that the whole population crowded to their doors, and remained watching until he disappeared. It served as food for conversation long afterwards; on such a day, said they, " we saw a man!" For miles round none but women were left at home: the lands lay uncultivated, and famine gradually consumed the aged and the helpless. As to children, my informant added that none below a certain age remembered their fathers, and, although familiar with the name, they knew not its meaning.

wages and somewhat else, so that I trust they shall be pleased. Sir, I beseech you to take the pains for me this time, and I shall do you that service that lyeth in me, by the grace of Jesu — which preserve ye. — ROGER L'ESTRAUNGE. — Monday, April 16th, 1492."

The three famous archers mentioned below, often figure in scraps of ancient poetry. They seem to have stood equal, in popular estimation, with Robin Hood and his co-mate John Little; since, in Shakspeare's days — and no doubt long before and after — the name of one of them was used to compliment an expert archer. "*Benedict.* He that hits me, let him be clapt on the shoulder and called Adam."

> Merry it was in fair forest,
>   Among the leaves green;
> Where as men hunt east and west,
>   With bowes and arrowes keen.
> To ryse the deare out of their den,
>   Such sights hath oft been sene,
> As bye three men of the north countrie,
>   By them it is I mene.
> The one of them, hight Adam Bel,
>   The other, Clym of the Clough,
> The third was William of Cloudeslie,
>   An archere goode enow.

Among the monuments in Clewer church are some memorials to the family of Hayes of Hollyport. One of these celebrates, in indifferent poetry, the exploits of Martin Expence, a famous archer, who shot a match against a hundred men, near Bray. In Glinton church, also, we have the effigies of a bowman, wearing his bugle horn and other insignia of the craft. Leland tells an interesting story of John Pearson, a Coventry archer, who, being at the battle of Dixemunde, had one of his legs shattered by a cannon ball: but such was the indomitable spirit of the man, that he continued to use his bow kneeling or sitting; and when the French took to flight, addressing a comrade, he said, "Have these three arrows which remain, and continue thou the chase, for I may not."

"Here," observes the author of "The Troubles in New England," "I cannot but record the valliancy of George Forest, one of my soldiers, who, with seventeen arrows sticking in him, still stoutly resisted the foe; and then, for want of a chirurgeon, died."

The author of "The Lay of the Last Minstrel" has immortalised the fame of Wat Tinlinn, "who in my younger days," says he, "was the theme of many a fireside tale." This person was a retainer of the Buccleugh family, and held, for his border service, a small tower on the frontiers of Liddesdale. Wat was by profession a *sutor*, but by inclination and practice an archer and warrior. Upon one occasion, the captain of Bewcastle, military governor of that wild district of Cumberland, is said to have made an incursion into Scotland, in which he was defeated and forced to fly. Wat Tinlinn pursued him closely through a dangerous morass: the captain, however, gained the firm ground; and seeing Tinlinn dismounted, and floundering in a bog, used these words of insult, "Sutor Wat, you cannot sew your boots; the heels risp, and the seams rive." "If I cannot sew," retorted Tinlinn, discharging a shaft which nailed the captain's thigh to his saddle, — "if I cannot sew, I can *yerk*." This latter word, signifying the twitching or tightening of the thread, practised by his trade, alludes also to the act of letting off the bowstring. It may be here remarked that Lancashire Rawson, who still lives in the remembrance of many of my seniors, the best among modern archers, was also a shoemaker.

Carew, the ancient historian of Cornwall, alludes to the dexterity of one Richard Arundel, an intimate friend and countryman of his own, who, like a Parthian, could shoot twelve score from behind his head, with the right hand or the left. He, presently afterwards, tells a quaint anecdote of another archer, in language equally quaint. "I have heard," says he, "by credible report, of those who professed and protested themselves to have been eye-witnesses, that one Robert Bone, of Antony, shot at a little bird sitting on his cowe's back, and killed it—the bird I mean, not the cowe;—which was very cunning in the performance, or very foolish in the attempt. The first of these somewhat resembles Menelaus, mentioned by Zosimus, lib. ii., who, nocking three arrows, and shooting them all at once, would strike three several persons; and might have deserved a double stipend in the Grand Signior's guard, where the one half of his archers are left handed, that they may not turn their tail upon their sultan when they drawe."*

Among the troops which composed the Floridan expedition, herein-before referred to, there were only two archers: one an Englishman, named Coles; the other a Spaniard, who, being in London until the age of twenty, had acquired an Englishman's adroitness with the bow and shaft. These were the only adversaries truly formidable to the Indians, who, also, chiefly depended on their archery, but laughed to scorn the confined range of a Spanish cross-bow. The arquebuses, indeed, might have been more formidable; but these the Christians, having no iron, had been compelled to convert into "horse-shoe nails." Coles relates that, in their disastrous voyage up the river Chicagua, he received two dangerous arrow shots, and only escaped death by a miracle. At the same time, Don Gusman, one of the Spanish officers, was struck by above fifty arrows in his head and shoulders, and expired in the arms of his associates as they bore him from that scene of slaughter.†

---

* A bowman, left-handed, is undoubtedly the most ungainly of monsters, to whom the recommendation of even so grave an authority as Plato fails to reconcile us. The Greek philosopher considered that children should be taught to use both hands with equal dexterity, and attributes it to the imprudence of mothers and nurses that there is any difference; for among the Scythians, he says, men draw the bow equally with both hands. I repeat, however, that it has a very contemptible appearance, and is unpardonable, because any one may cure himself of the bad habit in a week.

† Commentarios Reales de el Origin de los Incas.

Many centuries ago, the barons of Berkeley Castle were at feud with Lord de Lisle. Having come to a resolution of putting their irreconcileable differences to the arbitrament of the sword, both parties met near Nibley Green, Gloucestershire, where the Berkeleys came attended by a large reinforcement from Bristol, whose citizens, at that period, were as famed for a turbulent martial spirit as for commercial enterprise. To these were added a band of archers from Dean Forest, who, secure in their native fastnesses, like the Kent woldsmen, owned vassalage to none, although they usually maintained an alliance, for mutual protection, with the neighbouring barons of Berkeley. Dwellers within the purlieus of a royal chase, stocked with countless herds of deer, each man, from infancy, had become well accustomed to the yew bow and grey goose shaft, which they handled with an adroitness that made them the terror of the west country. There is a circumstantial narrative of the battle of Nibley Green among the castle archives, from which it appears that their leader, Black Will, marked the Lord Lisle, when he lifted the visor of his helmet for fresh air, and loosing against him an arrow, it pierced his brain, and he fell dead from his horse. Du Carell's poem of De Wyrale makes this redoubtable personage confess and glory in the feats of arms he performed during that sanguinary fray.

> And note, advancing through the tall trees' shade,
> A stranger bold and armed, a bow who bare
> Some six feet long, of toughest yew-tree made.
> A goodly sheaf of arrows bright and keen,
> Were deftly stuck beneath his baldric green.

Thus accoutred, he falls in company with the "chief forester in fee."

> 'Say, who and whence art thou?' De Wyrale* said.

---

* A tomb of Newland churchyard, which is within Dean Forest, represents an archer, bow in hand, and with a single arrow beneath his belt.

    ' I reck not,' he replied, and careless laughed,
       Of Briton, Saxon, Norman, or of Dane,
    If I compacted be; so I my craft
    Well know, nor ever do dismiss in vain,
    Drawn to my ear, the unerring cloth yard shaft;
       Nor know I fear — nor crouch to sword or lance,
    As many a daring deed might testify.
       He too, the Lord of Lisle, who dared to prance, —
       At his life's cost, in an ill-omened day,
       Joining with Berkeley's earl in deadly fray: —
    'T was I that drew the bow, the shaft that sent,
    And planted deep its steel point in the brain
    Of that proud lord, what time Fitzharding* vent
       Gave to the wrath he did perforce restrain,
    Rankling long time within his bosom pent;
    Nor proved the cherish'd hope of vengeance vain.'

I will here offer a few words respecting the mode by which Lord de Lisle met his death. A petition, presented to the king by his widow, states that the arrow entered his left temple, for, like Cæsar's soldiers at the battle of Pharsalia, our English yeomen were prone to strike at the visage, although from very different motives. Strong mail protected the person of knights and men-at-arms, over and above which a triangular shield, fenced with steel plates, and suspended by a strap round the neck, gave additional protection to the vital parts. None but very "strong and sinewy bows" could drive an arrow through this panoply of metal, so the archer, keen-sighted as the lynx, and no less cruel, constantly directed his aim at face and throat, when the foeman, who played his game of war beneath a summer's sun, unwarily lifted visor, or removed gorget, to breathe

---

Another shows a figure recumbent, reposing his head upon a lion, his feet upon a hound. Around is sculptured the following legend: —

      Here lyeth Jenkyn Wyrale, chief forester in fee,
      A braver fellow never was, nor ever will there be.

* The family name of the earls of Berkeley.

a cooler air. Few who ventured to do so ever lived to close them again; and this favourite manœuvre with archers of our own and other countries, is repeatedly adverted to in the chronicles. At Towton, the most fatal battle in all that long quarrel of the Roses, when the Lord de Clifford, fainting with pain, heat, and thirst, took off his gorget, instantly an arrow — tradition says a headless one — passed through his neck; "and thus," adds the chronicle, "he rendered up his spirit." — Again, during the same wars, John Paston, writing to a friend, relates, as a piece of news, that the Earl of Oxford, making a sally from a castle where he was besieged, was shot through the bars of his helmet. "This day," says Paston, laconically enough, "I saw the man who did it; and there I leave him."*
In his first engagement with Hotspur's forces, Hollinshed states that Harry the Fifth, then Prince of Wales, received a shot in the face; and Shakspeare introduces him upon the stage, immediately after that accident.

Enter the Prince of Wales wounded.

Westmoreland. Come, my lord, I'll lead you to your tent.
Prince. Lead me, my lord! I do not need your help.
And heav'n forbid! a shallow scratch should drive
The Prince of Wales from such a field as this. †

One instance more, and I have done. Some pirates, from the Orcades, once entered the port of Anglesea in their long vessels; and the Earl of Chester, apprised of their approach, boldly met them, rushing into the waves upon a spirited horse. Magnus, the commander of the expedition, standing upon the prow of the foremost ship, aimed at him an arrow: the earl was completely equipped in a coat of mail, which guarded every part of his person except the eyes; but the unlucky weapon struck him in the right eye, and, entering his brain, he fell a lifeless corpse into the sea. The victor, seeing him in this state,

* Paston Letters. † Henry IV.

proudly and exultingly exclaimed, in the Danish language, "Leit loup" — let him leap; and thenceforward the power of the English ceased altogether in Anglesea.*

From the fragment of a humorous ballad, entitled "The Kynge and the Hermyt†," we have a droll insight into the character and mode of life peculiar to many a jovial friar of the fourteenth century.

> Arise up, Jack, and goe with me,
> And more of my privitie
>   Thou shalt see somethinge.
> Into a chamber he him led:
> The kynge saw about the hermyt's bed
>   Broad arrowes hang.
> The frère‡ gat him a bow in hande:
> ' Jack,' said he, ' draw up the bonde §;'
>   He ∥ might only stir the stringe.
> ' Syr,' he said, ' so have I blisse,
> There's no archere may shoote this
>   That's with my lord the kynge.'—
> An arrowe of an elle longe,
> In hys bowe he ¶ it throng,
>   And to the head he gave it hale:
> ' There is no deere in this forest,
> An it would on him feste**,
>   But it should spill his shale. ††
> Jack sith thou can of fletcher crafte,
> Thou mayst me ese with a shafte.'‡‡

* From Sir R. C. Hoare's elegant translation of Giraldus. Among the Cotton Collection of MSS. is a Danish poem, reciting the exploits of Oddus the Archer, which that hero composed whilst in the agonies of death.

† Library of Corpus Christi College, Cambridge; supposed to have been written about the year 1384.

‡ *Frère*, brother; *i.e.* a monk.

§ *Bow;* " draw up" means pull the arrow to its head.

∥ The king.

¶ The monk; it will be seen that he shows himself the more sinewy archer of the two.

** Light.

†† Blood.

‡‡ " Me ese with a shafte:" — accept an arrow from me as a present.

> 'Then,' said Jack, 'I shall.'
> 'Jack, an you will a' of my arrowes have,
> Take thee of them, and with thy leve,
>   Now go we to our play.'
> And thus they sate with fustie bandy,
> And with strike partner in that place,
>   Till it was near hand day.

From this and many similar passages, which occur in old books, it would appear that the class of "lazy, lozel, roystering monks," of whom Tuck, Robin Hood's celebrated confessor, may be considered a type, abounded in England from the Conquest to the Reformation. Indeed it could hardly be otherwise. However unfitted for the sacred office, the cowl was the most obvious resource of the junior branches of our ancient country gentlemen. "Younger sons," they were, "of younger brothers," whom the feudal system, in most cases, left entirely destitute. They could not dig, and were ashamed to beg. As Englishmen, an ardent love of field-sports was inherent in their nature: even with their mother's milk, they imbibed a taste for those manly exercises which constitute nearly the sole occupation of a martial age.

> The Curtall friar of Fountain's Abbey,
>   Well can a good bowe draw,
> He'll beat you and your yeomen,
>   Set them all on a row,

says Scadlocke to his master, Robin Hood. The earliest recorded incident in the life of the famous Thomas à Becket, archbishop of Canterbury, is his being put in the stocks for getting drunk, and fighting with his quarter-staff at a village fair. In the records of the exchequer[*], we find Savory, a clerk, that is, a friar, fined and imprisoned for wresting a bow out of the hands of one of the royal foresters. Whilst going his rounds, he convicted him of "stable stand;" or in the act of shooting at the king's deer. The burley friar forth-

[*] Madox's Exchequer.

with threatened his captor with the vengeance of the church. Too ignorant to understand, or too cunning to believe, the man insisted on bringing him before the lord warden; whereupon his holiness showed fight, disarmed the keeper, and belaboured him stoutly with his own bow.*

A prior of Winchester, in the reign of King John, appears to have been more deeply read in the "Booke of St. Alban's" than in his breviary. The most renowned chase in England was near at hand, where many "a stag of ten" fell beneath his arrows. At length these depredations became so notorious that the king, whose veneration for monks seems not to have been very profound †, ordered his convent to be searched, and fined him heavily for every bow discovered there.‡ What a pretty piece of drollery to have encountered the portly abbot and his merry freres, in shaven crowns and priestly frocks, plying their sturdy bows and cloth yard shafts, among the verdant recesses of the Hampshire forest!

> And of these merry *monks* there was not any one,
> But he could kill a deer, his swiftest speed upon.

Doubtless there stood within their lordly domain of Winchester

> Battes both fayre and longe;

that is to say, full fifteen score apart: for, under all circumstances, we do these holy fathers little injustice in presuming their fingers infinitely more ready with arrow nock than bead roll.

---

* Madox's Exchequer.

† Being abroad to hunt one day, whilst the kingdom stood interdicted, it chanced that there was a great stag or hart killed, which, when he came to be broken up, proved very fat and thick of flesh. "Oh! oh!" quoth the irreverent monarch, "what a pleasant life this deer hath led, and yet in all his days he never heard mass." — *Hollinshed*, vol. ii. p. 339.

‡ He could not plead the statute commanding every Englishman to be possessed of four shafts, because it expressly exempts "all holy men."

Before entering upon what may be properly styled the drill exercise of an archer, I may be allowed a remark or two respecting "modern gymnastics," and the substitution of archery in their place at schools. A more dangerous *, vulgar, stupid plan than the former, for exercising the limbs of boys, could hardly be devised. Let proper targets be erected on playgrounds, with the presence of teachers, to control and prevent the pupils from shooting in any other direction, or at any other objects, and all fear of accident is obviated.

That a recreation eminently conducive to health should not yet have been revived in all our private educational establishments is to be regretted. That it should be abolished in those public ones, where the rules not only expressly command its observance, but actually provide the scholars with the whole apparatus, is very strange, but very true. At Eton, Westminster, and Harrow schools, Greek and Latin orations or plays have been substituted. Thus, the original intention is altogether perverted. To relax the pupils' minds, after the arduous course of study dictated by the rules of our ancient grammar schools; to comply with the laws which enforced upon every instructor of youth and head of a family the superintendence of their initiation into this important means of national defence; and to gratify their own partiality for an accomplishment dear to Englishmen—were the reasons which

---

* "Westminster Medical Society. — Dr. George Gregory in the chair. Disease of the heart occasioned by violent gymnastic exercises.

"Mr. Smith related the case of a young gentleman, who was sent to a school where gymnastic exercises were much practised by the scholars. The youth, being desirous of emulating his companions in their feats of strength and activity, applied himself violently to their exercises, and was shortly afterwards seized with palpitation of the heart, pain in the epigastrium, and other symptoms of hypertrophy. He believed that this disease was not uncommonly the result of great excitement and over exertion, and thought their consequences should be carefully guarded against in constitutions where the fibre was lax, and a predisposition existed towards the complaint."
— *Lancet.*

made "arms for the boys" to be classed by the founders among the necessary calls upon their liberality. Foremost in the list of those writers on education, who zealously inculcate the propriety of mingling athletic with mental exercises, is Roger Ascham, sometime tutor to Queen Elizabeth, well known as the author of "Scholarca;" still better by his "Toxophilus." "Would to God!" he exclaims*, "that all men did bring up their sons, like my worshipful master Sir Henry Wingefield, in the book and the bow." "He that shooteth in the free and open fields," observed Mulcaster†, the first tutor appointed to the Merchant Taylor's School, "may choose whether between his marks he will run or walk; daunce or leape; halloo or sing; or do somewhat els, which belongeth to the other either vehement or gentle exercises. And whereas hunting on foot is much praised, what moving of the bodie hath the foot hunter in hilles and dales which the roving archer hath not in variety of grounds? Is his natural heat more stirred than the archer's is? Is his appetite better than the archer's, though the proverb help the hungry hunter? Nay, in both these, the archer hath the advantage, for both his houres be much better to eat, and all his moving is more at his choice. In fine, what good is there in any particular exercise, either to help natural heat, to clear the body and the senses, to provoke appetite, to strengthen the sinews, or to better all partes, which is not altogether in this? This exercise do I like best of any round stirring without doores upon the causes before alledged, which if I did not, that learned man, our late and worthy countryman, Maister Ascham, would be half angry with me, though he were of a mild disposition; who both for trayning the archer to his bow, and the scholar to his book, hath shewed himself a cunning archer, and a skilful maister."

* See " Toxophilus, or Scholè of Shewtinge."
† " Richard Mulcaster's Positions; wherein those primitive circumstances be examined which are necessary for the training up of children, either for skill in their book, or health in their bodie." — A.D. 1560.

A perusal of those laws which, until within the last two centuries, make the use of the bow compulsatory on all male children *, will show there is nothing "strange or singular" in the

* Many of the old black letter volumes, compiled for the instruction of country justices, have allusions to the manner in which the laws respecting archery were to be enforced. One of the least known of these † directs that butts are to be made in every village and hamlet, with a penalty of twenty shillings, recoverable every three months whilst the same should be neglected. The magistrate is further required to make inquisition as to how many possessed bows and arrows, and to fine every householder one noble per head for each male found unprovided. The " man child, from seven years of age to seventeen," to have a bow and two shafts; and each man, from seventeen to three score, a bow and four shafts. In cases where the farm servants neglected to equip themselves, their master was compelled to purchase what was necessary, and deduct the cost from their yearly wages.

" Eastington Manor, Gloucestershire, A.D. 1605. The jury present, that no one had exercised the art of archery with bows and arrows."— *MS. copy of Court Rolls.*

The legislature, which thus enforced the practice of archery by various statutes, and visited its neglect with fine and imprisonment, would have been guilty of great injustice had it not devised some protection from monopoly, and enabled the poor shooters to purchase their apparatus at a price proportioned to scanty means. At a time when the wages of farm servants amounted to no more than a groat per day, it was preposterous to expect them to hand forth their rose noble (6s. 8d.) for the purchase of a foreign yew bow, half that sum for one of inferior description, or even two shillings for a bow of common English yew. Laws were therefore enacted compelling the bowyers to manufacture for every yew bow four of other reasonable woods, to be sold at a very low rate.

To prevent the monopoly of foreign bow-staves, numerous regulations were also passed, one of which I here present to the reader, because it has escaped the notice of previous writers. It is found in a volume of statutes, without date, in the library of Earl Spencer. — " Item, for as much as the great and ancient defence of this realm hath stood by the archers and shooters, which is now fallen to decay from the dearth and excessive price of long bows, it is therefore ordained, that if any person or persons sell any long bow over the price of three shillings and four pence, then the seller or sellers of such bow to forfeit, for every bow so sold, the sum of x shillings to' the king."

---

† A treatise concerning the office of a sheriff, A.D. 1641.

shooting matches which once prevailed at all our public schools, and which were retained by a small number until within a comparatively recent period. At many, as Eton, the college school of Warwick, &c., the custom may be recognised in the appellations still borne by a portion of their respective playgrounds: in the former styled "shooting fields," in the latter "butts."

As the institution where this ancient regulation was longest respected, and even within memory of the present youthful generation, I shall introduce a description of juvenile archery as practised at

HARROW SCHOOL.

" You shall allow your child at all times bow, shafts, bowstrings, and bracer, to exercise shooting," is the founder's third rule addressed to parents who wished their sons to enjoy the advantages of education there.

John Lyons flourished as a wealthy Middlesex yeoman in the reign of Queen Elizabeth. His rank in life is at once decisive of his being a bowman; the descendant of one of the heroes alluded to by our delightful poet Drayton, when he describes a warlike rustic elder exhorting his boy to acquit himself manfully beneath Henry's banner on the plains of hostile France.

> The man in years preached to his youthful son,
> Pressed to this war, as they sat by the fire,
> What deeds in France were by his father done,
> In this attempt to work him to aspire;
> And told him there how he an ensign won,
> Which many a year hung in the village choir.

In the time of Edward II., a good bow cost about 3s.: thus, it is stated in a MS. of the Berkeley Chiefrents, that " a sturgeon taken within the lordship was to be carried up to the castle of Berkeley; howbeit, the lord of custom gives the taker, upon delivery of the sturgeon, half a mark in money, and a long bow and two arrows; or half a noble in lieu thereof."

In addition to the above regulation, Lyons has perpetuated his love for archery by the representation of an arrow which appears sculptured on many parts of the old school-house, and is, or used to be, stamped on the covers of all books, &c. provided by the foundation.*

Many ancient allusions to

> The arrow with a golden head,
> And shaft of silver white,

as the meed of successful archery, will be seen in future portions of this work. That annually provided for the Harrow boys was in like manner the founder's gift, and appears to have been a rather costly affair. The twelve competitors assembled at the butts, attired in dresses of white, green, and sometimes even scarlet satin, ornamented with spangles in various fanciful devices : they were also equipped with braces, gloves, and belts, beneath which

> Their shafts were buckled fast.

The juvenile who planted an arrow within any of the circles was each time saluted with a concert of French hunting-horns; and he who shot twelve times in or nearest to the centre came off victor, and claimed and carried home the silver arrow, followed by the music, and a procession of his school-fellows. A ball in the spacious school-room, which was attended by all the families in and near Harrow, concluded this happy day;

---

* I extract the following paragraph from " The Sun " newspaper for Nov. 12. 1792, a period of great scarcity and national distress : —

" The captain of Harrow school presents his compliments to the editor of ' The Sun ;' has the pleasure of informing him that a subscription is now commenced among his companions, from the amount of which he hopes to send him fifty flannel waistcoats in the course of a fortnight. The waistcoats will be marked with an arrow."

when, in selecting partners for the dance, where beauty sat, the victorious archer

> Claimed kindred there, and had his claim allowed.

We can trace back the winners' names, and other circumstances connected with the Harrow bow-meetings, for upwards of a century. I believe the first on record is the following, which occurs in the "Country Journal," or "Craftsman," for August 5th, 1727: —

" On Thursday a silver arrow, value 3*l.*, was shot for at Harrow by six youths of the free-school, a custom annually performed on the first Thursday in August; being the gift for that purpose by Mr. Lyons, an inhabitant of Harrow, and founder of the free-school there. Mr. Chandler, a captain in the *tame army* (militia?), marched thither from London, with about thirty or forty of his company, and performed a fine exercise in honour of the day and his son, who is one of the scholars."

Mr. Lyons fixed the 4th of August annually as the period on which the prize should be contested: and the archers were limited to six. Subsequently they enlarged the number to twelve, and selected the first Thursday in July, as more convenient than the original day. The following paragraph refers to the ancient arrangement: —

" The silver arrow was shot for at Harrow on the Hill, on the 4th of August, by the twelve following gentlemen: — Messrs. Thomas Swale, Owen Brigstock, Robert Tomlinson, His Grace the Duke of Gordon, the Right Honourable Lord W. Gordon, the Right Honourable Lord Mountstewart, Messrs. Thomas Clerk, Wright, Henry Rooke, Darby, and Denham Skeet.[*]

" August 4. 1758. The silver arrow was won at Harrow by Master Middleton.[†]

---

[*] London Chronicle. [†] Ibid.

"August 4. 1760. By Master Earle.*

" July — 1764. The silver arrow, annually shot for by the gentlemen of Harrow school, was won by Master Mee.

"July 5. 1765.† Won by Master Davies, from twelve competitors. On this occasion some Irequois Indian warriors attended to witness a sport, in which they were themselves such admirable adepts. When the game had been about half won, one of them intimated to the young gentlemen, through their interpreter, that he thought he and his friends could win the prize, if they were allowed a chance of doing so.

"July — 1766.‡ The silver arrow was shot for by the scholars of Harrow school, according to annual custom, and won by Master Alex."

After July 1771, from motives for which I am unable to account, the children were allowed to enjoy no more of these delightful anniversaries during the remainder of that century. The accustomed prize was indeed provided against the ensuing year, but, being never shot for, is now in the possession of the Rev. Henry Drury, of Harrow. The summer of 1816 saw the practice again revived, as appears from the following paragraph § :— " On Thursday, according to annual custom, the silver arrow was shot for at butts, at Harrow on the Hill, by twelve of the young gentlemen educated at that school. It was with difficulty won by Master Jenkins, who contested the prize for nearly three hours, owing to the equality of three of the young gentlemen, who gained nine each, *ten* being the winning number."

From that day the arrow ceased to be given, and with it expired the ancient practice of archery at public schools. Most persons familiar with the environs of London remember the pleasant butt-fields which formed the theatre of this romantic spectacle. They stand at the entrance of the village,

* London Chronicle. † Gent.'s Mag.
‡ Universal Museum. § Morning Herald.

on the left-hand side of the road leading from the metropolis, but retain nothing of their original appearance: the name alone remains. Those ancient earthern mounds, against which the targets rested, have been dug down; the beautiful isolated eminence, crowned with lofty trees, which once rose behind them, and down whose sides ranges of grassy seats sloped gradually to meet the turf below, was first stripped of its wood, and then (proh pudor!) consigned to the tender mercies of that ancient fraternity—the brickmakers. Altogether, the scene is one of disgusting devastation, universally regretted, except by those who sanctioned it. In the true spirit of modern utilitarianism, one link more has been wrested from the chain which connects the present and the past. By fostering a love for the robust amusements in which our martial ancestors delighted, we help to keep alive that spirit of fortitude and patriotism which they bequeathed to us as a heirloom. The prize-shooting contests at Harrow appear an unexceptionable mode of promoting health and cheerfulness among schoolboys, and of reconciling them to the performance of many a dry imposition by the anticipated pleasures of another "first Thursday in July." I consider, however, the "embryo statesmen and unfledged poets" there, exhibited unpardonable apathy whilst this inroad upon their ancient privileges was in agitation. A spirited remonstrance, arranged, for obvious reasons, after the fashion of what our sailors term a round robin, might have arrested the spoiler's hand. Failing there, we opine the malcontents would have been justified, *foro conscientiæ*, in pushing the matter a *leetle* further,—usque ad fori pessulis exclusionem, —even to a BARRING OUT, conformable to Miss Maria Edgeworth's most approved recipe. As it is, one generation more, and the "match for the silver arrow," after surviving upwards of two centuries and a half, will become a matter of mere uncertain tradition.

SECTION II.

JUVENILE BOWMEN

continued.

Scholar. What handling is proper to the instruments?
Toxophilus. Standing, nocking, drawing, holding, and loosing, whereby cometh fai shooting, which belongeth neither to wind nor weather; for in a rain, and at no mark, a man may shoot a fair shot.
Scholar. What handling belongeth to a mark?
Toxophilus. To mark his standing, to shoot compass, to draw ever more alike, to loose ever more alike, to consider the posture of the mark in hills and dales, in straight and winding places. — ASCHAM.

AND now, boys, having shown that our ancestors of every rank and profession practised archery, regarding it as an important branch of manly education, I will next teach you to become their rivals in dexterity. Provide a good bow, of any wood* you most fancy, and of a weight proportioned to your age and strength. Now the mode by which bowyers determine the relative powers of bows is this; having braced them, they either use a steelyard, or rest the handle upon some ledge, and suspend weights from the exact centre of the string, until the bend is sufficient to allow of an arrow standing between wood and string. They mark each just above the handle, according to the number of pounds necessary to accomplish this,

---

* See " Yew-trees and Yew-bows " in another part of this work.

and call it a fifty, sixty, or one hundred pound bow. The custom is of comparatively recent introduction among us, being borrowed from the Chinese, who manufacture bows of four different powers. The weakest draw seventy pounds; the others being of eighty, ninety, and one hundred. Beyond the latter weight they are used for show merely, or by persons of extraordinary muscular power. Tchien Lung, emperor of China at the time of Lord Macartney's embassy, had the reputation of being an expert bowman, and inferior only in drawing this weapon to his grandfather Caung Shee, who boasts, in his last will, that he drew one of 150 pounds. The price paid by the emperor for an ordinary bow is a tact, 5s. 3d. of our money.

But to return. Get, also, half a dozen shafts of the proper length; some spare strings, belt, bracer, and shooting gloves. Examine diligently the manner in which the string is attached to the upper and lower horns, that you may be able to put one on yourself when occasion requires. Remember that it is fixed to the lower and shortest horn by a peculiar knot or running noose, which seamen call a "timber hitch," because used in landing large beams of wood; and the tighter it is drawn the more secure it becomes.

A few minutes' inspection of your first bow will teach all this; so it is unnecessary to attempt an explanation here. I will just mention that, after forming the eye through which the string plays, you must make three turns at least, to secure it from slipping. Ascham says the same, and gives an important reason why you should attend to his caution. The opposite end of the bowstring, being already formed into a loop by the manufacturer, requires no preparation.

I would have my young archer as much distinguished for the trim neatness of his equipments as for dexterous shooting. Attention to this "fitness of things" conveys a pleasing impression to the spectator's mind; on the other hand, nothing more disparages an archer than its neglect. Instead, then, of coming to the target ground, as I have seen many of your seniors do, with unpolished bow, and the string's lower end untwisted, ragged, and streaming "like meteor in the troubled air;" the centre unwhipped, frayed by friction of the bracer, and putting the bow in jeopardy at every shot*; do you take the trouble to entwine the upper and lower noose with fine kid leather, either white, red, or green. After making the two or three turns recommended above, cut off all that remains except about a couple of inches, which may be secured by a whipping of crimson silk: the centre also will require your attention. Brace the bow, in order to ascertain how much of the string meets the sleeve, after an arrow has been shot. Closely wrap this with crimson silk, slightly rubbed with shoemaker's wax. The space of two hands' breadth will be sufficient, and about one quarter of an inch of the exact middle of this whipping must be again overlayed with silk of a light colour, to mark the nocking point. Lastly, secure the string from being drawn downwards when the bow is taken from its case, or when unstrung, by looping it to the upper horn by a piece of green riband, secured with a handsome bowknot. About once in a fortnight pass some white wax twice or thrice from end to end. It serves to keep the fibres down, and was an ancient practice.

> And, as before, they stretched their well-waxed strings
> At the French horse that cometh with the wind. †

Good taste is as perceptible in trifles as in matters of greater moment, and such will ever be the arrangement of the bow in the hands of those gifted with it. The proper distance between wood and string in a braced bow, being determined by the distance from an arrow's nock to the top of its feathers, is

---

* Bows are broken through the string giving way more than by any other accident, except over-drawing.

† Battle of Agincourt, 1625.

called a shaftment, an ancient archery measure of six inches. The rude peasants ascertained this by the ready characteristic expedient of resting their clenched hand, with the thumb erect, inside the bow handle. If the thumb nail reached the string, or nearly so, all was right; otherwise they altered it accordingly. In bracing very long bows an additional inch may be allowed. Having thus put his tackle in the best possible order for use, I will now proceed to instruct my little archer how to

STRING HIS BOW.

Grasp the handle firmly with your left hand, the back of the bow being, of course, outwards. Place the bottom horn against the hollow of the left foot, turned a little inwards to secure it from slipping. Then press the thumb and forefinger closely against the sides of the bow, beneath the upper noose, and, while you pull smartly at the handle, force the string upwards towards its proper place; the operation is perfectly easy, and will become familiar enough when practised half a dozen times. Do not remove your fingers until, by turning the noose repeatedly to the right and left, you ascertain that it is secure within the horn, and also that it lies exactly in the centre of the bow. Inattention to the former of these hints might cause you to receive an uncomfortable slap in the face from its recoil: and, if the string is allowed to remain awry, it will probably *cast*, or warp, and consequently spoil the bow. Look to this occasionally whilst shooting; particularly if you brace and unbrace the bow, at those times a very judicious custom. In England such has been the manner of stringing a bow for the last century and a half. It is one of the archer's most graceful positions, but applicable only to bows of a certain strength. Anciently they found it difficult so to brace the tall sturdy weapons brought into the battle field. Some, laying the end of the bow upon the ground, and pressing the knee or foot upon its belly, forced the other end upwards with the left hand, while they slipped the string into its place with the right. In Ingham church there is a very remarkable painting of two foresters hunting in a wood, habited in

The coat and hose of green,

exactly as Chaucer describes his woodsman, in the Canterbury Tales. One of them carries his ready strung bow in an easy, graceful position; the other is in the act of bracing his. This he does by holding it perpendicularly, with the inner side turned toward his body, and, whilst pressing his knee against the centre, he forces the string into the upper nock by the exertion of both hands.

The manner in which the Orientals bend their bows, though altogether different from our own, is equally picturesque.*

There are certain wild tribes in Hindostan who manage this business after a fashion very different from any of the foregoing. With them, as with many other savages, the feet perform the duties of a second pair of hands, for they sometimes even direct the arrow between their toes.

When one of these Indians wishes to string his bow, he lies upon his back on the ground, and grasps the extremities with either hand. Then pressing the middle against the soles of his feet, elevated into the air for that purpose, he bends the bow, whilst a companion fixes on the string.

There is something very characteristic of savage indolence in this, unless indeed the bow proves too powerful to be managed otherwise. Then, indeed, I conceive *we* might adopt the hint with advantage. The modern English archer, who finds a bow difficult to brace, employs another person to draw down the upper horn with his forefinger, while he exerts himself to force the string upwards in the usual manner. But this should be performed discreetly; for, unless your assistant keeps his finger

---

* See "Female Archery."

low upon the nock, he may chance to split and tear away the horn. With this caution I conclude the archer's first drill.

The preceding lessons may be practised as effectually in the drawing-room as elsewhere. Let us now adjourn to the

Smoothly shaven lawn,

where, gay and glistening, our targets repose beneath the giant limbs of tall ancestral trees. Shaded by this verdant skreen, both the archer and his marks will escape the fierce glare of a noontide sun. The dazzling splendour of a summer's day, is very unfavourable to shooting.* Our old English bowmen took special care to secure themselves, if possible, from this disadvantage. At the battle of Cressy, very soon after the signal to engage was given, a partial shower fell on that portion of the plain where the French army was drawn up. At the same instant, a sudden gleam of sunshine burst forth behind the English, and its beams, besides dazzling the eyes of the enemy, flashed upon their polished shields and corslets with a lustre so brilliant, that our archers discharged their first flight of arrows with more than usual certainty of aim. Wind and weather likewise exercise a certain influence to aid or mar a well-directed shot. Let not the reader, however, give implicit credence on this point to Ascham, who pushes his remarks even to the verge of folly. A calm, clear, balmy evening, with little or no air stirring, in those months, too, when every zephyr comes loaded with the perfume of the hay-field, is ever most propitious to the archer's sport. But an exact description of such an one has ever been the poet's darling theme; see, therefore, how a master hand doth set it forth:—

> Clear had the day been from the dawn,
> All checkered was the sky;
> Thin clouds, like scraps of cobweb lawn,
> Veil'd heaven's most glorious eye.

---

* See " Welsh Archery."

> The wind had no more strength than this,
>   As leisurely it blew,
> To make one leaf the next to kiss
>   That closely by it grew.

For shooting in boisterous weather a comparatively heavy arrow does best. Ascham says so; Shakspeare likewise, whose illustration, for obvious reasons, we will adopt. When the king is devising the ruin of Hamlet's popularity with the multitude, he grows mistrustful of his weak and shallow calumnies, fearing they might recoil upon himself. The manner in which he puts this, is as true of archery as of morals.

> —— So that my shafts,
> Too lightly timbered for so loud a wind,
> Should have reverted to my bow again,
> And not where I had aimed them.

Every person accustomed to this exercise has probably remarked his own superior shooting between sunset and twilight, in comparison with any previous portion of the day. The atmosphere seems to have then acquired additional clearness: by an optical illusion the surface of the target appears enlarged, and its colours more vivid and distinct.

String up your bow! turn the left foot a little more inwards;—steady—so. Now, draw stoutly at the handle, pressing the ball of your thumb close upon the back. All's well. Just glance along the string, that there be no twist at either horn, and then away to the target, where you shall learn how an archer

TAKES HIS FOOTING;—

the first *step* in Ascham's celebrated "five points." The bowman, who turns his front towards the object aimed at, as when discharging a fowling-piece, will assuredly never touch it, except by mere accident. The side only is to be presented to the target, with which your eyes will be brought exactly parallel,—

remember to keep both wide open, — by turning the face over the left shoulder, until your chin rests just above it. Don't stand bolt upright; but incline the head and neck slightly forward; a position which not only brings your bow and shaft-hand in a line with each other, but affords a more distinct view of the gold; for in the target ground — and only there — seem as much influenced by the "auri sacra fames" as though you were among the most ardent and devoted of Mammon's wretched slaves.

I have here described the mode of standing familiar to our old British bowmen. All representations of archers, which occur in illuminated manuscripts of the 13th, 14th, and 15th centuries, — and I have examined some scores of them, — identify the ancient with the modern practice. The pen and ink drawings of John de Rous, a bowman as well as contemporary biographer of that Earl of Warwick who, during the wars of the red and white Roses, was the setter up and destroyer of many kings, will furnish amusement and information to the curious. The necessary slight inclination of the head and neck — "this laying of the body in the bow," the drawing with two and with three fingers — are there correctly delineated. They may be found among the MSS. in the British Museum.

When preparing to draw, the archer should plant his feet upon the ground, so that the body's weight may bear equally firmly upon both. His heels ought to be about six or eight inches apart, and anciently the left foot was a little in advance of the right. The grace, confidence, and strength, which adorn every position of this exercise, are very aptly described in the following quaint lines by a poet of the sixteenth century : —

> How is it that our London hath laid downe
> This worthy practice, which was once the crowne
> Of all her pastime, when her Robin Hood
> Had wont each year, when May did clothe the wood

> With lustie greene, to leade his younge men out,
> Whose brave demeanour, ofte when they did shoote,
> Invited royall princes from their courts
> Into the wilde woods to beholde their sports!
> Who thought it then a manlie sight and trim,
> To see a youth of clean compacted limb,
> Who with a comely grace, in his left hand,
> Holding his bow, did take his steadfast stand,
> Setting his left foot somewhat forth before,
> His arrow with his right hand nocking sure,
> Not stooping, nor yet standing straight upright,
> Then with his left hand little 'bove his sight,
> Stretching his arm out, with an easy strength,
> To draw an arrow of a yard in length.

OF NOCKING THE ARROW.

The usage of centuries sanctions our adoption of this phrase instead of notching, with which it is synonymous.

The following hints comprise a regular gradation of positions, all of which the archer performs whenever he discharges an arrow. I therefore recommence with my pupils where I left them; viz., before the target, equipped with shooting-glove, bracer, belt, &c., containing three arrows. Draw out one of these by grasping it two or three inches *above the feathers;* pass its steel point beneath the string, and over the upper edge of the bow handle, now held in a horizontal position across the body, towards which the string is turned. Confine the arrow head there with the forefinger of the bow-hand, whilst shifting your shaft-hand down to the nock. Turn that round with the thumb and two first fingers, until the cock feather* is perpendicular, the other two being flat or parallel with the bowstring, upon which you now place the arrow nock, exactly at that spot indicated by the whipping.

Every archer who aims to keep his shafts in good preserv-

---

* Usually distinguished by being grey or black, when the others are white, and vice versâ.

ation will carefully avoid handling the feathers, that delicate beautiful portion of an arrow being easily torn and ruffled, by which its flight and appearance will be equally damaged. One is sometimes thrown into a fever of impatience, on witnessing the absurd heedlessness of bowmen, who violently snatch from the ground such arrows as miss the mark, or twist them out of the target-bass by grasping at the feathers. I once observed a stout elderly gentleman busily engaged in brushing his altogether the reverse way from that in which nature had disposed them, until

> Each particular *plume* did stand on end
> Like quills upon the fretful porcupine.

This extraordinary procedure he justified, by observing, he considered it materially improved an arrow's course through the "liquid yielding air."

Your hand ought not and need never come in contact with the feathers. In taking an arrow from butt, ground, or target, grasp it firmly as near the pile as possible, and by a gentle twist it may easily be drawn forth.

Thus, then, do the skilful manœuvre their tackle. But accidents sometimes occur to the archer which no care or forethought can avert; and for these Shakspeare shall aid me in suggesting an ingenious and appropriate remedy, as well inserted here as elsewhere. It is from the Merchant of Venice.

> In my school days, when I had lost one shaft,
> I shot his fellow off the self-same flight*, the self-same way,
> With more advised watch, to find the other forth;
> And by adventuring both I oft found both.

During summertide, whilst the ground is baked by the sunbeams to an almost stony hardness, arrows, unless shot at a considerable elevation, do not penetrate, but glide along the turf, until all trace of them is lost amongst the herbage.

* Equally heavy or light.

Archers call this accident by the expressive term " snaking ; " and a great annoyance it is to lose a valuable arrow entirely, or, what is as bad, to find it warped and unfeathered by remaining out a whole night among the damp grass, because darkness had rendered the previous evening's search ineffectual. No person unacquainted with the details of archery could understand the singular manner in which an arrow threads itself among the short fine sward, and remains undiscovered, in spite of a search carried on unremittingly for hours, during which the owner passes a score times to and fro over the spot where it is thus "snaked."

On meeting with the object of your search, never drag it rudely from the matted grass, but first draw your knife on both sides from pile to nock. I will just add, that all possibility of moisture bringing off the feathers of my own arrows is obviated by oil paint applied on either side the stem of each. Their flight is by no means affected by the process, for which crimson is a very appropriate colour. Possibly Indian-rubber varnish would answer still better.

" Nihil tetigit quod non ornavit," seems equally applicable to Shakspeare, when speaking of archery, as of almost every other subject. The curious recipe for discovering a lost arrow, given in the passage to which I have already directed the reader's attention, is afterwards resumed in the following beautiful strain : —

> I urge this childish proof, because what follows is pure innocence.
> I owe you much; and, like a wilful youth,
> That which I owe is lost: but, if you please to shoot
> Another arrow that self-way which you did shoot the first,
> I do not doubt, as I will *watch the aim*, or to find both,
> Or bring your latter hazard back again.

I shall render this very ancient and familiar resource of archers more intelligible by a passage from Crescentius's " De Re Rustica," or Treatise on Country Life, a curious Latin work of the fifteenth century, but of which the King's library has a splendid MS. French translation, written on vellum, and adorned with beautiful water-colour drawings.

" Qu'il veult tirer aux coulons, ou aultres oiseaulx sur arbres, il doit avoir matras ou bongons gros en la teste devant, et quils soyent d'un mesme poix. Et quant il veult tirer, il doit signer au precise lieu ou il est, et noter le lieu ou le coulon est ou autre oisel semblable, et lors traire ; et s'il l'assomme, il a son content. Et ainsi par ceste maniere il pourra trouver son matras. Si il note ces deux lieux ou il fault et pert sa sagette, il la retrouvera bien par en traire une d'un tel poix, à la place ou lui et loisel estoient." P. 270.

" He that purposes to disport himself with killing doves, and other birds perched upon trees, must have bolts all of *equal weight;* and when about to let fly an arrow, he should note the exact place where he stands at the time, and also the place of the bird; and if he succeed in bringing her down, then hath he his desire, and shall get his arrow again. So, if he miss, and have duly marked his standing, and the place where his game was when he shot, let him return back and loose another arrow towards that spot, and there is no doubt but he shall recover both."

So in Decker's " Villanies discovered by Lanthorn ;"— " and yet I have seen a creditor in prison weep when he beheld his debtor, and to lay out money of his own purse. To free him he shot a second arrow to find the first." There is also an allusion to this practice in Howel's " Familiar Letters."*

OF HOLDING, DRAWING, AND LOOSING.

Your expert archer, gazing steadfastly at the mark, combines these three divisions of his manual exercise into one

* Vol. i. p. 183.

deliberate, continuous action; I have, therefore, arranged them under the same head.

Although the bow is held across the body during the preparatory action of nocking, it must be ever raised perpendicularly when you shoot. Elevate your arms slowly to the level of the mark, and, whilst drawing the arrow steadily with your right, with the left hand press your whole strength into the bow. By so doing, the English yeoman was enabled to pull his cloth-yard shaft up to the head; and to this Bishop Latimer partly alludes, when he tells us " his father taught him not to draw with mere strength of arm, as other nations did, but *to lay his body in his bow.*"

When about to loose, never look at your arrow's point; it is unnecessary: for constant exercise will so accustom your hand to obey and act in conjunction with your eye, that a wonderful precision of aim is the result. Your whole attention must be directed towards the golden centre of the target, where *both* eyes are to be intently fixed. Again, I remind you that drawing and loosing are to be performed together. Grasp your bow with the firmness of a smith's vice; draw steadily, until the steel pile of your arrow rests upon the knuckle of the bow hand, while the thumb of the drawing hand grazes against the upper part of the right ear. That instant of time, in which the sight suddenly concentrates itself upon the target's centre, whilst every other object grows dark and indistinct, is the critical moment of your aim. Loose, then, without a second's pause, by gently relaxing the fingers of your shooting glove, and, ere your arrow has made half its flight, you may determine that its direction-point will be where every archer is ambitious to see it placed. *

Modern English bowmen generally draw with three fingers.

---

* The practised eye will foretel an arrow's fate long before it arrives at the mark.

The Flemings use the first and second only — a method adopted by some of our bowmen also. Those strong bows in use during the reign of military archery must have required the former number; yet it is remarkable that in most of the drawings before alluded to, the Flemish custom prevails.* Ascham, however, orders the shooting glove to be made with three fingers; and when Henry the Fifth harangued his troops previous to the battle of Agincourt, he endeavoured to exasperate their minds by dwelling on the cruelties in store for them. Addressing his archers, he said that the French soldiers had sworn to amputate their three first fingers, so that they should never more be able to slay man or horse. †

The Indians of Demerara use only the thumb and fore finger for this purpose. Practice from early youth will necessarily strengthen the muscles of the hand; still, by their mode of drawing, none save men of great bodily power can ever shoot with force. We consequently get few bows from that part of the globe beyond fifty or five-and-fifty pounds. Their chiefs sometimes have bows which draw eighty or ninety; but these barbarians never select any individual for a leader ungifted with thews and sinews. One of our old English archers, who settled in America, makes an observation illustrative of their feeble archery. " Forty yards," says he, " will they shoot level; one hundred and twenty is their best at rovers." ‡

---

* See De Rous's MS.

† All nations appear to have held the shaft hand in some respect. Thus, in the middle ages, a severe punishment awaited youth or man who designedly injured either of the three first fingers of his right hand. Dr. Southey says, that one tribe of cannibal Indians superstitiously abstained from eating the thumb, even of prisoners taken in war, because of its use in their method of drawing the bow; and when a certain horde of Tartars celebrate the funeral of their khan, each person of distinction present, shoots an arrow into the right hand of the royal corpse. See *Dr. Southey's Brazil.* — *Lind. Gloss. art. Digitus.*

‡ Unpublished MS., Sloane Collection, No. 444.

To hold the bow perfectly steady whilst loosing the arrow seems indispensable to accurate shooting. I will therefore describe a somewhat feeble archer's mode of fortifying the left arm, which proved very successful. He procured a bow of some common English wood — well seasoned elm or mountain ash answers sufficiently well; six or eight pounds of sheet-lead were wrapped above and below the handle, and secured by strong whipping of waxed thread. With this ponderous instrument he exercised himself in shooting at a level mark, with heavy arrows, for the space of two hours every morning during three months. The result was most satisfactory, *Crede experto me Roberto.*

Shooting straight and keeping a length are equally indispensable. The best, and indeed the only, expedient for attaining perfection in the former, is to shoot in the evening at lights. To this end fix a black circular or lozenge-shaped mark in the centre of two common paper lanterns, in each a lighted candle, and place them sixty, eighty, or one hundred yards apart. The above number of hours of nightly practice, during a similar period, will amply recompense the assiduity of any enthusiastic archer, since a line drawn from target to target will not be more unerring than the flight of his arrow. Your town resident may become equally expert by a much easier process. The gas-lamp opposite his sitting-room furnishes as good a mark as any: I do not mean he is to shoot at it — merely to elevate his arms in the attitude of drawing a bow will assuredly produce the same effect.

" For keeping a length" no certain rules can be laid down. This phrase, borrowed from Roger Ascham, signifies the art of raising the bow hand always to one certain pitch, at unvarying marks, so that your arrow may neither fly over nor fall short of its object. Every kind of missile, whether stone, arrow, or bullet, describes a parabola or section of a circle in its flight through the air, if aimed at remote objects. Confining my observations to the weapon under discussion, I have merely to add, that as the degree of elevation necessary for planting an arrow in a mark, at any given distance, must wholly depend on the power of the bow, theory can render the archer little assistance. Every man equips himself according to his individual strength, so that incessant observation and practice can alone determine this point. He has, however, one certain rule for aiming at very remote objects. The arrow has reached its extreme flight when it descends to the earth, after being discharged at an angle of forty-five degrees; and, as ten degrees *above* or *below* that number will diminish the extent of its range, we always elevate thus in flight shooting.

I'll give my young friends a curious illustration of the fatal accuracy in " keeping his length " to which a youth arrived when vengeance prompted him to its attainment. Fordbhuide, the young son of Conner, an ancient Irish monarch, instigated by some trivial insult which he had received from the Queen of Connaught, set himself to study means of revenge. Having heard that she came every morning, without attendants, to bathe herself in one of those magnificent lakes scattered along Shannon's banks, he concealed himself in a spot where he could see without being seen. He was there during several successive days; and finding that the queen always selected the same spot, a small, shallow, sandy bay of clear water, as soon as she departed he tied the line, with which he had come provided, to the trunk of a tree growing at a convenient spot on the opposite side of the lake, which tree he carefully marked with his sword, and then plunging in, swam across to the queen's bath. The exact distance from shore to shore being thus ascertained, this young demon returned to his father's hall, and deliberately prepared to execute his murderous scheme. When he had marked off the exact length of the line on the side of a green hill, he fixed up two stakes, and setting an apple on one, and taking his station at the other, passed several hours daily for some months in hurling pebbles at it with his sling, never varying his standing one single yard. At length the inhabitants of Ulster and Connaught agreed to hold a conference at Ilis Cloithroin, upon one side of the river Shannon. The son of Conner, who came with his father's deputies, and was the principal person there, thought it a good opportunity for executing his revenge upon the queen. She came, as usual, one sultry morning, to divert herself in the pure cold waters, and the prince, from his hiding place, slung a stone so expertly that he smote her full on the forehead, when, sinking instantly to the bottom, her body floated into the depths, and was seen no more.*

The youthful bowman, being thus initiated into all the preparatory mysteries of his art, may next proceed to exercise himself in shooting at the targets. The first distance should not exceed ten yards; at which, after a month's diligent practice, he will be able to strike a tennis ball suspended from a string, many successive times. Let him then remove it to twenty yards; and on acquiring a similar degree of dexterity at that distance, his next step will be the extreme *point blanc* range of his bow.

From shooting horizontally, proceed to acquire the habit of mechanically lifting your hand to the degree of elevation required by your bow at various distances. Your expertness in this, one of the most difficult branches of the archer's discipline, must be in proportion to the time devoted to it. Three months of assiduity will, however, effect wonders: at the expiration of that little period of probation, you may confidently take your station among the competitors for gold medal, silver arrow, and bugle horn.

In private societies, six or eight archers are usually considered the complement for a single pair of butts or targets. The novice only, who has never witnessed an exhibition of this

* Psalters of Tara.

kind, need be informed that two marks are employed, the party standing in front of one whilst aiming at the other. When all have shot, they walk in a body towards the opposite mark, and each individual draws out his successful arrows, and gathers up those which have alighted over or under the target. When carefully wiped, he replaces them in his belt; and the archers, resuming their station in front of the target near which they then are, aim at that they have just quitted. The number of arrows shot at each round is called an end, and the shooting up and down a double end.

Rank, courtesy, or lot, decides the order in which a group of archers stand at the commencement; after that, merit alone gets precedence. Thus, if I hit *any* part of the gold, I am coryphæus of the bowmen, provided no other arrow is nearer than mine to its exact centre. The same rule applies to each of those concentric rings of which the target is composed. If, on the contrary, my arrows fly over, or fall short of the target, or, even hitting it, are still in colours of less value than those struck by my associates, I take a position in the rear of all.

And here I think I cannot do better than introduce some rules for the guidance of young toxophilites in the formation of large, or more select, societies; because all such knotty points of precedence, &c. are there accurately enlarged upon.

In the first place, then, they shall have those of the Kentish Bowmen, to whom his Majesty George the Fourth was captain general*; secondly, those of the United Society of Woodmen

---

* The Kentish Bowmen rendered themselves highly popular by the alacrity with which, when the French threatened to invade us, they abandoned their sportive pursuits, and fled to the arms of the day, in order to battle " pro aris et focis." Many spirited jeux d'esprits, complimentary to the loyalty of its members, of both sexes, were circulated at the period, but now lie hidden in the portfolios of the curious, or have perished with the fraternity and the occasion. In one of them, the " Thunderer" of Olympus suggests to its assembled deities the peculiar favours each should

of Arden, Broughton Archers, and Lancashire Bowmen, because their regulations specially refer to the ladies; and, thirdly, those of the Derby and Kiddleston Archers, because distinguished by a laudable brevity.

SOCIETY OF KENTISH BOWMEN.

MEETINGS.

That the Society of Kentish Bowmen be continued on Dartford Heath.

That the meetings commence annually the first Saturday in

---

bestow upon England's patriotic bowmen. The ladies are unanimously consigned to the tutorage of the little archer god: —

"His bow shall he bend, and a lesson impart,
Expertly to shoot at their target, the heart."

The poet then alludes to the British nation in general: —

"Then bestow'd each celestial some habits of worth,
And mercy descended triumphant to earth.
New Henries and Edwards did swarm on the plain,
And Cressys and Agincourts conquered again;
And many a fair, darting love from her eyes,
As Captain of NUMBERS!* soon bore off the prize.
Favour'd thus by the gods, by the king, by the fair,
May ye Britons have peace. Yet should trumpets speak war,
Of a nation insulted, beware — the bow's bent —
Then make from the shafts of the Bowmen of Kent."

Some of the prizes offered by the Royal Kentish Bowmen were truly magnificent. In August, 1802, they assembled on Dartford Heath, to shoot for an elegant Indian bow, quiver, and twelve arrows, valued at fifty guineas. Distance 100 yards. It was won by George Maddock, Esq., who pierced the gold centre.

---

* In its ordinary signification, captain of numbers means the archer who scores highest, according to the value of the target rings; but an equivoque is here intended.

May, and continue every Saturday during the months of May, June, July, and August.

That twelve members form a meeting competent to transact all business, except the repeal of the rules.

ELECTION.

That every candidate be proposed by a member; and, upon his being seconded, such member shall cause his name to be hung up in some public part of the rooms; that he shall be balloted for at the next meeting, twelve members at least being present, and two black balls excluding.

That if any candidate is rejected, the member who proposed him shall be at liberty to have the ballot tried once again, and no more.

That no candidate who has been rejected be again proposed that year.

That the ballot be brought forward immediately after dinner, and at no other time.

SUBSCRIPTION.

That every member, upon his election, shall pay ten guineas; which sum shall include his entrance money and first annual subscription.

That every member shall pay annually 1*l.* 11*s.* 6*d.*, out of which, he shall be allowed part of the expenses of his ordinary at every meeting; and he shall pay one guinea annually for his four target dinners.

That every subscriber for one year be considered as such for each subsequent one; and be liable to be called upon for such year's subscription, unless notice of his intention to withdraw his name be sent to the secretary or treasurer in writing, on or before the first day of May each year, on which the subscription shall become due.

That in case any gentleman elected does not pay his subscription, the member who proposed him shall be called upon for it.

That every member who does not pay his subscription and all arrears to the Society by the first of June, every year inclusive, shall forfeit the sum of one guinea.

ATTENDANCE.

That if any member shall neglect attending at some one meeting each year, or sending an excuse for such neglect, the admissibility of which shall be determined by the members present at the last target day, on or before which day the excuse must be sent, he shall be no longer considered a member of the Society.

UNIFORM.

Ordered by his Royal Highness the PRINCE OF WALES, Jan. 1789—

A grass green coat, buff linings, and buff waistcoat and breeches; black collar to the coat, uncut velvet in winter, and tabby silk in summer, with yellow buttons.

Resolved,—

That there be a forfeit of 2s. 6d. for not wearing the uniform coat at all meetings of the Society, and of 5s. for not appearing according to the above resolutions upon target days; and such member not to be permitted to shoot.

That the fines for not appearing in uniform be remitted to those members who appear in family mourning.

That an R.K.B. button, with a gold loop to a black round hat, and small black feather, be part of the shooting uniform; and no member to shoot without it, under the penalty of 2s. 6d.

That all captains, captains of numbers, and lieutenants, shall wear a gold or silver arrow embroidered in their collar.

That all clergymen belonging to the Society do wear a uniform button of *papier maché*.

LIMITATION.

That the number of ex-county members be limited to thirty-six.

That any member or candidate possessing any of the under-written qualifications be considered as a county member or candidate.

1st. A freehold of 10*l.* per annum in the county of Kent.

2d. Any person resident and holding a lease of 20*l.* per annum in the county of Kent for no less time than three years.

4th. Sons of leaseholders as above, resident with their fathers.

5th. Any person entitled to a freehold of 20*l.* per annum in the county of Kent, either in reversion or remainder.

ORDINARY.

That the bill be called for at eight o'clock.

That every member appearing upon the ground, either before or after dinner, shall pay 10*s.* 6*d.*; and that every member who dines shall pay the like sum, to clear his expense till the bill is called; the surplus, if any, to go to the general fund; the deficiency, if any, to be paid out of the general fund.

That every member, upon his marriage, shall present the Society with three dozen of claret.

That no stranger be admitted to the dinners of the Society but such as, at the time of their appearance, are resident with the members who introduce them.

OFFICERS AND COMMITTEES.

That there be appointed to the Society, every year, the following officers:—

President, Antiquarian,
Vice-President, Four Standard Bearers,
Secretary, Chaplain.
Treasurer,

SHOOTING.

That none but members be permitted to shoot.

That no greater number than six shoot rubbers, or games at any of the butts; and that the same set do not shoot two rubbers together, if any other wishes to occupy them.

That the large targets are never shot at a less distance than one hundred, nor the small at a less distance than sixty yards, under the penalty of 1s. each shot.

That any member who shoots games at the small targets forfeits 2s. 6d. for each game.

That the order of shooting rubbers or games be determined by the oldest member concerned.

That any member shooting out of his turn shall not reckon the arrow so shot, and the rest to shoot according to the first order.

That the side which won the last end shall always lead.

That seven be the game, and two games in three the rubber.

That if any member borrows any implement of archery, and does not return it safe, or pay the prime cost, and if the member from whom it is borrowed refuses to accept the prime cost, they shall forfeit 5s. each to the Society.

TARGETS.

That there be four targets every year, to be shot in the four respective months during the continuance of the meetings.

First target in May, to be fixed by the Society at the first or second meeting, to be shot for at three different distances according to the rules of shooting for the Prince of Wales's prize; and the three distances then determined upon shall be the distances at which his Royal Highness's prize shall be shot for.

Second, his Royal Highness the Prince of Wales's prize to be shot for in June, with his approbation.

Third, anniversary target, July 15.

Fourth, institution target, August 28.

[N. B. There are in the Society three pair of medals for three of the above named targets, and the Prince's prize for the fourth.]

That the officers of the last target deliver the medals to those who hit the gold and red circles first, who shall again deliver them to better shots as they are won; by which means, the two shots nearest the centre in the course of the day are the captain and lieutenant of the target.

That the members who win the medals be obliged to produce or send them to the first meeting upon the Heath in the following year, or forfeit 5s.

That no one member shall receive the captain's and lieutenant's medals at one target.

That the members in possession of the medals appear with them at all the meetings, or forfeit 1s.

That the members in possession of the medals forfeit one guinea if they do not produce or send them to the respective targets.

That the two last targets, namely, the anniversary and institution targets, be shot at the distance of one hundred yards.

That after the targets are pitched, and the shooting commenced, any two members may continue it.

That any member, having once loosed an arrow, be called upon for his target money.

That the subscription, or target money, may be enlarged, first beginning with 2s. 6d., and when the first subscription is shot out, any member may withdraw his name, being only answerable for such subscription.

That a separate committee be appointed to conduct every target on target days, consisting of seven members at least.

ORDER OF SHOOTING

To be observed at all Targets belonging to the Society of Royal Kentish Bowmen.

Captain of the respective Target,
Lieutenant of the respective Target,

Captain of Numbers,
Lieutenant of Numbers,
President,
Vice-president,
Winners of the Prince of Wales's prizes,
Secretary,
Treasurer,
Antiquarian,
Chaplain,
Four Standard Bearers,
Captain and Lieutenants possessing medals,
Captains and Lieutenants in the Society,
Honorary Captains,
Rest by lot.

That when the captain and lieutenant either of the last target, or for the time being, part with their respective medals to a better shot, those who receive them shall take the lead, and those who part with them retain their original places.

WINTER MEETINGS.

That there be two winter meetings between the last target in August, and the first summer meeting following.

That the committee for the time being, or the majority of them, shall have the power of appointing the times and places for such meetings.

That no business be done at such meetings, except the proposition of candidates, to be balloted for at the first meeting upon the Heath in the ensuing season.

STANDARD BEARERS.

The Society of Royal Kentish Bowmen having been presented with two standards, — one by the Hon. H. Fitzroy, the other by George Grote, Esq., — have, according to Mr. Fitzroy's motion, appointed four standard-bearers, to be elected according to the rules.

And, in common with other corporate bodies, deeming the colours most sacred and honourable, and feeling the necessity of securing them, have thought proper to prescribe the following regulations, to be adopted by the standard-bearers: —

That it be the duty of the standard bearers to guard and keep safe from damage the standards of the Society.

That the standards be carried to and from the ground with the members attending in full uniform, on every target day, and at the first meeting in each year.

That the hour for beginning to shoot targets being fixed at twelve o'clock, it be required that two standard-bearers attend every target day, on which the standards are to be borne, properly accoutred, at a quarter before twelve o'clock.

That the standard-bearers appear in full uniform, with a cross belt of black leather and swivel affixed, for the more convenient carrying the standards, and an epaulet of gold according to the pattern first produced.

UNITED SOCIETY OF WOODMEN OF ARDEN, BROUGHTON ARCHERS, AND LANCASHIRE BOWMEN.

I. Agreed and resolved, that all subscribers to this meeting of the United Archers shall pay the ordinary of two shillings per day, from Monday the 5th July, 1792, to Friday in the same week, inclusive.

II. That all those who have already subscribed to this meeting, if they object to the above rule, are at liberty to withdraw their subscription.

III. That no money be received upon any pretence for admission into the ground during the archers' meeting; and any constable or other person employed by the

Society who breaks this rule be immediately discharged.

IV. That no person be admitted but at the front gate.

V. That no person be admitted to the outer booth at dinner, but those producing tickets signed by the mayor or secretary.

VI. That only ten tickets* be issued for each day; and that no member be allowed more than two tickets the same day.

VII. That no person be admitted into the ladies' booth, except those who are invited by the ladies.

VIII. That the secretaries of the respective societies, which constitute this meeting, be requested to send to the mayor or secretary of United Bowmen the number of persons subscribing to the Society one month before it begins.

IX. That two butts at the distance of eight roods be made for the ladies.

At the meeting in July, 1792, a silver bow was shot for at the distance of one hundred yards, by the gentlemen of the United Society of Bowmen.

DERBY AND REDDLESTON ARCHERS.

RULES AGREED TO BY THE DERBY AND REDDLESTON ARCHERS, ESTABLISHED A.D. 1790.†

I. To meet one day in each month during the season.

II. Dinner to be on the table by four o'clock.

III. The bill to be called for and settled at seven.

IV. The ordinary not to exceed two shillings and sixpence.

V. The absent members to pay for their ordinary.

VI. The number of members to be limited.

* This, of course, applies to visiters. † From MS.

VII. Candidates to be balloted for the day they are proposed, but no ballot to take place except at the monthly meeting.

VIII. No ballot to take place except seven members are present; and three black balls to exclude.

IX. That no person who has been black-balled, shall be proposed again the same season.

X. That no person be admitted, nor any meeting suffered to use the butts, unless introduced by a member; and it is to be hoped no member will introduce any person except his own visiters, or officers quartered at Derby.

XI. The monthly meeting to be advertised in the Derby papers, under the direction of the secretary.

XII. No alteration to be made in the rules of the Society except seven members be present.

XIII. That the annual subscription of each member for defraying extra expenses be one guinea.

XIV. That no honorary members shall be admitted into the Reddleston and Derby Archers.

N.B. Their uniform is a green coat, and black collar, with a button inscribed D. A. for Derby Archers. They had their anniversary on August 26th. The highest prize was a silver arrow, retained by each winner during one year. Inferior prizes — bows and arrows, which become the property of those who gain them.*

I do not conceive any thing advantageous to the young archer can be added to the foregoing plain and simple instruc-

---

* Anniversary of 1793.
Silver arrow. — Rev. Edmund Wilmot.
Of 1794.
Silver arrow. — C. Hope, Esq.
Bow and arrow. — Rev. J. Clarke.

tions. His first essays, necessarily constrained and awkward, may excite the mirth of such of his companions as are conscious of superior skill. Let him not regard their laughter; be "nil desperandum" his motto, and a few weeks' assiduity will entitle him to laugh at others. We have all passed through a similar ordeal. The queerest of us never displayed one tithe of the ludicrous antics and gaucherie, which Ascham charges upon that "bold yeomandree," who frequented the shooting grounds during some of England's palmiest days of archery; and as the Toxophilus is not in the hands of every one, I will extract a portion of it for the reader's consolation. Hear him when he describes *his* awkward squad of bowmen.

" All the discommodities which ill custom hath graffed in archers can neyther be quycklye poulled out, nor yet sone reckoned of me, they be so many. Some shooteth his head forward, as though he woulde byte the mark: another stareth with his eyes, as though they shulde fly out: an other wynketh with one eye, and loketh with the other: some make a face with wrything theyr mouth, as though they were doing you wotte what: another bleareth out his tongue: another byteth his lippes; another holdeth his neck awrye.

"In drawing, some fetch such a compasse, as though they woulde turne rounde and bless all the feelde : other heave their honde now up, now downe, that a man cannot discerne whereat they would shote: another waggeth the upper end of his bow one way, the nethyr ende an other waye: another will stand poynting his shafte at the mark a good whyle, and by and by he wil give him a whip, and awaye or a man wite* : an other makes such a wrestling with his gere, as though he were able to shoote no more as long as he lyved : an other draweth softly to the myddes, and by and by it is gon, you cannot tell how : an other draweth his shaft low at the breast, as though he would shoote

---

* Before you are aware of him.

at a rovyng mark, and by and by he lyfteth his arm up pricke heyght: another maketh a wrynchinge with his back, as though a man pynched him behynde: another cowereth down and layeth out his buttockes, as though he would shoot at crowes*: another setteth forward his left leg, and draweth backe with heade and shoulders, as though he pouled at a rope, or els were afraid of the mark: an other draweth his shafte well, untyll within two fingers of the head, and then he stayeth a little, to looke at hys marke, and that done, pouleth it up to the head, and lowseth; which waye, although summe excellent shooters do use, yet surely it is a faulte, and good mennes faultes are not to be followed: summe drawe too farre, summe too shorte, summe too slowlye, summe too quickley, summe holde over longe, summe lette go over sone, summe set their shafte on the grounde, and fetche him upwarde: another poynteth up towarde the skye, and so bryngethe him downwardes.

"Ones I saw a man that used a bracer on his cheek, or els he had scratched all the skynne of the one syde of his face with his drawinge hande; another I saw, whyche, at every shoote, after the loose, lyfted up his righte leg so farre, that he was ever in jeopardy of fallynge; summe stampe forwarde, and

---

* " That fellow handles his bow like a crow-keeper," says Lear, *i.e.* cowereth down, that the birds may not see him. Perhaps Shakspeare had read the Toxophilus; perhaps his own perfect acquaintance with the bow suggested the comparison. The allusion, however, was not an uncommon one with poets of that day.

>Cupid I hate thee, which I'd have thee know:
>   A naked starv'ling ever may'st thou be.
>Poor rogue, go pawn thy fascia and thy bow
>   For some few rags wherewith to cover thee;
>Or, if thou 'lt not thy archery forbear,
>   To some base rustic do thyself prefer,
>And when corn's sown and grown into the ear,
>   Practise thy quiver, and turn crow keeper.
>   JOHN HEYWOOD.

summe leape backwarde. All these faultes be eyther in the drawinge, or at the loose; with many other mo, whych you may easylye perceyve, and so go about to avoyd them.

" Nowe afterwarde, when the shafte is gone, men have many faultes, whych evyl custom hath brought them to, and speciallie in cryinge after the shafte, and speakinge woordes scarce honest for such an honest pastime. Such woordes be verye token of an ill mynde, and manifest signs of a man that is subject to unmeasurable affections. Good mennes ears do abhor them, and an honest man wil avoyde them.

" And besydes those whiche muste nedes have theyr tongue walking, other menne use other faultes; as some will take their bowe and wrythe and wrynche it, to poul in his shaftes, when it flyeth wyde, as yf he drawe a carte. Summe wyll gyve two or three strydes forwarde, dancing and hoppynge after his shafte, as longe as it flyeth, as though he were a madman. Summe, which feare to be farre gone, runne backwarde, as it were to poull his shafte backe: an other runneth forwarde when he feareth to be shorte, heaveynge after his armes, as though he woulde helpe his shafte to fly. Another wrythes or runneth aside, to poule in his shafte strayghte. One lifteth up his heele, and soe holdeth his foote styll, as long as his shafte flyeth. Another casteth his arme backwarde after the lowse: another swynges his bow about him, as it were a man with a staffe, to make roome in a game place; and many other faultes there be, which come not to my remembrance.

" Nowe ymagen an archer that is clean wythout all these faultes, and I am sure every man would be delyghted to see him shoote."

BELT, BRACER, AND SHOOTING GLOVE.

> A sheaf of peacock's arrows bright and keen,
> Under his belt he bare full thriftilie.
> CHAUCER'S *Squire's Yeoman.*
>
> And on his arm he wore a gai bracer.
> *Ibid.*
>
> A white dove sat on the castle wall,
> I bend my bow, and shoot her I shall.
> She's safe *in my glove*, feathers and all.
> RITSON'S *Old Ballads.*

THE belt worn by our English archers was often called their girdle. Those who preferred the baldric suspended their arrows by a sort of running noose, or a small additional strap and buckle, which they tightened as its contents were gradually expended.* The latter contrivance is thus noticed by Drayton: —

> " Their baldrics, set with studs, athwart their shoulders cast,
> In which, under their arms, their sheafs were buckled fast."

Modern bowyers, who supply this, as well as every other article of our equipment, might greatly improve upon their present designs. Some alteration, for instance, is desirable in the arrow-pouch attached to the belt; the belt buckle, also, should be larger, and of cut polished steel.

The bracer is a well known contrivance for protecting the archer's wrist from being bruised by his bowstring. Its form and materials have varied little, though anciently a leathern gauntlet, fitting close to the arm, was worn by many archers, and with a thin oval leaf of ivory, or mottled horn, sewn upon the cuff, I know nothing which looks or answers better. The

* See ancient illustrated MS. edition of Froissart in the British Museum.

old bowmen sometimes had bracers formed entirely of ivory, as is shown by a unique and very elegant specimen preserved among the rarities at Goodrich Court. Where the bowstring strikes, you have a smooth polished surface only; but every other part is covered with rich carving and scroll-work. The initials M. R., and the arms of a society of bowmen, appear in the lower corner; the upper one is adorned with a medallion, containing the head of a Roman soldier; altogether, it forms a relic very interesting to the lovers of archery.

There is, also, an ancient black leathern bracer in possession of the Honourable Miss Grimstone, which exactly illustrates my motto from Chaucer. It resembles a half sleeve; the part frayed by the bowstring (the marks of which are still visible) being without ornament; but a rose, with many curious devices beautifully embossed cover the other portions, and the words 𝔍𝔢𝔰𝔲𝔰 𝔥𝔢𝔩𝔭𝔢 are inscribed on a gilt ground. This curious specimen of an old English archer's shooting gear was found at Boulton Hall, Yorkshire, where it had been left by one of Henry the Sixth's followers, when retreating from the fatal field of Hexham. Oriental bracers are described in the treatise on female archery. The North American Indian uses a piece of badger's or black fox's skin fastened upon his arm by slips of beech bark; and the Matryas, a nation of Brazil, are said by Dr. Southey [*] to twist plaited horse-hair round the arm. A number of quill feathers from the macaw or paroquet's wing constitutes the bracer of another South American tribe. These entirely encircle the wrist, their quills pointing towards the hand, the plumed ends towards the elbow. A more effectual, elegant expedient could hardly be devised; and of an Indian warrior, thus equipped, it may be truly said, —

> Upon his arm he wore a gai bracer.

But the ancient bowman not unfrequently dispensed with

[*] History of Brazil.

this part of his shooting gear. When a bow is highly braced, it becomes unnecessary. Ascham seems to have thought so:— "In my judgment," says he, "it is best to give the bow so much bending, that the string need never touch the arm, and, consequently, that a bracer should become needless. This is practised by many good archers with whom I am acquainted."

Most of my readers know that the modern shooting-glove consists of three leathern finger stalls sewn to corresponding straps, and buckled round the wrist. Anciently it was a leathern gauntlet, of which the cuff reached nearly to the elbow. "Leather," says Ascham, "if it be next the skin, will sweat, wax hard, and chafe; therefore *scarlet*, on account of its softness and thickness, is good to sew within a glove."

In the reign of Queen Elizabeth, the finest woollen cloth imported into England was that mentioned by Ascham. We should at present call it superfine; but our native looms were then unequal to its manufacture.

The same writer puzzled his commentators, by directing that the glove should have a "purse," to hold some waxed cloth for polishing the bow. An old French work of rural sports advises the archer to carry a file, or small whetstone, there also, for sharpening his arrows, when engaged in the chase. Surely, says a modern author*, very gravely, a bowman of the present day would never think of putting these things in his shooting glove.

At the present day he could not; but the long leathern cuff, anciently worn almost to the elbow, was a receptacle for these little items. According to my motto, the archer appears to have sometimes carried even his game there. The frontispiece to an early edition of "An Ayme for the Finsburie Archers," represents a bowman equipped with a gauntlet in the manner here described. †

* Roberts.   † See plate.

The contrast between the prices of the foregoing articles two centuries ago and those common at the present day is so well illustrated by the following document, that I am sure the reader will be pleased with its insertion : * —

10th Aug. 1627.

		s.	d.
Item.	Given away at the Tower	14	6
	To see the lyons	2	0
	For the shooting-gloves	2	6
	For a *Turkey* bowstringe †	1	0
	Paid for feathering an arrowe	0	2
	For mending an arrowe	0	$0\frac{1}{2}$
	For heading arrowes	0	3
	For six bowstringes	0	8
	For a bracer	0	6
	For seven butt shots	3	6
	To Ed. Terry for five prick shots	4	4
	To the bowyer for bow cases	4	8
	Given him for coming down	2	0
	Paid to Trustrum the bowyer	6	8
	Paid for the bow-cases	2	6
	For marks for the arrowes	2	6
	Paid for arrowes	12	6
	Paid for velvet for bow handles	3	0
	A quiver	11	0
	Paid to Dennis for twelve bow-strings	1	6
	Paid to Trustrum for mending of bowes	5	6

* From an old account book once belonging to Sir John Franklyn, Knt. of Wellesden, Middlesex.

† Of silk.   " Their strings of silk full sure."
                                     Ballad of Robin Hood.

		s.	d.
For two bow-cases for Master Richard and Master John	- - -	10	0
For two shooting gloves and bracers		3	6
For a quiver and 12 arrowes	- -	7	0

OF THE BOWSTRING.

The Ancient and Worshipful Company of Stringers still survive. They possess a hall somewhere in the city of London, although their vocation has long ceased. I believe few bowstrings are now made in England, the great mart being Flanders, where both materials and workmanship are excellent. In selecting them, see that the eye is large and thick; inferior strings being always weak at that part, and therefore liable to break themselves and your bow. When thinner at the centre than elsewhere, they are worthless also, because the whole strain of the bow acts on that part; though a bowstring equally slender throughout, the noose excepted, proves good and far casting. Choose such as feel hard, and are of a very dark brownish-grey colour.

The sinews of deer, cord made from the silk grass of Guiana, a thong of undressed hide, and even a strip from the outside of the bamboo, are severally used by various uncivilised people. The ancients say their archers had leathern thongs for the same purpose : —

Ελκε δ' ὁμοῦ γλυφίδας τε λαβών καὶ τό ξα βόει.
He drew the arrow by the leathern string.

The Roman Sagittarii seem to have preferred the sinews of a horse : —

Reciproca tendens nervo equino, concita tela, &c.

Drawing the arrow with a horse's nerve,
They reciprocally spring forwards.

Every one of you, my boys, has read of those heroic Carthaginian ladies, who, during their husbands' and lovers' struggle for independence, actually cut off their beautiful long hair, and devoted it to stringing up the catapultæ! According to Lady Mary Wortley Montague, the fair dames of some place she visited in Austria were at one time not a whit inferior in patriotism to these heroines of the ancient world. The lasses in question are remarkable for exceedingly beautiful hair, at all times their greatest embellishment; and once, like that of Samson, the strength and safeguard of the land. Historians relate — in whose reign, I believe, is rather dubious — that the city, during a long siege by the Saracens, was ill provided with provisions; but a total want of the materials for making bowstrings appeared almost as likely to cause a surrender. In this dilemma, a patriotic beauty stepped forth and proposed that the whole of the women should devote their glossy tresses to the bowmen, a proposition which was adopted with enthusiasm.

"The hair of our ladies," observes one of their quaint poets, "is still employed in the same office; but now it discharges no other shafts but those of Cupid, and the only chords it forms are chords of love."

I remember De Vega tells a story of an Indian cacique, who, being defeated in a great battle, and seeing himself surrounded by heaps of his fallen countrymen, and all hopes of escape cut off, resorted to a very characteristic expedient for terminating his existence and his despair. After the battle of Mauvilla, this Indian alone remained in the town, and, the fury of the combatants having subsided, he became conscious of his danger, and hurried to the walls, with the design of escaping into the forest; but, espying the Spanish cavalry and infantry scattered far and near over the plain, all hope forsook him. He then loosed the string from his bow; and having tied one end to the branch of a tree, and the other around his neck, leaped desperately from the wall, and was strangled. Some soldiers who hastened to his assistance found him already dead. Such is the invincible courage of a Floridan warrior.

To rush upon an archer and sever his bowstring by the stroke of a sword, or otherwise, seems to have been a common expedient in ancient battles, either to place an enemy *hors du combat*, or check the impetuous valour of a brave companion in arms. From numerous instances which are scattered throughout early writers, I shall content myself with selecting the two following: —
" Eltchi Behader eut son cheval tué sous lui, et cependant combattoit toujours avec un extrême valeur, son arc à la main. Timour, qui vouloit partager la gloire, et menager un si brave homme, lui arrachoit l'arc, et en rompit la corde, de peur qui son intrépidité le fist périr." [*]

" I seized hold of a firebrand," says George Hubbard, when describing an attack upon an Indian fort, in his History of the Troubles of New England, " at which time an Indian, drawing an arrow, would have killed me, had not one Davis, my sergeant, rushed forwards and cut the bowstring with his courtlace."[†]

[*] Vie de Behader Khan.   [†] A.D. 1673.

OF THE ARCHER'S MARKS.

Mistress Openworke. Did'st ever see an archer, as thou walk'st by Bunhill, look asquint whilst he drew his bow?
Mistress Gallipot. Yes; and when his arrows flew towards Islington, his eyes went clean towards Pimlico. — ROARING GIRL.

How ugly is a bald pate! It looks like a face wanting a nose, or like ground eaten bare by the arrows of archers; whereas a head all hid in hair gives ever to a most wicked face a sweet proportion. — GUL DECKER'S HORN BOOK, Dr. Nott's edit.

  The second shot had the wight yeoman,
  He shot within the garland;
  But Robin he shot far better than he,
  For he clave the good white wande.
      GUY OF GISBORNE.

THE ancient public butts, observes Dr. Nott[*], were in general so thronged with archers, particularly at holiday times, that they raked up the surrounding turf by the very arrows that missed, in such a manner as never to suffer the grass to grow there.

The continual trampling of feet as the bowmen circulated about the marks also contributed to destroy the verdure. In the vicinity of large and populous towns, the concourse must have been prodigious, and for this reason each archer used but a single arrow. Besides the impossibility of getting a second shot amidst so much confusion, he found it necessary to hurry away to the opposite butt, in order to catch up his shaft, before it was trodden under foot.

Peers and churchmen were privileged by law, but no other persons, aliens excepted, could absent themselves from these

---

[*] Of Bristol, a genuine admirer of our old English literature. His edition of "Gul Decker's Horn Book," quoted above, besides containing much antiquarian lore, is a fine specimen of provincial typography.

public exercise grounds without incurring what was then considered a serious penalty. Thither the lordly baron sent his vassals, and thither came the independent franklyn, the wealthy yeoman, the rude peasant, and the unwashed artizan. Distinction of rank was for the time lost sight of, and adroitness alone gave a title to superiority.*

In 1570, Catharine Stanton bequeathed a piece of ground at Andover called "Common Acre," for the recreation of its inhabitants. A lease of this acre, for twenty-one years, was granted to William Gold, on condition that he should keep a pair of butts for men to shoot at, and permit all persons to take their pastime there. Also, in 1603, Robert Aubie devised one rood of land for providing butts for the exercise of archery in his native place. Indeed every town, small and great, had one or more pairs; and changed as may be the aspect of the ground where they once stood, their names in many instances survive unaltered. Thus, we have Newington Butts in London; St. Augustine's Butts at Bristol; and many closes of pasture land in the vicinity of country towns still retain the appellation of "butt fields." In the parish accounts of Faversham, there is an entry for a new pair then recently erected in the parsonage mead near the church. †

* Some time in the early part of his reign, Charles the First granted permission to one Benjamin Andrews to set up public marks, and demand a penny for eight shots, from every archer willing to pay for the same. The patent to continue in force during the space of fourteen years. — *Patents of King Charles I.*

It is a curious, but hitherto unnoticed, fact, that, before the Reformation, our Roman Catholic parish priesthood sometimes raised a trifling fund for pious uses, by the loan of bows and arrows to those who could not afford to purchase them. Thus, in an old churchwarden's account of the time of Henry the Seventh, found in the muniment chest of Shure Church, Surrey, a schedule of the parish property mentions "two bowes, one in the keepynge of Robert Wornham, the other of Thomas Astone, under surety of John Astone, smythe and archere. These were to maintain a lampe before the rode."

† Carlyle's Charity Commissions, 234, 235.

What the expense was about the time of Queen Elizabeth, will be seen by the following extract from some MS. accounts by the churchwardens of Eltham:—

	s.	d.
1583. Paid for felling 3 trees for the butts, and cutting them out	0	12
For carting the same timber	0	12
To Hampshire, for 2 days' work to make the posts and rails, and set them up	2	4
Paid to 4 men that digged turf and labred at the butts, and for one hundred and a half of nails	4	9
Paid in charges for the suppers of all them that wrought at the butts, which were three or four more than we hoped, becas we could end them in one day	2	2
For the two barres for the butts with the staplest iron works thereto	2	2
Paid to Henry Byrde for ditching before the butts in Easterfylde	0	12

The moderns have not departed from the old fashion, except that our butts, like those who use them, are rather more precise. Earth taken from a heath, common, or turbary, is preferred, because its fibres render it more tough and adhesive than meadow turf. Butts are wedge-shaped, and taper somewhat towards the summit. Crown clods, that is to say, three pieces of sod rudely cut into the form of an urn, give a finish to the modern butt; and a piece of white pasteboard generally forms the mark. They are arranged in sets, at four, eight, twelve, and sixteen roods, in this manner: one hundred and twenty yards being measured, a butt ten feet broad, eighteen inches wide at the top, and about six feet in height, is erected at the two extremities. Thirty yards distant from one of these, and a little to the right hand, they place a second; sixty yards to the left, a third; and ninety to the right, a fourth; which forms a complete set, no one of which impedes the view of the others.

The Cheshire and Lancashire mode of shooting the " paper game " at butts is this : —

Seldom more than three pair of arrows are allowed on each side, which do not reckon except when within the inches; that is, when they pierce a square paper-mark of the following proportions. The weight of the arrows used at each distance is also added.

At 4 roods or	30 yards	4 inches, arrow	5s. 6d.	} Silver weight.*
8 —	60 —	8 —	4s. 6d.	
12 —	90 —	12 —	3s. 6d.	
16 —	120 —	16 —	3s. 6d.	

Seven the game. No lurch.

The archers usually draw lots to determine the order in which they shall shoot. Each maintains his original place during the contest, without reference to the position of their arrows. The diminutive size of the clout renders a marker necessary, at the twelve and sixteen rood length. Like the person who attends, for a similar purpose, during Swiss rifle matches, he stands near the butt, holding in his hand a white wand, which is placed, for a few moments, near each arrow. The signs made use of also much resemble those of his Alpine brother.

For the best arrow, the wand is thrice shaken above his head; second ditto, the same towards the ground. When the paper is pricked, he uncovers and bows; for the outer circle, once; the white, twice; the pin, thrice. For over-arrows, the wand moves briskly upwards; for wide arrows, horizontally; for short arrows, downwards.

Such appears to have been the usage of centuries. " A school of cross-bowmen," engaged at their exercise in a beau-

---

* This arrow scale applies equally to all other archery games.

tiful green alley, with butts at either end, figures as the illumination of an old French MS. dated 1450 *, at present in the King's library. A marker attends, and is represented making one of the signs specified above. Two centuries ago, they merely fixed a very diminutive *blanc* in the centre of the butt by a wooden peg, from which the marker measured to the arrow, before giving his signal. We have this custom plainly alluded to in the following rather ludicrous paragraph :—" Upon a time, being in the king's pavilion, who was desirous of partaking some novelty, there instantly appeared upon the table a pair of butts and whites to shoot at, where suddenly came in six dapper pert fellows like archers, in stature not above a foot high, and all other members accordingly proportioned. Their bows were of the side-bones of an overgrown pike; their strings of a small sleevy silk, not bigger than the thread of a cobweb; their arrows less than picktooths, feathered with the wings of small flies, and headed with the points of fine Spanish needles. These gallants made a show as if they were to shoot a match, *three to three*, and roundly they went about it. In the middle of the game, there was a shot that rested doubtful, which, as it appeared, the gamesters could not well decide. Then Merlin called one of the servants, who had a somewhat big nose, and bade him measure to the mark, and give it to the best. To which, when he stooped and inclined his face, the better to umpire the matter, one of the pigmy archers that had an arrow to shoot delivered it from his bow, and pierced him quite through the nose, at which he started, and the king heartily laughed; for there was no room to be seen, the butts and the archers having together disappeared." † Hitting the white was considered the feat of a very adroit archer; but to split the peg which fastened it to the butt, ranked as the *ne plus ultra* of his skill.

* See plates at the end of this volume.
† Heywood's Life of Ambrosias Merlin, edit. 1609.

>   ——— Hold out, knight! —
> I'll cleave the black pin in the middle of the white.
> *No Wit like a Woman's.*

Give me town wits that deliver jests clean from the bow; that whistle through the air, and cleave the pin at twelve score. — *Lady of Pleasure.*

The ancient marker had also certain terms to express the flight of arrows which entirely missed the butt. When they flew over he cried " gone." " Short" is sufficiently expressive; " wide," too much on either hand, right or left. In their fondness for archers' phraseology, the old writers applied these words in a figurative sense, to express failure of any kind.

> Eschewing short, and gone, and on either side, — wide.
> MASSINGER.

Giving or crying aim, an obscure phrase, rendered still more obscure by Ascham's interpretation, and which greatly puzzled Roberts, merely alludes to the marker's office. An old dramatist thus unlooses the Gordian knot of it: —

> The silver game shall be yours; we'll stand by, and give aim, and halloo, if you hit the clout." — GREEN's *Tu Quoque.*

Money was always staked during the archery matches of our ancestors. At times, the wager amounted only to a few pence; on other occasions, to half a mark.

TARGETS are of comparatively modern invention; I can discover no earlier notice of their use, than occurs in the records of the Finsbury archers, A.D. 1671, when they presented their brethren of London and Westminster with one of a novel construction. Not quite a century afterwards, we find them shooting at a square pasteboard covered with cloth, round the centre of which was drawn a circle, and about that circle four concentric rings. A black border ran around the outside.

Our modern target base is a flat circle of straw, manufactured by the beehive makers; painted canvass forms the face or covering, the centre being gilt, and surrounded by circles, usually named the red, inner white, black, and outer white; while dark green distinguishes its exterior edge, or petticoat. The relative and respective value of these colours shall be decided by the original targets adopted by the Royal London Toxophilites, who used them of three different sizes, painted as above.

Gold	9
Red	7
Inner White	5
Black	3
Outer White	1

The Cheshire targets differ from those common to other parts of the kingdom; their colours are —

Gold (small),
Black,
Red,
White,
Green,
Yellow.

The following may be used as a correct scale for regulating the breadth of the various circles * used in painting a target three feet and a half in diameter. Gold, seven inches, the entire surface being of that metal; red and inner white, each three inches and a half; black, one inch and a half; outer white, which also may be termed the petticoat, one inch broad.

The following colours and value belong to a species of blazon used for the cross-bow in France: — Yellow, 1; white, 2; red, 3; yellow, 4; white, 5; red, 6; yellow, 7; white, 8; black, 9: game, 35.

* The breadth of the *belt* or *band*, not the *diameter* of the whole circle formed by it.

The target varies in size according to its distance from the archer. When of four feet diameter, they are fixed 100 yards in the south, and 120 in the north of England, apart from each other. At eighty yards, the diameter should be three feet; at sixty yards, two feet.

In counting the target, the invariable rule is, that an arrow piercing the edge of the gold must come forth unmarked by the slightest tinge of red, the approximating colour, otherwise it is considered to have been in the red, and will reckon only as such. The same custom prevails in reference to all other circles.*

My information on this subject would be still incomplete, were I to omit showing my young archer how the target card is kept during prize-shooting. It enables each party to ascertain exactly the state of the contest at any time of day, and is generally worn suspended to a button-hole of the coat. Each of the compartments being coloured as a duplicate of the target, we mark the hits with a pin attached to the card by a silken thread.

Archers' Names.	Gold.	Red.	Inner White.	Black.	Outer White.	Number of hits.	Value.
A.	6	10	19	15	34	84	298
B.	4	11	13	20	31	79	269
C.	4	10	25	31	48	148	372
D.	2	14	19	27	31	90	323
Total Hits and Value						401	1262

The smallest possible honour arises from hitting the corners without the circles, and the person who does this is presented, by very ancient custom, with a horn spoon, which he must wear in the button-hole of his coat until won from him by the next archer who plants an arrow in the same division of the target. †

* The target, properly so called, is bounded by the exterior circle; all beyond counting as nothing.

† The horn-spoon is used at the meetings of the Woodmen of Arden.

A stranger merely seeing the trophy won, and unacquainted with the laws of archery, would possibly mistake the honour for a disgrace.

When flight-shooting, place your marks upon the greensward without triangles. There is no object which suggests so perfect an idea of complete and beautiful repose as do these broad circles, like the disc of a full moon, when arranged upon an extensive lawn of smooth velvet turf.

Many substitutes for the regular target will suggest themselves to him who resides some six or ten score miles from the metropolis. We may choose the old Roman expedient, a large bundle of brushwood tied together, and suspended to a stake, from which the archer stood at the distance of 600 feet; or a good thick sheaf of haulme, that is, thatchers' straw. If bound tightly at the centre and the two extremities, this answers well while nothing better can be commanded. Place any neat round mark on each, and elevate them by stakes fixed slopingly in the earth.

A military writer of the 17th century, while strongly advocating the adoption of " fire shafts," suggests a most atrocious substitute for the common target, at once to render soldiers expert, and inure them to accidents and perils of the field. " Fire shafts are so neat, portable, and manageable," says he, " that even children may make their sport with them, and youths of any growth do good service. So if, at festival times, a bull, instead of baiting him with dogges, were tyed to a stake, or sheweled in with archers conveniently placed upon a common or other spacious place, men might then make trial with their fire shafts, a brave and manlie sport! where, haply, the maddening of the enraged beast, besides enuring them to conflict, would teach some profitable stratagems of war."

I will now offer a few words upon several peculiarities in the marks at which Oriental nations display their archery. The Mantchou Tartars, who practise with whistling arrows, use a target consisting of two parts. A cushion, or roll, of cloth, well stuffed with wool, and about a foot in breadth, is nailed round the edge of a circular hole of the same diameter, cut from the middle of a square board. The bull's eye, painted red on the outer edge, and black in the centre, is then made to fit tightly into this aperture, being confined there by the elasticity of the cushion. On hitting the latter, only the arrow falls uninjured to the ground, and no arrow is accounted a shot but the one which dislodges the bull's eye, by striking it out behind the target; when it does not fall to the ground, but drops a few inches, being sustained by a string attached to an upper projecting rod.

Altogether, this seems not a bad contrivance, as it must obviate much ill blood among a people fierce and irascible like these Tartar savages, who might otherwise be tempted, in case of a disputed shot, to "loosen the Gordian knot of it" with their dagger's point.

One is a little startled to find a treatise on the bow among the lucubrations of a grave philosopher like Confucius. Yet the Huor Yu, or Book of Sentences, contains some curious allusions to its practice among the author's countrymen. In the third article of that work, he speaks of the adoration due to spirits; of the imperial laws of music; and the manner of drawing the bow.* When engaged at this exercise, they fixed up the skin of some beast as a mark. For the emperor, it was that of a bear; for a king, that of a stag; for a mandarin, that of a tiger; and for literary gentlemen, that of a wild boar. The first aimed 120 yards from the butt; the second, 80; the third, 70; the fourth, 50.

Every Chinese who purposes entering the army is required to possess some previous knowledge of military tactics; to exhibit proofs of personal strength and adroitness in aiming

* Du Halde.

with the bow*; and to recite from memory the following precepts of archery addressed to his officers, by Yong Tcheng, third emperor of the reigning dynasty : —

"Warriors! from the moment you assume the garb of a soldier, the state provides for your subsistence, and provides for it with parental care. Doth it become you, then, to be negligent of your chief duties, — those for which you are maintained at so great a cost?

"The accomplishment of being able to draw the arrow with precision, whether on foot or on horseback, — to know either exercise perfectly, — can be acquired only by incessant application.

"Relieved from the necessity of following uncongenial occupations, nothing should distract you from the exercise of arms; everything you see, everything you hear, incessantly reminds you of your obligations. Wherefore is it, then, that, instead of devoting all your energies to their fulfilment, you seek to dissipate those hours in enervating pleasures, which alone should be solely dedicated to bending the bow and launching the arrow at its mark? Of what monstrous ingratitude are you not guilty towards the state?

"To draw the bow with energy and skill was an art ever highly cherished by the Mantchous. By that alone did we acquire of old a mighty name amongst the nations of the earth; by that only have we been entitled to rank among the chiefest of mankind; and although, in the present degenerate age, we fall away from the discipline of our ancestors, time was, when a Mantchou who drew his arrow unskilfully, would have been exposed not only to severe personal chastisement from his officers, but to the universal derision of his comrades; he would have been regarded as a disgrace to his name and an opprobrium upon his country. In the silence of the night, then, when the hollow

---

* These exercises consist in shooting dismounted, and also riding at full gallop, against a very large target. Such as acquit themselves with *éclat* are elected doctors, or licentiates, in archery. — *Art. Mil. Chinois.*

drum announces to you the commencement of the various watches, meditate deeply on a subject so important.* May each of you be animated by a noble emulation; may he incessantly direct his energies to acquire perfection in an art on which not only his own preservation, but the safety of the state, so materially depends!

"In all the contests in which you indulge, whether private or in public, be still unsatisfied if with your shaft you pierce not the centre of the butt; and when at the chase, be ever emulous to transfix the fleet objects of your aim. Remember that by your address in the noble exercise of archery the nation will measure out the portion of esteem you are destined to enjoy.

"We shall bestow on you military honours and promotion exactly in reference to your adroitness in the use of the bow. Thus, soldiers will become officers,—officers will be elevated to a more distinguished rank, — and all will partake the glory of shedding equal lustre on your ancestors and on your posterity."†

When Sultan Mohammed Khan became master of Constantinople, he distributed the chief booty among his rapacious followers, and caused the idols Vudd Yaghús, Yaaf Surá, and Nesr, which the infidels had encrusted with jewels, to be carried to the Okmeydan, or Place of Archers, and set up there as marks for every soldier of the Faithful to level his arrows at. Hence it arose that, even at the present day, a well-delivered arrow, which hits the mark, is styled by archers Pútch Oki, an idol's shaft. One of these images remained, until knocked to pieces, about the time of Sultan Ahmed Khan; another was called Aymaïsh, because it stood on the south side, and the arrows hit it when shot with a northerly wind. A third, called Heki, near Kaás-kói, was also most easily hit from the same quarter; hence the phrase a " Heki shot," so common in Turkey. A

---

* The Chinese divide the night into four portions, by *vielles*, which they sound upon the tambour. The first is at midnight, the last at daybreak.
† L'Art Militaire Chinois.

fourth, named Pish, stood on the north-west side of the Okmeydan, and being commanded only from the south-east, gives its name to such a shot. From Pelenk, erected on the west side, and, of course, aimed at from the east, we derive the bowman's phrase, Pelenk. In short, having fixed twelve different idols on the four sides of the exercise ground, a grand archery match was proclaimed, and all the veteran bowmen, each showing his skill in taking aim at them, made a magnificent show; and hence originated the custom among the people of Istamboul * of meeting there on holidays, for the purpose of exercising their adroitness in archery.†

These repeated allusions in this passage to an allowance for the wind, so strongly recommended by our own Ascham, have probably not escaped the reader's attention. For private practice, the modern Turks place upon their butts a small white mark about the size of a dollar. Standing at the distance of thirty feet, they will place five or six successive arrows around its outer edge, never touching the centre, unless by design. At this species of short butt, one of their favourite recreations, the most dexterous receives an embroidered handkerchief for his reward.

Splendid exhibitions of archery formerly took place in the Hippodrome, or Horse Course, at Constantinople, one of which an eye-witness, thus describes ‡: — "A brave troop of archers, mounted on the finest Arab steeds, now arrived, and their presence excited an universal murmur of applause. Indeed, their skill and adroitness were most extraordinary. Having finished several courses with the target and jareed, they again put their horses to the gallop, sheathing and unsheathing their cymetars without stopping. In the same manner they shot thrice with the bow. Each archer first aimed at and struck the hinder shoe of the horse immediately in advance of him. At the

---

* Turkish name for Constantinople.   † Evliya Effendi.
‡ Translated from Vertomannus's Travels in the East.

second course, they planted their arrows in a gilt ball, fixed on the top of a lofty mast that stood in the centre of the Hippodrome. And, lastly, they shot through a ring at which some Albanians had been previously exercising with the lance. One noble cavalier took off his saddle, placed it upon his courser's neck, and then re-fastened the girths while going at the top of the animal's speed. This same Turk laid an orange on the turban of one of his slaves, and, spurring his courser, struck it in pieces with an arrow, repeating the experiment a second and even a third time, without drawing bridle, or injury to him who acted target.

Equestrian archery was likewise much practised in Persia by the Shah and his nobles. A mark, about the size of a plate, is fastened against a tree, at which they discharge their arrows whilst riding full gallop. "I have seen the Shah," says Shirley, "tire out six or seven horses successively at this kind of pastime. He often continued on the ground from noon until four or six o'clock; and it was really astonishing how he could endure such violent exercise during the ardour of the sun, and the dust raised by the horses' feet. He once gave me an astonishing proof of his dexterity and strength. Stretched on the earth with his face downwards, he took one of the strongest bows, and drew it, as if about to discharge an arrow. Then, unassisted by his hands, and without putting them to the earth, he rose up briskly with his bended bow, — certainly an instance of prodigious muscular power."*

In the centre of the Meidan, or market-place, at Ispahan, stood a high pole, much resembling those set up in some European cities for the popinjay game. Instead of a bird, however, they place on its summit a small melon, an arpus, an apple, or a trencher filled with small silver coin. At this they shoot whilst the horse is going at full speed. It is by no means

* Relation d'un Voyage en Perse, 1590, par un gentilhomme de la suite du Seigneur Scierley, ambassadeur du roy d'Angleterre.

unusual to see the Shah himself gallop unexpected into the Meidan, and mingle unceremoniously among his subjects whilst engaged at this sport. When the plate falls, its contents become the perquisite of the king's footmen; and the most successful shot has the honour of feasting the whole company, even to the Shah himself, should the royal bow have been put in requisition.

When Karib Shah fell into the hands of his enemies, after an unsuccessful effort to throw off the Persian yoke, he was condemned to die under circumstances of the most revolting cruelty. They first shod his hands and feet with iron, like a horse, scoffingly observing, that, as he had been accustomed to the soft roads of Kilan, he would otherwise hardly endure the stony and rugged ways of Persia. After being suffered to languish in that condition for three whole days, he was brought into the Meidan, and bound to the summit of the mast. When the king had set an example by discharging at him the first arrow, he called loudly to his assembled lords, telling them that every true and loyal man should follow his example. Upon the word, he was instantly so covered with arrows that the body retained no shape of a man, and, after remaining thus during three days, was taken down and interred. On the suppression of Karib Shah's revolt, the people of Kilan were disarmed; neither have they since dared to possess any sort of weapon,—not even the *sefin*, or ring, with which the Persians bend their bows.*

I shall close this chapter with a lively anecdote of Persian butt shooting, which furnishes a general idea of the mode in which these matters are conducted throughout the East.

Whilst Shah Abbas remained encamped at Casbin, he held a grand review of cavalry, which lasted nearly a fortnight. Every day the king took his station upon an elevated throne, under the portals of the royal gardens, with his nobility and principal officers ranged on his right and left hand. The last day of this

* See Female Archery.

magnificent spectacle being devoted to an exhibition of archery, a select number of the finest and most expert soldiers were ordered to ride in single file before the Shah. Only one cavalier passed by at a time on the gallop, which he commenced at some distance; and, passing the throne, turned about in his scarlet morocco saddle, and drove his arrow into a butt of sand, placed on the king's left hand. At the close of the review it was usual to reward the most expert archer with a considerable increase of pay. One cavalier, however, instead of galloping and shooting as the others did, only walked his horse by, and placed his hand on his breast, and afterwards on his head, according to the Oriental mode of saluting the monarch. He possessed a singularly forbidding mien; for he had coarse, flat, Tartar features, and a complexion changed almost to blackness by the heat of the sun. On witnessing this act of audacious disobedience, the Shah's indignation burst forth; and, in allusion to his unprepossessing appearance, he fiercely exclaimed, "that they should immediately discharge the black-looking scoundrel from his service."*

The guards flew to execute his commands. After being dismounted, and deprived of his arms and accoutrements, he was on the point of being severely bastinadoed, when the commanding officer rode up, and, by a sign, interfered. Then, respectfully approaching the throne, he represented that this cavalier, so ill-looking, was, in reality, one of the best soldiers in the army. At the sieges of Erivin† and Candahar he had fully proved his undaunted courage; and his father was one of those who thrice led a storming party to the gates of Bagdad.

A representation so favourable had due weight with the offended Shah, and he commanded his horse and arms to be restored. The archers, whose progress was suspended by this

---

* The Persians, in general, have a very noble physiognomy.

† A town in Persia, celebrated for its manufactory of gilded and painted bows and arrows.

occurrence, again resumed their bows, and the disobedient soldier received a command to place himself at their head. He obeyed, and pushed his horse past the throne with the speed of the wind, but again reined him up on coming opposite the butt. There he remained stationary, turning first to the right hand, then to the left, and looking about on all sides, without uttering a word. His commander, who justly anticipated another burst of indignation from the monarch, when in all likelihood he would have ordered the guards to cut him in pieces, called, in a loud and peremptory tone, that he should shoot.

The soldier immediately exclaimed, "My lord, whither would you that your servant direct his arrow?"

"At the butt, dog of a slave!" shouted the enraged Satrap, "as your comrades have already done."

"What doth it advantage," resumed the veteran, shaking his head, "thus to waste and spoil my good shafts against a lump of earth? Fain would I use them against the bodies of my sovereign's foes; then should you see me discharge five ere another could find time to shoot one!"

He had drawn two arrows from his quiver whilst speaking these words, and held one of them in his teeth as he fitted the other to his bow. Then pushing vigorously across the plain, until the earth seemed to tremble beneath his courser's hoofs, he passed the butt; and turning in his saddle like a Parthian[*], drove the first arrow directly into the hollow centre.[†] After contemplating this successful shot for an instant, he wheeled

---

[*] Their mode of training for this Parthian manœuvre has been well described by Busbequius, an eye-witness. They erect a high pole in the centre of a plain, having a brass ball fixed on its top. Around this they spur vigorously, until a little beyond it, the horse still galloping, when suddenly they turn in their splendid morocco saddles, and drive an arrow into the globe as they fly. The constant practice of this manœuvre renders them so expert, that the bow being turned in the sight of the unwary pursuer, he is instantly shot through and through.

[†] See "Female Archery," p. 111.

round, flew past the same spot, and fixed the second shaft in the hole, whence, an instant before, the attendants had drawn out the first.

The officer, who had already interceded for him, now again approached the Shah, and, touching the earth with his forehead, ventured to express a hope that the soldier's bearing justified the expectations he had raised. His Highness loudly declared his admiration of his adroitness. He was ordered to approach and kiss his royal master's feet, who forthwith increased his pay to fifteen tomas, instead of the five he had previously received.

SECTION III.

FEMALE ARCHERY.

> As that word was spoken, Clorinda came by,
>   The queen of the shepherds was she ;
> Her kirtle was velvet, as green as the grass,
>   And her buskin did reach to her knee.
> So modest her gait, her person divine,
>   And her countenance free from all pride !
> In her hand was a bow, and a quiver of arrows
>   Hung gracefully by her fair side.
> Said Robin Hood, " Lady fair, whither away ?
>   Oh whither, fair lady, away ? "
> She smilingly answered, " To kill a fat buck,
>   For to-morrow is Tutbury day."
> And as we did wend all towards the green bower,
>   Two hundred fair stags we espied ;
> She chose out the fattest of all that brave herd,
>   And shot him through side and side.
> " By the faith of my body," said bold Robin then,
>   " I never saw woman like thee ;
> Or com'st thou from east, or com'st thou from west,
>   Thou need'st not beg venison from me."
>
>   *Ballad of Robin Hood's Marriage.*

From her golden quiver Camilla has drawn forth the light and varnished shaft. She bends the fatal yew by thrusting it from her, until the curved extremities approach; and elevating her hands equally, she touches her left hand with the arrow's barb, and with her right, and with the string, her left breast. — VIRGIL.

STAR of the Archers*, fairest Clorinda, and queen, not of shepherds only, but lady paramount over all the blithe foresters of merry England to boot ! That is, provided you were something more than a mere offspring of the poets' imagination, — a being

---

* " That Moorish queen was so skilful in drawing the Turkish bow, that it was held as a marvel ; and it is said that they called her in Arabic, Nugueymat Turga ; which is to say, ' Star of the Archers.' " — DR. SOUTHEY's *Chronicle of the Cid.*

of flesh and blood, possessing form, figure, and local habitation, as well as music-breathing name.

That passion for the martial festivities of tiltyard and banqueting hall, which distinguished our stately dames of the chivalrous ages, has often been painted by the romantic pen of Froissart. Whether they appeared in the shooting-ground, prior to the last half century, equipped with bow and quiver, to take an active part in its amusements, is a question certainly interesting to archers, but, perhaps, to them only. Such evidence as I have been able to collect, shall be presently laid before the reader, who will perhaps consider it a satisfactory elucidation of the point in dispute.

Previously, however, to entering upon the inquiry, let us take a hasty glance at those regions where the early existence of female archery cannot be questioned. Magnificent and spirit-stirring as are the details of its progress in many a distant clime, the reader will turn from their perusal with renewed pleasure to the unsullied and not inglorious records

> Of home and native land.

Unlike Teucer, Merion, Pandarus, and other illustrious bowmen of antiquity, we seek not inspiration by incense or hecatomb:

> No firstling lambs, unheedful, do we vow
> To Phœbus, patron of the shaft and bow.

Still will we evince our respect for the archer god, by commencing our inquiries in the land on which he loves to shed the lustre of his earliest beams.

To the EAST, then, where, within the rose gardens of Teheran, the dark-eyed houris of Persia launched their varnished shafts at the distant butt, equipped in all the magnificent apparatus of their native archery.

Some remarkable changes have recently taken place in the social condition of the women of two distinguished oriental nations. I allude to Persia and Turkey. In the latter, we see the fair tenants of the harem daily promenading the public quarters of Constantinople. At home, a French *maître de ballet* attends to initiate them into the mysteries of his art. Unencumbered by the odious *yasmak*, and guarded by a few female slaves only, they whisk it,

> Upon the light fantastic toe,

through all the tortuous mazes of waltz, gallopade, quadrille, mazourka, and contre dance.

And is not any amelioration in the condition of these lovely, helpless beings a subject of general interest? The recent innovations of his majesty the Shah, however, are alone connected with the subject of this chapter.

Badinage apart, it is a well known fact that the harem of the Persian are permitted, nay, encouraged, to disport themselves with archery. These oriental bow meetings take place within the recesses of the royal gardens, where, their black-bearded tyrant and a bevy of female attendants excepted, no spectators are allowed to be present. Thus secluded, however assiduously the fair toxophilites may pursue this novel pastime, still, it can hardly be asserted they are occupied in drawing the *bow* [*], at least in that equivocal sense, in which we often apply the expression to their fair sisters of Britain, whose proceedings in this sort are as embarrassing as they are successful; and the consequent hymeneal arrangements sadly destructive of mine. To preserve any correct list of our fair toxophilites, as far as *names* are concerned, seems just as hopeless — owing to those inroads of matrimony — as was a certain long-desired consummation to Penelope's suitors, when dependent on the progress of her distaff and shuttle. The catalogue arranged so accurately to-day, shall be nearly all undone within the space of six months. Let them, therefore, be taken with the usual

[*] Beaux.

mercantile proviso, — " errors excepted," — and don't hold me responsible where I cannot control. Not satisfied with triumphing over us in every contest, these remorseless syrens, like the famed Amazonian queen, level at their victims a battery of darts, far more potent than those previously exhausted upon the target.

> The bold Penthesilæa durst
>   The Danish fleet oppose;
> And from her bow sharp arrows sent
>   To gall her harnessed foes.
> No sooner was the battle done,
>   Her golden helm laid by,
> But whom by arms she could not take,
>   She slaughtered with her eye.

And what's the result? Let cooler heads determine whether an exercise, in itself all gracefulness, invests our fair enslavers with some mystic fascination, more potent than laughing eyes and blooming cheeks, when sun and summer breeze, echoing bugle, and other romantic accessories, invite them to the target field, making

> Their bosom's lord sit lightly on his throne.

This much, however, is certain. Recommence acquaintance with a bevy of fair dames after a few seasons' absence, and mark what change comes o'er the spirit of your dream! Worse than Babel confusion of names; matronly graces; while in addition to Waring's burnished shafts, which, as vivacious spinsters, they handled so adroitly, many a fair *arrow* besides, thus beautifully alluded to by the Psalmist: " Happy are they who have their quivers full of them; they shall not be ashamed when they speak with their enemies in the gate." I presume the attractions are, and ever have been, reciprocal in both sexes; at least there is evidence that, four centuries ago, your archer was the truest, most loyal, and most chivalrous of lovers. " Thomas Boyd, Earl of Arran," says John Paston, in a letter to his brother, dated about the year 1470, "is one of the lighterest, deliverest *, best spoken, fairest archer; devoutest, most perfect and truest to his lady, of all the knights that ever I was acquainted with. So, would God my lady liked me as well as I do his person and most knightly condition!" †

But in this digression we had nearly lost sight of our fair Persian dames, whose place of exercise, I have said, is within the shady recesses of the pleasure-grounds attached to the royal residence. The butts consist of moistened sand, inclosed in a wooden frame, and beaten into a hard compact mass. These are set up in a slanting direction at the boundary of some verdant alley, where the over-arching branches of vine and orange tree exclude the fierceness of an eastern sun. Consistent with that gorgeous taste so prevalent throughout the East, the whole exterior of the butt is covered with elegant scroll-work and patterns of flowers. Gold and silver, intermingled with various pigments of the most brilliant hues, are lavishly employed to produce this effect.

A female Abyssinian slave stands beside the mark, provided with a large round pebble, to form and preserve an unbroken hollow in the centre, and at this cavity every arrow is directed. She repeats the operation several times whilst her mistresses are shooting; for the triumph of Persian archery consists not merely in a central shot, but also in making the arrow penetrate deeply into the sand at every discharge.

At the termination of their sport, these fair butt shooters scrupulously conform to a remarkable custom, which, from remote antiquity, has prevailed among Persian bowmen of the other sex. Know, ladies, the followers of the Prophet divide themselves into two great sects, who hate each other with a cordiality worthy of the most polished nation of Europe. The Persians are devout followers of the Caliph

* A lightly delivered arrow marks the skilful bowman.
† Paston Letters, vol. ii. p. 97.

F. P. Stephanoff.   J. Portbury.

Oriental Female Archers.

London Published by Longman & Co. Feb.y 1840.

Ali, and regard the Turks and other disciples of his antagonist, Omar, as a sort of Mahomedan heretic. To assist in perpetuating the memory of this religious feud, the Persian archer, on discharging his arrow at the mark for the last time, fails not to pronounce the charitable aspiration of, " Ter a kir dirdil Omar ! " — Would that this arrow might bury itself in the heart of Omar !

It must be highly amusing to witness the affected change which comes o'er the spirit of these orthodox beauties, whilst thus denouncing the heretical caliph. Gay, innocent, and thoughtless, it were absurd to suppose they have the least real feeling on such a subject. Still, like prattling parrots, their lesson is repeated, with many a pretty indication of displeasure, akin to that of the " wrathful dove, and most magnanimous mouse." Eyes which, a moment before, beamed with the softest expression, now dart forth flashes of anger, like the opening storm-cloud. Pretty mouths, so lately wreathed in smiles, are tortured into an expression of the most inveterate contempt. But, no sooner does the glancing shaft quiver within its destined mark, than Ali as well as Omar are consigned to oblivion; and songs, and laughter, merry and musical as the chime of silver bells, again re-echo through the perfumed walks of their magnificent pleasure-garden. Bows, arrows, and the costly sefin*, are speedily abandoned to the attendant slaves; and with a zest which their recent occupation is so well calculated to supply, the fair revellers hurry off to

Taste the good the gods provide them,

in the splendid luxuries of an Oriental banquet.

Leaving our beauties in quiet enjoyment of its festivities, we will endeavour, like true archers, to get a peep at their accoutrements, since we dare not peep at them. These form so com-

---

* Thumb-rings for drawing the bowstring. Their use, description, &c. are hereinafter fully explained.

plete a contrast to what has been, at any time, common to Europe that they merit a particular description.

Persia still boasts within most of her large towns a race of hereditary bowyers.* To judge from some specimens of their handicraft now before me, the art can have degenerated but little, if at all, since the period, when truth, good shooting, and a firm seat on horseback, were considered the all-in-all accomplishments of a Persian satrap.† The royal armoury of Teheran exhibits a number of bows of the richest description, many upwards of a century old, still retaining an elasticity worthy of their external elegance. But their power is enormous; and, although the Shah and his nobles manage them with ease and adroitness, the same could not be expected from the delicate strength of a female arm.‡ When, therefore, the monarch signified his wish that the harem be exercised in archery, the most celebrated bowyers of Teheran were employed to equip them suitably. But, as the material of which these Oriental bows have been made for ages could not be improved, the workmen

* Near the port of Ali, at Ispahan, is a bazaar, where live the manufacturers of bows and arrows. In India, the bowyers form a distinct caste. — STRUY's *Travels.*

† And of monarchs likewise, as the following quaint translation of an epitaph will show: —

> Darius, the Persian, lies buried here,
> Who in riding and shooting had never a peer.

Indeed, this consummate skill gained them a distinctive epithet among cotemporary nations. We have allusions to their archery in the Bible; and, among profane writers, Pollux preserves the following legend, which was inscribed on a picture representing several Grecian females, who had offered up prayers during the Persian invasion. " These are the women who prayed to Venus for the Greeks, more particularly for their countrymen of Corinth; since the goddess was concerned that we should not betray the citadel of Greece to the bow-bearing Persians."

‡ Khondemir says, that the art of archery had reached its highest perfection among Persians of all ranks, from the prince to the peasant, under the Kajan dynasty; so that, at this day, they call a strong bow, such as few men can draw, " Keman Kajani " — a Kajanian bow. — D'HERBELOT, i. 463.

merely aimed at fabricating a lighter instrument, still more ornamented.

Buffalo or wild goat's horn, jet black, and of a fine polish, forms the belly of a Persian bow. Glued to this is a thin slip of some hard wood, little inferior in toughness, which serves for the back.* The extreme points are fashioned to resemble a snake's head, the loops of the cord having the appearance of being held within its extended jaws. As the horn, with its dark rich lustre, needs not the aid of ornament, it is left entirely plain, the richness of Oriental taste being lavished on the splendid arabesque which decorates the wooden back. Birds, flowers, fruit, and all the graceful devices one sees in the most elaborate scroll-work of the ancients, are represented on its surface in vivid colours, intermingled with gilding: not that pale, thin, lack-lustrous article with which the English artist is compelled to be satisfied; but the real "red, red gold," unalloyed and brilliant as when drawn from its native mine; and the centre of the bow, serving for the grip of the archer's hand, is marked by several broad bands of the same metal, separated from each other by figures of flowers and fruit.

These beautiful weapons were formerly considered as the most acceptable offerings which one Oriental monarch could make to another. Thus, when the ambassador sent by the Shah to compliment Sultan Amurath the Second, had deposited before the Ottoman divan the munificent presents of his master, among them appeared nine splendid Persian bows, and a proportionate number of arrows of the same fine workmanship.† The Shah likewise presented our countryman, Sir John Shirley, with a similar one.‡ Again, in 1656, the Dutch East India Company

---

* Oriental bowyers use a peculiar kind of glue, made from a root called in Turkey *Sherisçhoan*, which they grind like corn between two stones, until it resembles sawdust. — THEVENOT.

† Hist. of Juss. Bassa, p. 11. ‡ See Travels.

sent to the Emperor of Ceylon, among other presents, "two Persian bows, with their arrows and quivers, richly adorned." *

The Oriental bowstring, from its peculiar construction and twofold use, is not less interesting than the weapon of which it forms a part. Many strong silken threads are laid together, until the whole equals the thickness of an ordinary goose quill. Whipping, composed of the same material, is then bound firmly, for about three or four inches at the centre, and also for a less width, equidistant from either end. Large loops of scarlet, or other colours producing an equally brilliant contrast, are attached to this middle piece by a very curious knot. Complicated and elegant as that by which King Gordianus perplexed his royal brother of Macedon, it is to be solved only by similar decisive means, for never yet saw I the fingers that could unfasten, much less imitate, it. The vivid contrast between the pure white silk, of which they usually make the centre of this bowstring, and its gaudy loops, produces quite a splendid effect.

I have hinted at the twofold purpose to which it was occasionally applied. To the Turkish Basha, sleeping or waking, whom "His Highness" suspected of growing rich in his pachalick, it was an object of continual dread. Under these circumstances, rarely did he escape a summons to Constantinople, where, within the seraglio walls, the bowstring freed him from l'embarras des richesses, and the life he esteemed worthless without them. Like our wolf in the fable, the sanguinary despot quickly found or invented causes of accusation. Brief, therefore, was the colloquy, ere, at a sign imperceptible to the predestined wretch, the mutes advanced. Placing him upon his knees, they passed their bowstring once round his neck, and, with their right hands in the loops, drew tightly, until appearances indicated their victim had ceased to breathe. At one period this practice prevailed very extensively throughout the East. It was used as a means

* Baldæus, Description of Ceylon.

Persian Archers.

London Published by Longman & Co. Feby. 1840.

of executing revenge as well as punishment; and we may attribute its adoption to the readiness with which the instrument of death might be procured, when every man carried at his back the weapon to which it belongs.

In nothing is the contrast between English and Oriental archery more manifest than in the manner of bracing the bow. The trowsered beauties of the East do this with equal grace and facility as the men, because the lower part of their dress is nearly similar in both sexes.

When an Oriental wishes to string his bow, he places himself firmly on his centre, and grasping the upper ear* in his left hand, passes the weapon behind the left leg and over the shin bone of the right. Then, bending it, by forcing the upper ear round towards the opposite side, he slips the string, which has been already secured on the lower horn, into its place, with the right hand. This operation requires considerable muscular power, and is by no means an easy one, until repeated attempts have rendered it familiar. I believe Sir Walter Scott makes Saladin string his bow in this manner whilst on horseback.

The Persian arrow is altogether worthy of its bow, being a small jointed reed, called, in Latin, Arundo Bambos, which is used almost universally throughout the East. Of this there are two species, one being much stronger, and of a texture very superior to the other. War arrows, and those designed for occasions where the chances of recovering them are small, are made of the latter kind: the former, which, besides its hardness, has a fine nutbrown, glossy surface, is reserved to replenish the quivers of princes and grandees. The heads take many forms, according to the purposes for which they design them. In butt shooting, a solid pyramid of steel seems to be preferred,

---

* The curved extremity of an Indian bow is so named by their bowyers.

" The man provided himself with several little rods, about the length of the ears of a bow." — *Autobiography of Buber Khan.*

and for about three inches below this point, the natural colour of the reed is entirely concealed by rich japan painting, intermixed with gold and silver flowers. Ornaments in a similar style of richness are repeated at the butt end, above and beneath the feathering. Indeed, the Persian arrow is altogether so delicate and costly that we consider them as objects of curiosity rather than use. When shot into damp ground, the friction gradually impairs their beauty, and for that reason I seldom use any out of the numbers I possess: substitute a light English pile*, however, for the solid Persian steel head, and you have a really superior flight and target arrow, which, from the extraordinary lightness of its hollow reed, may occasionally be observed to far outstrip the wind.

The *sefin*, or thumb-rings†, before alluded to, are one of the distinctions of an Oriental archer. Englishmen, it is well known, draw the bowstring with their three first fingers; the Flemings, with the first and second only; but neither use the thumb at all. The Asiatic method is the reverse of this. There the bowman draws altogether with his thumb, the forefinger bent in its first and second joint, being merely pressed on one side of the arrow nock, to secure it from falling. In order to prevent the flesh from being torn by the bowstring, he wears a broad ring of agate, cornelian, green marble, ivory, horn, or iron, according to his rank and means. Upon the inside of this, which projects half an inch, the string rests when the bow is drawn; on the outside it is only half that breadth; and, in loosing the arrow, he straightens his thumb, which sets the string free. These rings, with a spare string, are usually carried in a small box, suspended at the bowman's side; but,

---

* The iron point of an arrow.

† Sandys observes, that one of the early Turkish sultans occupied his leisure in manufacturing these rings. The produce of his industry, distributed among favourite pashas and officers, received of course an additional value from the distinguished rank of the donor.

from habit, many retain them constantly upon the hand, for ornament as well as for use.

Consistent with the splendour of their other appointments, the sefin worn by those dark-eyed houris, whose feats we have so recently been contemplating, are adorned with all the cunning of the jeweller's art. A stone called jadde *, chrystal, jasper, and even gold, inlaid with stones of varied hue, glitter in the sunbeams as each snowy hand strains up the silken bowstring. A quilted half sleeve of crimson velvet, or fine cloth, thickly embroidered with gold flowers, protects the arm from being bruised by the chord in its return. Did not a very curious relic, recently come to light, prove Chaucer's " gai bracer † " to be a purely English fashion, we might imagine he was describing one of these. The weight of the gold in one which I wore upon my arm for a short time was remarkable; it probably amounted to three or four ounces.

One other curious contrivance connected with the Oriental bow remains to be described. When flight-shooting, to which they are particularly attached, a grooved horn, about six inches long, is fastened upon the back of the bow hand by straps of crimson morocco buckled round the wrist. The bow is then, and then only, held across the body, and, by drawing several inches within this horn, they can use very short arrows. By thus diminishing their length, superior lightness, the chief quality of a flight shaft, is proportionably attained. On the 9th July, 1792, Mahmood Effendi, the secretary to the Turkish embassy, exhibited his great strength by shooting an arrow in this way 415 yards partly against the wind, and 482 yards with the wind, in a field behind Bedford House, London. He used a Turkish bow,

* Of this a considerable specimen may be seen in the figure of a tortoise found on the banks of the Jumna, in Hindostan, and preserved in the British Museum. Sefins of cornelian may easily be procured in the bazars of Constantinople.

† See page 102.

drawing 160 pounds; and this exploit was performed in the presence of three gentlemen, members of the Toxophilite Society. The arrow measured $25\frac{1}{4}$ inches, which he pulled 3 inches within the bow, so as to make the draught 28 inches. He said, upon the ground, that Selim, the then Grand Segnior, often shot 500 yards, the greatest performance of the modern Turks. However, the Sultan afterwards, in 1798, drove an arrow in the ground 972 yards from the spot where he stood, the distance being measured in the presence of Sir Robert Anslie, ambassador to the Porte. All these singular contrivances are, of course, common in the East to archers of both sexes; and their dissimilarity to every thing we apply to the same use in England, has induced me to detain the reader by a minuteness of description otherwise unnecessary.

The French traveller, Gentil, who visited India at the commencement of the seventeenth century, dwells with enthusiasm on the appearance of a body-guard consisting of 100 ladies, whom he saw in attendance on one of its native princes. Their weapon was a crossbow, in the use of which they exhibited remarkable dexterity. He asserts that he saw each of them plant an arrow, at a considerable distance, into a circle no larger than a French sol.* On other occasions, they would discharge three arrows at once, with such prodigious rapidity and violence, that, on piercing a tree, the steel points entered so deeply as no force of pulling could draw them out.

When the monarch quitted his capital, whether for war or the chase, this band of Amazons invariably accompanied him. They were styled Menaytas, were lodged within the palace, and annually drew a magnificent stipend from the royal treasury. Masters attended to instruct them in every kind of warlike accomplishment, which they studied with the utmost enthusiasm. One of them, whose age Gentil guessed to be about

* Halfpenny.

twenty-four, was, unquestionably, the most beautiful woman in India. Her complexion displayed a beautiful fairness; and her hair, black as jet, flowed in a profusion of natural ringlets upon a neck of ivory. In a mock combat performed by a detachment of these ladies, she acquitted herself so valiantly, that the enraptured monarch, unable to control his emotion, caused her to raise her casque, while he saluted her in the presence of his whole court. Then, with his own hands, he placed a chain of massive gold around her neck. She was called Langir. Her mother, Acosira, also a woman of extraordinary charms, had been so valorous, that in wrestling she never met her equal. On one occasion, being challenged by certain strangers, she quickly laid them prostrate on their mother earth; and, on their attempting to rise and resent this indignity, forthwith strangled them outright. Her own fate was as extraordinary: she was torn in pieces by a lion, which, during one of the royal hunting matches, she had the rashness to attack dismounted and single-handed. The king, her lover, being excessively grieved, gave her a royal funeral, abstaining for many days from the consumption of aneca, betel, and shaving his beard, with many other symptoms of mourning and regret.

In Usbec Tartary, the natives of both sexes ply their bows with equal dexterity. When invaded by the Russians, it is related by the historian of the expedition *, that they almost annihilated the enemy's cavalry, killing man and horse 100 paces further off than the best European musketeer. Travellers who visit their country are received with a rude hospitality; and when

> Sated Hunger bids his brother Thirst
> Produce the mighty bowl,

they amuse them with many extraordinary anecdotes of strong and skilful archery, the only subject on which they appear to

* Le Clerc.

converse with satisfaction. These, however, refer oftener to their wives and daughters than to themselves. They say that, when the emperor Aurunzebe invaded Usbec Tartary, it happened that a small party of his horsemen entered a village to plunder it; and whilst they were binding the inhabitants, preparatory to leading them off as slaves, an old woman spoke as follows: —

"Children," said she, " refrain your evil hands, and hearken to my words. Withdraw from the village while there is yet time. Should my daughter return, and find you thus occupied, you are undone." But the old crone's admonition only excited their laughter and ill treatment. They persisted in the work of devastation, until their beasts being fully loaded, they withdrew, taking with them the old lady herself. As she rode anxiously along, her eyes continually wandered in the direction she had left. By and by, she suddenly broke forth in an ecstasy of joy, exclaiming, " My daughter, my daughter! She comes, she comes!" The person alluded to was not then in sight, but the trampling of her horse, which every moment became more audible, and the clouds of dust, left no doubt on the poor woman's mind that her heroic child was hastening to the rescue. Presently the maid appeared, mounted on a fiery steed. A quiver hung at her side, and in her hand she held a bow. While yet a considerable distance off, she called aloud to the Indians that their lives would be spared if they restored the plunder and released the captives. But they continued to hurry onwards regardless of her offer. In a minute, then, she let fly three or four arrows, which emptied an equal number of saddles. The enemy had then instant recourse to their own bows; but the archery of India availed little in the plains of Tartary. Laughing at their impotent efforts, she continued to pour in her arrows with a strength of arm and accuracy of aim which appeared marvellous to her affrighted adversaries. At length, full half their number being slain, she closed in with the rest,

P. P. Stephanoff. S. Bull.

The Tartar Maid.

London Published by Longman & C.º Feb.ʸ 1840.

and, assisted by the released captives, put them all to the sword.*

In a battle between the Arabs and the citizens of Damascus, Thomas, the emperor Abubekir's son-in-law, greatly distinguished himself by his skill in archery. Amongst others, he wounded Abu Ibu Said with a poisoned arrow, of which he instantly died. The queen, who shared with her husband all the perils of war, was overwhelmed with grief on receiving the first intelligence of this fatal catastrophe, and, retiring to her tent, gave vent to her feelings in an agony of tears. But that heroic fortitude, for which through life she had been distinguished, quickly came to her relief. " What mean these vain lamentations?" she exclaimed. " Be it now my sole care to avenge thy death, my husband, and endeavour, with the utmost of my power, to gain the place where thou art, because I love thee! Henceforth I am indeed a widow, for I have dedicated myself to the service of God!"

She then armed herself with Abu's weapons, and sought the fatal field. On arriving there, she eagerly demanded whereabouts it was that Abu had been killed. They told her over against St. Thomas's Gate, and that Thomas, the emperor's son-in-law, was the man who did it. Hurrying towards the spot, with her first arrow she pierced the standard-bearer in the hand. The standard fell, and the Saracens instantly bore it away. When Thomas learned this, he was greatly enraged, and spurred into the depth of the battle, in the hopes of regaining his ensign. As the soldiers on both sides stood amazed at his gallant bearing, Abu's wife saw him, and demanded who he was? They replied, the same who had slain her lord. Instantly levelling an arrow, she shot him in the face, so that he was forced to retire within the city. On his wound being dressed, he again returned into the battle, where he

* Marco Polo.

engaged Serjabil, his former adversary. Abu's wife ranged herrelf among Serjabil's men, seeking in vain for a second opportunity of avenging her husband. Thus she did great execution with her arrows, until all were spent but one, reserved as a signal, should occasion demand it. But observing one of the Christians advance towards her, she was unable to refrain her hand. The arrow entered his throat. He fell dead, and the wife of Abu Ibu Said immediately after became a prisoner. *

From that land whose glowing atmosphere seems to inspire its daughters with a taste for feats of martial daring, turn we now unto the kingdoms of the West. It is remarkable that Tasso has sketched a very adroit female archer under the same appellation as the lady who figures in my motto, to whom, indeed, she proves no insignificant rival. The passage is written quite in an archer-like style, and contains much variety of action : —

> Her rattling quiver at her shoulder hung,
>   Therein a flash of arrows feathered weel.
> In her right hand a bow was bended strong,
>   Therein a shaft headed with mortal steel;
> So fit to shoot, she singled out among
>   Her foes who first her quarrel's strength should feel;
> So fit to shoot, Latona's daughter stood,
> When Niobe she killed, and all her brood.
>
> * * * * *
>
> While thus the worthies of the western crew
>   Maintained their brave assault and skirmish hot,
> Her mighty bow CLORINDA often drew,
>   And many a sharp and deadly arrow shot;
> And from her bow no steeled shaft there flew,
>   But that some blood the cursed engine got, —
> Blood of some valiant knight, or man of fame;
> For that proud shootress scorned the meaner game.

---

* Ockley's Hist. of the Saracens.

Lord Stephen of Amboise, on ditch's brim,
   And on a ladder high, Clotharius died;
From back to breast an arrow pierced him;
   The other was shot through from side to side.
Then, as he managed brave his courser trim,
   On his left arm she hit the Fleming's guide;
He stopped, and from the wound the reed out-twin'd,
But left the iron in the flesh behind.

As Ademare stood to behold the fight,
   High on a bank withdrawn to breathe a space,
A fatal shaft upon his forehead light;
   His hand he lifted up to feel the place,
Whereon a second arrow chanced right,
   And nail'd his hand unto his wounded face.
He fell, and with his blood distain'd the land, —
His holy blood, shed by a virgin's hand.

While Palamese stood near the battlement,
   Despising perils all, and all mishap,
And upward still his hardy footings bent,
   On his right eye he caught a deadly clap.
Through his right eye Clorinda's seventh shaft went,
   And in his neck broke forth a bloody gap.
He underneath that bulwark dying fell,
Which late to scale and win he trusted well.

Thus shot the maid.

During the reign of one of the Stuarts, the warlike and turbulent Douglas claimed as his "helpmete" a damsel, *non bella, sed bellicosa**, and well known to man, woman, and child of that period as Black Agnes. Whilst her fierce liege lord was over the English border, engaged in those "woful huntings" which form the subject of many a pathetic ballad, or, uniting his forces with those of other nobles, made open war upon the sovereign, this valorous wench kept effectual watch and ward at home. Perhaps the Chieftain of the Bloody Heart† himself never gave those who ventured to beard him

---

* Ladies are assured this is merely an unworthy play upon two Latin words, — "Not fair, but fighting."

† The cognizance of the Douglas.

in his own fortalice a rougher handling, than did his martial spouse, who at one hour was seen levelling a culverin, and in the next heading a sortie against the assailants. An old Scottish harper, one of those vagrant minstrels always welcomed to a seat at the feudal board, alludes to her extraordinary vigilance in the following quaint distich:—

> Came I early, came I late,
> I saw Black Agnes at the gate.

When beseiged by the royal forces, Agnes, ever on the watch, espied James, attended only by a single knight, riding round the castle walls at rather an unwary distance. Hastily summoning a bowman, she pointed to her foes, and desired him to take heed that neither of them escaped. The fellow, promising to do his best, loosed an arrow, which struck the king's companion dead from his horse. "That's one of Black Agnes's love tokens," exclaimed James; and leaving the knight where he fell, he dashed spurs into his horse's flank, and galloped off in the direction of the camp. Here, as the lawyers say, we gain nothing by our motion; for, had Agnes learnt

> To grasp the distant aiming bow,

she had, doubtless, scorned the aid of another, rejoicing, like a second Thalestris, to prove the temper of her own arrows upon the mailed bosom of Scotland's king. Therefore her summons to the bowman who slew the knight must, I fear, be received in evidence of her own lack of skill. Early British history furnishes many similar anecdotes, equally vague, and, of course, unsatisfactory.

Could we rest content with the poet's testimony, there would be no difficulty whatever, since the productions of very many of that privileged caste, furnish most decided and beautiful allusions to female archery. Thus, in the Aminta,—

> Son poteza, &c. &c.

"Though with the bow the snowy arm may wound,
 Yet in the eye the surest death is found."

Our own Gower, describing the various modes by which his heroine manifested her affection for a lover, says:—

> She took him all to venerie,*
> In forest and in wilderness,
> For that was all her business
> By day, and eke by nighte's tide,
> With arrows broad under her side,
> And bow in hand, with which she slew
> And took all that her list; enough
> Of beasts that be chaceable.

In Ben Jonson's Philaster, a lady of rank indulges in the pleasures of the chace, with all the wild woodland accompaniments of a genuine English hunting match of olden days.

King. What? are the houndes before, and all the woodsmen,
 Our horses ready, and our bowes bent?
Duke. All, Sir.   [*Exeunt.*

 Enter two Woodsmen, at opposite Sides.
1*st W.* Ho! have you lodged the deer?†
2*nd W.* Yes; they are ready for the bowe.
1*st W.* Who shoots? The Princess?
2*nd W.* No; she'll hunt.
1*st W.* She takes a stand ‡, I say. Who else?
2*nd W.* Why, the young stranger prince.
1*st W.* He shall shoot in a stone bowe § for me. — *Act 4.*

---

* An ancient term for hunting.

† "Lodged the deer." On the eve preceding a stag hunt, the foresters contrived to separate one or more deer of a "fair head" from the rest of the herd, and drive them into a thicket apart. As this was purposely delayed until dusk, the animals were sure to make their lair there, until the hunters appeared, at daybreak. In those days *fixtures* for ten or eleven o'clock were unknown; men who went to bed with the sun rose with the sun.

‡ "Takes a stand." Places herself in some convenient spot to shoot at the game when afoot before the dogs.

§ Stone bow, hereinafter described.

L

Among the Harleian manuscripts there is a musical piece, entitled, "A Description and Praise of Denham," written about the time of Queen Elizabeth. This curious old tract contains, among others, the fragment of a song, apparently very popular in that age: —

> Now, Robin, lend to me thy bowe,
> Sweet Robin, lend to me thy bowe,
> For I must needs a hunting with my ladye goe,
>   With my sweet ladye goe.
>
> And whither will my ladye goe,
> Sweet Wilkin, tell it unto me,
> And thou shalt have my hawke and hounde,
>   And eke my bowe,
> To wait upon thy ladye.
>
> My ladye will to Uppingham,*
> To Uppingham in sooth will she,
> And I, myself, appointed am
>   To wait upon my ladye, &c.

Still, mere poetry must be rejected as evidence in a literary as well as in a legal court; and, were my researches to terminate here, we should have no grounds for considering the Clorinda of our English Robin Hood less a child of imagination than the Clorinda of Tasso. But in Sir Harris Nicolas's Privy Purse expenses of Henry VIII. we have the royal bowyer's charges for three bows, a proportionable number of shafts, belt, braces, and shooting glove, provided for the Lady Anna Boleyn. The archives of Berkeley Castle, also †, furnish historical evidence that our female nobility, as far back as the commencement of Queen Elizabeth's reign, joined their feudal vassals at the bow butts, and even staked money on the flight of a favourite shaft, or the skill of some adroit yeoman present there.

"In July, 1st Elizabeth," says the Veel Manuscript ‡, "the Lord of Berkeley returned to Rising; and the first work done

---

* Rutlandshire.   † Gloucestershire.
‡ A MS. record of the Berkeley family, written by one of their household, named Smyth.

was to send for his buck hounds to Yate, in Gloucestershire. His hounds being come, away goeth he and his wife stag hunting to the Parks of Groby, Bockewell, Leicester Forest, and others on this side of his house. And so was the course of this lord, more or less, for the next thirty summers' months*; and his wife, being of like honour and youth, from the 1st of Elizabeth, 1588, to the beheading of her brother, the Duke of Norfolk, thirteen years after, gave herself to such pastimes as the country usually affordeth; wherein she often went with her husband part of these hunting journeyings, delighting with her cross-bow; keeping commonly a cast or two of merlins, which sometimes she mewed in her own chamber; which fancy cost her husband, every year, one or two gowns or kirtles, spoyled by their mutings; *used the long-bow, and was in those days, among her servants, so good an archer at the butts, that her side by her was not the weaker;* whose bowes, arrowes, gloves, bracer, scarfe, and other ladylike accommodations, I have seen, and heard herself speak of them in her elder years." And, lastly, Leland mentions that Queen Margaret of Anjou killed a buck with the broad arrow, a missile peculiar to the long-bow, at Alnwick Park, during her progress into Scotland. Shooting with the cross-bow, requiring infinitely less practice, and attended with greater certainty of aim, than its rival archery, was frequently sanctioned by the practice of England's queen.

I believe it was within Cadenham's great oak, a tree entirely hollow and decayed on one side, that the royal Bess sometimes

* The following passage presents a lively idea of the pursuits of an old English sportsman: —

" It now behoves to cast an eye a little back into this knight's age of puberty, in which he much delighted himself in hunting the deer, hare, foxe, and goat, wherein himself, and his next brother, John, would lye out in the fields whole nights in Michael Wood thickets, then stored with goats, and in the parts of Combe and Oselworth, then ever abounding with foxes; and in also running at ring, with other hastitudes, or spere plays, as the accounts of his father's officers doe call them, and was also, in his age of adolescency, prime minister of his father's falconry."— SMYTH's *MS. Lives of Berkeleys.*

stationed herself, to strike a deer with this weapon. The foresters had received previous orders to windlass up the game towards the queen's stand; and thus many a fair-headed buck, unconscious of his enemy, fell a victim to her quarrils. The sylvan recesses of Crowday Park, in like manner, occasionally witnessed the queen's adroitness, and that of her friend and favourite, Lady Desmond. When describing these splendid hunting matches, the "Court Journals" of that age amused themselves and their readers with frequent inuendos upon the courtly policy of the fair countess. They hint that many a "high-palmed hart" returned unscathed to his lair, after passing within cross-bow range, less from want of skill, than a fear of exciting her royal mistress's displeasure. And she was wise. The triumph of a successful arrow had been dearly purchased by, perhaps, months of exile to Leinster's desolate wilds, far from the sunshine of the English court.*

Our system of female education, from the beginning of the seventeenth until nearly the close of the eighteenth century, was a positive conspiracy against the moral and physical development of the sex. Nature, we are aware, in the assertion of her rights, occasionally broke through its absurd restraints; but the change was merely from evil to evil. With scarlet riding dress, masculine head-gear, flushed countenance, and dishevelled locks, the huntress came bounding to the covert side. Undismayed by showers of mud and snowballs from some five score horses' hoofs, — by hedge and fence, gate and stile, she scoured the country " thorough bush thorough briar," *screeching* forth a tallyho! at renard's departure, and a whoo-hoo-hoop! at his death.

To the honour of the sex, however, be it spoken, comparatively few ladies were found to unsex themselves thus; and, during a portion of that period, falconry ranked high among amusements chosen to dissipate the ennui of the fair. Lady Juliana

* Desmond is an Irish earldom.

Queen Elizabeth in Cadenham Oak.

London Published by Longman & Co. Feby 1840.

Barnes, the noble prioress of St. Albans, has obliged the world with an elaborate treatise on this princely art. She tells us that a peculiar species of falcon, more or less generous according to the possessor's rank, appertained to every man, from monarch and belted earl, to simple franklyn or holy clerk. Thus, the high-mettled gyrfalcon, thirsting for blood, and white as the snows of her native Iceland, was assigned to the two first; the sprightly sparrowhawk to the second; a hobby to the third; while the bold, but diminutive and graceful, merlin belonged to the fair sex.

> " A falc'ner Henry is when Emma hawks,
> With her of tarcels * and of lures he talks.
> High on her wrist the tow'ring merlin stands,
> Practis'd to rise and stoop at her commands.
> And when obedient, now, the bird has flown,
> And headlong pluck'd the trembling quarry down,
> Her Henry hastens to relieve the fair,
> And with the honour'd feather decks her hair."

Proud of his silken jesses and embroidered hood, the docile bird sat perched upon his mistress's hawking glove; now pluming his dappled breast; now answering her caresses by mantling wings, and the harmonious chime of his silver bells. The velvet kirtle of antique fashion, the heron's plume waving in her snooded hair, showed nothing inconsistent with female bashfulness. And, when she thus rode forth on ambling barb, schooled to obey the slightest motion of her hand, and encircled by a knot of obsequious cavaliers, far from appearing an outrage on decorum, there was something graceful and becoming in a lady's participation of this noble recreation. But, anon, loud shouts of " heron à la vol!" " heron on the wing!" proclaimed the approaching quarry. The falconer, unhooding his fierce gyrfalcons, cast them into the air; and then it is this

---

* The male hawk being a *tierce* or one third smaller, and far less courageous, than the female.

sport loses all its external gentleness, and becomes distinguished for danger, as, in the last century, it was for cruelty, perhaps beyond every other.*

Since, then,

> —— To range the wood,
> And follow hawk and hound,

are amusements subversive of that tender sympathy for all created beings, the meanest as well as the noblest, which forms the basis of so many virtues dear to womanhood, it becomes the duty of society to discountenance them. Still, nature having decreed the " healthy body, and the mind at ease," in either sex, shall mainly depend on pure air and active exercise, it was desirable to find some substitute for these robust pursuits equally healthful, and unsullied by their danger and their cruelty.

Eternal honour be the award of that distinguished society of archers who first made the happy discovery. To the good sense and discrimination of " the Woodmen of the Ancient Forest of Arden " are we indebted for the introduction of archery, as a perfectly unexceptionable recreation for ladies. It was fortunate their individual position in society entitled

---

* When a *cast* of well-trained falcons are thrown off, one of them exerts herself to climb above the heron. From this elevated position, she makes her stoop with greater vigour; whilst her partner hovers beneath, prepared to attack the devoted bird in its downward rush to avoid the beak and talons of the first. As the combat takes place in the clouds, the eyes of the spectators are necessarily there also. The heron's flight then becomes rapid, however sluggish it may be at other times. Your pace is therefore tremendous; for, in order fully to enjoy this animated sport, the falconer pushes forward his unguided horse, at a speed to which the first burst of a crack pack of fox hounds forms no adequate comparison.

When the game fell beaten to the earth, our ancient falconers galloped in to break its legs and wings, and pin it to the ground by means of its own long pointed beak. The hawks were then permitted to *tire* upon the quarry; that is, to tear her in pieces at their leisure. Modern falconry is unacquainted with this cruel finale to an otherwise very delightful recreation. We now take the bird alive, and with a label attached to its leg, setting forth when, where, by whose hawks captured, it is restored to liberty and its native groves.

them to dictate the laws of fashion; under whose all-powerful influence the bow again made rapid advances in the estimation of the British fair.

The example of the noble and the wealthy had, no doubt, considerable influence on the spread of archery; nevertheless, its own intrinsic excellencies were its chief recommendation. Requiring no excessive corporal exertion, a combination of the most graceful positions of all the bodily exercises, and invariably associated with refined and polished society, the bow appears especially adapted for relieving the sedentary occupations to which women are still far too much devoted. But why seek to justify the practice, when, in our own day, we see the name of HER GRACIOUS MAJESTY, ALEXANDRINA VICTORIA, QUEEN OF THE ISLES, AND A NATION'S HOPE, inscribed upon the Archer Rolls? That illustrious lady, in imitation of the warrior race of monarchs from whom she springs, has given a proof of real British feeling, by the appointment of a Master of Archery* among her household officers.

About sixty years have elapsed since the commencement of this era in the annals of *modern* archery. Our countrywomen, long rebels in heart, did not neglect so favourable an occasion for emancipating themselves from the ancient tyranny of harpsichord, spinnet, backboard, and embroidery frame; and

> In the good greenwode,
> Among the lilie flower,

they wandered, bow and shaft in hand, to seek that health and vivacity the pure breath of nature can alone bestow.

---

* Spon and Monfaucon have preserved the form of an ancient tablet, dedicated in the following terms to a Roman professor of the art:—

" D. M.
T. FLAVIO EXPEDITO
DOCTORI SAGITTAR:
FLAV: EUPHROS:
E ATTIC: TULLIÆ
P. B. M.

The ladies associated with the Woodmen, were originally limited to their immediate family connections. Soon, however, the admissions became more general; and they complimented the fair members of other societies with freedom of access to their grounds. The prizes distributed by the Foresters of Arden have always been remarkable for splendour and variety; but then the Mordaunts, the Adamses, the Morlands, and the Bagots, of the last, with the Boultbees, the Parkers, the Gresleys, and the Grimeses, of the present age, — those fair victors who have won, and who still " win and wear them," contest their possession with a skill and enthusiasm well worthy of their magnitude.

Among the ladies on whom, at an early period, these archers did themselves the honour to confer the freedom of their society, was the Marchioness of Salisbury. The diploma which conveyed this privilege, and of which I insert a copy, was richly emblazoned, and deposited in a box of heart of oak, made from a tree which grew in the Forest of Arden.

| " Riband, garter blue, with white border at each end. Suspended from it A gold crescent, bugle, and shaft. (*Signed*) AYLESFORD, Warden. | In a wreath of oak. AR A shaft on a gold ground. DEN. | Red riband, with black border at each end. (*Signed*) JOHN DILKE, Master Forester. |

FUGITUR IN JUSSO NOSTRA SAGITTA LOCO.
Striped riband, of pale violet blue.
WRIOTHESLEY DIGBY, *Secretary*.

TO THE MOST NOBLE THE MARCHIONESS OF SALISBURY,
PATRONESS;
AND ALL OTHER THE MEMBERS OF THE SOCIETY OF THE
HERTFORDSHIRE ARCHERS,
THE WOODMEN OF THE ANCIENT FOREST OF ARDEN
SEND GREETING:

BE IT KNOWN, that, in token of the great love we bear the Patroness and Members of the said Society, We have given and granted, and by these presents Do give and grant, to each and every of them, the free Use of all our Butts, Targets, and Marks now erected, or hereafter to be erected, within the Bounds, Purlieus, Privileges, and Assorts of the FOREST OF ARDEN, the property of the Woodmen of the said Forest.

"In Witness whereof we have hereunto set our Hands and Common Seal this sixteenth day of November, MDCCLXXXIX.

(*Seal*) " ARDEN."

The archery fêtes at Grove House, Camberwell, the residence of the handsome, witty, and accomplished Mrs. Crespigny *, still live in the remembrance of many a veteran toxophilite. This lady was an early and enthusiastic advocate for the adoption of the bow as a becoming recreation for her own sex; yet in her ardour to promote a fashionable amusement, she exhibited the same spirit of benevolence which rendered life one lengthened scene of active usefulness.† Selecting utile dulci as her motto, she very adroitly made her gay and thoughtless visitants contribute

* Lady patroness of the Royal Toxophilite Society.

† One fact of undoubted credit, but little known, will show that the heart of this fair archeress was just in its right place. Whilst passing over Westminster Bridge, Mrs. Crespigny observed a wretched crippled soldier, with an intelligent but half-famished countenance, sitting on the pathway. She stopped, and sent him a small sum of money by the servant, when the poor fellow returned a message of gratitude so simple and touching, as induced her to alight from the carriage, and personally inquire the circumstances of his distress. The tale proved by no means an uncommon one in those days. He was an American loyalist gentleman, who had lost all in fighting for his sovereign; and, after witnessing the destruction of his wife and children by the flames, which, in the dead of night, the hostile party kindled around his dwelling, he had sought an asylum in England, in the vain hope of being admitted into Chelsea Hospital. Mrs. Crespigny was deeply affected; and leaving a more ample supply, departed, with the exile's address.

After many days of fatiguing, unwearied solicitation, she managed to obtain from Sir George Younge, the then Secretary of War, a promise that the man should have an out-pensioner's order. Though not what she had hoped, it was a source of great rejoicing to this friend of the wretched soldier; and with eager satisfaction she conveyed to him the news. The sequel is distressing. When Mrs. Crespigny's servant silently entered his

largely to the support of a Sunday school, by levying fines on the unskilful. Her muse, too, was frequently put into requisition on these occasions; and many songs written by her, and sung to vary the pleasures of the entertainments, have survived in manuscript. We have, here, the two concluding stanzas of one of them, intended to be sung by a chorus of gentlemen, in which archery, on the score of humanity, is made to bear the bell from every other rural post.

> The huntsman pursues, too, an innocent foe,
> And drives the poor suff'rer with shouts to and fro,
> That, distracted by fear, and perplex'd in its way,
> Made bold by despair, e'en in death stands at bay;
> So I think, my good friends, I shall prove what I say,
> That the pleasures of archery carry the day.
>   Then, sons of the bow,
>   'T is meet, ere we go,
> That, to wish it success, ev'ry glass should o'erflow.
>
> For no devastation here follows our gain;
> Our pleasure 's to no one productive of pain.
> Though we pierce through the centre and bear off the prize,
> The wound never rankles, the victim ne'er dies.
> Where humanity points you will sure lead the way,
> So the pleasures of archery carry the day.
>   Then, sons of the bow,
>   'T is meet, ere we go,
> That, to wish it success, ev'ry glass should o'erflow. *

Fortunate did the votary of fashion esteem himself who received an invitation ticket to Mrs. Crespigny's archery break-

---

apartment, he overheard a pathetic prayer for the happiness of his benefactress. On recognising him, the white-haired veteran found strength only to pronounce a hasty blessing, ere he fell backwards, and in a few moments expired.

* As this specimen of Mrs. Crespigny's muse exhibits more playfulness than poetic talent, a mere *jeu d'esprit* of the moment, I add the concluding

fasts. The company shot "games" as they are termed in archers' language. Eleven was the winning number, and each arrow counted according to its position in the target. Thus, a shot in the gold centre reckoned as 9; in the red, 7; in the inner white, 5; in the black, 3; and in the outer white, 1. The targets lay 100 yards distant. After the gentlemen had shot, they escorted their fair associates within 70 yards, and at that unusual distance the latter drew their bowstrings. Half-crown forfeits were paid by the unsuccessful; and the little orphans of the charity attended in dresses of grass green, the whole forming a very interesting group. Each revolving summer witnesses the revival of many similar bow meetings throughout the sylvan glades of this romantic land. The presence of women is now regarded as indispensable to the perfect enjoyment of these genuine fêtes champêtres; for the trim shaft, launched from the hand of some fair toxophilite, faultless in face and figure, inspires us with an enthusiasm which belongs not to the most adroit display of archery in the other sex. It was this sort of gallant admiration that inscribed the following record of a fair victor's achievements upon the walls of the Royal Toxophilite banqueting room.

"October 1st, 1790. A match was shot at Mr. Wyborough's, Branhope Hall, Yorkshire, at one hundred yards, between Miss

---

lines of an effusion of a higher order, addressed by this amiable woman to Sir Harry Martyn, when a child, accompanied with the present of a knife:—

"Whilst there is so much cutting in high life,
No present, sure, is equal to a knife;
But you, dear boy, will very shortly know
How far your cutting may in reason go.
That tyrant, fashion, whom so many seek,
Can only govern, unrestrained, the weak;
So with its follies sometimes you 'll dispense,
And never cut good humour or good sense."

Mrs. Crespigny's Letters to her Son were once deservedly popular.

Littledale, Mr. Gilpin, and Mr. Wyborough, in which Miss Littledale was victorious. During the shooting, which lasted three hours, Miss Littledale hit the gold four times; and, what evinces superior skill, the three last hits made by Miss Littledale were all in the gold." *

Appropriate costume —

> To sport the gay sash of Toxophilite green —

is indispensable in both sexes; indeed, the verdant livery of the woods should, of course, be the predominant hue throughout;—

> We 're clad in youthful green, we other colours scorn; —

for I never knew but one exception to the rule: it was the Marquis of Blandford's Society of Bowmen, who wore purple, with white velvet collars; the buttons gold, with a bull's eye pierced in the centre by an arrow, and encircled with this well-conceived motto: —

> Je ne suis volage qu'à fixer.
> I am volatile only to become the more steady.

In reference to the ladies, I may observe that all such vital matters are arranged by the lady patroness, assisted by a committee of her own sex. On them, also, devolves the weighty responsibility of selecting a characteristic full dress costume where the pleasures of the ball-room succeed those of the target ground.

Although to hazard anything *original* on the subject of female attire is an act of presumption at which even the boldest of us might justly feel a trembling, I am resolved on omitting nothing essential to the general interest of my book. Three specimens of archery costume are therefore, with diffidence, presented to the fair reader's criticism, certainly distinguished by that simplex mundities † which I regard, as well as Horace, as the

---

* " This inscription is placed in a glass frame, and was copied April, 1798." — BANKE's *MSS.*

† Simple neatness.

basis of whatever is elegant in female attire. One of them was proposed to the ladies of the Royal Surrey Archers, by their patroness, as a ball dress, about *five and forty years* since.

White muslin round gown, with green and buff sash: white chip hat, bound with narrow green riband. Riband of the same colour as the sash encircled the crown, on which were two bows, rising one above the other. A magnificent snow-white ostrich plume waved over this tasteful head-gear, and a sprig of box was so arranged beneath, as to appear just above the wearer's left eyebrow.

The second was worn by the fair members of a very happy, well-conducted, hospitable little band, who, about the year 1792, assembled among those scenes of rare beauty, the Piercefield domain, in the vicinity of Chepstow, and were called, "Bowmen of the Wye." Their dress, then, like the former, consisted of plain white muslin, bound with green satin riband; a green and white sash; small green satin hat, with a white feather tipped with green, and having a motto inscribed on the bandeau.*

"Oh, the horrid frights! Is this your simplex mundities?" some fair reader may possibly exclaim. Even so, lady; according to my poor judgment. Naithless, chacun à son gout; and the third, perhaps, may be destined to the honour of your patronage. It belongs to the present age, being that of a numerous and distinguished society, who style themselves the Harley Bush Bowmen.

Robe, a judicious arrangement of white and green; white hat and feathers; shoes of grass green. The bow and quiver slung gracefully over their shoulders.

Right glad am I to make my escape from the subject; for in treating it, one feels like a man treading among eggs in a taperless room, or the wretch who, unable to swim, finds the current every moment hurrying him beyond his depth. Once more on terra firma, let us

* Letter from Mrs. Jones of Monmouth to Sir Joseph Bankes.

next examine in what manner the dexterity of our fair toxophilites is rewarded at these archery fêtes. The Hertfordshire archers, who met at Hatfield House, gave, as the principal ladies' prize, a gold heart, enriched with a bow and shaft set in diamonds, a costly stake, first won by the Marchioness of Salisbury. But a list of the presents distributed, during a series of years, by one leading society, will be most satisfactory, since it affords an opportunity of recording the names of many a lovely votaress of the shaft and bow.

WOODMEN OF THE FOREST OF ARDEN.

September, 1794.	Gold bugle,	-	Miss Mordaunt.
	Gold arrow,	-	Miss Moland.
September, 1795.	Gold bugle,	-	Miss Boultbee.
	Gold arrow,	-	Miss Croxhall.
September, 1797.	Gold bugle,	-	Mrs. Bree.
	Gold arrow,	-	Hon. Miss Summerfield.
August, 1798.	Gold bugle,	-	Mrs. Col. Pack.
	Gold arrow,	-	Miss Mordaunt.
August, 1799.	Gold bugle,	-	Miss Beresford.
	Gold arrow,	-	Miss Digby.
September, 1800.	Gold bugle,	-	Miss C. Mordaunt.
	Gold arrow,	-	Miss Ayre.
August, 1801.	Gold bugle,	-	Mrs. Carter.*
	Gold arrow,	-	Miss Bree.
August, 1802.	Gold bugle,	-	Miss Mordaunt.
	Gold arrow,	-	Miss Hartopp.

* Daughter of the Laird of Arran.

FEMALE ARCHERY.

August, 1804.   Gold bugle,   -   Miss Moland.
                 Gold arrow,   -   Mrs. H. Grimes.

September, 1805. Gold bugle,⎫
                    Gold arrow,⎭ - Miss More.

September, 1806. Gold bugle, - Miss Boultbee.
                    Gold arrow, - Miss Sharpe.

August, 1807.   Gold bugle,   -   Miss C. Grimes.
                  Gold arrow,   -   Miss Boultbee.

August, 1808.   Gold bugle,   -   Miss Greenway.
                  Gold arrow,   -   Miss Bourgeois.

August, 1811.   Gold bugle,⎫
                  Gold arrow,⎭ -   Miss Greenway.

August, 1812.   Gold bugle,⎫
                  Gold arrow,⎭ -   Miss Birch.

August, 1816.   Gold bugle,   -   Mrs. Tongue.
                  Gold arrow,   -   Miss Knightly.

August, 1818.   Gold bugle,   -   Miss Bradish.
                  Gold arrow,   -   Miss Payne.

August, 1832.   Gold bracelet, - Miss E. Gresley.
                  Torquoise gold knot, Miss Isabel Simpson.

The following are the names of some skilful Female Archers of the present day, with the Societies to which they belong.

ARCHERS OF THE ABBEY OF BURY ST. EDMONDS.

Misses Jane Roy and Wilkinson.

HEREFORDSHIRE BOWMEN.

Lady Cornwall, Misses Walley, Jane Salway, —— Miney, Margaret Salway, &c. &c.

Melksham Foresters.

Misses Hale, Merewether, &c. &c.

Selwood Foresters.

Mesdames Medlicot and Plunket; Misses Talbot, Doveton, &c. &c.

West Somerset Archers.

Miss Guerin, &c. &c. &c.

Staffordshire Bowmen.

Honourable Mrs. Beaumont, Misses Child, Broughton, Lefroy, Wheeler, Reddlestone, &c.

Newton Villa Archers.

Mesdames Blake and Powell, Miss Sarah Lawton, &c.

South Saxon Archers,
Conyborough Park.

Ladies Gage and Shiffner; Honourable Mrs. Trevor; Honourable Mrs. Thomas; Misses Wilde, Partington, Irvine, and Syms.

Derbyshire Archers.

July, 1829.   Gold medal,   -   Miss Crumpton.
                     2d Prize,   -   Mrs. Julia Fox.

Carisbrook Archers.

Mrs. Hastings, Miss Glynne, &c. &c.

West Berkshire United Archery Club.

Misses Pearson, Meyrick, Catherine Bulter, &c.

Royal Sherwood Archers.

The bracelet presented by his Royal Highness the Duke of Sussex, to be shot for as the first ladies' prize, was originally won by Mrs. Colonel Wildeman.

Lady Bromley, Mesdames Hull and Nixon; Miss Barron, &c. &c.

SECTION IV.

WELSH ARCHERY.

Nyd hyder ond bwa.
There is no dependence but on the bow.
Ancient Welsh Adage.

By yon castle wall, midst the breezes of morning,
  The genius of Cambria strayed pensive and slow :
The oak wreath was wither'd, her temples adorning,
  And the wind through its leaves sigh'd its murmur of woe.
She gazed on her mountains with filial devotion,
  She gazed on her Dee as he roll'd to the ocean, —
And Cambria! poor Cambria! she cried with emotion,
  Thou yet hast thy country, thy harp, and thy bow.

Sweep on, thou proud stream, with thy billows all hoary ;
  As proudly my warriors have rush'd on the foe ;
But feeble and faint is the sound of their glory,
  For time, like thy tide, has its ebb and its flow.
E'en now, while I watch thee, thy beauties are fading,
  The sands and the shallows thy course are invading,
Where the sail swept the surges, the sea bird is wading ;
  And thus hath it fared with the land of the bow.
                            BISHOP HEBER.*

IT is a remarkable, but hitherto, I believe, an unnoticed fact, that while Englishmen were carrying the terror of their archery through all the principal kingdoms of Europe, proving themselves, as the old chronicle expresses it, " the best allies or the very worst foes," they found, even at their own doors, some most formidable rivals in its practice, — I mean the Welsh. To the strength and skill with which they handled the bow, as

* Mr. Reginald Heber sometimes promoted, by his pen, the harmless merriment of the bow meetings of his neighbourhood. From the songs which he wrote for this purpose, the above passage is selected for its imagery and historical allusions. It was sung at Harwarden Castle, in Flintshire, the seat of Sir Stephen Glynne, Bart.

much as to the inaccessible character of their native fastnesses, may be attributed the successful struggles by which their independence was long preserved.*

A knowledge of the bow appears to have existed in Britain from the remotest antiquity. In one of the Triads, mention is made of a mythological or fabulous person, called " Gwrnerth Ergydlym," or Powerful Sharpshot; who slew the largest bear that ever infested his country with a straw arrow. And in a composition of the 14th century, the author refers to a tradition of a character somewhat similar. Speaking of an improbable event, it is asked, " When will that be?" — " When worthless Deikin † of Gwynedd is as good an archer as Mydr ap Mydvydd ('Aim, the son of Aimer'), who could shoot the wren through his claw, from Caenog, in the Vale of Clwyd, to Esgair Vervel, in Ireland."

The discovery of arrow heads of flint and metal in the ancient cairns and tumuli, so abundantly scattered over the open downs of Britain, is better evidence that its aboriginal inhabitants were acquainted with these missiles. A considerable number has been lately added to the antiquarian collections of the British Museum. A still larger quantity exists at Stourhead, the seat of Sir Richard Colt Hoare, Bart. One regards these interesting relics with feelings of deep interest. Their construction is most ingenious, and the lapse of twenty centuries has made not the slightest change in their original form and appearance.

Indeed, the compositions of even the most ancient Welsh bards make frequent mention of bow and arrow. These al-

---

* The Normans greatly dreaded the effects of the Welsh arrows. William de Brensa, having convened a meeting of the principal chiefs of South Wales at Abergavenny Castle, under some colourable pretence, made them purchase their liberty by swearing they would not, in future, permit any of their followers to travel armed with the bow. " Ne quis gladium ferret viator vel arcum."

† David.

lusions, however, are not sufficiently explicit to suggest any idea of the state of archery when they wrote. A poet of the sixth century, apparently advocating the arts of peace, says,

<blockquote>Better is the work of the sickle than of the bow.</blockquote>

Neither Cæsar, nor any succeeding writer who has treated of British affairs, describes the ceremonies practised by the aboriginal inhabitants, in their declarations of peace and war. During the reign of Howel Dha, the blast of a horn, and in a more improved state of the arts, that of a trumpet, borne by a herald throughout the land, summoned its warriors to the battle.* But a more ancient plan appears to have been adopted by the Welsh, equally distinguished by its efficacy, its elegance, and its simplicity. In no composition of prose or poetry is this specifically described; yet, traces of ancient but obsolete customs may frequently be discerned in the proverbs of a nation. These, though used in an indirect sense, and without any reference in the speaker's mind to the literal or original application, frequently allow that, as well as the cause of it, to appear. Thus Lewis or Glynn, alluding to a proclamation of says,

<blockquote>Bwa rhadded drwy holl Brydain.
A bow was sent throughout Britain.</blockquote>

And in some remote districts of North Wales, where the most primitive modes of thought and action still prevail, the inhabitants thus recommend the straight path to a stranger's choice.

<blockquote>Ewch ar hyd y bwa hedd.
Go along the bow of peace.</blockquote>

Here, by the use of an elegant and highly poetical metaphor, the path is compared to an unstrung bow. The natural inference to be drawn from the two proverbial expressions is, that different conditions of this weapon were symbolical of

* Roberts.

peace and war. If threatened by hostile aggression, a speedy messenger perambulated the country, bearing the bent bow, a signal no one dared to disregard. When peace again extended her olive branch, the joyous tidings were communicated by the same weapon, unstrung.

> There was heard the sound of a coming foe,
> There was sent through Britain a bended bow,
> And a voice was poured from the free winds far,
> As the land rose up at the sign of war.
>> 'Heard ye not the battle horn?
>> Reaper, leave thy golden corn!
>> Leave it to the birds of heaven,
>> Swords must flash, and shields be riven!
>> Leave it for the winds to shed,
>> Arm, ere Britain's turf grow red.'
> And the reaper armed like a freeman's son,
> And the bended bow, and the voice pass'd on.
>> 'Hunter, leave the mountain chace,
>> Take the falchion from its place;
>> Let the wolf go free to-day,
>> Leave him for a nobler prey!
>> Let the deer ungall'd sweep by,
>> Arm thee, — Britain's foes are nigh!'
> And the hunter armed ere his chace was done;
> And the bended bow, and the voice passed on.
>> 'Chieftain, quit the joyous feast!
>> Stay not till the song hath ceased.
>> Though the mead be foaming bright,
>> Though the fires give ruddy light,
>> Leave the hearth, and leave the hall —
>> Arm thee, Britain's foes must fall.'
> And the chieftain armed, and the horn was blown,
> And the bended bow and the voice passed on.
>> 'Prince, thy father's deeds are told,
>> In the bower, and in the hold!
>> Where the goatherd's lay is sung,
>> Where the minstrel's harp is strung! —
>> Foes are on thy native sea! —
>> Give our bards a tale of thee!'
> And the prince came armed, like a leader's son,
> And the bended bow, and the voice passed on.

F. P. Stephanoff. J. Hollis.

Bow of Peace and War.

London, Published by Longman & Co. Feby 1840.

> ' Mother, stay thou not thy boy!
> He must learn the battle's joy.
> Sister, bring the sword and spear,
> Give thy brother words of cheer!
> Maiden, bid thy lover part,
> Britain calls the strong of heart.'
> And the bended bow, and the voice passed on;
> And the bards made song for battle won.

Traces of this singular expedient may likewise be found among nations with whom the Welsh could never have had communication, unless, indeed, we assign them an oriental descent. Of this there is a remarkable instance in the history of the Seljukian princes.

Mohammed and David, the sons of Seljuk, king of Bokhara, by their ambitious and warlike character, had excited the jealousy of Mahmoud of Gazneh. Desirous of ascertaining indirectly the extent of his rivals' military resources, the sultan requested them to send to his court some confidential person with whom he might treat of an important affair. They despatched their uncle Ismael. Mahmoud inquired of this personage how many troops the Seljucides could furnish him, in case circumstances rendered an alliance expedient on his part. Ismael, who at that time held a bow and two arrows in his hand, replied, " Send one of these arrows into our camp, and 50,000 of your servants will mount on horseback; and if that number should not be sufficient, then send this other arrow to the horde of Balik, and you may reckon on 50,000 more." But," said the Gasnevede, dissembling his anxiety, " if I should stand in need of the whole force of your hundred tribes?" " Despatch my bow," firmly replied Ismael, striking the weapon with his shafts, "and as it is circulated round, the summons will be obeyed by 200,000 horse." *

* M. de Guigne's Hist. of Huns. D'Herbelot, Bib. Orient. Albupharagius, Dynast. 221, 222.

It may occur to the reader that the more distant hordes would not be likely to recognise Ismael's from any other bow. But nothing was more

The use of the bow as a declaration of hostility is common in many other parts of the East. When the king of Bisnagar designs to make war against any neighbouring prince, he issues from the capital in great state, surrounded by his nobles, with cavalry, infantry, and elephants, as if about to commence a distant march. Then, detaching himself from his attendants, he mounts a war horse, superbly caparisoned, and riding towards the hostile country, discharges an arrow in the direction of its frontiers. Immediately a band of cavaliers, well mounted, scour the surrounding country with burning torches, to announce the days on which the inhabitants are required to repair to the royal city.*

In the customs of the most ancient nations we discover traces of the same expedient. When Cambyses had subdued Egypt, his ambition prompted him to the invasion of Ethiopia. Under pretence of carrying presents to the king, spies were despatched thither to ascertain its strength and its resources. But the monarch quickly penetrated into their real character,

---

easy. Orientals of rank have short and pithy Arabic sentences — generally an extract from the Khoran — inscribed with their names upon the horns of their bows, and also upon their arrows, expressive of remote and steady flight. The Damascus bladed scymetars are marked in this way. His Majesty George the Fourth had exquisite swords of this description among his splendid Oriental armoury, which he once displayed to the Grand Signior's ambassador at our court. On being presented with one of more than ordinary beauty, the Turk hesitated, and bending over it, pressed the hilt first upon his forehead, and then to his lips, with indications of the profoundest respect. Being questioned as to the cause of this singular ceremony, he replied, that, by the inscription on the blade, he knew it once belonged to the grandfather of the present Sultan. It had been received with some other presents from Constantinople.

"Strength to the arm that wields this blade in a righteous cause, and death to him it reaches," is one of the sentences occasionally found on Turkish swords.

Arabic characters are inscribed on the points of a very elegant Persian bow in my possession.

* Voyages fameux de Sieur Vincent le Blanc. 1649.

and addressed them as follows: — " If Cambyses were an honest man, he would desire no more than his own; nor endeavour to reduce a people under servitude, who have never done him any injury."

Then, taking a splendid bow, suspended at his right hand, upon a corner of the golden throne whereon he sat, he thus continued: — " Give your master this weapon, and say the king of Ethiopia advises the monarch of Persia to make war against his country, when the Persians shall be able thus easily to bend so strong a bow; and, in the mean time, to thank the gods, that they never inspired the Ethiopians with a desire of extending their dominions beyond the boundaries of their native country." Saying this, he again unstrung the mighty weapon, apparently without an effort, and delivered it to the ambassadors.*

I need scarcely add, that the Persian desisted from his design of attempting the conquest of Ethiopia. But let us return to the Welsh. Their ancient maxims of jurisprudence enumerate three weapons with which it was incumbent on every householder to be constantly provided, against foreign aggression and domestic plunderers. These are — a sword, a spear, and a bow with twelve arrows in a quiver.

The Laws of HOWEL DHA, or the Good, were framed in the tenth century. He fixes the price of a bow at one penny; of an arrow, at a farthing. It is therefore evident that the ancient Britons manufactured the apparatus of archery at home. If procured from England, they could not have been sold at so low a price; for, there, even the most ordinary bow never cost less than eightpence. It must be remarked, however, that we have no means of deciding whether the penny was of silver or brass; nor is it clear that the farthing was a fourth part of the penny. The former is a Saxon, the latter, a Welsh word. However, we may acquire some idea of the relative value of

* Herodotus.

these articles, from the following general list of prices current in that age: —

A spear, 4d.; a broad axe, 4d.; a filly fourteen days old, 4d.; ditto, three years old, 6d.; a calf, till All Saints, 4d.; a chicken, ¼d.; a water bottle, ¼d.; a spindle, ¼d.; a pair of fetters for cows' legs when milked, ¼d.; a hayrake, ¼d.; a wooden shovel, ¼d.; a fork, ¼d.

Archery was included among the four-and-twenty Welsh games, and in hunting they adhered to the following regulations. No one was permitted to shoot at a beast under chase, or whilst reposing *, on pain of forfeiting his bow and arrow to the lord of the soil. He might shoot at and kill the game, if he could, while the dogs were after it, but was not allowed to shoot among the dogs. † These laws must be of considerable antiquity, the bear and wild boar being enumerated among the animals of chace. That the bow was used with considerable adroitness by the ancient Welsh sportsmen is evident from the writings of Giraldus Cambrensis. In his Itinerary, he says that Einion, Lord of Gwrthrynion, being out hunting, one of his attendants killed, with an arrow, a hind as she was springing off, which proved to be fatter on the haunches and every other part than a stag —

Quidam ex suis arcum tenens [qy. tendens?] carvam exsilientem sagittâ perforavit.

Like their English neighbours, the Welsh archers relied on foreign importation for a supply of superior bow-wood. It is worthy of remark that Flanders, celebrated at the present day for producing all the apparatus of archers in great perfection, should have enjoyed similar repute nearly two centuries and a half ago. The following anecdote, extant in the Welsh lan-

* Just as a modern sportsman is forbidden to shoot a sitting hare.
† In France, at the present day, the hunter carries a fowling-piece at his saddle bow, with which even the *fox* is shot, when the dogs are running in to him at full cry.

guage, is given in support of this assertion. Rhys Wyn, a gentleman advanced in years, came with William Cynwal on a visit to Edmund Prys, archdeacon of Merioneth*, they found him engaged in archery, shooting thirty yards, or point blank distance. After the usual salutations, Rhys Wyn spoke thus: "Had I a bow weak enough, old as I am, you should not shoot alone. Then William said he had a bow that would reach thirty yards, which Rhys could draw with *his little finger*. And the latter replied, " With your permission, I will request this man (the archdeacon) to compose a poem, soliciting the loan of it." Cynwal assented, on condition that he himself should name the subject of these verses, because his bow was the gift of William Clwtch, who brought it from Antwerp. However, Rhys Wyn, finding William did not send the subject in time, solicited the archdeacon to compose the verses upon any subject he might choose; and the answer of William by letter was, that the bow had been lent to Master Thomas Prys, but when returned, it should be sent, or else he would purchase the best bow to be found in Chester.†

I may observe, *en passant,* that we have here one of a thousand instances which might be adduced to show the extreme fondness entertained for poetic composition by the Welsh. The birth of a child, or its departure from the world; the marriage of a friend; a successful hunting match; the ordinary occurrences of domestic life; an interchange of courtesy, were celebrated, or replied to, by a copy of verses. In this talent for unpremeditated composition they were in nowise inferior to the Italian improvisatori. Gynddelw, the Homer of Welsh bards — and right well is he entitled to the distinction — ad-

* One of the early translators of the Bible into Welsh. The date of this transaction is somewhere about 1590.
† "Many a good bow, besides one in Chester," is an old English proverb, meaning that merit belongs to no exclusive rank or locality. I request the reader to bear in mind, here, and in other passages from Welsh annals and poetry, that the translations are rendered literally.

dresses one of these complimentary effusions to the son of Madog ap Meredudd Llywelyn. It seems the chieftain, desirous of testifying his respect, had sent in the whole carcass of a stag which his hounds chanced to kill before the poet's threshold. In like manner, he pours forth his acknowledgments —

> In never-dying verse —

to Blaid, or the Wolf, another munificent patron, who had gratified his martial tastes by the present of a glittering sword, —

> The ice-brook's temper.

And in the following lines addressed by Gwffudd ap Tudor, a bard of the thirteenth century, to one Howell, thanking him for a handsome bow, the reader will see a further illustration of this remarkable propensity. It appears in its original dress, because assuredly doomed to suffer in my hands by translation. The Saxon must rest satisfied that it has poetic merit; while the vast body of archers, with which the Principality, north and south, abounds, are fully competent to form their own opinion : —

> Erfid newid nwyf arfer cler a'm clwyf,
> Efyniaid i'm rhwyf ydd wyf eidda,
> A rhwydd wawd erfyn aroed un flwyddyn
> A warawd toppyn felyn fwla;
> Arwyddion rhoddi a wna haeloni,
> Caledis cronni, crynu a wna;
> Eraill a roddai arwydd, rhwydd fydd rhai,
> Ped fai a'i dyrrai mor i derra
> Eryr, gwyr gwarani arwyr moliant,
> Ardunniant ffuiant ytty ffynna;
> Edrydd gweinydd gwawd adneu cerdd dafawd,
> Arawd o'm meithwawd ytt ni metha,
> Er mwyn mirein son morwyŋawl ddynion,
> A son llatheion a'i llettya;
> Er mwyn llif ddwyn llaith, gwawr geinllawr gynllaith,
> Gwawd obeith gweniaith a'm gweinydda;

Er lliw lluch Ianawr, er nef llef a llawr
Er mwyn gwawr Faelawr nam gofala,
Er cof dof dy frwys ban loywlan lin lwys;
Canwyll Bowys lwys a'm dilyssa,
Fy rhwyf a'm rheufedd o'roi'r gair gommedd;
Rhiannedd Gwynedd a'th ogana,
Celi a droses wrthyd fy neges,
Culwydd a'th roddes lles nyw llaesa,
Colofn Prystallum, coel finian Awrtun,
Catgun cain eiddun ail cunedda,
Calan ddydd pan ddel celenig ddigel.
Howel aer drafel ni wer drofa,
Cydwedd buelin cadedig hadin,
Cyfryn car iessin newn côr assa;
Cirried nawdd ged nudd car prudd far preidd fudd,
Can nidd Gruffudd ha'th rudd na'th ra,
Cader ar curbost cadarn lawfarn lost,
Cad'r ffrost da fuost eithr dy fwa;
Cynnal gwyrirdeb, ac enu, ac wyneb,
Er neb rhyw atteb na'm rhy oetta,
Dos gennad teithfad tuthfa poen dethrol poni ddoethosti etwa:
Duw a rhydd i ddedwydd dda,
Diau mi biau 'r bua.*

Chester, to which reference is made in the anecdote of Rhys Wyn, anciently formed a portion of North Wales. No part of the Principality was then so famed for the excellence of its bowyers, or the number and frequency of its bow meetings. Among the Sloane MSS. is preserved a collection of Moralities enacted by the " Bowyers, Fletchers, and Stringers," of that ancient town, about three centuries ago. Archery also held a place among the festivities which ensued on the election of its civic officers, and a very ancient document† gives the following description of what the writer quaintly styles " A Sheriff's Breakfast."

" There is an ancient custom in the city of Chester, the origin of which is now unknown. On Easter Monday, every year,

* Tribes of North Wales.
† Bankes's MS. Collections.

commonly called Black Monday, the two sheriffs of the city do shoot for a breakfast of calf's head and bacon; commonly called the sheriffs' breakfast. This is the manner of it. The day previous, the drum soundeth through the city, with a proclamation for all gentlemen, yeomen, and good fellows, that will come with their bowes and arrowes, to take part with one sheriff or the other; and upon Monday morning, on the Roodday, the mayor, shreeves, aldermen, and other gentlemen being there, the one sheriff chooseth one, and the other sheriff chooseth another, and so of all the archers; then one sheriff he shooteth, and the other sheriff he shooteth; the mark being twelve score yards distant. Thus they proceed, until three shots be won. Then all the winner's side go up together first, with arrowes in their hands; and all the loser's, with bowes in their hands, together to the Common Hall of the city. There the mayor, aldermen, gentlemen, and the rest take part of the said breakfast in loving manner. This is yearly done, it being a commendable exercise, a good recreation, and friendly assembly. Another curious regulation once existed in this ancient city. Every man who chanced to be married there on a Shrove Tuesday was required to deliver to the Drapers' Company, in the presence of the mayor, a silver arrow, valued five shillings or upwards, instead of the football of silk and velvet, which they had been accustomed to present time out of mind, according to the ancient customs of Chester. The arrow was given by the authorities as a prize for the encouragement of shooting with the longbow." *

We have very erroneous ideas, or rather no idea at all, as to what extent civilization prevailed among the ancient Welsh. Generally speaking, my Saxon countrymen conceive them to have been little better than a nation of cannibals, and their language is *rather less* understood than the Sanscrit or the Chinese. Yet, whilst England, in common with the rest of Europe, was

* Bankes's MSS.

sunk in the darkest ignorance, there flourished in Wales a succession of men of genius, whose compositions, in my estimation, were scarcely surpassed during the brightest epoch of lyric poetry in Greece. Foremost amongst these stands Davyth ap Gwilym, the archer bard, an equally ardent votary of Apollo in his two-fold capacity as god of the bow and the lyre. Of his enthusiasm for the latter I shall hereafter present my readers with some pleasing instances. And if splendid original imagery united to the most harmonious versification exalt their possessor to the highest walks of poetry, the following passages alone will be amply sufficient to confirm the pretensions of one at least of Cambria's early bards.

TO SUMMER.

And wilt thou, then, obey my power,
Thou summer, in thy brightest hour?
To her* thy glorious hues unfold,
In one rich embassy of gold!
Her morns with bliss and splendour bright,
And fondly kiss her mansions white;
Fling wealth and verdure o'er her bow'rs,
And for her gather all thy flow'rs.
Oh! lavish blossoms with thy hand
On all the forests of the land,
And let thy gifts, like floods descending,
O'er every hill and glen be blending;
Let orchard, garden, vine express
Thy fulness and thy fruitfulness.
Around the land of beauty fling
The costly traces of thy wing!
And thus, 'mid all thy radiant flowers,
Thy thick'ning leaves and glassy bowers,
The poet's task shall be to glean
   Roses and flowers that softly bloom,
   (The jewels of the forest's gloom!
And trefoils wove in pavement green,
With sad humility to grace
His golden Ivor's resting-place.

---

* Glamorganshire.

MAY.

Many a poet in his lay
    Told me May would come again;
Truly sang the bards, for May
    Yesterday began to reign!
She is like a bounteous lord,
    Gold enough she gives to me;
Gold — such as we poets hoard —
'Florins' of the mead and tree,
Hazel flowers, and 'fleurs de lis.'
Underneath her leafy wings
I am safe from treason's stings.
I am full of wrath with May
That she will not always stay!
Maidens never hear of love,
But when she has plumed the grove.
Giver of the gift of song
To the poet's heart and tongue,
May! majestic child of heaven,
To the earth in glory given!
Verdant hills, days long and clear,
Come when she is hov'ring near.
Stars, ye cannot journey on
Joyously when she is gone!
Ye are not so glossy bright,
Blackbirds, when she takes her flight.
Sweetest art thou, nightingale;
Poet, thou canst tell thy tale
With a lighter heart, when May
Rules with all her bright array. *

Davyth ap Gwilym flourished about the middle of the thirteenth century. Gifted with an unlucky taste and talent for satirical composition, he embroiled himself with his relatives at an early period of life, and, quitting their protection, sought refuge in the castle of Ivor, surnamed Hael, or "the Generous," where he was received with affectionate kindness. His characteristic pursuits at the court of the chieftain, who resided at

* Maelog.

Basaleg in Monmouthshire, are aptly described in the following lines : —

> Honours great for me are stored,
> If I live, from Ivor's hand;
> Hound and huntsman at command,
> Daily banquet at his board.
> Princely baron! at the game
> With his piercing shafts to aim;
> And to let his falcons fly
> On the breezes of the sky.*

Besides being an elegant poet and minstrel, for he played admirably upon the harp, his national instrument, he may be regarded as the very *beau ideal* of a man of fashion in that age. According to a tradition current in the reign of Queen Elizabeth, he was tall, slender, and wore his fair yellow hair flowing in ringlets upon his shoulders.† His dress was equally foppish, in conformity with the practice of the age in which he lived.

Thus accomplished, and connected by the ties of birth with many an ancient family, he spent his time very pleasantly, as he himself tells us, in strolling from the court of one chieftain to that of another, happier than his entertainers, though they enjoyed the possession of a mansion in every district of Wales, as he fancied he might secure the affections of every beauteous maid. Here, however, as in many an ardent youthful aspiration besides, and notwithstanding his great bodily and mental endowments, anticipation seems either to have outrun the cold realities of success, or, else, poor Gwilym, like greater heroes, found

> Increase of appetite to grow with what it fed on.

---

* Literally, hawking, singing with the harp, shooting at marks, and shooting the bounding deer."

† Gwilym himself alludes to this, with the curious addition that the girls, instead of attending to their devotion, used to whisper at church that he had his sister's hair on his head. — MAELOG.

He became utterly dissatisfied with his progress in these love passages, and then, as usual, poured forth his chagrin in melodious verse.

> The archer who aims at the target his blow,
> Shakes the dust from his arrow, the dust from his bow; *
> And ne'er shall he loose forth his brave shaft in vain,
> If he aim but aright, if he shoot but with pain.
> But, poor bard! if one maiden but fall to thy lot,
> In a thousand, alas! 'tis a mere random shot.

Gwilym was an enthusiastic, and therefore a skilful, archer; and an allusion to this accomplishment furnishes us with a curious illustration of the manners of his age. It appears that to possess a costly bow of foreign wood, was as indispensable to the modish equipment of a young and handsome Welsh gallant five centuries ago, as a polished steel-hilted rapier to the modern visitant at court. "Yesterday," says he, "I was in anxious mood and ardent expectation, beneath a shadowy tree, with the gold and jewel upon my brow†, waiting the arrival of Gwenllian." Whilst thus engaged, there appears in the distance, what he elsewhere styles "a harsh-voiced, dog-hating, poultry-eating fox." He then adds, "I aimed between my hands‡, with a valuable yew bow, which came from abroad, intending to send a keen arrow from the forest, dark headed, to dye his

---

* I have elsewhere said that the ancient archer kept his tackle over the chimneypiece.

† So expressed in the original, and worn either in compliment to his mistress, or intended as a present to her, which the gallantry of Gwilym renders probable. She it was perhaps whom he invites to "the house of leaves," in one of his most graceful sonnets, commencing,—

> Maid of dark and glossy tresses,
> Humbly I request,
> In Dol Aëron's green recesses,
> Thee to be my guest, &c. &c.

‡ The archer shooting at an elevation aims between his left and right hand.

hair with blood. I drew — oh, unlucky shot! it passed by his head altogether; alas! my bow is splintered into a thousand pieces."*

From another passage contained in his works, it appears that the Welsh bow was sometimes adorned with gilding, a practice nowhere alluded to by the writers of our own country.† Animadverting upon the fashion of young women overloading themselves with ornaments, which appears to have been very prevalent in the fourteenth century, he signifies that real beauty has no occasion for them, and that they are assumed only to conceal some glaring defect.

" The yew bow," says he, " which is so unsound, that it will presently break in two halves, is covered with gold on the back; and then, appearing an undamaged article, is sold at a high price." I have here rendered the words literally from the Welsh; he afterwards pursues the same sentiment, in the following beautiful strain of poetry, translated by Maelog: —

> Would the pure lustre of the warlike mail,
> That hangs on yon white wall ‡ with glimmerings pale,
> Gleam brightly thus, if muffled and concealed
> In the long tabard — that with many a shield
> And many a rich emblazonry is dyed
> By painter's hand, and all diversified
> With rare devices? On the brow of snow,
> E'en thus, no diadem fresh glory can bestow!

This bard is inexhaustible in his allusions to an accomplishment in which he excelled as much as he did in poetry. He

---

* Literal translation.

† When James the First, in his progress from Scotland, came to Rippon in Yorkshire, the townsmen presented him with a gilt steel bow, and a pair of spurs of native manufacture. But that is quite a different affair.

‡ The interior, as well as the outside, of Welsh country dwellings, is kept most assiduously whitewashed. The occupants extend this care even to the gates and stone stiles of their vicinity.

instructs us that the Welsh archer shot at flying game with the confidence and dexterity that distinguishes a modern sportsman. When lamenting the ill success which had attended his addresses to his mistress, he compares himself to a man standing on the beach " with a yew bow* in his hand," and shooting at the sea-gulls; who neither recovers his shafts, nor gains possession of the objects at which he aims. " My poetic strains," says Davyth ap Gwilym, " are all sent forth in vain; as well might I discharge an arrow at the stars." In the original Welsh, this sentiment, as well as the following lines, addressed to the sea gull, are distinguished by great felicity of expression : —

> Bird, that dwellest on the spray,
> White as yon moon's calm array,
> Dust thy beauty ne'er may stain,
> Sunbeam gauntlet † of the main !
> Wilt thou, lily of the sea,
> Draw near, and, hand in hand with me,
> To the beauteous maiden's home —
> Nun that dwellest in the foam,
> With thy glossy figure climb
> Round her castle walls sublime?

Even in the most trifling matters he introduces allusions to the bow, so as to make them highly picturesque. When addressing the roebuck, which he despatches with a letter to the object of his affections, he tells the animal not to allow any obstacle to impede his course, nor to fear

> The grinded ‡ arrow.

Sending the skylark on a similar errand, the poet admonishes

---

* The Welsh writers of this period, generally add this epithet, when naming the bow.

† The bird, with its indented wings spread over the sea, is here compared to the open fingers of a gauntlet.

‡ If my memory does not fail me, Sir Walter Scott makes Richard invite Saladin " to run three courses with grinded spears."

his messenger, should he be exposed to the archer's aim, to turn his flight above his hand, whilst the arrow passes by."*

> Sentinel of the dawning light,
> Reveller of the spring!
> How sweetly, nobly, wild thy flight —
> Thy boundless journeying.
> Far from thy brethren of the woods, alone,
> A hermit chorister before God's throne!
> O wilt thou climb yon heavens for me,
> Yon starry turret's height,
> Thou interlude of melody,
> 'Twixt darkness and the light!
> And find — Heaven's blessing on thy pinions rest! —
> My lady love — the moonlight of the West!
> No woodland caroller art thou,
> Far from the archer's eye;
> Thy course is o'er the mountain's brow,
> Thy music in the sky!
> Then fearless be thy flight, and strong,
> Thou earthly denizen of angel song. †

After he had fallen into the sear and yellow leaf, the poet evinces the same predilection for the manly pursuits of his early youth. With a natural pleasing satisfaction, he alludes to the period when he could rapidly ascend the hill, leap, swim the torrent — literally "the eye of the pool," — and shoot with the bow. Indeed, if the following passage, from one of his latest poems,

---

* Literal translation.

† Maelog observes, that, in the original, the imagery is so rich and diversified, it is almost impossible to give a close translation. The preceding, therefore, must be considered in the light of an imitation, an expression of the leading ideas, rather than as a complete and accurate translation.

Of similar character are some stanzas addressed to the wind, commencing: —

> Bodiless glory of the sky,
> That, wingless, footless, strong, and loud,
> Leap'st on thy starry path on high,
> And chauntest midst the mountain cloud;
> Fleet as the wave, and fetterless as light!

be received as a faithful picture of his mental condition towards the close of life, we can hardly conceive a more melancholy contrast to that bold and vivacious spirit which had previously animated this most distinguished of our old Welsh bards.

> Youth has fled, and, like a dart,
> Grief is planted in my heart;
> All the joy of life is gone,
> Strengthen me, thou Secret One.*
> * * *
> In the grove no more I doat
> On the cuckoo, and the note
> Of the nightingale — no more
> Pine for the maiden I adore —
> For the kiss and murm'ring voice
> Of the lady of my choice!
> Age's pangs are on my brow,
> (Love is not my sickness now!)
> Love and all his joys are o'er,
> E'en his memory I deplore!
> All my strength like chaff is sear;
> Death is threateningly near!
> Near is the impending doom —
> Earth, and darkness, and the tomb.
> Christ, my thoughts — my footsteps lead!
> Amen — no other guide I need.

The "History of the Gwydir Family," alluding to the style of living, and amusements, common to persons of rank and fortune, in Wales, during the reign of Edward IV., says it was the fashion of those days for gentlemen and their retainers to assemble daily, to shoot matches and masteries. There was then no individual of any note in the country, who had not a cellar well stocked with wine, which was sold for his profit. Thither came his friends to meet him.† They spent the day in wrestling, shooting, throwing the sledge, and other feats of activity.

* A Welsh epithet for the Deity.
† Traces of this custom may still be seen in the *Cwrw bach*, or private drinking matches of the Welsh peasantry. Their liquor is, of course, of a homelier description — the bonnie nut-brown ale.

Even in times of peace and apparent security, the Welsh chieftain never laid aside his bow. One Jevan ap Robert was returning on horseback from Chirkland, to his residence, near Galt-y-morfa-hir, by moonlight. Unconscious of present danger, he rode onwards, chatting carelessly with his men. Suddenly, an arrow lighted amongst them, from the hill side, which was then clothed with wood. They immediately halted, and, drawing their bows, shot all seven together towards the spot where they conceived the archer to be secreted. On searching the wood, it was discovered that one of their random arrows had killed their assailant, who proved to be the third brother of a family with whom Jevan ap Robert was at deadly feud. The whistling of the shaft, as it flew through the air, and the direction in which the feathers pointed after alighting on the ground, may have indicated the spot whence the archer aimed, yet, even with this assistance, it is most extraordinary they should have killed him.

That the inhabitants of a country like ancient Wales should have gone continually armed, cannot be a matter of surprise. A man's person and property were liable to continual aggression, and he naturally carried with him those weapons in the use of which he felt the greatest confidence. But when sent to court the Muses, within "academic bowers and learned halls," it is reasonable to suppose the formidable bow and shafts might be laid aside. Not so, however, in our English universities, where the young Welshman retained them as pertinaciously as when traversing the wildest glen of his native land.

Whilst Cardinal Otho was holding a synod at Oxford, he lodged in the Abbey of Osney. One day, a number of students thronged about the gates of that edifice, and commenced an affray with the legate's men, who vainly endeavoured to repel them with their staves. It so happened, that a poor Irish scholar made good his entry into the Abbot's kitchen, and approaching the dresser, besought the cook, for God's sake, to give him something to satisfy his craving hunger. But the brutal fellow, whose pampered stomach prevented his feeling for the distresses of another, in a great fury took up a ladle full of hot broth, and cast it into the Irishman's face. Seeing this, a Welsh scholar, who stood by, exclaimed, "What, mean we to suffer this villany?" Then seizing an arrow, he set it in his bow, which he had caught up at the beginning of the fray, and drawing it to the head, let fly at the cook, and slew him outright.*

The portraiture of an accomplished bowman has been so admirably sketched by one of their early writers, that its insertion here becomes a matter of course. Aware, however, that a Welshman of the fourteenth century, speaking only his native language, would in the nineteenth be scarcely intelligible to one English reader of a thousand, it is requisite somebody should act as his interpreter.† This task has been undertaken by one well qualified, who has the pleasure of introducing to their acquaintance Iolo Goch, "Iolo the Red," bard of the chieftain Glendower.

I will first state, by way of prologue, that a considerable degree of jealous enmity existed between the chieftains, as well as people, of the two divisions of Wales.‡ When Dafydd ab Owen Gwynedd, prince of the north, had honourably received some fugitives from the south, his courtiers insinuated that such an act of condescension was too great towards the subjects of a rival, who would not show the least respect to any of his; whereupon Dafydd swore a great oath, that he would not rest until satisfied whether the Lord Rhŷs of South Wales would not honourably receive an envoy sent from his court. Some

* Hollinshed.

† To the kindness of the Rev. Thomas Price, of Crickhowel, Breconshire, a name long familiar to the admirers of ancient British lore, I am indebted for this remarkable passage. The original MS. is in the library of the London Welsh School.

‡ "Tribes of North Wales," twelve copies, for private circulation only.

P. P. Stephanoff. R. Staines.

y Paun Bach.

London Published by Longman & Co. Feby 1840.

time elapsed before he could meet with a person qualified for, or willing to undertake a mission so delicate; and at length Gwgan the Bard was fixed upon as his messenger. But Gwgan then dwelt in Powysland, and the exact place of his retreat was unknown. As a preliminary step, therefore, Dafydd ap Owen despatched a shrewd active fellow called y Paun Bach, to make the necessary inquiries. On arriving in Powysland, it was speedily ascertained that Caer Einion, Gwgan's abode, lay in a sequestered valley bordered by a forest. Towards the close of a summer's day, y Paun Bach entered this lonely spot; and as he rode slowly forwards, the sounds of music broke upon his ear. He halted to listen. It was a harp, whose sweetness, and the style of modulation, told that his errand was accomplished. On reaching the snow-white cottage, where on a fragment of rock the minstrel reclined with his harp, Dafyd's messenger, desirous of opening a conversation, demanded, with a bold ruffling air, where he could put up his horse.

Gwgan, laying down the harp, replied in a similar strain:—

"Turn him loose into the forest," said the bard, "where some night prowler will save ye the trouble of catching him again, for he'll take a spring upon his back, and give him such a heel-stab (sawel frath) as will send him to Nictref beyond Seis nictref."*

"But," replies the other, "suppose I were in yonder sloping wood opposite, and in my hand a bow of red yew ready bent, with a tough tight string, and a straight round shaft with a well rounded nock, having long slender feathers of a green silk fastening†, and a sharp-edged steel head, heavy and thick, and

* *Nictref beyond Seis nitref*, a sort of punning unmeaning expression, as if we said, " to Sack town beyond Saxon town."

† The common Welsh word for the feathers of arrows, and that used here, is *bon-cawiad;* compounded of *bon*, the butt end, and *cawiad*, a whipping or lapping round. The same word *cawiad*, and the verb *cawiaw*, are used for whipping on a fish-hook, so that the meaning cannot be mistaken. Previously to gluing on the feathers, the arrow-makers, Flemish as well as En-

an inch wide *, of a green blue temper, that would draw blood out of a weathercock. And with my foot to a hillock, and my back to an oak, and the wind to my back, and the sun towards my side; and the girl I love best, hard by, looking at me; and I conscious of her being there;—I would shoot him such a shot, so strong and far drawn, so low and sharp, that it would be no better there were between him and me a breast-plate and a Milan hauberk, than a whisp of fern, a kiln rug, or a herring net!"

Bravo, y Paun Bach! thou Mercutio of bowmen; worthy associate art thou of that splendid conception of Avon's bard: the same in reckless humour and daring courage; equal, too, in skilful use of your respective weapons. He with the glittering toledo, you with gallant grey goose-wing.

It is a very natural supposition, that the author of the above passage was one who had himself proved the sharpness of his arrows against the harness of our English knights. " Drawing blood out of a weathercock," is a bold and original idea; while the ineffectual protection which even the steel hauberk afforded against shafts so vigorously aimed, renders the allusion to a whisp of fern, &c., strikingly apposite.

---

glish, wind a small portion of green or scarlet floss silk round the butt end of the stele, for the breadth of a quarter of an inch, exactly where the two extremities of the feather will lie. Its use is to afford a firmer hold. They also wind several turns of the same over the upper end of the stem, pared away fine, in order to prevent its catching the archer's flesh. This custom is very ancient, and affords a full interpretation to the phrase, "green silk fastening."

The Orientals wing their arrows by sewing on the feathers with fine threads, stripped from the tendons of deer and other animals. But this plan has never, to my knowledge, been adopted in Europe. It is very insecure, and the delicate fibres of the feather suffer by the operation. If we imagine a thread of green silk to have been so used by the Welsh, here is another explanation. The other parts, however, so much resemble the English arrow, that it seems highly probable the allusion is as I have stated it to be.

* The usual breadth of an ancient barbed arrow.

The shot contemplated by this adroit bowman would naturally be a very distant one. How admirable is his enumeration of the requisites for such an exploit. His arrow must have the well-rounded nock, with the slender or low feathering, peculiar to a flight shaft; the hillock and the oak give firmness to his position; a "down wind" will assist the arrow's flight; and to avoid fighting with the sun in front, was one of the most important manœuvres of our old English archers. Again, the arrow is to be strongly and far drawn; because, when well aimed, it is pulled even close up to the head.* He looses sharply, since that is equally essential to success. By the lowness of its range, we judge of the extraordinary power of his bow; for the parabolic curve in which an arrow flies towards a distant object, is diminished in proportion to the force of the weapon whence it is discharged. Lastly, that no favourable influence might be wanting, the maiden of his affections must witness his dexterity; her smiles, at once its inspiration and its reward.

The termination of Gwgan's embassy may as well be added. On arriving at Lord Rhŷs castle, he found him in a furious temper, beating his servants and hanging his dogs. Gwgan knowing it was no time to appear, delayed his business until the following day; and then, in a long speech, still extant in MS., he let the noble descendant of Rhŷs ab Tewdwr know that his master had made him the bearer of a complimentary message; and if he were well received, he had commission from his prince to thank the Lord Rhŷs; if not, he had commission to act on the reverse. Struck by his boldness, Rhŷs asked him in what would his honourable reception consist. Gwgan replied, "In giving me a horse better than my own, to carry me home; in giving me five pounds in money, and a suit of clothes; in giving my servant who leads my horse by the bridle, a suit of

---

* " Draw archers, — draw your arrows to the head." — *Shakspeare.*

clothes, and one pound." "Marry," cried the prince, "I will give thee the noblest steed of my stud, for the sake of thy royal master; and, above thy demand, I will double the sums, and treble the suits of apparel." So Gwgan returned home, having executed his commission to the mutual satisfaction of both princes. Some curious references to the household arrangements of our ancestors are scattered through the history of this embassy. He speaks of dinner beneath a canopy, to prevent the dust and cobwebs from falling upon the dishes, and of a screen for protecting his shins from the scorching embers of a green ash wood fire.

Before we bid adieu to Iolo Goch, it is but fair to justify our preference, by permitting a rival—one of the bards of England — to stand upon his defence. We have a pleasing description of the old English archer in Chaucer's Canterbury Tales. La voici!

THE SQUIRE'S YEOMAN.

A yeoman had he and servants no mo
At that time, for him list to riding so.
And he was clad in coat and hose of green;
A sheaf of peacock's arrows bright and keen
Under his belt he bare full thriftily;
Well could he dress his tackle yeomanlie.
His arrows drooped not with feathers low,
And in his hand he bare a mighty bow.
A nott head had he, with a brown visage;
Of wood-craft well couth he all the usage.
Upon his arm he ware a gay bracer,
And by his side a sword and bokeler;
And on that other side, a gay dagger
Harnised well, and sharp as point of spear;
A Christopher on his breast of silver shene,
A horn he bare, the baldric was of green.
A for'ster was he, soothlie as I guesse.

Among the Welsh, a robust and hardy race of mountaineers, instances of strong and distant archery were doubtless common enough, though a solitary example only occurs to me at the present moment. It relates to one of those private feuds which, both in Wales and England, retarded the progress of civilisation during the fourteenth and fifteenth centuries, and which, like the lex talionis of the Arabs, demanded blood for blood. Robin ab Gruffydd Goch lived at the Graianllyn. At that time, Rhŷs ab Gruffydd Goch was slain at Tal y Sarn. Then went Robin, and Howel his brother, across the ferry; and having scaled Conway Castle, they entered, seized the constable, and cut off his head on the garreglas (grey rock), in front of the town. Llewelyn of Nannau, had shot across the river Conway, at a man from the upper side of the town — the parson of Disserth, — and had killed him. This was accounted one of the longest shots by which a person was ever slain; and, on that account, Robin ap Gruffydd Goch took his revenge.*

The Conway is one of the few Welsh rivers I have never seen; but an individual in the camp of Henry III., A.D. 1243, describes it, under the castle, as a small arm of the sea. This river separated the English from the spot where the Welshman lay encamped. He adds that, at full tide, its breadth was about a bow-shot. Doubtless, what passed for good shooting at Conway, must have been so in reality. No place in Europe witnessed finer displays of archery; for there the best troops of England, headed by the English kings, had often encountered the Welsh, also fighting under their Prince's banner. I have recently seen another account of this transaction. It is there said that Llewellyn of Nannau shot from Carnarvon Castle, and that the man at whom he aimed was standing upwards of eight hundred yards off. The archer's elevated position renders this account as by no means improbable, for Robin Hood is traditionally reported to have cast an arrow a mile at one flight, from the battlements of Whitby Abbey.†

* From a collection of Historical Notices on the Welsh Language.
† See Ritson.

From numerous facts recorded by their native historians, we learn that, renowned as was the skill of the English archers, they stood in considerable dread of the Welsh bow. In the Welsh chronicle of Caradoc of Llancarvan, written in the Welsh language, it is said that, about the year 1120, Henry II. undertook an expedition into Wales. He was opposed by Meredith ap Blethyn, and his nephews, Einon, Madoc, and Morgan, sons of Cadwgan ap Blethyn. And as the king approached the confines of Powys, Meredith despatched a few young archers to a woody pass to meet him, that they might with their arrows annoy his army. When the king arrived at the pass, it happened that the young men were there to meet him, and they opposed the king and his army with much tumult, discharging their arrows among the troops. After killing many and wounding others, one of these youths drew his bow and loosed an arrow amongst the host; and it lighted upon the strong part of the king's armour, opposite his heart, without his knowing the person who struck him; and the arrow did not injure the king, on account of the excellence of his harness, for he was breast-plated*; and the arrow glanced against his armour. But nevertheless the king became exceedingly terrified, being seized with as great a dread as if he had been pierced through. And he ordered his army to encamp, and demanded who had the boldness to assault him so daringly. It was told him, some young men belonging to Meredith ap Blethyn. Then sent he messengers requesting they would come to him on truce. And they came. And he asked who sent them there; and they said, it was Meredith, &c. Then sware Henry, " By the death of our Lord," his usual profane oath, that the arrow came not from a Welsh, but an English bow. He perhaps considered

Nor helm nor hauberk's twisted mail,

---

* *i. e.*, wore a breast-plate independently of the ordinary chain mail.

to be any protection against the former; and, like Falstaff, regarding discretion as the better part of valour, made peace with the Welsh prince, and immediately returned to England. Meredith agreed to pay him ten thousand head of cattle; but this tribute appears to have been merely nominal, to save the king's credit with his own subjects.*

During the expedition of Henry II. into Wales, a Norman baron, named Hubert de St. Clare, constable of Colchester, distinguished himself by an act of heroic self-devotion to that monarch. Whilst the English army were attempting to force the passage of a bridge, the king was aimed at by a Welsh archer, who recognised him among the assailants. The arrow must inevitably have transfixed him, had not this valiant knight sprung forward, and received it in his own bosom, of which wound he instantly died.

In reference to the first of these anecdotes, it is reasonable to presume Henry and his body guards to be protected by the best armour of that age. The same remark will apply to a baron so wealthy and powerful as Hubert de St. Clare. Such, then, was the extraordinary vigour with which these Welshmen plied their bows.

The "yew-bow," — "the bow of red yew†," with the characteristics of drawing and loosing, are sufficiently explicit of the kind of archery in use among these sons of Cambria's death-clad hills. It was therefore the long-bow, not the arbalist, to which the chronicler and the bard refer. Indeed, wherever mention of the cross-bow occurs, it is spoken of contemptuously, as a weapon peculiar to the Flemings and French. There is a

* Caradoc of Llancarvan, the author of this history, wrote about the year 1140, only twenty years afterwards. He consequently must have been minutely acquainted with all the details of that event.

† I may here remark that Ossian, describing the hue of health upon one of his hero's cheeks, compares them to a "red yew-bow." Does not this say something for the authenticity of the poems? The comparison would never suggest itself to any but an archer, which Macpherson was not.

striking illustration of this national difference in the poems of our old friend David ap Gwilym. A wealthier and more fortunate rival, whom the poet contemptuously styles " Hunchback," had succeeded in winning from him the affections of his Morvyth.* Alluding to the departure of this person, with

* Will the reader digress a few moments from the subject in hand, to peruse the following exquisite address of Gwilym to his mistress. The constancy of his affection, united to the glowing harmony of his versification, have justly earned for him the appellation of Cambria's Petrarch.

All my life time I have been
Bard to Morvyth, " golden mein!"
I have loved beyond belief;
Many a day to love and grief
For her sake has been a prey,
Who doth wear the moon's array!
Pledged my truth from youth till now,
To the girl of glossy brow.
Oh, the light her features wear,
Like the bursting torrents glare!
Oft by love bewildered quite,
Have my aching feet all night
Stag-like tracked the forest shade
For the foam complexioned maid,
Whom with passion firm and gay
I adored mid leaves of May!
Mid a thousand I could tell
One elastic footstep well!
I could speak to one sweet maid —
(Graceful figure!) by her shade
I could recognize till death,
One sweet maiden by her breath!
From the nightingale, could learn
Where she tarries, to discern;
There, his noblest music swells
Through the portals of the dells!
When I am from her far away,
I have neither laugh nor lay!
Neither soul nor sense is left,
I am half of mind bereft;

three hundred men, to join Edward III. in France, previous to the battle of Cressy*, he calls upon the arbrysiwr, that is, the

> When she comes, with grief I part,
> And am altogether heart!
> Songs inspired, like flowing wine,
> Rush into this mind of mine;
> Sense enough again comes back
> To direct me in my track!
> Not one hour shall I be gay,
> While my Morvyth is away!
>
> MAELOG.

* Great numbers of Welsh served at Cressy and Poictiers, and it is somewhere said that a considerable portion consisted of archers. Among those who distinguished themselves at Poictiers, was a gentleman of North Wales, called SIR HOWEL Y VWYAL, "Sir Howel of the Battleaxe." By the Welsh, he is said to have been the identical person who captured the French king, and this remarkable tradition is confirmed by a passage in the Harleian MS., No. 2298. "Sir Howell y Fwyall, ab Einion, ap Gruffith, ap Howell, ap Meredith, ap Einion, ap Gwgan, ap Meredith Goch, ap Collwyn, ap Tangno, called Sir *Howell y Fwyall* or Sir *Howell Pole Axe*, from his constant fighting with that warlike instrument. It is said he dismounted the French King, by cutting off his horse's head at one blow with his battle-axe, and took him prisoner; and that as a trophy of victory, he bore the arms of France, with a battle-axe in bend sinister argent."[1] However this may have been, his valour and conduct on that occasion induced the Black Prince to reward him with the constableship of Chester and Cricketh castles, with the rent of Dee Mills[2] in Chester, and other matters of profit. He also bestowed a mess of meat to be served up before his battle-axe, or partisan, for ever; which was afterwards to be carried down, and given to the poor. The following lines commemorate the event:—

> "Seiger fy feigyr fwyall, — doeth pon gar bron y Brenin
> Gwedy'r maes, gwaed ar ei mîn; ei dysaig a'i dewiswr
> A'i diod oedd waed a dwr."

Serve up the feast before my gallant battle-axe, — this came before the king, after the foughten field, with blood upon its edge; its banquet and its choicest beverage was then the streaming gore.

---

[1] And on the same manner of wyce, a poor archer might have taken a prynce or noble lord; and so, the armes of that prisoner, he may put to him and his heyrs."—*Book of St. Albans,* by DAME JULIANA BERNERS.

[2] "If thou hadst Dee Mills, thou wouldst spend all," is a Cheshire proverb, indicative of their profitable revenue.

arbalister, or cross-bowman, to despatch him with his albras, " that short stirrup stick : "*

> And thou, cross-bowman true and good,
> Thou shooter with the faultless wood,
> Send me an arrow through his brain,
> (Who of his fate will ere complain!)
> Then from thy quiver, take and aim
> A second arrow through his frame;
> Well will the varlet's corpse be known
> By the stiff beard so scantly sown;
> Haste with thy stirrup fashioned bow,
> To lay the hideous varlet low!

Foreign service, and the abatement of prejudices consequent upon it, seem to have reconciled the natives of this country to the use of the cross-bow. When Edward I. invaded Scotland to take possession of its crown, there was about his person a Welsh servant named Lewin, the most expert cross-bow man in the whole army, of whose fidelity he entertained a very high opinion. On one important occasion the king wrote letters to his council at home, to advertise them of his proceedings, and delivered the packet to Lewin, commanding him to proceed to London with all possible despatch, for he knew him to be a very speedy messenger. The possession of a liberal sum, given him to bear his charges, proved too strong a temptation for one who had never been remarkable for his sobriety; he therefore betook himself to a tavern, and riotously consumed the money in play and good cheer, until the night was far spent.

At day-dawn the following morning, he affected to prepare for his errand; but pretended an unwillingness to depart until he had once more " wrought some displeasure" to the Scots with his weapon. He therefore bribed a companion to

---

* The cross-bow had an iron stirrup, in which the foot was placed to steady the weapon, whilst the archer bent his steel bow by means of the windlass.

take a target* and bear it before him to the castle walls, whilst he followed with his cross-bow.

On reaching the gates, he called loudly to the warders on the walls to let down a cord and draw him up, for he had important communications to make to their captain, "touching the secrets of the King of England." The guards complied with his request; and on being introduced to the commanding officer, who was at breakfast, he addressed him thus :— " Behold, sir, here ye may peruse the King of England's papers ; and now appoint me to some corner of the wall, and you shall straightway see whether I can handle a cross-bow, or not, to defend it against your adversaries," — at the same time offering a box in which the letters were contained.

When all present, except the captain, eagerly desired to see its contents, he interposed, and, like a man of honour, declared the box should remain untouched. Then going to a high tower, he called aloud to the companions of the traitorous messenger, desiring them to inform the King of England that one of his servants had fled to the castle with an intention to betray his despatches, intimating, at the same time, a desire to deliver up him and the letters. Intelligence was accordingly conveyed to Lord John Spencer, who immediately sent a guard up to the walls, from which Lewin was let down and marched off to the English camp.

" As soon as the King understood this," says Hollinshed, " he much commended the honest respect of the captain ; and whereas he had caused engines to be raised to annoy them within, he commanded the same to cease ; and withal, upon their captain's suit, granted them liberty to send unto John Baliol, to give him to understand in what sort they stood. As touching the Welshman, he was drawn and hanged upon a high

---

* The soldier armed with a cross-bow, was generally accompanied by another, bearing a *pavoise*, or large wooden shield, to protect him whilst charging and discharging his weapon.

gallows prepared for him on purpose, as he well deserved." *
It must be recollected that the Welshmen in Edward the First's
army were, many of them, serving against their will, and the
nation in general had not become reconciled to his government.

Before we entirely lose sight of the archery of North Wales,
let us take a glance at Nannau Park †, for the sake of an ancient
tradition preserved among its family archives.

Within the precincts of that domain once stood a venerable
oak of vast dimensions, and entirely hollow, called, by the super-
stitious peasantry of a wild mountainous district, Ceubren yr
Ellyll, or,

The goblin's hollow tree.

Its girth, as far as I can recollect, measured upwards of
twenty-seven feet; while its prodigious antiquity appears from
the fact, that a lapse of four centuries made no change in its
appearance. During the wars of the Roses it was a huge
decayed trunk, nearly in the same condition as when prostrated
by the tempest only a few years since. Scattered over the
turf, at some distance from the spot where grew this forest
patriarch, are the ruins of a once considerable mansion, black-
ened and scorched by fire. Their appearance plainly indicates
the manner of its fall; a history of that conflagration being, in
fact, a history of the Nannau oak.

Howel Sele was of gigantic stature, and enjoyed the reputation of being the strongest and most skilful bowman, where
excellence in archery was an accomplishment possessed by very
many. Rarely was he seen to launch a second arrow at the
same object; the twang of his bowstring sounded as the knell
of his victims, whether in war or in the chase.

Sele was a strenuous partisan of the House of Lancaster in

---

* Vol. ii. page 517.

† Near Dolgellan, Merionethshire, the seat of a highly respected gentleman, Sir Robert Williams Vaughan, Bart., M. P. for the county, until his
resignation of that honour.

England; his cousin, the celebrated Owen Glendower, had as zealously espoused the cause of the rightful heir of the deposed Richard. This will sufficiently account for a mortal feud which raged between these powerful chieftains and near kinsmen.

Sanguinary brawls were of daily occurrence amongst such of the retainers as had not accompanied their respective lords to the English camp. For the general peace, and in the hope of eventually detaching Howel from the Lancastrian interest, the venerable abbot of Cemmes attempted a reconciliation. It is said their interview took place before the altar; but, unawed by the sanctity of the place, these haughty rivals, instead of extending the right hand of fellowship, broke forth into loud and angry recrimination. Daggers were unsheathed, and the sacred edifice seemed on the point of being polluted with blood. At that instant the abbot rushed forwards, and extending towards them the sacred symbol of the cross, vehemently denounced their conduct as an unatoneable insult to the Holy Mother Church.

The terrors of excommunication acted upon their excited passions as oil when poured upon the raging waters. The glittering weapons dropped from their grasp, and in an instant hands were united in apparent friendship which, a moment previous, had thirsted for each other's blood.

It was then proposed by Howel Sele that Glendower should visit him on the morrow at his house of Nannau, and partake of its hospitality. The festivities of the day commenced with a grand hunting match, to which the cousins came, attended by a numerous body of their respective vassals. The park was then, and I believe continues, well stocked with deer; small, indeed, but remarkable for the fine flavour of their venison. As soon as the hounds were uncoupled, and whilst the two chieftains stood within a short distance of each other, Owen Glendower espied a stag. Calling to Howel, he pointed out the animal which now came bounding towards them, with a request that he would exhibit a specimen of his archery. The latter immediately placed an arrow on his bowstring, and elevated his arms as if to shoot in the proposed direction, but wheeling round suddenly, he launched it full at his cousin's breast. The shaft rebounded, and fell broken to the ground, for Owen, suspicious of treachery, wore that day a breastplate of treble proof beneath his hunting garb.

In an instant all was tumult and confusion. The perfidy of this attempt roused the latent passions of Glendower, and, drawing his sword, he rushed towards his adversary. Sele, equally furious at being baffled in his revenge, and aware he must now conquer, or die a felon's death, cast away his bow, and, calling loudly on his followers to maintain the combat, stood resolutely on his guard. They fought long and desperately. At length the men of Nannau, originally inferior to their assailants, being considerably thinned by the sword, attempted, with their chief, to take refuge in the house. They succeeded in gaining it, but the defences were too weak to afford them protection; and when Owen caused his men to kindle a large fire against the gates, they quickly fell to the ground. The infuriated victors put all within to the sword, except Howel Sele himself, the treacherous author of this catastrophe. Disarmed, and covered with many a ghastly evidence of the desperation with which he had maintained the conflict, he was led forth and placed under a guard, whilst his adversaries busied themselves in the work of destruction, by firing his house in four quarters. Glendower remained until its entire demolition was certain. He then marched off, bearing with him his vanquished kinsman.

From that day, until the lapse of about thirty years, Sele's fate was wrapped in mystery. His friends and partisans vainly endeavoured to tempt the captor with offers of a splendid ransom, but the inexorable Glendower deigned not even a reply to their solicitations. Whether, therefore, his cousin had fallen beneath his dagger, or still lingered within the dungeons of some one of his numerous strongholds, none could tell. Accident at length unfolded the mystery.

An old forester, one of Howel's retainers, had been hunting within the domain of his absent lord, and in passing near the great oak, he observed a heron perched among its branches. The flesh of this bird, at present neglected, was anciently esteemed the chief delicacy, even of a monarch's table; its feathers, also, enjoyed some reputation among the arrow-makers. The man, therefore, levelled his cross-bow, and the heron fell transfixed into the hollow trunk. Willing to recover both, he climbed the tree, and descended after them. All within was dark; and while groping about at the bottom, his hands came in contact with many strange uncouth substances; with one of these, which he imagined to be a large shell, and the objects of his search, the forester reascended. But how great was his consternation when, on bringing his prize in contact with the light, he discovered in his grasp the upper half of a human skull!

The tale quickly circulated: numbers crowded to the place; and when the tree was again searched, the gigantic skeleton of a man came forth, which, from its position, appeared to have been entombed in this living grave head downwards. Conjecture pointed them out as the remains of Howel Sele, — a suspicion confirmed shortly afterwards by the confession of one of Glendower's vassals, present at that fatal hunting-match. Exasperated by the threats and defiance of his prisoner, the wrathful Owen commanded a halt, and drawing his dagger, buried it to the hilt in Howel's side; then with his own hands dragged the body to the tree, and tumbled it headlong into its hollow trunk. Long before this discovery Owen Glendower had paid nature's debt; but his vast feudal influence placed him beyond the power of the law, had he been living. The revelation of his guilt, therefore, only served to perpetuate the mortal feud which raged between these two families previous to Howel's death.*

* When the Nannau oak fell, it was, like Shakspeare's celebrated mulberry-tree, preserved in various small articles of taste and utility; picture-frames made from its wood, and enclosing an engraved portrait of the tree, are usual in many respectable residences of the county.

The following anecdote of a domestic feud, in which a similar expedient is resorted to, also furnishes a deplorable insight into the manners of other times: — " Enmitie did still continue betweene Howell ap Rys ap Howell Vaughan, and the sonnes of John ap Meredith. After the death of Jevan ap Robert, Gruffith ap John ap Gronw [cosen german to John ap Meredith's sonnes of Gywnfryn], who had long served in France, and had charge there, comeing home to live in the countrey, it happened that a servant comeing to fish in Stymllyn, his fish was taken away, and the fellow beaten by Howell ap Rys his servants, and by his commandment. Gruffith ap John ap Gronw tooke the matter in such dudgeon, that he challenged Howell ap Rys to the field; which he refusing, and assembling his cousens John ap Meredith's sonnes and his friends together, assaulted Howell in his owne house, after the manner he had seene in the French warres, and consumed with fire his barnes and his outhouses. Whilst he was afterwards assaulting the hall, which Howell ap Rys and many other people kept, being a very strong house, he was shot out of a crevise of the house, through the sight of his beaver, with an arrow into the head, and slayne outright, being otherwise armed at all points. Notwithstanding his death, the assault of the house was continued with great vehemence, the doors being fired with great burthens of straw; besides this, the smoake of the outhouses and barnes, not farre distant, annoyed greatly the defendants, soe that most of them lay under the boordes and benches upon the floore of the hall, the better to avoyd the smoake. During this scene of confusion, only the old man Howell ap Rys never stooped, but stood valiantly in the middest of the hall, armed with a gleve in his hand, and called unto them, and bid them ' arise like men, for shame, for he had known there as greate a smoake in that hall upon a Christmas even.' In the end, seeing the house could no longer defend them, being overlayed with a multitude, upon parley between them, Howell ap Rys was content to yeald himself prisoner to Morris ap John ap Meredith, John ap Meredith's eldest sonne, soe as he would sweare unto him to bring him safe to Carnarvon Castle, to abide the triall of the law for the death of Gruffith ap John ap Gronw, who was cosen german removed to the said Howell ap Rys, and of the very same house he was of; which Morris ap John ap Meredith undertakeing, did put a guard about the said Howell of his trustiest friends and servants, who kept and defended him from the rage of the kindred, and

Among the archers of South Wales, none enjoyed a higher reputation than the men of Gwentland.* As the vicinity of a fine river makes the skilful angler, so one might naturally attribute some portion of this predilection for the bow to the great abundance of fine yew scattered over many districts of Monmouthshire. But my hypothesis, somewhat plausible, is at once overturned by the pages of Giraldus Cambrensis, who tells us they made no use of this tree, and as he flourished at a very early period, and describes what he actually witnessed, his authority is altogether unquestionable. Though a monk, he well knew the difference between a yew and an elm bow; indeed, judging from his language, I conceive he could handle either to good purpose. "The bows of the Welsh," he observes, "are not made of horn, or white wood, or yew, but of wych elm plants; they appear neither handsome nor polished, but, on the contrary, rude and mis-shapen. Yet are they stiff and strong; not so well calculated to cast far, as to give a weighty blow in close fight."† By the bye, what could Warrington have dreamt of, when he translated *ulmellis sylvestris*, "slight twigs joined and twisted together."? Who ever heard of this expedient for manufacturing a bow?

The Welsh historian has recorded several extraordinary instances of powerful shooting, attributed to the men of Gwent. During the siege of Abergavenny Castle, a party of Welsh

---

especially of Owen ap John ap Meredith, his brother, who was very eager against him. They passed by leisure thence like a camp to Carnarvon: the whole company being assembled, Howell's friends posted a horse-backe from one place or other by the way, who brought word that he was come thither safe; for they were in great fear lest he should be murthered, and that Morris ap John ap Meredith could not be able to defend him, neither durst any of Howell's friends be there, for feare of the kindred."— Miss AGHARD's *Gwydir Family.*

* The ancient name of Monmouthshire, and a part of Glamorgan.

† Sed ad graves cominus ictus percutienda tolerandos. — *Itin. Camb.* c. 3. p. 835.

archers perceived two Norman soldiers running towards a tower, situated some distance off; they were immediately assailed by a storm of arrows. He does not tell us whether they were killed, but merely observes that some of the arrows penetrated through the oak doors of a gateway, four fingers in thickness. The heads of these missiles were subsequently driven out and carefully preserved, to perpetuate the memory of such extraordinary force in shooting with the bow.

He next gives an anecdote told by William de Breusa, a Norman knight, one of the followers of Fitzhammond in his conquest of South Wales. A Welsh archer aimed at one of De Breusa's horsemen, who wore armour, under which was also his buff coat. The arrow, besides piercing through his hip, stuck also in the saddle, and mortally wounded the horse on which he rode. In the same battle, another cavalier, also protected by strong armour, had his hip nailed to the saddle by a Welsh arrow. Then, as the soldier drew his bridle, in order to wheel round, a second shaft penetrating his other hip, firmly fastened him to the saddle on both sides. Giraldus adds, "What more could be expected from a balista?"

This occurrence, though sufficiently remarkable, is by no means unlikely. The Inca Garcilasco de Vega records an accident, somewhat similar, which happened to a Spanish trooper. In marching towards the banks of the river Chircagua, the Spaniards had again a considerable number of their comrades wounded. Of these, the principal was the cavalier St. George, who, as he rode through a rivulet, received the arrow of a concealed Indian, which was shot with uncommon force. After breaking through his mailed coat, it penetrated his right thigh and the pommel of the saddle, until it wounded his horse. The terrified animal, maddened by pain, dashed out of the stream, and, bounding away, endeavoured, by violent and repeated plunges, to free himself from the arrow and his rider. St. George's comrades hastened to his succour, and perceiving that he was nailed to the saddle, they led him to his allotted quarters, as the army was encamping by the water side. Lifting him gently from his seat, they cut the shaft between the saddle and the wounded limb; and, on stripping the horse, there arose an exclamation of astonishment from all present, to find that a weapon, apparently so insignificant as a reed tipped with a point of hard wood, should have been able not only to penetrate so many substances, but to inflict a serious wound upon the rider and his horse.

The popularity enjoyed by Harry of Monmouth, among his Welsh subjects, owing to the circumstance of his being born in the principality*, induced numbers of the South Wales archers to join the expedition to France. Among the most distinguished of these were Roger Vaughan of Bedwardine; Watkin Lloyd of the lordship of Brecknock; and the renowned David Llewellyn, better known by the soubriquet of David Gam, or "Squint-eyed David." † He also was a gentleman of good estate, descended from Einon Sais, or Einon the Saxon‡, whose property lay in the parishes of Garthbrengy and Llandew, Breconshire. §

Like too many of his class in that age and country, Gam had embroiled himself in a violent domestic feud. During an affray which took place in the High Street of Brecknock, he unfortunately killed his kinsman, and, to shun the threatened consequences, sought an asylum in England. The dependency of his estate on the honour of Hereford rendered him, like Howel Sele, a determined partisan of the Lancastrians; like him, too, he made an ineffectual attempt on the life of Owen Glendower.

* At Troy House, near Monmouth, a seat of the Duke of Beaufort, the oaken cradle which rocked the hero of Agincourt, is still preserved.

† *Gam* also signifies left-handed, but is more generally applied to a one-eyed person.

‡ So named from having resided in England. The family is Welsh, and traces its descent from Caradoc Fraichfras.

§ Dr. Meyrick.

David Gam held a command of archers on the field of Agincourt; and it is said that, being despatched by the King to reconnoitre the enemy, and report upon their numbers, he returned with this laconic estimate: "an't please your highness, there are enow to be killed, enow to be taken prisoners, and enow to run away." Historians have passed many encomiums on his valour and conduct — Sir Walter Raleigh even goes so far as to compare him to Hannibal — but they make no mention of this circumstance, which might perhaps be known only to his fellow countrymen in arms; unless, indeed, Elmham has given a false colouring to the transaction. He mentions that scouts were despatched by the Duke of York, to gain intelligence of the enemy's approach, when one of them, who had climbed to the summit of a hill, saw the whole French host, to the number of sixty thousand, stretching far and wide over the plain beneath, which seemed on a blaze, as their polished harness reflected the beams of a splendid noontide sun. Astonished at the sight, he retreated with a trembling heart and the utmost speed of his horse, and, breathless, reached the English camp: — "Quickly," said he, "be prepared to do battle, for you are about to fight against a world of innumerable people."

These three valiant Welshmen, Gam, Vaughan, and Llwyd, fell covered with wounds whilst defending the person of their monarch, and Henry knighted them as they lay extended in the agonies of death upon the gory bed of honour. Sir S. R. Meyrick remarks, that the above Sir Roger Vaughan was married to Gwladis, Sir David Gam's daughter. Agincourt made her, as it made many besides, a widow; but she afterwards married another hero of that day, Sir William Thomas, of Ragland, one of the ancestors of the present Duke of Beaufort.

I have been induced to enter thus largely into the biography of these three individuals, because their chivalrous self-devotedness stands so conspicuous in the annals of that memorable contest. Their heroism, no less than Henry's Welsh extraction, gave rise to the following spirited burst of poetry, entitled —

OUR CAMBRO-BRITONS TO THEIR HARP.

Fair stood the wind for France,
When we our sails advance,
Nor now to prove our chance,
    Longer will tarry.
But putting to the main,
At Kaux the mouth of Seine,
With all his martial train,
    Landed King Harry.

And taking many a fort,
Furnished in warlike sort,
Marched towards Agincourt,
    In happy hour.
Skirmishing by day
With those that stopped his way,
Where the French general lay,
    With all his power.

And turning to his men,
Quoth our brave Henry then,
" Though we be one to ten,
    Be not amazed:
Yet have we well begun;
Battles so bravely won
Have never seen the sun,
    By fame been raised.

" And for myself," quoth he,
" This my full rest shall be,
England ne'er mourn for me,
    Nor more esteem me.
Victor I will remain,
Or on this earth lie slain;
Never shall she sustain
    Loss to redeem me.

" Poictiers and Cressy tell,
When most their pride did swell,
Under our swords they fell.
   No less our skill is,
Than when our grandsire great,
Claiming the regal seat,
By many a warlike feat
   Lopt the French lilies."

They now to fight are gone;
Armour on armour shone,
Drum now to drum did groan;
   To hear was wonder;
That with the cries they make
The very earth did shake;
Trumpet to trumpet spake,
   Thunder to thunder.

Well it thine age became,
O noble Erpingham!
Who did the signal aim
   For our brave forces;
When from a meadow by,
Like a storm suddenly,
The English archery
   Struck the French horses.

With Spanish yew so strong,
Arrows a cloth-yard long,
That like to serpents stung,
   Piercing the weather.
None from his fellow starts,
But playing manly parts,
And like true English hearts,
   Stuck close together.

When down their bows they threw,
And forth their bilboes drew,
And on the French they flew,
   Not one was tardy;
Arms were from shoulders sent,
Scalps to the teeth were rent;
Down the French peasants went:
   Our men were hardy.

This while our noble king,
His broadsword brandishing,
Down the French host did ding,
  As to o'erwhelm it;
And many a deep wound lent,
His arms with blood besprent,
And many a cruel dent
  Bruised his helmet.

Glo'ster, that duke so good,
Next of the royal blood,
For famous England stood
  With his brave brother
Clarence, in steel so bright;
Though but a maiden knight,
Yet in that furious fight,
  Scarce such another.

Warwick in blood did wade,
Oxford the foe invade,
And cruel slaughter made,
  Still as they ran up.
Suffolk his axe did ply,
Beaumont and Willoughby
Bare them right doughtily,
  Ferrers and Fanhope.

Upon St. Crispin's day,
Fought was this noble fray,
Which fame did not delay
  In England to carry.
Oh! when shall Englishmen
With such acts fill a pen,
Or Cambria breed again
  Such a King Harry?

The enthusiasm attendant on the revival of archery in England towards the close of the last century, quickly reached the Principality. Of the numerous societies formed there, the first in rank and consequence is the Royal British Bowmen. It includes nearly all the leading families of North Wales, and was originally founded by Sir Watkin Williams Wynne, Bart., in whose park of Wynnstay, Denbighshire, the Royal British Bowmen hold their meetings. His Majesty George the Fourth, when Prince of Wales, not only condescended to become their patron, but presented them with several beautiful prizes. The prize arrows, for both ladies and gentlemen, were first shot for, October the 6th, 1788, when Sir Foster Cunliffe, a well-known archer, won the former, and Miss Harriot Boycott the latter. His Royal Highness likewise presented them with a superb gold medallion, and a silver bugle. They were ably contested at Acton Park, when the former was gained by Lady Cunliffe, at 30, 60, and 70 yards; the latter by R. Hesketh, of Rossell, Esq., at 64, 96, and 128 yards.

The Society of Royal British Bowmen still survives in all its original splendour. Their uniform is green and buff, with black hat and feather. I may minister to the "hæc olim meminisse juvabit" of many an ancient bowman, by adding a list of those ladies and gentlemen who early joined this society.

Sir W. W. Wynne,	Lady Wynne,
Sir Foster Cunliffe,	Lady Cunliffe,
Lord Carysfort,	Lady Carysfort,
Messrs. Bunbury,	Mrs. Cooke,
St. Leger,	Mrs. Puleston,
P. L. Fletcher,	Mrs. Apperley,
Maurice Wynne,	Miss Parry,
O. Bridgeman,	Mrs. Hammerston,
Jones,	Miss Hammerston,
Warrington,	Mrs. Fletcher,
Hammerston,	Miss Fletcher,
Master Wynne.	Mrs. G. Warrington,
	Mrs. Jones.

Oh loyal in grief, and in danger unshaken,
For ages still true, though for ages forsaken;
Yet, Cambria, thy heart may to gladness awaken,
Since thy monarch has smiled on thy harp and thy bow!

SECTION V.

FRENCH ARCHERY.

Sometimes I gallop o'er the ground,
Upon my well-breath'd nag, to cheer my echoing hound.
Sometime I pitch my toils the deer alive to take,
Sometime I like the cry the deep-mouth'd kennel make.
Then underneath my horse I stalk, my game to strike,
And with a single dog to hunt him eke I like.
* * *
The stately hart his hind doth to my presence bring,
The buck his tawny doe, the roe his dappled mate,
Before me to my bower, whene'er I sit in state.
I' the morn I climb the hills, where wholesome winds do blow;
At noontide, to the vales and shady groves below.

DRAYTON.

" God thee save, my dear mastyr,
  And Chryste thee save and see." —
" Raynold Greenleafe," said the sheriffe,
" Where hast thou now be?"

" I have been in the forest;
  A fayre sight did I see,
It was one of the fayrest shewes
  That e'er yet sawe I me.

" Yonder there stood a ryght fayre hart,
  His coluere was of greene;
Seven score deere upon a herd,
  Be with him all bedene:

" His antlers are so sharp, mayster,
  Of sixty and well mo;
That I durst not shoot for dreade
  Lest they would me sloo."

Old Ballad.

IT was in the sports of the field only, that the ancient inhabitants of France used the long bow with any considerable address. Their princes, indeed, with the warlike dukes of

Burgundy, and other independent nobles, laboured for centuries to create efficient bands of military archers in their respective dominions. Sensible of the advantages which would result from being able to combat the English with their own weapons, during the scourging visitations of those "nock shotten islanders," they heaped honours and rewards upon all who excelled in drawing the bow.* "Ordonnons," says the decree issued to promote this object by Charles VII. "qu'en chaque paroisse de notre royaume, y aura un archer qui sera, et se tiendra continuellement en habillement suffisant, et seront appellés les francs archers. Et seront tenus en habillement sous dit, et de tirer à l'arc, et aller en leur habillement toutes les fastes et jours non ouvrables," &c. &c. But experience at length convinced them of the vanity of these attempts. "In the end," says a passage from one of the Harleian MSS., " the French king and the captains of many nations did manifestly see, that neither his, nor any other people, could attain to shoot so strong, and with that dexterity and excellence which the English bowmen did. Whereby they, seeing our archery in our sort of long bowes, was a very peculiar gift of God given to our nation, they left off the practice and use of that weapon." While Englishmen, from childhood to age, retained an enthusiastic attachment for the bow, the French abandoned it so soon as the penal enactments were relaxed, returning to the use of the arbalist, which in course of time gave place to the arquebuse. †

The preference thus given to an arm requiring no exertion of bodily strength, would seem to imply a difference in the physical conformation of the two nations. When exercising with the same weapon, the one exhibited a vast superiority of manly vigour over the others, the French archer rarely considered his arrow effective beyond one hundred and forty, and found its extreme range limited to three hundred yards; the

* Speed. † Père Daniel, Milice Françoise, tom. i. liv. 4.

Englishman sometimes killed man or horse, at two hundred and forty, and cast his flight shaft a full quarter of a mile.

Drayton, probably availing himself of popular traditions of his own age, has a very remarkable allusion to this amazing vigour of arm. He states that old men encouraged their descendants to join the standard of Henry V. by recounting the valorous deeds of their yeomen ancestors, who fought in the Continental war, and introduces a veteran endeavouring by these arguments to work upon the martial feelings of his son.

> Upon their strength a king his crown might lay,
> Such were the men of that brave age quoth he.
>
> The good old man with tears of joy would tell,
> In Cressy's field, what prizes Edward play'd;
> As what at Poictiers the Black Prince befel,
> How like a lion he about him laid.
>   *   *   *
> "And boy," quoth he, "I've heard thy grandsire say,
> That once he did an English archer see,
> Who shooting at a French, twelve score away,
> Quite through the body nailed him to a tree."

The French had a considerable number of archers at Agincourt*, but the narrow space occupied by their army forbade their being brought into action. After the battle, many carts, laden with bows which had never been even unpacked, fell, with other warlike munitions, into the hands of the victors.

Since then, the history of French archery, in a military point of view, has little to interest our attention: we will now consider it in reference to the destruction of sylvan game.

That pre-eminence in all matters of *vénerie*, by which England is at present distinguished, seems to have been conceded to her by most of the Continental nations five or six centuries ago. Not only were our dogs and horses considered vastly superior to theirs, but our implements of archery were gifts worthy the

---

* Sir N. H. Nicolas's "Agincourt."

acceptance of a monarch. In the reign of the second Richard, Sir Peter Courtney obtained leave from the king to send Northampton herald, and Anlet pursuivant, with the following present to the French court:—Six small (*i. e.* hunting) bows, one sheaf of large arrows, and a sheaf of quarrils, for the crossbow.* These, with a greyhound and other dogs, were intended for the use of the king's head gamekeeper.† Sir Peter Courtney was allied by blood to the royal family of France, which may account for his desire to compliment them with these gifts.

Among the books preserved in the Royal Library at Paris, there is a treatise on the use of the bow in hunting, written about two centuries and a half previous to the "Toxophilus" of of Roger Ascham.

I am not aware that any English writer has made allusion to this curious work; and to the archer corps, for whom chiefly such a subject has attractions, I am convinced it is wholly unknown. Indeed, the whole external aspect of "King Modus" appears so unprepossessing, that, with even a large share of the enthusiasm possessed, more or less, by all bowmen, not one in fifty would have resolution to turn the second page. Let the reader figure to himself a book printed in coarse wooden black letter types of the fourteenth century, filled with vague and constantly recurring abbreviations, and words not only long obsolete, but sometimes changing their orthography three or four times in the course of a dozen lines; he will then properly estimate the difficulty of "doing" the old savage into intelligible English. Having thus interceded for the reader's indulgence, without further preface I will place before him —

---

* The Commons of England, always extremely averse from allowing the exportation of these weapons, petitioned Edward III. that no "French alien priors, be permitted to reside within twenty miles of the coast, to prevent their sending bows and arrows abroad." — *Rolls of Parliament*, 47 Ed. III.

† Prince's "Worthies of Devon."

The Book of King Modus.*

This brief treatise on archery setteth forth how King Modus instructed his scholars that the bow is an instrument not only profitable for recreation, but also for defence. And he likewise taught them, that the man who invented it was named Fermodus, whose son, Triquin, was the best archer that ever lived; and so greatly did he affect this weapon, and the art of shooting in it, and so well had he profited by his father's lessons, that he became marvellously firm and steady in his bow-hand, and could, at every discharge, strike with a bolt an apple placed on the top of a pole at the distance of thirty fathoms or more. And Modus likewise set forth, that when the said Triquin was yet but eight years of age, Fermodus, his father, furnished him with a bow, and taught him the use thereof.

Here follows a particular chapter, entitled "Instructions in the Art of Archery," containing the elements of that exercise as it was anciently practised in France. And now, continues Modus, he taught his son more things respecting the mystery of the bow.

The first was, that the string thereof should be of *silk*, and nothing else, for three reasons: because it is strong and endures a long time without breaking; because, when the threads thereof are properly united together, and well set on, it is so stiff and hard, that it will drive an arrow or bolt farther, and strike a heavier blow, than any string made of flax or hemp; because it can be made of whatever strength and thickness the shooter pleaseth.

The second instruction in archery is, that you endeavour

---

* The author is unknown; but the following extract from the work itself will show that he lived towards the close of the thirteenth, or at the beginning of the fourteenth, century: —

" And on my right hand I saw the King, Charles the Handsome, who hunting one day in the forest of Bertelly, in a thicket called La Boule Gueraldel, took twenty-six wild boars, without a single one escaping." Charles le Bel died in 1328.

always to shoot straight; to which end, be careful, when placing the arrow upon the bow, that the feathers run flat thereon, otherwise your shaft will assuredly fail of the mark.

The third instruction in archery is, that you draw the arrow with three fingers, holding the nock (coche de la flèche) between the forefinger and the next thereto.

The fourth instruction in archery is, that the steel point of your arrow be not too heavy, and that, in ordinary, the feathers thereof be cropped short and low; nevertheless, if it is a weighty shaft, you may shear them proportionably higher and larger.

The fifth instruction in archery is, that your arrow be headed so as the barbs may answer to, and run parallel with, the nock.

The sixth instruction in archery is, that the arrow be ten handsful* in length, measuring from the end of the nock to the barb of the steel head.

The seventh instruction in archery is, that a well made bow ought to have exactly twenty-two handsful between the upper and lower notch.†

The eighth instruction in archery is, that when your bow is braced, there be a full palm and two fingers' breadth between its belly and the string.

The ninth instruction in archery is, that you draw the bow with your right, and hold it in your left, hand.

Then King Modus's scholars demand how archers take stand, to shoot deer in a forest. And Modus replies, this mode of hunting may be practised two ways, either with hounds or without.

When an archer designs to hunt in a thicket where he perceives game is harboured, let him carefully notice from what point the wind cometh, that he may place himself with advantage, and so the animals may not get vent of him. And if several archers follow this chase together in an open country,

---

* The hand is three inches. † Six feet six inches.

they must station themselves much farther apart than where the trees and underwood are more abundant. The chief forester who manages the dogs should be on horseback, and his hounds must be taught to couch and cower down, until he has appointed for each bowman his respective station.

This done, if the cover be large and thick, they must let loose from three to five dogs, according to its extent. Those who are appointed to drive the deer should now talk loudly and call to each other, that they may not attempt to pass between them. When an archer espies a deer approaching his stand, he must order himself after this fashion:—Let him endeavour to keep out of sight as much as possible, while he raises his bow perpendicularly, holding the drawing hand with the arrow ready nocked, directly before his face; and if the animal continue to approach without stopping, he should very silently and cautiously extend his arms, and draw his bow softly, that the arrow may be pulled up to its head, before the game come near; and his bow should be very weak and gentle*, so that he may hold it drawn a reasonable space; and he must pull the bowstring ever to his right ear; and whilst the deer is passing by a few paces, the archer should follow him with his bow, drawing and redrawing the shaft. Then, having made sure of his aim, he is to let fly with a sharp and steady loose.

---

* The following are the rules laid down by Gaston Phebus, that most illustrious Nimrod of ancient France: —

"The sportsman's bow should be of yew, and measure twenty palms (five feet) from one notch to the other, and, when braced, have a hand's breadth between string and wood. The string must ever be of silk. The bow should be weak, because an archer over-bowed cannot take aim freely and with address; besides, such a bow may be held half-drawn a long time without fatigue, whilst the hunter stands in wait for the deer.

"The wood of a well-formed arrow measures eight handsful in length from the end of the nock to the barbs of the head, which will be exactly four fingers broad, from the point of one barb to the point of the other. It must

If the beast come very leisurely, and in a direct line, the hunter must aim his arrow straight at the breast: but if it cross him unexpectedly on the right or left hand, let him shoot in a slanting direction behind the shoulder, about the centre of the ribs, allowing the game to pass him a few paces, as before mentioned.

And now I will set forth why the crafty and cunning archer should ever do thus: for to shoot in any other manner is wholly unsportsmanlike, and a violation of the laws of archery, for these four reasons following:—Firstly; should the arrow pass straight through her body, it may fail to wound a vital part, and the deer will not die near so quickly as when shot obliquely just behind the shoulder, and in the direction of the heart. Secondly; because, having seen the archer, she will make a

---

be duly proportioned in every part, well filed and sharpened, and five fingers in length.[1]

" When a deer is discovered approaching the archers, as soon as they hear the hounds are slipped, they ought to set their arrows on their bows, bringing the two arms into such a position as to be prepared to shoot. For, should the animal espy the men in motion whilst nocking their shafts, he will assuredly escape in another direction. Thus, a keen sportsman is ever cautiously on the alert, ready to let his arrow fly without the slightest motion, except that of drawing with the arms."

He then goes on to describe the different modes of shooting at game in every possible position, somewhat after the fashion of the text; and gives a remarkable reason why an archer should point his shaft in a rather slanting direction when the aim is at the stag's broadside, in preference to straight forwards. He says,—" There is peril to him who shoots directly *at* the side, independently of great uncertainty of killing when the arrow does prove fatal, it sometimes passes through and through the beast, and may thus wound a companion on the opposite side. Such an accident I did myself see once happen to Messire Godfrey de Harcourt, who was pierced through one of his arms."

This is a rough translation, the original being, like old Modus, in very obscure and difficult French.

---

[1] We have here an explanation of the true size of an ancient " broad arrow."

bound, and most probably cause him to miss his aim. Thirdly; from the flurry produced by her sudden appearance, he cannot point his arrow so deliberately as when shooting after her. Fourthly; if the game cross the hunter very swiftly, and at any considerable distance from his stand, the arrow shot in a direct line may fail to reach it before it passes by.

Thus have I explained the reasons why the hunter should manage his bow according to the peculiar circumstances of the case.

And if the deer at which he aimed be struck by the arrow and mortally wounded, the huntsman should whoop loudly for his bloodhound, which is abiding with the other dogs. Let him also blow a note upon his horn, to warn his comrades to cast down the *blinks*.* Should the wound, on the contrary, be only a slight one, not the bloodhound only, but the other dogs must be slipped, the forester on horseback spurring after them with all the speed he may.

And now I will explain how the cunning archer may discover, by the colour of the blood which falls from the stricken deer, whether the wound be fatal or not.

When dark red, and slightly covered with froth, it is a sure token that the arrow has met her in a good place, and she shall die quickly. Item, if the blood be clear and thin, with a few bubbles on its surface, be satisfied that your arrow, having struck upon a bone, has done little hurt. If the game be hit in the belly, then small portions of grass or other food, on which she has been feeding, shall flow with the blood. When this is the case, you may allow her to repose a considerable time before laying on the bloodhound, for two reasons: firstly, because she cannot live long thus; secondly, because where she lyeth down, she will remain, and permit the hunter to take her.

* Branches of trees broken off and thrown upon the paths of a wood, to impede the flight of a wounded deer, and enable the hounds more easily to come up with him.

But if, when you follow with the bloodhound, she should happen to spring up from her lair, loose four or five steady dogs, and you shall see her taken with much pleasure.

If the arrow enter at the loins, she will die in an hour. If at the chine, between two joints, she will void herself and fall, but not die. If among the great ribs, in a slanting direction towards the shoulder, she shall die briefly; but if the arrow points towards the haunches, she shall run a long time. If struck high up behind the shoulders, she shall not die; but if lower down towards the ribs, instant death follows. If in the middle of the neck, death will not ensue; nearer the setting on of the head, your weapon shall be fatal. If the arrow enter right through the neck, three fingers from the shoulders, that is among the vitals, she shall fall instantly. An outside wound in the thick part of the haunch is not mortal; but on the inner part of the same, just the reverse. Lastly, an arrow passing directly through the throat, severs the windpipe, and causes instant death.

A DEVICE HOW TO HUNT IN WOODS AT STAND, WITHOUT A PACK OF DOGS, AND THE MANNER OF IT.

When the archers have taken their stand, as before indicated, the chief forester should station those who are to drive the deer right across the thicket, at a stone's throw from each other; then should they gradually walk towards the archers, whistling and shouting as they proceed, to alarm the herd. And when a deer is struck, he who is inclined to the love of archery should have with him one good dog trained to hunt upon the blood. And farther, I will describe other things peculiar to this mystery. First, then, the bow with which an archer shoots at stand, should be more elastic and easier to draw, than that used by him who shoots at view, or when a beast is in chase, for three reasons: because he who shoots with too strong a bow, will be compelled to incline his body forwards from the tree, and thus expose himself to the view of the approaching game; because he cannot hold the arrow when drawn up to the head, for any length of time; because his bow hand will be unsteady, and his loose uncertain and irregular. These are the reasons why every archer who shoots at stand, should be master of his bow. There are yet other requisites for a chief of the game; viz.: — a file wherewith to make his arrow heads sharp and pointed, some spare strings carried in his pouch, and a coat of green; or, in summer and autumn, of russet colour, resembling that of the woods.

Then King Modus's scholars demand what the second chapter of archery shall contain. And Modus answers, that the second chapter shall treat of killing deer with the bow, by riding in upon them unawares.

When archers go to the forest to take deer after this manner, two horses will be amply sufficient; for where there are more, the game, becoming restless, straightway decamps. Two mounted foresters, skilful in discovering the haunts of deer, each followed by a small party of archers, are to proceed into those glades and open woodlands which afford an easy passage to the horses; and if they discover the herd feeding at a distance, let them ride cautiously one a little in advance of the other. On arriving as near as prudence will admit, both archers and horsemen should stop. The former then station themselves in a semicircle, about a stone's throw apart, and so as to gain the vent* of the beasts; their bows, ready braced, are to be held perpendicularly before the body, with an arrow on the string, the right hand should hold the nock of the arrow before the archer's face, very near to it; and they are to remain in this position, keeping their eyes fixed on the deer. In the mean time, the two mounted foresters, having made a large circuit, on arriving opposite the archers, should walk their horses for-

* Wind.

wards in a direct line. The deer, startled at their appearance, will rush towards the ambuscade, when each bowman, singling out the one which likes him best, discharges his arrow with a cool and deliberate aim. Such as do not fall directly, are tracked by the bloodhound, kept waiting at some convenient spot.

Then King Modus's scholars demand of what the third chapter on archery consists. And Modus replies, that the third chapter treats of shooting deer at view, both on foot and on horseback.

The foot archer who designs to shoot at view, must order himself in the following manner: let him seek the game among the forests, with bow in hand, and shafts buckled under his belt. And here the bow may be much stronger than that used by the archer on horseback, for three reasons: because he will have to take aim from a greater distance; because his mark being a flight shot, he may extend his arms more fully, and lay his body in the bow; because he will have no occasion to hold the arrow drawn up, even for an instant, as he is directed to do when at stand. On discovering a stag, let him forthwith brace his bow, and place an arrow upon the string, approaching him as near as he can; and if the stag raise up his head to gaze around, at that instant must he pull the string to his ear, and having drawn and redrawn the arrow for an instant, to secure his aim, he is then to let fly. If the shot take effect, the archer should speedily fetch his bloodhound from the place where he left it.

The sportsman who shoots at view on horseback, must provide himself with some sober jade, that will, when necessary, remain quiet without moving. As soon as the game is in sight, let him brace his bow, which should be a weak one; then placing his arrow on the string, he is to hold both in his left hand, by throwing the fore-finger over the arrow to secure it, and guide the horse with his right. Then, putting him to the gallop, the archer should make a wide circuit around the whole herd, in order to select the best opening through which to direct his shot. If the deer grow restless and alarmed, which he will be presently aware of, by their raising up their heads, let him halt until they recommence feeding. When he preceives they are quiet, he may approach very cautiously, until in a favourable position for shooting; in other words, until he can discern the side of the fattest of the herd fully exposed to his arrow: let him then halt, and handle his weapons. Now, the skilful archer will so order himself, that he may conveniently draw his bow behind him, and not on one side, or directly in front, supporting himself in the left stirrup, which should be a little shorter than the other. Let him shoot with all his force, drawing the arrow fully up to its head, and levelling his bow-hand at the spot where he wishes to pierce the game. If the shot be fatal, he may go and seek his bloodhound, as before said, or slip his deer dogs, which latter will be better able to pull down the stag, in case he be but slightly hurt.

King Modus's scholars demand of what the fourth chapter on archery is to consist. And Modus replies, the fourth chapter treats of shooting in covert during the prevalence of windy weather.

The best season is from the middle of August to the middle of September, for two causes; because in these months deer are yet in full season; and because they go forth very early in the morning, and bray so loudly at one another, as to be heard afar off. A strong wind, accompanied by rain, is, for two causes, the most favourable weather for this kind of shooting: the deer being then more a-foot, and less able to discern the archer, by reason of the force of the wind. Let the hunter proceed alone, early in the morning, creeping from stand to stand, through the overgrown bushes of that part of the forest where he suspects the game is harboured. Having got sight of a stag, he cannot be too wary; if seen, it is all over with him, his shot is spoiled. But should he succeed in creeping unperceived within range, let him kneel behind a bush, and there brace his bow; then placing an arrow on the string, he is to hold both of them in the left hand, while with each blast of wind he changes his position, taking notice if the animal continues to feed.

When two stags are braying and fighting together, the hunter may approach exceedingly near; indeed, it often happens that they are so blinded by fury as to be easily killed with a sword. And when the archer has got so near that he cannot possibly miss, let him move cautiously from his hiding-place and discharge his arrow. This is best done whilst kneeling on one knee, the bow being short and weak. He should hold a small green branch in his mouth to conceal his features, and the habit he wears must be the colour of the woods.

In a country well covered with lofty trees, stalking will afford the archer much diversion. Procure a piece of linen sufficiently large to admit the figure of a hind * being painted on it, and fasten its extremities to a couple of poles, like those of a stalking horse. The hunter keeps this device extended, while he advances very cautiously down wind upon the deer, which he discovers by looking through the eyelet-holes made in its centre. Let him creep from tree to tree under cover of his disguise, until within bow-shot; then fixing the poles in the ground, so that the painted deer may be fairly displayed, let him rise cautiously and shoot over the upper edge of the cloth. This is a very agreeable mode of hunting, and the archer cannot fail of sport in a country tolerably well furnished with stags.

King Modus's scholars demand what is the pastime of shooting wild boars at soil.† And Modus replies, that to shoot at soil is the fifth chapter of archery, and the finest sport a single archer can enjoy.

The proper season extends from mid-October to the end of

---

* The female stag.

† " At soil," *i. e.*, whilst wallowing in the mire.

November. And now it is proper the archer be informed that "a soil," in hunter's language, means a standing pool of mud and water. Thither the boars assemble while roaming in search of food, to drink, wallow, and rest therein.

Having discovered such a place, look out some moderately sized tree, growing on the edge of the water, and as nearly as possible opposite to the path by which wild boars make their approach. Then select a bough of four forks, a couple of feet at least from the ground, which may serve for a seat. And now I will inform you why it is necessary to be placed thus high. Rest assured, if the wild boars are near, either with the wind or against it, they will neither see nor smell the hunter, who is lifted above the ground. Mount then, to your seat, with your bow ready bent, and a good tough-shafted arrow, well headed and sharpened. Keep good watch, looking narrowly around, and there is a certainty of sport, for not only wild boars, but every other description of game, will pass by your hiding place, and you may kill them quite at hand; more especially the former, for they will dash into the pool, and wallow therein before your eyes.

Lastly, King Modus's scholars demand what is the pleasure of shooting hares sitting. And Modus replies, that to kill a hare on her form* is a pleasant diversion in a favourable country.

The season for this sort of hunting is the month of April, when hares resort at daybreak to the green corn, to feed thereon. Let the archer mount on horseback, and ride forth, bow in hand, with a varlet at his side, leading a brace or a leash of greyhounds. Then let him ride up and down the corn, until he espy a hare, when the hounds are to be placed in front, that the sight of them may occupy her attention. And as soon as she sees the dogs, straitway will she tap with her foot among the corn, a sure sign

* " Ah! the poaching old savage!" exclaim our sportsmen.

that she is squatting close: then make a wide circuit, with the bent bow in your left hand, and an arrow nocked upon the string; draw up and shoot, without stopping the horse; and know, that as soon as the hare espies the dogs, she will allow the hunter to approach as near as he listeth. This is a marvellously pleasant amusement in a country abounding with hares.

And now my friends and pupils, ye will be duly qualified and skilled to practise and enjoy all the pastime which I and Queen Raco have taught; provided ye give heed unto our words.

Thus far the Book of King Modus. Altogether, it may be considered an interesting production; nothing similar existing among the literature of our own country.

There are at present, in the suburbs of Paris, one or two feeble " réunions des Tireurs," as the modern French term our bow-meetings. Yet, not a few of their nobles of the last age practised archery during the usual summer sojourn at their maisons de campagne, and green alleys, decked with flower-beds, and having butts at each extremity, may still be found within the precincts of many a dilapidated château. Those familiar with Chantilly and its magnificent forest, will remember a double set, for shooting the eight and twelve rood lengths, which stand upon *La Pelouse*, a delightful range of lawn attached to that now untenanted edifice, once the palace of the " great Condé."

In Belgium one rarely sees a village, never certainly a market town, unprovided with a tall mast for the exercise of an amusement common to nearly the whole male population, from 12 to 70 years of age. Of the younger people's dexterity, I witnessed many pleasant examples, especially when disembarking one very delightful July evening at Ostend, from the treckskuyt, which plies between that city and Bruges. A merry party of youngsters were amusing themselves shooting at a small wooden bird, the size of a sparrow, perched upon the summit of a tall pole, which stands upon the magnificent canal bank. They used bolts tipped with horn, as, indeed, all Flemish arrows are; in this case, about the circumference of a shilling. I loitered near, an interested spectator of course; since, if truth be spoken, my five weeks' ramble through Brabant, terminating at Ostend, had been projected under the influence of pure toxomania.* After many clever shots, the bolt belonging to one juvenile got entangled in the small cord, contrived for replacing their popinjay upon its perch without the trouble of an ascent. Seeing this, a little brown visaged, curly pated urchin, scarcely twelve years old, but perfectly equipped for the sport, set himself to bring down the lost shaft. Accordingly, he adjusted his aim with the adroitness of an old hand, and, releasing the imprisoned bolt, at a second attempt, sent it spinning, in company with his own, to the distance of a dozen yards. That lovely summer's eve, the broad and glassy bosom of the magnificent Canal de Bruges, the beautiful little lawn, on which stood the tall white maypole, are associated in my recollections with the pigmy archer's feat, and have helped to impress it there.

Flemish bows and arrows are truly excellent. For perfect straightness and seasoning, with beauty of feathers, the latter cannot be surpassed. In their bows they are a little fanciful; I saw many formed of two pieces, united by an iron hinge; and to construct them so as to be put together like the joints of an angling rod, seems a favourite fancy. In most Flemish bows, the upper horn is of beautiful and even classical form, imitating the heads of swans, griffins, snakes, &c. &c.

Archery prevails very generally throughout Brabant, and that portion of French Flanders bordering upon it. I recollect,

* May not toxomania, or bow-madness, be as legitimate a coinage as the bibliomania of Dr. Frognal Dibdin?

whilst seated in a carriage which rumbles along between Paris and Brussels, to have seen a stalwort peasant unbending a magnificent yew bow, nearly seven feet in height, at the door of a woodbined road-side cottage. It was about dusk, in the month of July, and apparently, he had just returned from shooting "matches and masteries," as did our merry English yeomen five centuries ago. In butt practice, they rarely exceed seventy paces, the distance between the Ostend marks; which, by the bye, are dated 1673, and made of haulm straw, set endways, and pressed tightly.

At Brussels you find butts of earth, well rammed and moistened daily, within flower gardens, at the rear of many an auberge in that town. The archers shoot under a portico at each end, passing from mark to mark by a second alley bordered with frequent knots of the gaudy tulip; so, there being no danger, the sport never stands still. A small sheet of cartridge paper, which I have often brought away as a trophy, forms the mark, for most of the elders loose their arrows with the precision of riflemen. They shoot games, and a flagon of "Louvain," or "bonne bierre double," forms their stake. Every town has similar companies, and similar accommodations, together with their salles des archiers, often very tastefully embellished. Those of Ghent, Bruges, and Antwerp, are worth a visit; there being, four fraternities existing in the latter place: —

> The Ancient Company of Bowyers.
> The Modern Company of Bowyers.
> The Ancient Company of Bowmen.
> The Modern Company of Bowmen.

Ghent has two celebrated toxophilite societies, respectively styled, the Knights of St. Sebastian[*], and St. George. The former wear an uniform of green, the latter of scarlet cloth.

---

[*] St. Sebastian, the patron saint of archers, owing to his martyrdom by arrows.

Independently of frequent assemblies for ordinary practice, there is an annual rendezvous of all the archers of Ghent, Bruges, and the surrounding towns, villages, and hamlets, which lasts for several days. A hundred lofty poles are erected in the suburbs, to receive the same number of popinjays, of which each society produces its own; and for the chief prize, the wooden bird is elevated to a height equalling that of the cathedral. The crossbow, still popular in Brabant and the rest of Flanders, is used in the contest for this principal stake; and the bowman who strikes the popinjay from its iron peg, gains a certain number of napoleons, besides a superb gold cup or medal. With these he returns into the city, at the head of his brethren, with drums beating, trumpets sounding, colours flying, and all the pride, pomp, and circumstance of triumphal archery. There he is duly fêted and feasted; and after gratifying his friends and kindred with a sight of the precious trophy, he deposits it in the Archery Saloon of his native town, in commemoration of victory; there are also many inferior prizes, such as watches, gold keys, chains, and pieces of silver plate, distributed to competitors in shooting with the bow. These knights of St. George and St. Sebastian also give splendid fêtes and balls to the ladies of their acquaintance during the period of this celebration, and attend mass at the cathedral in full costume. Indeed the whole spectacle is grand and imposing, and realises our ideas of those ancient festivities, " when English kings and princesses, with the lords and ladies of their court, patronised similar manly exhibitions, to welcome in

<blockquote>The merry month of May.</blockquote>

SECTION VI.

THE CROSSBOW.

> I'm clad in youthful green, I other colours scorn;
> My silken baldric bears my bugle or my horn,
> Which setting to my lips, I wind so loud and shrill,
> As makes the echoes shout from every neighbouring hill.
> My dog-hook at my belt, to which my lyman's tied;
> My sheaf of arrows bright, my wood-knife at my side;
> My crossbow in my hand, my gaffle* on the rack
> To bend it when I please; or if I list, to slack.
> My hound then in my lyam, I by the woodman's art,
> Forecast where I may lodge the goodly hie palmed hart.
>   *   *   *   *
> The sylvans are my true subjects—I their king!

THE longbow was the national weapon of England; the arbalist, or crossbow, of the French, Flemings, Germans, Italians, and Spaniards. In describing the latter, therefore, I shall chiefly confine myself to its practice among those nations.

This instrument, anciently used both in war and the chase, is but a modification of the longbow, the latter being a simple, the former a very complicated weapon. The crossbow, properly so called, was unknown to the ancients, though they had something like it in the Balista.

In the brief description of Père Daniel, it is treated merely as a weapon of war; so Alonzo Martinez de Espinar, the author of a delightful Spanish work on field sports, must be considered the only real historian of this arm comparatively so little known in modern times.†

---

* A lever for bending the steel bow of an arbalist.

† Arte de Ballesteria y Monteria en Madrid, en la emprenta real, 1644. 4to. Sir S. R. Meyrick, the great antiquarian of our own country, should also be consulted.

THE CROSSBOW. 227

The oldest specimens now in use, are those of the Chevaliers Tireurs d'Anneci, in Savoy. This society, formerly called the Jolly Companions, is so ancient that the period of its institution is entirely lost. Their exercises were sanctioned by a patent from Prince Philip of Savoy, dated the 15th of May, 1519; and cotemporary with them there existed at Chamberry a fraternity which obtained a similar charter from Duke Manuel Philiberg, about fifty years afterwards.

There were formerly as many companies of crossbowmen in the principal cities of France, as there are of riflemen at the present day; and in some of its northern towns, and in Brabant, these two arms are still practised alternately. According to archives preserved in the Town Hall at Lisle, a fraternity of crossbowmen flourished there as far back as 1379, and was suppressed by an ordinance of Council, about half a century subsequently, during the reign of Francis I., its property and possessions being given to the chief hospital of that town.

Similar societies still exist at Lennoy, Le Quesnoy, Comines, and at Roulaix, a little town one league from Lisle, instituted by Pierre de Roulaix, lord of that place, in 1491. Those of Valenciennes and Douay are only very recently abolished, companies of cannoniers, archers, and riflemen, commonly called jouers des armes, having arisen in their stead.

There are exercises with the great and with the little crossbow; the first being weapons of a very large size, which contest the prizes at much longer distances than the second. At La Basée, and Hautbourdin, near Lisle, the arbalisters have adopted the smaller kind, in imitation of several societies at Antwerp, Gand, Bruges, Louvain, Malines, Alost, &c.

Besides the hand crossbow, there were anciently others, of monstrous proportions, called *arbalétes de passe*, or *ribeaudequins*. This appellation, according to Fauchet*, belonged

---
* Antiq. Gauloises.

to an enormous engine, the lathe * of which measured twelve or fifteen feet. It was fixed upon a stock of proportionate length, and at least a foot in diameter, containing a groove sufficient to receive an arrow, or rather javelin, of two fathoms, winged with thin leaves of horn, or some kind of light wood.

These huge contrivances were permanently fixed on the walls of towns, castles, forts, &c. To bend them, a windlass, managed by one, two, three, or even four men, according to their magnitude, was necessary. Their arrows flew with prodigious violence, frequently traversing the bodies of several successive men.

Many modern crossbows are constructed with a stock, similar in shape and dimensions to that of the common fowling piece. Our ancestors generally preferred them straight, and much longer; and in taking aim, rested the stock upon the shoulder, while its extreme end projected behind †; a method retained by most of the before-mentioned Continental societies. A few, however, not only substitute the gun-stock for the ancient tiller, but have made many alterations in other parts of this weapon. Thus, at Valenciennes, instead of the old-fashioned nut for receiving the string turning on a pivot when the trigger was pulled, they have a notch in the stock itself, and the cord is confined there by a flat piece of steel, opening and shutting like a valve. To free the string and discharge the arrow, it is only necessary to touch a trigger which communicates with a spring within the body of the stock.

Having given this brief description of the French crossbow, ancient and modern, I will next remark upon the arrows discharged from it. Of these there are several kinds, differing greatly from each other, in length, thickness, manner of feather-

---

* Lathe, steel bow.

† In a collection of old engravings after Stradia, illustrative of the chase, entitled "Venationes Ferarum," 1562, we see a sportsman shooting in this attitude.

ing, and shape of their heads. Some were winged with horn, some with leather. Others, again, had merely three triangular projections, of the same wood of which the arrow was made. The heads of many were exceedingly sharp; many resembled a lozenge, being obtuse, and indented at the sides. All these bolts * receive different names, according to their form; as, vire, vireton, sagette, garrot, bougon, &c., and they are usually only half the length of the long-bow arrow, which in France measured two feet and a half. The wood was of various kinds; in the statutes of the Gunmakers' Company of Paris, formed about the middle of the sixteenth century, it is recorded that the chef d'œuvre of the master of that company was a crossbow complete, with its gaffle†, a dozen well-brazed quarrils, duly and properly made of good seasoned yew, and a quiver for the arrows, garnished with a cover.

It now remains to treat of the purposes to which the arbalist was applied. And here, making little reference to its warlike character, I shall confine my remarks to the more pleasing considerations connected with sylvan sport. The principles of its construction, and the requisite attention on the part of the

---

* " Bolt in Tun," — the sign of a well-known London tavern. Few persons are aware that it represents a crossbowman's target. A tun or barrel of wine, sometimes of ale, being set upon a wooden horse, the shooter aimed at the bung, which was rubbed over with chalk. If his arrow pierced it, he had the liquor, and sometimes that of many others, for his reward. When properly represented, the sign should be a barrel with an arrow sticking in it.

> What is the wager? said the Queen,
>   That must I know here:
> Three hundred ton of Rhenish wine,
>   Three hundred ton of beer;
> Three hundred of the fattest harts
>   That run on Dallom Lea; &c.
>   *Ballad of Queen Katharine.*

† A contrivance for bending the steel bow.

workman to form a perfect crossbow, will be accurately detailed.

It appears that the arbalist was formerly in Spain what the long bow was in our own country — the popular amusement of all ranks. By no other European nation was it brought to so high a degree of perfection, and none more excelled in its use. Espinar has preserved the names and marks of those ancient Spanish crossbow-makers who acquired a high degree of consideration in their art; though, it may be observed, there were very few who could make the entire instrument. While one set of artisans devoted themselves to the construction of the steel bow (verger), others only made the stock (tablero), and the bender (gafa). The manufacture of arrows was likewise a distinct branch of the art. These, as in France, bore names indicative of their form; — verote, jara, sostrore, passadore, &c.

A Spanish crossbow, when intended for the chase, generally measured two feet in length. The stock in its most ancient form was square and somewhat flat, tapering gradually towards the extremity. It is thus represented in a collection of costumes belonging to the fourteenth and fifteenth centuries, preserved in the royal cabinet of engravings at Paris.

As all sportsmen cannot accommodate themselves to one level, some crossbows had stocks perfectly straight, whilst others were slightly curved from the nut to the extremity of the butt. The former appear to be most favourable to correct shooting. Their mode of taking aim with the straight stock was this: whilst the sportsman's left hand supported the upper end of the crossbow, he grasped the butt with his right, placing the thumb above, and the forefinger below upon the trigger; the thumb was then drawn just sufficiently under the eye to enable the shooter to discern the head of his quarril. On covering his mark he pressed the trigger, and away flew the arrow. The crossbow with a crooked stock was not raised to the eye, but to the cheek; a difference easily comprehended by those familiar with the effects of a greater or less curvature in the stock of a modern fowlingpiece.

In a perfect crossbow, the recoil against the sportsman's cheek is so trifling as not in the least to incommode him. Espinar expresses this quality by the word *sobrosa*, — gentle, agreeable. Its trigger should be easy, and not liable to go off accidentally when the string is stretched upon the nut. The lathe must be truly and accurately proportioned, for therein a crossbow's principal excellence consists; from this its force and certainty are derived: for when the quarril twists and wabbles, instead of flying straight, not only will its range be greatly diminished, but the sportsman is never secure of his shot.

This fault may arise from various causes; as when, through the ignorance or carelessness of the workmen, the bow is not well fitted in the stock, one of its arms being higher than the other. The force of the impulsion on either side is then unequal; and the higher arm, being mistress of the other, disorders the quarril's flight. If this disparity be considerable, there results from it another capital inconvenience. Owing to the bow not lying level, the string will never strike the arrow exactly in the middle, and the aim, however correctly taken, must be unsuccessful in consequence. It is also of primary importance that the notch in the nut of the crossbow hold the string exactly at its centre, so that the mark which the nut impresses on it, trespass not the breadth of a horsehair on one side more than on the other.

There are many other defects; as when the cord, pressing too tightly on the surface of the stock, diminishes the power of the arms of the bow, prevents their playing freely, and causes the cord to act not upon the centre of the quarril's butt, but lower down. The reverse of this fault is equally disadvantageous to its flight. In the one case, it will go whirling and wriggling through the air; in the other it is forced downwards, and quickly falls to the earth. Finally, a crossbow will shoot incorrectly, when there is any considerable friction of the arrow upon the surface of the stock. The ancient arbalister was very particular upon this point. Whilst the butt of his quarril rested in the notch of the nut, he took care that its head only should be upon the upper end of the stock, none of the intermediate portion coming in contact with it.

The point-blank range of an ordinary crossbow was twenty-five paces. At thirty, the arrow began to lose its force, and to descend; this was, of course, in proportion to the strength and goodness of the bow. The weaker sort, at merely an increase of five paces in the distance, dropt the arrow two fingers' breadth; the stronger, one finger only. The crossbowman, by repeated trials, made himself thoroughly acquainted with the range of his weapon, and levelled higher or lower according to the distance of his mark.

The next question which naturally arises is, what was the remotest flight of a bolt discharged from a well-constructed arbaliste de chasse. According to the Spanish author, it would kill at one hundred and fifty paces, or more. The military crossbow, of much larger dimensions, threw an arrow considerably further, killing man or horse two hundred paces off. " Our archers and crossbowmen," says the author of the " Discipline Militaire," " will slay a naked man, ten or even twenty score further off than the best arquebusiers; even harness, if not very strong, will at that distance be unable to resist their quarrils." A celebrated modern French sportsman remarks, that this statement is by no means an exaggerated one. He adds, that Mons. the Abbe Collomb, canon of Anneci, to oblige him and gratify his curiosity, caused several of the best crossbows belonging to the society of archers there to be tried before him. Certain of them, at a very small elevation, threw the arrow four hundred paces; others three hundred and twenty, the smallest distance being two hundred and sixty. These shots were measured by the ordinary military pace of from eighteen to twenty inches.* The reader, however, will bear in mind that I am here speaking of the French arbalist. In the Dunstable Chronicle, preserved in the Harleian collection of MSS. No. 24., it is stated, that Henry V. came to the city of Rouen by forty rods length, within shot of quarril. The rod is five and a half yards. †

Fire-arms doubtless possess some advantages over the crossbow, being more manageable, as well as more rapid in their discharge. Yet there is one characteristic which gives a decided superiority to the latter: I mean its silent discharge, which enables the hunter to get a second, and even a third shot, should the first be unsuccessful, or the game abundant on any particular spot. Dominique Boccamazza, who wrote a treatise on field-sports applicable to the country around Rome‡, complains that the use of the arquebuse had so alarmed and dispersed all animals of the deer kind, that the sportsmen of his day rarely returned home satisfied with their chase.

When the ancient Spanish huntsman used the crossbow for the destruction of the larger species of game, he shot with poisoned arrows, prepared by steeping their points in the expressed juice of white hellebore, veratrum album, gathered in the month of August. Like the vegetable poisons used by the barbarous nations of Africa and South America, it produces death by coagulation of the blood, and however slightly the animal may be wounded, its operation is so sudden, that the victim never flies beyond 150 or 200 paces, and expires in a few minutes.

---

* This proves the inferiority of the arbalist to the old, and even to the modern, English long bows. He is, indeed, a weak-armed archer who cannot drive a flight-shaft 450 of the paces described in the text. Many a ladies' bow (English I mean), will beat the two last-mentioned distances.

† Sir S. R. Meyrick.

‡ Caccie della Campagna di Roma, cioè della Trasteverina, dell' Isola de Latio, &c. &c. Roma, 1548. 4to.

For this reason, the white hellebore is still called yerta da ballestero, or crossbow plant, by the country people of Spain, who are proverbially tenacious of ancient usages.

It is generally asserted by those who have treated upon missile weapons in use previous to the invention of gunpowder, that the custom of poisoning arrows never prevailed in Europe. Espinar, however, has thus set the question at rest, as far as relates to his own countrymen; though there is good reason for believing the practice was confined to Spain. Neither Modus, nor Phebus Comte de Foix, make mention of it in their circumstantial details of the chase of the boar, the wolf, and the stag. It is true, they speak of the long bow, and not of the arbalist; but if poisoned arrows had at all been familiar to the sportsmen of France, they were as applicable to the former as to the latter.

The crossbow, then, before the invention of fire-arms, formed the chief dependance of the hunter. It was in much more general use than the long bow, over which it possessed the advantage of shooting further*, and with a truer aim. The sportsman could also adjust to it arrows of various descriptions, according to the species of game of which he was in pursuit.

It will be readily understood what extreme accuracy of aim belonged to those who prided themselves on their expertness with this weapon. To strike an object with the crossbow bolt is infinitely more difficult than with a single rifle ball. As the crossbowman never shot flying †, and very rarely at running game, a setter dog was infinitely more necessary for him than for the modern fowler, especially when in pursuit

---

* This remark applies only to French and Spanish archery. In England the long bow has ever maintained its superiority.

† Although they certainly never shot flying with the crossbow, yet, attached to a MS. copy of the "Marson Rustique du Laboureur des Champs," a work of the fourteenth century, there is a vignette representing a crossbowman aiming at a bird in the air; but it is only a fancy of the engraver.

of the hare or partridge. To train and break this dog required the utmost skill and patience; and even when the animal was brought under a proper degree of subjection, his sagacity availed little, unless his master also possessed a natural quickness of eye to discover the game through all its concealment, while the dog held it at point; besides which, many little expedients, with much adroitness and precaution, were requisite to obviate defects it was scarcely possible to remedy altogether. Yet the crossbow continued to survive the invention of the arquebuse, even for a considerable period after the latter was rendered far more manageable than at its first introduction. In Spain, and also in Italy, they made occasional use of it during the seventeenth century. Espinar repeatedly alludes to the crossbow, when describing certain royal hunting-matches at which he was present, and he tells us that Philip IV. of Spain, to whom he acted as gunbearer, had in his service a maker of these weapons, called John de Lostra. As to Italy, we see frequent representations of huntsmen armed with the crossbow in the plates attached to Olina's Natural History of Birds, A.D. 1622; and in a Treatise on the Chase, by Eugenio Raimondi, published in 1626. Salnovius, the author of a book on hunting well known in France, who wrote during the reign of Louis XIII., complains that, in his time, the sovereigns of Europe killed the noble hart and fallow-deer with the crossbow and fusil, instead of manfully chasing them with hound and horn, as their ancestors were wont to do.

Although this weapon has now been superseded by the fowlingpiece, in Spain, as elsewhere, the word ballastero, or crossbowman, is still there used to signify a sportsman. Its application, however, is not indiscriminate. For instance, they call him who occupies himself only in the chase of small game, cozador. Montero, is a hunter who pursues the stag, the fallow-deer, and the wild boar, on horseback, with dogs and gun; for, owing to the mountainous character of Spanish landscape, they are unable to run the game down, as in more level countries. But ballestero, is one expert and skilled in every description of chase, great and small; or, as we express it, a thorough-bred sportsman. It has been remarked that shooting with the crossbow was more followed, brought to greater perfection, and attended with higher honours in Spain, than in any other European country. Indeed, by an enactment of James I. of that country, no knight's son, not being a knight himself, or a crossbowman, was deemed worthy to sit at table with knights or their ladies.*

Hitherto, I have spoken only of the crossbow for discharging bolts or quarrils. It remains briefly to describe that called in French, arc à gallet; or, in England, the rodd, or stone-bow. They were of a much lighter, and, in many respects, of a construction very different from the others, the stock in its upper part being either hollowed out, or formed into a semicircle. The cord was double, its two portions being separated right and left by little cylinders of ivory placed at equal distance between the two horns and centre of the bow. In the middle of this cord, was a contrivance for holding the ball, called purse or cradle in English; in French, la fronde, or the sling. To charge the weaker sort of stone bows, the hands alone suffice; but for the stronger, a bender is as necessary as for those intended to cast arrows.

The stone-bow was used to kill small birds, as thrushes, blackbirds, larks, ortolans, or, at the utmost, partridges and quails. Espinar, who enters so fully into every detail connected with the arbalist properly so called, says not a word of the stone-bow, as if he disdained to speak of a thing so insignificant.

Several of our ancient English dramatists were less fastidious;

* See Sir S. R. Meyrick's work on armour.

in Shakspeare's "Twelfth Night, or What you Will," Sir Toby exclaims—

> O, for a stone-bow! to hit him in the eye. — *Act* ii. *sc.* 5.

Children will shortly take him for a wall, and set their stone-bows in his forehead. — FLETCHER's *King and no King.*

Who ever will hit the mark of profit, must be like those who shoot with stone-bows, wink with one eye. — MARSTON's *Dutch Courtezan.*

I will now present the reader with a translated passage from Le Plaisir des Champs *, a poem by Claude Gauchet D'Ampmartinois. It minutely describes the manner by which the ancient sportsman manœuvred his stone-bow: —

> Lors, avec l'arbalestre à la main, je m'approche,
> Je bonde, et le boulet dans le fronde j'encoche;
> Et l'œillet dans le noix; puis par le trou je voy,
> Et le merle et le point; alors m'arrestant coy,
> Je desserre la clef. La serre se desbande,
> Et l'arc se rejette avecque force grande,
> Envoye en l'air le plomb qui vers l'oiseau dresse,
> L'atteinet, el l'abat mort, d'oultre en oultre perce.

Then, with stone-bow in hand, I draw near, and placing a bullet in its sling†, and the loop upon the nut of the lock, I bend it. Through the little sight-hole therein, I espy my blackbird, and having covered her with the bead, I touch the trigger. The spring flies; and the steel bow, recoiling with prodigious force, drives the ball through the yielding air, directly towards the bird. It strikes; and, O lucky shot! my game falls to the ground, pierced through and through.

Should there be, as I suspect, no poetical exaggeration here, the bow must have been a very extraordinary one, to pierce

* Paris, 4to. 1583.
† La fronde has been explained already. The loop, which lies immediately behind it, is slipped over a hook at the moment of drawing down the lever. The stone-bow has also a single bead strained across an iron fork at the end of the stock. With this the marksman covers his game, looking through a small hole made for that purpose in a part of the lock.

even so small an object through and through. It may be remarked, that Gauchet speaks of the leaden bullet, instead of a clay ball; because, perhaps, plomb, a monosyllable, agreed better than boulet, with the measure of his verse. In the sixteenth century, the stone-bow was charged with clay balls and pebbles only, as its name imports.

The rodd is still commonly seen in the shops of the gunmakers, both in London and the north of England. Warrington retains its ancient celebrity for manufacturing the steel part or lathe, whence, or from the Continent, the crossbow makers of London, who rarely made any, had their supply. To the latter kind, there is an allusion in Harris's *Ariosto* : —

> But as a strong and justly temper'd bow
> Of Pyrmont steel, the more you do it bend,
> Upon recoil doth give the bigger blow,
> And doth with greater force the quarril send, &c.

John Paston, writing to his brother, thus expresses his uncertainty of getting some necessary repairs done to some arbalists, which belonged to himself and several other members of his family : —

" Also, sir, we poor sans derniers (moneyless men) of Caister have broken three or four steel bows; wherefore we beseech you, if there be any maker of steel bows in London which is very cunning, that ye will send me word, and I shall send you the bows that be broken, which be your own great bow, and Robert Jackson's bow, and John Pampeny's bow; these three last have cast so many calvys, that they shall never cast quarrils till they be new made." A pun seems here to be intended. To cast calves, means to kill enemies; styled calves in contempt. Quarrils are square-headed arrows.

When the bead, which answers to the sight on the muzzle of a fowlingpiece, is properly set, these modern stone-bows shoot with the greatest nicety. About twelve years ago, an individual at Liverpool made a considerable bet, that he would break a wine-glass with a bullet discharged from one of them, at the distance of sixteen paces. So far the feat involved nothing marvellous. The most singular part of the affair was, that any man could be found sufficiently foolhardy to place this glass upon his head, and stand with his face towards the shooter who aimed at it! The bet, however, was duly won; the glass having been broken into fragments, without the slightest injury to him who acted target. I have myself known persons whom practice had rendered astonishingly expert, even with the ordinary crossbow of ancient times. Such was a late head keeper of Lord de Clifford, at King's Weston, Gloucestershire, who rarely failed to strike down two rooks out of three with the common bird-bolt, shot from a rodd which appeared to have been made about two centuries ago.

This instrument was well known to Englishmen more than two centuries ago. A traveller who visited the western coast of Africa about that period, relates with considerable glee how he astonished the natives by his expertness with this instrument. "I have," says he, "with my stone or pellet bow, in two hours, killed twenty pigeons, even among the houses, which manner of shooting they had in wonderful admiration."* By the exercise of some little taste and ingenuity, the young archer may construct himself, or get constructed, a crossbow entirely of wood, far preferable to one of steel, which shall throw a bolt with effect thrice the distance shot by any common fowlingpiece. It will answer admirably for rabbit-shooting in a warren.

The great military crossbow, introduced into England by the Normans, was never very popular with our Saxon ancestors.† Their princes of foreign race, however, held it in the

* Golden Trade, or Discoverie of the River Gambia, 1623, p. 156.
† In the thirteenth century they charged 3s. 8d. for an English crossbow, and 1s. 6d. per hundred for its quarrils. Even in this age of gunpowder,

highest estimation. William the Conqueror was an expert arbalister; and it is very remarkable that Rufus and Cœur de Lion, two of his immediate descendants, both equally skilful, should have died by it.

During his expedition to Palestine, the favoured crossbow was Richard's constant companion in the field, and with it he caused many a haughty Saracen to bite the dust, from off the lofty towers of renowned Ascalon. Even when wasted with a burning fever, and incapable of taking an active part in the game of war, he exhibited a singular proof of his predilection for this weapon. Having caused an immense shed to be constructed of strong planks, he ordered it to be pushed forward to the trenches, and thus protected, his engineers continued to work in security. Thither, also, was Richard himself carried on a silken mattress; and there he pointed and discharged his crossbow, killing and wounding a number of the enemy. Observing a Saracen parading the fortifications, clothed in the armour of a valiant Christian knight, he levelled his weapon so accurately that the quarril buried itself in the bosom of the presumptuous miscreant.*

Richard owed his death to a singular accident. A vassal of the crown turned up a golden statue of Minerva, whilst ploughing a field in the province of Compeigne. Willing to secure a portion of this valuable discovery, he divided it into halves, and sent one of them to the king, who, as superior lord, conceived he had a right to the whole, and despatched a haughty message to the French nobleman, commanding its instant surrender. The order not being obeyed, Richard went over to Normandy, and having assembled a body of troops, laid

---

we could not purchase such of the former as have survived the corroding tooth of age for twenty times that sum.

* *Miscreant*, unbeliever. — Vinesauf, p. 338. Sir S. R. Meyrick, Ancient Armour.

siege to the castle of Chalus, where he understood this treasure was concealed. Whilst riding alone round the walls, to ascertain where the assault might be commenced with the best prospect of success, he was aimed at from a turret, by Bertram de Jourdan, a famous crossbowman, who formed one of the garrison. The practised ear of Richard enabled him to distinguish the twang of the bowstring. He instinctively bent forward over his horse's head, in the hope of avoiding the shot; and but for this precaution, the arrow would have struck his head, instead of his shoulder. In itself, the wound was not dangerous; but the square pyramidal head of the quarril rendered its extraction an operation of great skill and patience. Unhappily, there was no regular surgeon in attendance, and the individual who attempted to cut it out, so rankled the wound, that mortification ensued. Whilst thus lying in the agonies of death, word was brought that the place had been carried by assault. Richard instantly ordered the archer who had shot him to be singled out and brought into his presence, and writhing in agony, turned round to demand what injury he had done him, that he should seek his life.

"You slew," retorted the captive, "with your own hands, my father and my two brothers, and you intended to hang me. I am now in your power, and my tortures may give you revenge; but I shall endure them with pleasure, happy in the consciousness of having rid the world of a tyrant."

Liberty and a munificent present were the return made by the hero for these bitter taunts of his destroyer. But De Jourdan was never permitted to enjoy either; for Marcadee, a brutal mercenary, who commanded a portion of the besiegers, enraged at this unlooked-for termination of the expedition, ordered the poor crossbowman to be flayed alive, and then

> Hanged to feed the crow,
> Spite of his arrows and his bow.

> But see the man whose mad ambition gave
> A waste for beasts, denied himself a grave.
> Stretch'd on the land, his second hope survey;
> At once the chaser and at once the prey.
> Lo, Rufus tugging at the deadly dart,
> Bleeds on the forest like a wounded hart.

That the King fell by the hand of Sir Walter Tyrrel, his bow-bearer, is a fact pretty generally known. The following details of that catastrophe, chiefly derived from tradition, may by their novelty amuse the reader.

Charningham, one of the wildest and most romantic portions of the New Forest, is, by oral and written testimony, assigned as the spot where Rufus received his death wound. Here, until within a little more than the last half century, stood the decayed and mutilated remains of that ancient oak from which the fatal arrow is said to have glanced towards its victim's breast. Almost every visitant to this tree endeavoured to carry off some fragment in memory of his having been there; and it seemed probable that the spot would be eventually forgotten, unless some more lasting memorial were raised.* With this view, the then Lord de la Warre, forest-ranger, living in one of the neighbouring lodges, caused a triangular pillar to be erected, bearing the following legends:—

I.

Here stood the oak tree, on which an arrow shot by Sir Walter Tyrrel at a stag, glanced and struck William II., surnamed Rufus, in the breast; of which stroke he instantly died, on the 2nd August 1100.

II.

William II. being thus slain, was laid in a cart belonging to one Purkiss, and drawn from hence to Winchester, and buried in the cathedral church of that city.

* A fragment of Rufus's oak, is or was preserved in the Litchfield Museum.

III.

That the spot where an event so memorable occurred, might not hereafter be unknown, this stone was set up by John Lord de la Warre, who has seen the tree growing in this place.

Of all our princes of the Norman race, none more rigorously enforced the laws of the chase than the Red King, or more cruelly persecuted his English subjects for their transgression: even his father had been less unrelenting; and the poor Saxons had no revenge but that of contemptuously styling him, "Wood-keeper," and herdsman of wild beasts. No man of that despised origin could enter the royal forests with dogs, or weapons calculated to destroy game, except at the peril of his life.

In consequence, it soon became a popular superstition among the Saxons, that the devil frequently appeared to their tyrants, under the most appalling circumstances, whilst they were re-creating themselves in these hunting grounds.* Reports so consonant to the feelings and prejudices of a barbarous age, received a most extraordinary confirmation from the chance which made hunting in these English forests — the New Forest especially — fatal to the descendants of the Conqueror. Richard, his eldest son, there received an arrow in his heart. In May 1100, the nephew of Rufus, son to Duke Robert, was also killed here by an arrow discharged inadvertently†, and, strange to say, about three months afterwards, the Conqueror's other son fell by the same weapon, in the same place, in the manner I am now about to describe.

The scene of this event is a lovely secluded hollow, exposed to the sun only on the west, where a small portion of the heath slopes gently downwards to meet it. A beechen grove rears

---

* Ipse etiam in sylvis, diabolus subhorribili specie Normannis se ostendere, plura eis de rege ab aliis palam locutus est. — *Simio Dunelmensis*, p. 225.

† Ailredus Rievalliensis. — *Ord. Vital.*, p. 780.

itself on the east, and clumps of various trees of irregular growth form a shelter on every other side. Among these, winding avenues of greensward afford access to every part of the forest; and it is altogether just the situation where a hunter might be tempted to repose, when heated and fatigued with the chase.

That was already concluded, and William, dismounting from his horse, had thrown himself upon the verdant turf, with his crossbow on one side, and faithful hounds on the other. So he appeared when found weltering in his blood. A stag suddenly dashed across the heath. The king turning towards it, lifted up his hand to shade his eyes from the sunbeams. At that moment he received the arrow, and as it was found buried up to the feathers in his breast, there can be no doubt but he died instantaneously. Now the common belief is, that when Sir Walter Tyrrel levelled the crossbow, he was not aware of his vicinity to his master. At first the deer had approached at full speed, but not seeing any enemy halted, and began grazing quietly just behind the oak. At that moment the arrow of Tyrrel, who lay in ambush*, coming in contact with the body or a branch of the tree, — some say it grazed upon the back of the stag, — flew off at an angle towards the spot where the king was sitting. A good arrow is always worth the trouble of looking for; and when Tyrrel found that he had missed the game, most probably he went in search of his. The King's horse, feeding at large, first attracted attention, and then the horrible truth soon became apparent. Terrified at the accident, he lingered not upon the spot; but, setting spurs to his horse, galloped to the sea-side, embarked for France, and joined the Crusade, just then setting out for Jerusalem.

Such is the substance of a tradition, partly furnished by the

---

* This scene and this mode of forest hunting are well elucidated in the Book of King Modus, p. 217. of this work.

descendants of the very man who found and conveyed away the King's body in his cart. The accounts of contemporary chroniclers differ from it only in being less circumstantial: they perfectly agree as to the principal facts. Yet, plausible as the tale appears, it suggests more " historic doubts " to the archer, than even that famous question respecting the alleged deformity of our crooked-backed Richard.*

I allude to the arrow and the oak, which, from all antiquity, has been assigned as the direct and indirect occasion of Rufus's death. By what means could it possibly be ascertained that the former was turned from its course by glancing on the latter? The King was alone. He never spoke after receiving the fatal wound. Had he even lingered, or been surrounded by the companions of his day's pastime, neither he nor they could possibly have known that the weapon struck upon any thing in its course. It was unexpected and invisible, until it penetrated the King's body. An arrow glancing from a tree, leaves no mark behind, because the wooden shaft, and not the head, comes in contact with the opposing body. As the sportsman of our day cleans his fowlingpiece, and refits it with a new flint previously to going into the field, so the ancient archer made the steel points of his arrows perfectly keen and sharp on every similar occasion.† If one of these struck a tree, it would certainly go no further, but remain sticking in the bark. The oak, therefore, could furnish no evidence, and Sir Walter Tyrrel died in the Holy Land; independently of which, it is very improbable he would recur to an event, whose consequences he had fled from England to avoid. Admitting, however, that he had returned, it would be exceedingly difficult, after the lapse of years, to recognise, among all the trees of that portion of the forest, the particular one which is said to have turned the course of his arrow.

* Walpole's Historic Doubts. † Book of King Modus, p. 220.

An authority recently quoted *, gives a different, and, in my opinion, a much more probable version of the story, although it obtains little credit, solely because no mention whatever is made of Rufus's oak. He tells us, that Henry the king's brother, a Norman baron called William de Bretail, and several other chiefs, were invited to accompany him in that day's chase. Early in the morning a workman brought six crossbow arrows, exceedingly well made, and keenly pointed, as a present to the King. William, having examined them, greatly praised their workmanship; and keeping four for his own use, delivered the other two to Walter Tyrrel, saying, "Bon archier, bonnes fleches." † Walter Tyrrel was a Frenchman, the inheritor of large estates in Ponthien, and being a most dexterous archer, became on that account the chief favourite of his victim.

On arriving at the forest, each of the attendants took up his respective stand, according to the mode of hunting pursued in those days, which was to lie in wait for the game, and shoot as it passed.‡ Tyrrel alone remained near the King, opposite to whom he was stationed. Both held their crossbows bent, with an arrow upon the nut. § Suddenly a large deer, driven by the foresters, whose duty it was to windlass up the game, passed between them. William drew the trigger of his crossbow; but owing to the string breaking, his arrow fell short. The animal startled at the noise, stood still, gazing around him on all sides, as deer are wont to do. ‖ At that instant the King motioned Tyrrel to shoot; but the latter did not obey, not observing either the game or the signal. Rufus growing

* *Ord. Vital. Henric. Knighton,* p. 2573.
† "A good marksman deserves good arrows" "Justum est ut illi acutissimæ dentur sagittæ, qui letiferos exinde noverit ictus configere." — *Ibid.*
‡ See Book of King Modus, p. 217.
§ "Cum arcu et sagittâ in manu expectanti." — *Henric. Knighton, Ord. Vital.* p. 2373.
‖ "Sed fracta cordâ, cervus de sonitu quasi attonitus, restitit, circumcircà respiciens."— *Ibid.*

F. P. Stephanoff. Augt Fox.

The Death of William Rufus.

London Published by Longman & Co Feby 1840.

impatient, and fearful the stag would escape, hastily exclaimed, 'Tirez donc, Walter! Tirez donc! comme si même c'étoit le diable."* Scarcely had the words passed his lips, when an arrow, either that of Tyrrel or some other person, struck him on the breast. He instantly fell, and expired without uttering a word. His favourite rushed to the spot, but finding life utterly extinct, fled towards the sea-coast, as before stated.†

The body of William the Red, thus abandoned, as the Conqueror's had been, was found lying on the turf, which had become saturated with his blood. A man named Purkiss, and his sons, first made this discovery, in returning home through the forest from their daily occupation of charcoal burning. Ignorant of the rank of the deceased, and considering his fate a mere hunting casualty — as indeed it was, — they placed the corpse in their cart, wrapped in a piece of old linen, with the arrow still sticking in the wound, and in this sordid condition, were the remains of the second Norman king conveyed towards the city of Winchester. On its arrival there, not one of the splendid cavalcade who had ridden so obsequiously at his side to that morning's chase, was found to assist in performing the last duties of humanity. On the first rumour of his death, each fled to his respective residence, to place it in a posture of defence, fearing lest the royal succession might be decided by an appeal to the sword.

It is remarkable that when the late Duke of Gloucester was head ranger of the New Forest, a cottager named Purkiss still resided upon the spot occupied by his ancestor at the period

* Shoot, Walter, shoot! as if it were the devil.
Trahe, trahe arcum, experte diaboli.
Henric. Knyghton, p. 2374.

† In the face of all this, the Abbot of Seguin, prime minister of Louis le Gros, who wrote a life of Louis VII., relates that Tyrrel positively assured him he had not seen Rufus on the day he was killed. — *Sir S. R. Meyrick.*

of this history.* His calling and condition of life were in all respects similar, having suffered no alteration during a lapse of more than six centuries. It seems that a wheel of the identical cart used to convey the body of Rufus to Winchester, had descended as a heirloom from father to son. When this came to the knowledge of his Royal Highness, he desired to become its purchaser, and application was made to Purkiss, who expressed a perfect willingness to part with the relic, had it been still in his possession. But the previous winter was a severe one; fuel proved scarce and dear; the ancient wheel shared the fate of some old palings surrounding the hovel, — having blazed upon the chimney hearth!

But to return. It was doubtless very judicious policy in the English legislature to discourage the use of any inferior weapons, which withdrew men from the exercise of the long bow. Yet even this motive can scarcely account for the vigorous measures adopted to suppress them, which, upon the whole, appear exceedingly absurd. Whilst thousands of crossbows, with all their necessary appliances, occupied our public armories, the clerical councils repeatedly denounced them as " instruments hateful in the sight of God and man." Several acts of parliament were also passed, rendering it penal for persons of a certain rank to have them in their houses; the qualification being limited to such as possessed a hundred marks annual income. The preamble to one of these statutes declares, that many wicked and dissolute persons were accustomed to ride along the public highways with crossbows ready bent, and quarrils fixed thereon, committing wanton outrages on the property †, not unfrequently on the persons, of his Majesty's

---

* I believe some of them reside there still.

† " In the meantime Lord Stourton's men went to the pasture of William Hartgill, took his riding gelding, carried him to Stourton Park pales, and shot him with a crossbow, reporting that Hartgill had been hunting in his lordship's park upon that gelding."— *Trial of Lord Stourton for murder of the Hartgills.*

peaceful subjects. Here was certainly good reason for legal interference; but the same crimes might have been committed with the long bow, an instrument far less unwieldy, more rapidly discharged, and, if of small dimensions, equally capable of concealment.

A correspondent of the Gentleman's Magazine *, who furnishes the editor with a fac-simile of Henry VIII.'s autograph, states that the original signature is attached to a licence granted to one of his ancestors, to use and exercise his crossbow, notwithstanding any act or proclamation to the contrary.

That our parkers and woodsmen, as the English anciently styled their gamekeepers, were permitted to carry this proscribed instrument, will be fully evident from the subsequent narratives. It was applicable to the destruction of all game now killed with rifle and fowlingpiece; and Shakspeare has a highly graphic picture of two keepers, thus armed, lying in wait for the venison : —

Enter SKINKLO *and* HUMPHREY, *with crossbows in their hands.*

Skinklo. Under this thick-grown brake we'll shroud ourselves,
For through this laund anon the deer will come;
And in this covert will we take our stand,
Culling the principal of all the deer.
　Humphrey. I'll stay above the hill, so both may shoot.
　Skinklo. That cannot be; the noise of thy crossbow
Will scare the herd, and so my shot is lost.
Here stand we both, and aim we at the best;
And that the time shall not seem tedious,
I'll tell thee what befel me on a time
In this same place were now we mean to stand.

The piety, virtue, and learning of George Abbot, who filled the see of Canterbury during the reign of James I., shed a brilliant lustre on our ecclesiastical history. But while these

* November, 1792. This periodical frequently contains very interesting papers on the ancient and modern history of the bow.

are sufficiently familiar to most men, the remarkable incident which threw a cloud over the latter portion of his comparatively blameless career, is known to few.

In order to counteract the effects of a very painful disorder to which this archbishop had long been subject, his physicians prescribed active, even violent, exercises, and among these the chase. During one of his summer journeys through Hampshire, he sojourned for a few days at Bramshall, the seat of a dear friend and associate, the Lord Zouch. His constitution and habits of life being well known to the family, it was arranged that a grand stag-hunt should take place in the park soon after his arrival. One of the foresters, named Peter Hawkins, desirous to show his respect for a guest whom his master delighted to honour, was more than ordinarily zealous in his office on that day, and it being his duty to windlass up the deer towards the place where the archbishop's party had stationed themselves, he soon assembled a herd of between forty and fifty. Among them was a buck of a noble head, which this ill-fated man greatly exerted himself to separate from the rest, and drive within shot. Meanwhile each of the hunters sought out a convenient stand; and the archbishop, holding his crossbow bent, stationed himself within a few paces of a large oak, the leaves of which partially concealed him from view. As Hawkins continued in front of this tree, galloping in circles around the deer, he was twice warned by Lord Zouch to remain behind, the game being then near enough. Just as the archbishop levelled his weapon, with his finger on the trigger, the stag made a rush on one side to escape, seeing which, the poor keeper again spurred forwards; but the arrow had taken wing, and meeting with a small bough, glanced aside and struck him in the arm. "It was but a flesh wound, and a slight one," says the MS. which furnishes the substance of this anecdote; "yet being under the care of a heedless surgeon, the fellow died of it in the course of one hour." Externally, the injury might have appeared trivial, as here represented; but in reality, the steel head of the quarril must have divided one of the great arteries, and in consequence the man bled to death.

No domestic occurrence of that period excited more attention than the unhappy accident of Archbishop Abbot. His own conduct on this trying occasion is the highest encomium on his humanity and goodness of heart. The forester left behind him a widow and four children, upon each of whom he settled a comfortable annuity; and then, "being utterly incapable of consolation," observes his unknown biographer, he retired to an hospital at Guilford of his own foundation, and passed the remainder of his life in penitence and prayer.

A commission of twelve bishops was appointed, by the special command of King James, to deliberate and report upon this untoward occurrence. They were required to say whether an act of homicide, however unintentional, committed by a minister of religion whilst engaged in field sports, was calculated to bring scandal on the church. The report, grounded on Scripture and the canon law, is distinguished for eloquence, learning, and deep research. Altogether, it is a most interesting document, fully establishing the clergy's right to hunt, hawk, shoot, and fish whenever the pursuit of these amusements interfere not with the performance of their sacred duties. From the original and unpublished MSS. formerly in the possession of Dr. Zachariah Gray, I extract a short passage by way of specimen:—

"Touching the death of Peter Hawkins, wounded in the park of Bramfield by a crossbow, July 24th, 1621,—"It is certain that, in foro conscientiæ, this case may not only deservedly produce a fear and trembling in him who was the accidental cause thereof, but justly make the tallest cedar of Lebanon to shake, in debating with his inward man what crime it is that hath provoked God to permit such a rare and unusual action to fall out by his hand; an action which maketh him for the time to be fabula vulgi, and giveth opportunity to the enemies of religion of all kinds to rejoice; which furnisheth a source to fill their books and libells within the realme, and perhaps beyond the seas, and that concerning his calling as well as his person, not only for the present, but also for future ages, besides grief to his friends, and some scandal to the weak, who do not rightly apprehend things, but raise questions which few men can resolve. To all which may be added, the interpretation of it to his Majesty, graciously or otherwise; and the forfeiture that in rigorous construction of law may be put upon him, although held for no great delinquent; beside the providing for a widow and four fatherless children; all which may well pierce a heart that is not senselesse, and day and night yield him matter enough for troubled meditations."

Those personal inconveniences he naturally anticipated; but they were very properly averted by an exercise of the royal prerogative. "And you may be sure," says Dr. Hackett, in his life of Archbishop Williams [*], " the King thought it more pardonable, because it was a hunting casualty; and was very humane to all those harms beyond prevention, which fell out in that sport wherein he greatly delighted. Therefore his Majesty resolved to give it him in a consolatory letter under his hand, that he would not add affliction to his sorrow, nor take one farthing from his chattels and moveables, which were confiscated by our civil penalties."

Alban Butler, in describing the festival of St. Jane Francis de Chautal, mentions a case very similar to this of Archbishop Abbot. The Baron de Chautal, husband of the saint, was accustomed to follow the chase in a habit made of deer's hide, dressed with the hair on, the better to deceive and approach his game. On one occasion he had stationed himself within a thick tangled brake, to await the coming of the deer. His

[*] Page 65.

friend, who was hunting with him, actually mistook him for one, and levelling his crossbow, the arrow pierced him in the thigh. He survived the accident nine days. Whilst dying, he caused his pardon of the person by whom he had been shot to be recorded in the registers of the parish church, strictly forbidding any man to prosecute or bring him into danger.

A tradition extant in the West of England commemorates an extraordinary act of suicide perpetrated by means of the weapon under consideration. The victim inflicted the fatal wound, not with his own hand, but by the instrumentality of his servant.

Sir William Hankford, a gentleman of ancient family and competent fortune, in Devonshire, was Chief Justice of the King's Bench in the reign of Henry V. Much of his life had been afflicted by periodical attacks of nervous dejection, — a complaint of extremely rare occurrence, however, among Englishmen of that period. On returning from London, at the commencement of the holidays, just before his death, this malady appeared to influence him with all its force, aggravated, as it is supposed, by some disappointments he had endured at court. His family and domestics, shocked at the air of sorrowful anxiety visible in his countenance and deportment, vainly endeavoured to banish his distress by every art of social kindness, and to encourage that taste for rural pleasures, in the pursuit of which alone he appeared to derive satisfaction. One morning, whilst engaged hunting, he suddenly quitted the pack, and, galloping homewards, ordered a domestic to summon the park-keeper to his presence in the hall. It was with no small glee and satisfaction the ruddy old woodsman obeyed the call, not doubting but that, heartily tired of the chase, his master was desirous of varying the day's pastime by a flight at the heron or a mallard of the brook. He therefore cheerfully entered his presence, surrounded by a leash of docile spaniels, with the hooded falcon on his wrist. Sir William Hankford, however, assumed an air of stern severity, and pretending to have discovered during his morning's ride extensive depredations upon the venison, rated this domestic soundly for neglect. The man, however, respectfully persisted that he never omitted his nightly rounds; and, moreover, that any decrease in the herds of deer was not apparent to him. These remonstrances appeared only to heighten the displeasure of his master, and he was dismissed with a peremptory order to go forth every night, having his crossbow ready charged, and shoot any person, unchallenged, whom he caught trespassing within the precincts of the park. The very next evening, the unhappy individual who had issued this command, stationed himself disguised at the edge of a thicket, where he was certain to encounter his armed domestic. The keeper drew near, his self-devoted victim sprang forwards into the path: when, faithful to the instructions he had received, the man levelled his weapon, and Sir William Hankford lay weltering in blood! The author of the "Worthies" makes allusion to this catastrophe, adding, that the stump of the oak near which it occurred had been shown to some eminent lawyers riding the western circuit in his time. He was buried in America church, and appeared on his tomb in a kneeling posture, with the two following lines inscribed upon a label issuing out of his mouth.

> Miserere mei, Deus, secundum misericordiam tuam.
> Beati qui custodiant judicium, et facerent justitiam omni tempore.

"No charitable reader," well observes the pious and discreet Fuller, commenting on this act of self-destruction, "will condemn his memory, who, while living, was habited with all requisites for a person of his place."

To kill poachers upon the spot without ceremony, appears to have been a general practice during the feudal ages: thus, the Veel MS., before quoted, states that William Wicock, servant to Thomas, second Lord of Berkeley, having caught

William Goyle netting hares in his master's wood, killed him with an arrow." And Walter How, an under-keeper to the same, slew one Clift stealing deer, with a forker * out of his crossebowe.

The Inca Garcilasco de Vega preserves the particulars of a singular duel between an Indian and a follower of De Soto, the one armed with the long, the other with the crossbow. In all probability similar conflicts were not unfrequent during our own ancient military expeditions to the Continent, though historians have omitted to record them.

Whilst the Indians were in complete rout, after the siege of Alambano, a warrior, suddenly detaching himself from the fugitives, walked down to the water-side, armed with bow and quiver. There he shouted to his foes, intimating, by signs and a few words of broken Spanish, that he challenged any crossbowman among the Christians to approach and try a shot with him from shore to shore. Hearing this, Juan de Salinas, an Asturian hidalgo, who, with some of his comrades, had screened himself from the arrows within a small clump of trees, quickly stepped forth, and stationed himself opposite the Indian, armed with his crossbow. Here we have an almost solitary instance where the followers of De Soto respected the lofty chivalrous spirit which certainly animated these Floridan warriors; for when one of Juan's companions shouted that he should stay until he brought him the protection of his shield, the brave Salinas peremptorily refused to take any advantage of his naked foe; whilst the Indian, therefore, was selecting an arrow from his quiver, he also carefully placed one upon his arbalist. Both levelled and discharged their weapons at the same moment; but our hidalgo proved himself the better marksman, and his quarril buried itself in the Indian's bosom. The dying warrior was received in the arms of his countrymen,

* The forker is a bifurcated arrow.

who quickly bore him from the scene of action; but he fell not wholly unrevenged, for his arrow passed through the nape of the Spaniard's neck. Fearful lest irritation might ensue from drawing it out precipitately, he hastened back to his comrades with the shaft crossed in the wound. None of the other Indians attempted to molest him in his departure, as the challenge had been avowedly man to man. On another occasion, the Spanish commander directed his troops to attempt the passage of a lake or morass, bordered by a thick forest, on the further side of which the savages were observed to be collecting in great force. Each trooper, therefore, took a crossbowman behind him upon the crupper, that an imposing force might be assembled more quickly, to protect the landing-place, and seize upon the only passage into the interior; but as the soldiers were yet in the middle of the water, a storm of arrows descended upon them, while the most hideous yells issued from all sides.

At that instant, the horse of Alvarez Fernandez fell dead under him, and many more were mortally wounded; whilst the remainder, maddened also with pain, plunged and reared in the water, which reached beyond their saddle girths. The foot-soldiers were quickly dismounted; and as the wheeling and plunging of the horses exposed their riders' shoulders to the enemy, not one had escaped arrow wounds. And now the savages, observing their helpless condition in the water, raised the war-hoop, and rushed forwards to despatch them, shouting victory to their comrades. It was a scene of the wildest confusion. Up to their armpits in the current were seen the Christians engaged in mortal struggle with their tawny adversaries; horses galloping masterless along the shore; and hordes of natives crowding to the combat. Recovered at length from their first terror, the nearest Spaniards crossed over an Indian bridge of logs, and hastened to the succour of their companions. It was then a large body of warriors met them, led by a chief perfectly naked, armed with a formidable bow, and having his head decorated with lofty plumes. He marched about twenty paces in advance of his men, and was evidently manœuvring to gain the protection of a large tree, behind which he could securely gall the Spaniards with his arching. A soldier, named Gonzalo Silvestre, seeing this, hailed his comrade, one Anton Galvon, a crossbowman, who, though unhorsed and wounded, had, soldier-like, kept possession of his weapon. Preceded by Silvestre, holding before him a quilted surcoat, used by the Spaniards as body armour, which he found floating in the water, he managed to reach the tree before his Indian adversary. Enraged at being thus defeated, the latter in an instant let fly three arrows with an unerring aim, and they had certainly proved fatal, but for the garment still used by Silvestre as a shield; which being wet, effectually deadened the force.

When the practised eye of Galvon perceived the savage was within crossbow range, he levelled his weapon and lodged its quarrel in his adversary's heart. The dying Indian staggered only a few paces, ere he exclaimed to his followers, "The traitors have slain me." With mournful cries they received him as he fell, and passing his body from one to another, conveyed it from the fatal field.

Vitachuco, a Floridan cacique, had fallen into the hands of the Spaniards, by whom he was detained a prisoner. Many of his people shared his captivity, some of them having been taken at the same time, others came voluntarily to undergo the fate, and minister to the wants of their beloved chief. With these he entered into a plot to attack the Spaniards about the time of their mid-day meal, slay as many of them as possible, and then escape into the surrounding woods. Sticks and stones, but chiefly some culinary utensils of their captors, were the only weapons these savages could lay their hands on; nevertheless they wielded them with terrible energy; numbers of the Christians had their limbs broken; or were burnt, bruised, and scalded beyond a chance of recovery. One man had nearly the whole of his teeth knocked out; his head was terribly cut; and his assailant was in the act of giving him the *coup de grace*, as some comrades arrived to his rescue. Snatching up a spear, which accidentally lay against the wall, the Indian then took to his heels, and ran up a hand-ladder into a loft, the door of which opened upon a sort of basse court. Thither the Spaniards eagerly pursued him; but it was not possible to ascend, as he occupied the top of the landing-place, and with the lance threatened destruction to any who should molest him. At this juncture, a relation of the general, named Diego de Soto *, entered the court-yard, bearing his crossbow. Though fully aware of the power of this weapon to wound or kill him from afar, the savage unshrinkingly maintained his post: death in some shape or another he foresaw was inevitable; he therefore only sought not to fall unrevenged. As was usual in case of present danger, the Spaniard had come with crossbow ready bent, and an arrow upon the groove. Whilst resting the butt upon his shoulder †, preparatory to shooting, the savage collected all his force, and discharged the lance with prodigious violence. Its steel head grazed De Soto's shoulder; and the reverberating shaft, as it penetrated the ground, about half length behind, struck him upon his knees. But at the same instant his adversary fell to the earth, transfixed by the quarril, which had entered his left breast.

I shall conclude this chapter with an anecdote not wholly dissimilar to the last, except that the Spaniard encountered an adversary differing somewhat in species from the Floridan warrior.

"A bowman of our company," says the author of "Decades

---

* Killed at the battle of Mauvilla, where an arrow pierced his eye, and came out at the back of his head.

† See p. 233.

of the Ocean*;" " bent his crossbow against an old ape with a long tail, bigger than a baboon. This ape made as though she would wait for the arrow; but as soon as she saw it directed by shutting one eye, casting down a stone upon the archer, she shrewdly bruised his face, and brake his teeth out of his head. Yet the monkey was punished for her strange stratagem; for at what time the stone fell down upon the archer, the quarril ascended into the ape, and they eat her for a dainty dish. In truth, so great hunger oppressed them, that they had eaten toads, or any other worse meat."

* Page 592.

SECTION VII.

SOCIETIES OF MODERN ARCHERS.

> " What is the wager ? " said the queen,
> " That must I now know here ; "—
> " Three hundred ton of Rhenish wine,
> Three hundred ton of beer ;
>
> Three hundred of the fattest harts
> Which run on Dallom Lea."
> " That's a princely wager," said the king,
> Needs must I tell to thee."
>
> With that bespake one Clifton then,
> Full quickly and full soon,
> " Measure no marks for us, my sovereign liege,
> We'll shoot at sun and moon."
>
> " Full fifteen score your mark shall be,
> Full fifteen score shall stand."
> " I lay my bow," said Clifton then ;
> " We cleave the willow wand."
> *Robin Hood and Queen Katharine.*

A SMALL body of archers accompanied the Duke of Buckingham in his expedition against the Isle of Rhé in 1627; a few fought also at the siege of Devizes, during the civil troubles which ensued shortly after; one Neade and his son, both veteran bowmen, having been commissioned to raise a body of archers for his majesty's service. The besieged also had a similar force within the walls, and to these reference is intended in the following extract: — " I, having the guard of the river side," says Captain Gwynne, " and standing by Sir Jacob Ashley, a bearded arrow stuck into the ground betwixt his legs. He plucked it out with both his hands, saying, 'Ah! rogues, you missed your aim.'"* Bowmen formed part of the forces commanded by the gallant, but unfortunate, Marquis of Montrose, during the contest between King Charles and his Scottish subjects, some few years afterwards; and these are stated by modern authorities to have been the last who carried the warbow and barbed arrow into the battle-field. But does not the honour of being one of the latest upholders of military archery more properly belong to a redoubtable old soldier of the church militant, mentioned in my account of the Royal Scottish Body Guard? Could we trace his subsequent history, is it not more than probable he would be found to have actually done battle with his "artillery †" in defence of protestantism and the sacred order to which he belonged?

However this be, we have abundant means of knowing that archery, as a national English pastime, never became wholly extinct. Even whilst our bowmen were carrying a scourging hand in France, and the statute of Queen Elizabeth declared their weapons to be "God's special gift to our nation," the fraternities of St. George and Prince Arthur were bowmen incorporated for pastime only, both owing their origin to

* Memoirs, p. 39.

† It is one among many proofs how entirely time and circumstances have changed our language, that the word *artillery*, at present specifically applied to cannon, anciently meant bows and arrows only: " And David gave his artillery to the lad."

> Then some would leape, and some would runne,
> And some would use artillery.
> Which of you can a good bow draw,
> A stout archer for to be?
> *Robin Hood and the Curtall Friar.*

The Artillery Company of London was originally a body of archers.

Henry VIII, who appointed Sir Christopher Morris master of the ordnance, and Antony Knevit overseer of the former. For the latter he selected a title as romantic as it was appropriate. "Let them be called," said he, "The ancient Order, Societie, and Unitie laudable, of Prince Arthure's Knightes and his Knightlie Armory of the Round Table;" and wherever he saw a good archere and a fair, he chose and ordained such an one to be entered on their list. The associates were fifty-six in number, each assuming the name of one of the illustrious worthies in that brotherhood of chivalry. When Robinson published his "Famous History of Prince Arthur's Knights," during the succeeding reign, every archer, as we learn from a MS. catalogue of his typographical labours, bought a copy, commencing with Master Thomas Smith, her Majesty's Customer, who being Prince Arthur himself, payed 5s., his fifty-six knights 1s. 6d., and every esquire 8d. each, for the volume.* A no less personage than Justice Shallow claims to have been one of these archers: "I played Sir Dagonet," says he, "in Prince Arthur's shew," by which Shakspeare clearly meant a meeting of the toxophilites, and not an ordinary pageant. They assembled at Mile-end Green, near London. Probably Shakspeare himself was often among them.

Their charter authorised them to shoot at "all fowls and game"— in that age, no trifling privilege—within the suburbs of the metropolis; and it was further declared, that during their weapon shewings, each archer should, by way of caution to the spectators, pronounce the word "fast," before he loosed his arrow: which done, provided public proclamation had also been made that the populace should abstain fifty paces from either side of the butts, none of the fraternity were liable to prosecution, even for manslaughter, in case of accident from their arrows.

* Bankes's MS.

At the very commencement of the seventeenth century, we had the Royal Edinburgh Bowmen, and shortly afterwards the Richmond Archers, who possess a record of their silver arrow having been won by Henry Calvert, of Eyreholme, Esquire, as far back as the year 1673, and both still flourish as connective links between ancient and modern days. It is scarcely just, therefore, to term the numerous bow-meetings established at various recent periods, a revival of archery; since, speaking figuratively, the stream, though at times faint and low, has never, even for the shortest period, been wholly annihilated.

To the north of England, generally, must be assigned the merit of having preserved a traditional knowledge of the long bow, when its practice was extinct in other parts of the kingdom. Lancashire and Cheshire, counties once famous for recruiting our armies with those bands of tall archers, each one of whom boasted of carrying four and twenty Scotsmen under his girdle*, are at present conspicuous for numerous

---

* An allusion to the sheaf of twenty-four arrows usually carried into action. The establishment of a royal body-guard began with Henry VII., who ordered fifty tall picked archers to be selected out of Lancashire. It is remarkable that the guardsmen are still extensively recruited there; for, although the ancient motive for this preference has long ceased to exist, traditionary custom has perpetuated it. Queen Elizabeth doubled the number of her body-guard, showing much pleasure in being surrounded by the archers in all public processions; she also took great interest in their personal appearance and discipline, of which there is a curious instance in some letters preserved in the Bodleian Library, Oxford. " Queen Elizabeth loved to have all the servants of her court proper men, and, as before said, Sir Walter Raleigh's graceful presence was no mean recommendation to him, so I think his first preferment at court was captaine of her majestie's archer guard. There came a country gentleman, a sufficient yeoman, up to towne, who had several sonnes, but one an extraordinary proper handsome fellowe, whom he did hope to have preferred to be a yeoman of the guard. The father, a goodlie man himself, comes to Sir Walter Raleigh, a stranger to him, and told him that he had brought up a boy, that he would desire, having many children, to be one of her majestie's guard. Quoth Sir Walter, ' Had you spoke for yourselfe, I should readily have granted your desire, for your

and clever bow-meetings. In a day's journey through that portion of England, butts and marks erected upon the lawns, before the drawing-room windows of gentlemen's mansions, meet our eyes almost as frequently as rifle targets, along the shores of beauteous Leman's Lake.

I recollect a rather amusing proof of the laudable *esprit du corps*, existing among these Cheshire and Lancashire bowmen, a relic of ancient pride of skill, transmitted from their ancestors. Whilst target shooting with a small party at Tuttshill *, a lovely spot on the summit of Vaga's rocky bounds, the author of the History and Antiquities of Cheshire †, then residing at Sedbury Park, passed by. Being known as a good bowman, we challenged him to a shot; but, with ready wit, he made a familiar north country proverb to serve as his ex-

---

person deserves it; but I put in no boys. Said the father, ' Come in boye.' The son enters, about eighteen or nineteen, but such a goodlie proper young fellow, as Sir Walter Raleigh had not seen the like: he was the tallest of all the guarde. Sir Walter swares him in immediately; and ordered him to carry up the first dish at dinner, where the Queen beheld him with admiration, as if a beautifull young giant had stalked in with the service."

John Taylor, the Water Poet, thus describes this body from personal observation.

> Within these few yeeres, I to mind doe call
> The yeoman of the guard were archers all.
> A hundred at a time I oft have seen,
> With bowes and arrowes ride before the Queen.
> Their bowes in hand, their quivers on their shoulders,
> Was a most stately shew to the beholders.
> And herein, if men rightly doe observe,
> The arrowes did for two great uses serve:
> First for a shew of great magnificence,
> And trustie weapons for to guard their prince.
>
> *Prayer of the Grey Goose Wing.*

* The seat of the worthy and hospitable James Evans, Esq.
† —— Ormerode, Esq., of Ormerode Hall.

cuse: "A Lancashire man should never miss." Just then he was more devoted to the book than the bow; his literary labours left no time for practice, and he was unwilling, by exhibiting at a disadvantage, to compromise the reputation of his countrymen.

The ancient renown of our northern archers has been the subject of much panegyric by their contemporaries. Hear Drayton's description of the Cheshire men engaged in civil broil at the battle of Blore Heath. The Earl of Salisbury, their leader, is the individual first alluded to.

> He caused a flight of shafts to be discharged first;
> The enemy, who thought that he had done his worst,
> And cowardly had fled in a disorded route,
> Attempt to wade the brook; he wheeling soon about,
> Set fiercely on that part which then were passed over. —
> There Dutton Dutton kills; a Done doth kill a Done;
> A Booth a Booth; and Leigh by Leigh is overthrown.
> A Venables against a Venables doth stand;
> A Troutback fighteth with a Troutback, hand to hand.
> There Molyneux doth make a Molyneux to die,
> And Egerton the strength of Egerton doth try.
> Oh Cheshire, wert thou mad? of thine own native gore,
> So much until this day, thou never shed'st before.

In Weber's tale of Flodden Field, Lord Stanley addresses those who fought under his banner in the following pithy style:

> My Lancashire most lovely wights,
>   And chosen men of Cheshire strong;
> From sounding bows your feathered flights
>   Let fiercely fly yon foes among.

Enumerating the different towns and villages from whence they proceeded, he says —

> All Lancashire, for the most part,
>   The lusty Stanley stout did lead;
> A stock of striplings, stout of heart,
>   Brought up from babes with beef and bread.

> From Warton unto Warrington,
> From Wigan unto Waresdale;
> From Wedicar to Waddington,
> From old Ribchester, to Rochdale.

In another place it is said, that Sir Richard Bold brought considerable succour of his tenants and archers, out of Brundall in Lancashire, to the assistance of the Earl of Surrey. He behaved with great gallantry at Flodden; and to the Lancashire archers the fame of that victory has been generally ascribed. To Bosworth also —

> A most selected band of Cheshire bowmen came,
> By Sir John Savage led, besides two men of name.
> DRAYTON.

I think it is in Weber's poem that a Lancashire man named "Long Jamie," one of the archer guard, shoots three of his comrades, in revenge for an insult offered to the Earl of Derby. Pleading his cause before the King, he first recounts the origin of his attachment to that nobleman; then the particular instance of skill and strength which led to his admission among the royal military attendants:—

> They called me craven to my face,
>   When I was to my supper sat;
> And bade me flee all from the place
>   Unto that coward, the Earle of Derbie.
> Whilst I was little, and had small geare,
>   He was my helpe and succour true;
> He took me from my father dear,
>   And kept me with his own,
> Tyll I was able of myself
>   Both to shoot, and prick a stone.
> Then, under Greenhithe on a daye,
>   A Scottish mynstrell came to thee,
> And broughte a bowe of eugh to drawe,
>   But alle the guarde might not stir that tree.

> Then the bowe was given to the Earle of Derbie,
>   And the Earle delivered it to me.
> Seven shots before your face I shot,
>   And at the eighthe in sunder it did flee.
> I bade the Scot bowe down his face,
>   And gather up the bowe, and bringe it to his kinge.
> Then it liked your noble Grace,
>   Into your guarde me to brynge.

It is remarkable that Sir Ashton Lever, to whose zealous exertions the revival of archery in the metropolis may be partly attributed, should have been a Lancashireman. Whether his well-known coadjutor in this good work, the elder Mr. Waring, was equally far north, I cannot state positively, but I fancy he was. The "English Bowman" thus alludes to the circumstances which induced them to turn their thoughts upon this fine old rural pastime, whilst surrounded by the hurry, turmoil, and absorbing interests of what is called London life.

"About the year 1776, Mr. Waring, who may justly be styled the father of modern archery, resided with Sir Ashton Lever at Leicester House. Having, by continual application to business contracted an oppression upon his chest, he resolved to try the effect of the bow in affording relief. Accordingly he made it a regular exercise, and in a short time derived great benefit from the use of it; and ascribes his cure, which was perfect, solely to the use of archery. Sir Ashton Lever, perceiving the good effects which so engaging an amusement had upon the constitution, followed Mr. Waring's example, and took up the bow. He was soon joined by several of his friends, who, in the year 1780, formed themselves into a society under the title of Toxophilites."

The patronage of his Majesty George the Fourth, and the gratification he seemed to feel, whilst Prince of Wales, in an amusement so many of his illustrious forefathers had delighted to honour, assisted in reviving the public taste for archery. Like Harry Percy —

> He was indeed the glass
> Wherein the noble youth did dress themselves.
> * * * * So that in speech, in gait,
> In diet, in affections of delight,
> In military rules, humours of blood,
> He was the mark and glass, copy and book,
> That fashioned others.

Among the odd collection of miscellaneous items, ancient and modern, suspended around the walls of the *den* where I am writing, is a full-length portrait of his Royal Highness, in the costume of Captain General of the Kentish archers. He is represented reposing himself after a shooting-match, and gracefully holds in his left hand a beautiful backed bow, the only correct representation of that instrument I ever met with in print or painting.

The northern archery societies, before Sir Ashton Lever's and Mr. Waring's time, were —

	Date.	Prizes.
The Royal Edinburgh Archers	- 1600*	
Richmond Archers	- 1673	Silver arrow, silver cup, &c.
Scroton Archers	- 1673	Silver arrow, horn spoon†, &c.
Darlington Archers	- 1758	{ Silver medal, silver cup, silver gorget and banner.

The enthusiasm which attended the revival of archery can only be compared to that which animated the admirers of Shakspeare and the ancient drama generally during the Garrick era. Soon after the Royal Toxophilites were established, almost

---

* Or thereabouts. The prizes of this company are described elsewhere.
† See p. 102.

every considerable city in the kingdom possessed its bow-meeting. The following may be received as a pretty correct list of the societies to which they gave birth, arranged alphabetically:—

Archers of Archinfield, near Hereford	-	Several valuable prizes.
Bowmen of Chevy Chase, Morpeth	-	Bugle, hornspoon, and medal.
Bowmen of Chevy Chase, Newcastle	-	Gold and silver medals.
Bowmen of Chevy Chase {Town Moor, Northumberland.}		Silver quiver, gold medal.
Cambridge Bowmen	- -	Silver arrow.
Essex Archers *		
Hainhalt Foresters	- -	Two splendid bugle horns, and two medals.
Hatfield Archers	- -	Several valuable prizes.
John o' Gaunt's Bowmen, Lancaster		Silver arrow, gold medals.
Kentish Rangers	- -	Gold medal.
Lancashire Bowmen, Cheetham Hill		Bugle horn and medals.
Lancashire and Broughton Archers	- -	Beautifully mounted quiver and four pair of arrows.
Liverpool Mersey Bowmen	- -	A silver bow and bugle horn.
Mercian Bowmen	- -	Several valuable prizes.
Musselburgh Archers	- -	A silver arrow.
Northumberland Archers	- -	Bugle horn, gold and silver medals.
Old Sarum Archers	- -	Gold and silver medals, silver arrow.
Robin Hood Bowmen	- -	Bugle horn, gold and silver medals.
Royal British Bowmen	- -	Silver arrow, tipt with gold.
Royal Company of Archers	- -	Silver arrow, silver cup.
Royal Kentish Bowmen	- -	Bugle horn, gold medal.
Royal Surrey Bowmen	- -	Silver arrow, gold medal.
Southampton Archers	- -	Gold medal.
St. George's Bōwmen	- -	Bugle medal.
Teucerean Society of Archers	- -	Silver bugle, four silver medals.
Toxophilite Society	- -	Queen's prize,—silver bugle, medals.

* Prizes unknown.

United Society of Archers, Cannock Chase	- -	Silver bow, silver medal.
Woodmen of Arden	- -	Bugle horn, silver arrow, medals, &c.
Woodmen of Hornsey	- -	Gold and silver medals.
Yeoman Archers	- -	Medals.
Yorkshire Archers	- -	Silver bugle.

Of still more recent formation, are the,

Archers of the Abbey of Bury St. Edmunds.	Needwood Foresters.
Beulah Spa Archers.	Newton Villa Archery Society.
Blackmoor Foresters.	Robin Hood Society of Gloucestershire.
Brompton Archers.	Royal Sherwood Archers.
Carisbrook Archers.	Stourhead Bow-meetings. *
Clapham Archers.	Staffordshire Bowmen.
Derbyshire Archery Society.	Selwood Foresters.
East Berkshire Archers.	South Saxon Archers.
East Somerset Archers.	St. George's Bowmen.
Gwent Bowmen.	Stoke Leigh Camp Archers.†
Glasgow Archers.	Wellsbourne Archers.
Herefordshire Bowmen.	West Berkshire United Archery Club.
Harlow Bush Archers.	West Somerset Archers.
Melksham Foresters.	Windsor Archers.

It is not pretended that the above catalogue comprises every society, large and small, within the compass of Great Britain. Many include merely a family party; others, though perhaps less exclusive, have still neither local habitation nor a name, and their proceedings never transpire beyond their own immediate circle. We find some excellent marksmen, of both sexes, among these little knots of archers, notwithstanding.

First in seniority among modern societies, are the Toxophilites, who originally erected their butts upon the lawn behind Leicester House; but alas! through the rapid journey which London has been making out of town for the last century, the

* Sir R. C. Hoare.   † Near Bristol.

place that knew them, now knows them no more. Reader, just fancy an honest country archer visiting the metropolis for the first time in his life, A. D. 1839. He had long previously discovered in Hargrave's anecdotes, perchance in those of little Oldfield, where this celebrated body shot in the days of Sir Ashton. Comfort, rather than the vagaries of fashion, has been, from youth up, the characteristics of his ancestral home in Wensley Dale, the romantic shores of Ulswater, or some spot equally remote and beautiful: he takes his "ease at his inn," at the Bedford, or other similar establishment within the purlieus of Covent Garden. Having indulged in a due degree of repose after the fatigues of a long journey, he enters upon its object, namely, to inspect the wonders of the Great Metropolis, but, above all, to witness some of its archery parades; and this he considers will be best done by a visit to the shooting-ground of the Toxophilites, as the chief society in town. Accordingly, whilst discussing a broiled chicken, and the remains of his bottle of Chambertin, many inquiries are directed to the waiter respecting the road to "Leicester House Gardens." These, however, he utters with an air of perfect nonchalance, anxious to escape being set down as altogether a greenhorn. The man, accustomed to the little inaccuracies of country gentlemen, when conversing about streets and places in London, directs him to the square of that name, and, buoyant with expectation, he sallies forth. The evening turns out such as archers love—calm, serene, cloudless; and, hastening onwards, he meditates upon his chances of catching the Toxophilites engaged at their sport, when he will be enabled to judge, from personal observation, how far the Scroton and the Richmond have the odds in a challenge they contemplate sending to their Metropolitan brother archers. Although the localities he is compelled to traverse, in conformity with the waiter's instructions, certainly do not exactly "babble of green fields," nevertheless he pushes on, little dreaming of disappointment. But imagine his vacant stare, whilst some good-natured passenger explains the irresistible march of brick and mortar.

"What, here!" exclaims our astonished countryman; "among granite flags, macadamised roads, ranges of dingy houses, and a human tide rushing by, as if each individual composing it bore the cares of three kingdoms upon his shoulders!"

"Even so, good sir;—these now usurp the green sunny lawns where Britain's prince charmed all hearts by his affability, and all eyes by the grace with which he drew the bow, as he excelled in every other noble accomplishment." *

I have already compared the ardour with which, towards the close of the last century, Englishmen resumed the ancient national weapon to the Shakspeare mania prevalent about the same period. A similar rage for possessing even the most trivial relic analogous to the objects of their respective idolatry possessed the votaries of each. The Tower of London, the castles of Windsor, Edinburgh, Dover, — every fortalice and gothic mansion in the three kingdoms,— were ransacked, in the expectation of discovering some remnants of old English archery. The search was in general but ill rewarded; though, whenever any thing did come to light, it was treasured up with eager fondness, or disposed of at a price ridiculously exorbitant.

My own feelings with respect to this subject are ardent enough; yet is it possible to avoid laughing, when one reflects on the overwhelming rage which possessed that honest toxophilite, who discovered the domestics of a certain Scottish mansion in the act of cooking their master's haggis with a parcel of bows long secreted there! My readers will compare it to the indignation excited in the dramatic world, when Warburton's cookmaid confessed to having devoted the rarest spe-

* Many persons yet living have seen the Prince shooting with the Toxophilites in the grounds of Leicester House.

cimens of his early English plays to a similar use. In both cases, it might be quite as well that the respective offenders had challenged every archer and playgoer summoned upon the jury, had either of these exploits periled life or liberty.

In imitation of the Stratford jubilee, instituted by Garrick in honour of Avon's Bard, the Toxophilites contemplated a similar festival in memory of the celebrated author of the "Toxophilus." Why they never carried their plan into execution, I am unable to state exactly; I believe some difficulty was experienced in ascertaining the date and place of his nativity. Perhaps they would yet like to know that he was born at Kirkley Whiske, an obscure village of Richmondshire, in the North Riding of York, about the year 1511, being the son of John Ascham of the same place, an independent freeholder, much esteemed by his contemporaries for probity and good sense, to which honourable endowments he owed his situation as steward to the Lord Scrope of Bolton House.

At an early age his son Roger became page to Sir Henry Wingfielde, in whose family he acquired that love of archery which adhered to him through life. He afterwards married Mrs. Margaret Howe, a lady of family and fortune, ancestress to the present noble family of that name. Ascham's constitution, naturally weak, had been long overstrained by study, the ill effects of which, as he tells us, he laboured to counteract by daily exercise at the shooting-butts. At length, about the close of the year 1568, having sat up very late, according to custom, in order to finish a poem intended for presentation to the Queen, he was attacked with a violent fit of the ague, which proved mortal.

The following passage in Abraham Darcie's " Annals of England" will likewise be perused with interest, as containing some curious information respecting Ascham's private habits. "The last day but one of this present year (1568), pardon me this short digression for the memorie's sake of an honest and virtuous man, who being borne in the countie of Yorke, and brought up at Cambridge, was the first of our nation that refined the Greek and Latin tongues, and the puritie of the style, with singular commendation of his eloquence. He was some time reader to Queen Elizabeth, and her secretarie for the Latin tongue; and yet, notwithstanding he was given to play and cockfighting, he both lived and died not very rich *, leaving behind him two elegant books, as monuments of his rare wit and understanding; one of which was styled "Toxophilus, or schole of shootinge," and the other, " Scholarca." From a letter not found, as I believe, in any published edition of his works, it appears that he owed his church preferment to the former of these treatises. "I once wrote," says he, "a little book of Shewtinge, which King Henry, her (Queen Elizabeth's) noble father, did so well like and allow, that he gave me a living for it." Henry's love and knowledge of archery have been already described elsewhere.

The author of the "Seasons" likewise, another man of genius, appears to have handled his shafts as adroitly as he did the angling-rod. Who that is acquainted with that exquisite passage, beginning —

> " Just in the dubious point, where with the pool
> Is mix'd the trembling stream; or where it boils
> Around the stone, or from the hollow bank
> Reverted plays in undulating flow,
> There throw, nice-judging, the delusive fly;
> And as you lead it round with artful curve,
> With eye attentive mark the springing game.
> Straight, as above the surface of the flood
> They wanton rise, or urged by hunger leap,
> Then fix, with gentle twitch, the barbed hook,"—

---

* With such tastes, his wealth would be infinitely more surprising than his poverty. It is very remarkable that the "Toxophilus" contains some serious admonitions respecting the destructive habit of gaming; with earnest exhortations, that the youth of his age should forego the dice-box, and follow "the harmless and manly exercise of the bow."

will deny his adroitness with the latter? And were there no decisive evidence of Thomson's reputation as an archer, we are justified in upholding it, from the pains taken by Mr. Chalmers, and some other of the original Toxophilites, to find out every particular respecting his early life. How far they were successful, I know not; but if the following trivial anecdote be thought worthy of a place in their records, they are also exceedingly welcome to it. About the year 1725 the poet kept an academy on Kew Green, and twice or thrice a week a few of his elder scholars were invited to the palace, as playmates for the Prince of Wales. One of them, named Littlejohn, being a great favourite with his Royal Highness, he once observed to him — "Littlejohn*, when I am king, you

* The prince alluded to the well-known comrade of that "strong thief" Robin Hood. Would the reader like to see the origin of his name?

> With all his bowmen, that stood in a ring,
>   And were of the Nottingham breed,
> Brave Stukely came then, with seven yeomen,
>   And did in this manner proceed.
> This infant was called John Little, quoth he,
>   Which name shall be altered anon;
> The words we 'll transpose; so wherever he goes,
>   He 'll be hail'd as my own Little John.
> Thou shalt be an archer, as well as the best,
>   And range in the greenwood with us;
> Where we ne'er want gold nor silver, behold, —
>   While bishops have aught in their purse.
> And so, ever after, as long as he lived,
>   Although he was proper and tall,
> Yet nevertheless, the truth to express,
>   Still Little John they did him call.
>   *Old Ballad.*

A portion of a bow, with his name scratched above the handle, hangs within the hall of Cannon Hall, an ancient mansion in Yorkshire, the seat of Walter Spencer Stanhope, Esq. It was brought from Hathersage, in Derbyshire, an old seat that once belonged to the Ashtons, where Little John was buried, and where his bones, of gigantic proportions, were recently dug up; those of the thigh measured $28\frac{1}{2}$ inches, being now in the possession of Sir George Strick-

shall be our bow-bearer in chief, and have Sherwood Forest."
The promise was given with all the sincerity of ingenuous
childhood. It were interesting to know if Mr. Littlejohn survived, and saw his royal friend the monarch of three kingdoms.* I would have petitioned for the head rangership at
all events.

That magnificent spectacle, the Grand Meeting of Archers,
which took place on Blackheath, May 29th, 1792, owed its
origin to the Royal Toxophilites. The weather was most propitious, and the novelty of the scene drew together an incredible
concourse of spectators. At noon the archers, clothed in Kendall green, met at their respective tents, which were pitched
in a line fronting the south. Immediately opposite these,
fourteen pair of targets ranged from north to south: a distance
of one hundred yards intervened between each; and they appeared in the following order when reckoned downwards from
the front of the tents:—

  Surrey Bowmen; two sets of targets.
  St. George's Bowmen.
  Royal Kentish Bowmen; two sets of targets.
  The Toxophilite Society.
  Archers' Division of the Artillery Company.
  Woodmen of Arden.
  Robin Hood's Bowmen; two sets of targets.
  Woodmen of Hornsey.
  Bowmen of Chevy Chase.
  Suffolk bowmen.

The following programme of the day's amusements was published by authority of the stewards:—

---

land, Bart., of Boynton. As regards the bow just alluded to, it is of yew, and of great power still, six feet seven inches long, although that portion of both ends where the notches for holding the string were, has been broken off.

* Since writing the above, I am informed that he died subsequent to the year 1799, a wealthy planter in Jamaica.

GENERAL ORDERS.

At eleven o'clock, the leaders of the targets are to arrange the archers to shoot at their respective marks, and to set down their names.

No greater number than TEN to shoot at any one pair of targets.

Two arrows to be shot at each end.

Two target papers to be kept at each target.

At twelve, the shooters to form a line in front of the tents, in the order of shooting. The signal for forming the line, to be a march of the music, playing the whole length of the tents. The line being formed, the command, to face to the right and march, to be given by three strokes of the kettle-drums.

The different societies will then proceed to their respective targets, and begin shooting when the music ceases. The leader of each target to advance ten paces when his party have done shooting, and proceed to the opposite target, on hearing the bands, which will continue playing until the shooting recommences.

At three, refreshments to be taken into the tents.

The signal to go into the tents will be, by the music halting in the centre of the ground, until the arrows are collected; when each society will fall into its own station. The line will then be formed, and the archers are to march back to their respective tents, the same signal being used as for the march to the targets.

At half-past three, the re-opening of the targets will be announced, by a repetition of the signals before used.

At six, the shooting will cease, by the same signal as before used for going to refresh; the whole line to halt in front of the tents, while the stewards collect the target papers; the archers are then to be dismissed, and to proceed to dinner. Tickets to be collected at the door of the dining-room, and the societies to be seated according to seniority, the stewards making the arrangements.

These, we must allow, were eminently conducive to promote the good order and success which distinguished this laudable effort to revive the masculine robust exercises of our ancestors. The scene was a truly magnificent one. In beautiful contrast with the gay greensward, appeared numerous snow white tents, above which floated banners and other emblematical devices of the different societies; but the view of fourteen pair of targets, occupying an unbroken line full half a mile long, I can well imagine to have been by far the most elegant portion of the spectacle; with their gorgeous colours, and the idea of perfect repose they suggest to the gazer's mind. Busy groups of bowmen in their finest garb; tens of thousands of spectators attired in all that beautiful costume which the inhabitants of the metropolis never fail to exhibit on a gala day; bursts of martial music floating through the air; — must have formed a scene equally novel and picturesque.

Amongst those who especially distinguished themselves by gallant attention to their fair visiters, I will not omit to name the Royal Artillery Archers, whose tent was lined throughout with green silk; and Robin Hood's Bowmen, for they had provided in theirs a temporary flooring of boards. Their uniform also attracted universal attention, as being the most elegant and appropriate in the whole field. The honours of the day fell thick upon this society; since, out of the four prizes, they became entitled to three, two being won by —— Anderson, Esq., as captain of numbers, and lieutenant of the target; the third fell to the lot of R. Glenn, Esq., as lieutenant of numbers. The captain of the target was a Woodman of Arden.

Among the nobility present, Lord Aylesford distinguished himself by some very close shooting; indeed the exploits of the day, taken as a whole, stand high in the annals of modern archery. The captain of numbers above mentioned, placed thirty-three arrows in the target; and the second in command, twenty-four. On every former occasion, the highest number had never exceeded twenty-one. It is remarkable that Mr. Anderson, who bore away the most considerable prize, should have been a Fleming; and though but of middling stature, shot with a Flemish long bow of six feet three inches. This gentleman appears to have been an incomparable archer, at that period esteemed among the best in England, and the feats of dexterity recorded of him, justify the distinction. In September, 1795, shooting with the Woodmen of Arden, he gained a captaincy of numbers. During the same month and year, he was challenged by a gentleman in the Isle of Thanet for the best of three days' sport at target-shooting. On the numbers being cast up, the result appeared as follows. First day: Anderson, 415; Gibson, 372. Second day, which proved excessively stormy: Anderson, 479; Gibson, 341. Third day: Anderson, 496; Gibson, 407. Anderson had much of the right spirit in him. He never declined a challenge, and rarely failed of a triumph. In the choice of his bows he was somewhat *recherché*, as became an archer who could handle them so well. Take the following memorandum extracted from the Bankes' MSS., in proof of this:—

March 15th, 1794. At the Custom-house to-day, I saw several bows, which, having been entered too low, were seized and sold. Mr. Anderson, a famous archer, went to look at them. He said he had been abroad on purpose to purchase one of the lot, for which he would give twenty guineas. Four of them (that Mr. Anderson valued so much was one,) sold for 16*l*. I understand he bought the lot, and also another parcel of bows. There were no arrows, only wood for them.

March 15th, 1794. Mr. Waring told me he did not buy the bows, as the price was too high. That he never sold one for more than 2*l*. 2*s*. There was wood for arrows, at the Custom-house, which he bought. 'The bows,' he said, 'did not appear to him better than usual, only they were well seasoned.'

Let us resume the history of the Toxophilites. When Clerkenwell church was being rebuilt, they manifested their respect for Sir W. Wood, an old marshal of the Finsbury Archers, by expending a considerable sum in the re-embellishment and removal of his monument, from the outside of the old to the interior of the new building.* His tombstone bears the following quaint and characteristic inscription: —

> Sir William Wood lies very near this stone,
> In's time in archery excelled by none.
> Few were his equals, and this noble art
> Has suffered now in the most tender part.
> *Long did he live the honor of the bow;*
> *And his great age to that alone did owe.*
> But how can art secure, or what can save
> Extreme old age from an appointed grave.
> Surviving archers much his loss lament,
> And in respect bestowed this monument,
> Where whistling arrowes did his worth proclaim,
> And eterniz'd his memory and name.
> Obijt   Sept. 4th.
> Anno   { D^{ni}. 1691.
>   { Ætat 82.
>
> THIS MONUMENT WAS RESTORED
> BY
> THE TOXOPHILITE SOCIETY OF LONDON,
> 1791.

Pennant makes the following witty allusion to the poetical merits of this epitaph, in his account of London.† "Now we are on the outside of the church, let me, in this revival of archery, direct the attention of the brethren and sisters of the bow, to the epitaph of Sir William Wood, a celebrated archer, who died in 1691, æt. 82. May their longevity equal his! but when they have made their last shot, I hope that the ROYAL BRITISH BOWMEN have provided an abler bard to celebrate their skill than fell to the lot of poor William Wood."

This, it is imagined, alludes to some wretched doggerel prefixed to his "Bowman's Glory," and commencing thus: —

* "Mr. Waring told me it cost the society twelve pounds."— *Notes, Bankes' MSS.*"
† P. 195.

> " Brave archery, what rapture shall I raise
> In giving thee thy merit and due praise!
> Divine thou art, as from the gods begot!
> Apollo with an arrow Python shot;
> And Cupid, the fair Venus' son, we know,
> Is always figured with his shafts and bow;" &c. &c.

These are the only verses, if verses they may be called, in Wood's book. Its chief contents are: " Patents of King Henry VIII., James and Charles I., concerning Archerie;" and descriptions of several shows, processions, and shootings, from the year 1583 to 1681. Maitland, in his 'History of London,' asserts that the honour of knighthood was conferred as a compliment by his brethren, for his dexterity in shooting. But it is more likely to have been conferred on him royally, as the titles of Duke of Shoreditch, Marquis of Clerkenwell, &c., were on some of his predecessors. The current tradition is, that Charles II. seeing an arrow remarkably well shot, inquired who the archer was, and immediately knighted him.[*] However this may be, it is very evident he was held in high esteem by his cotemporaries; for when Queen Catharine, queen consort to Charles II., presented to the Finsbury Archers that splendid silver badge now in possession of the Toxophilite Society, it was unanimously confided to his keeping. Afterwards, the oldest members of the fraternity undertook the charge of this ornament in succession, together with its case, and a pair of arrows, prizes won by them.

The case just alluded to, is by no means the least interesting object among these archery trophies. It resembles a cupboard with folding doors, having on the inside of each a portrait of the old knight in his official costume; the countenance indicates great intelligence and good humour; in his hand the marshal's staff, and the silver badge upon his breast. He is represented with mustachios, a fine flowing beard, and wears a

---

[*] Bankes' MSS.

handsome dark velvet hat, surmounted by a rich plume, whilst the lower part of his dress, which is equally picturesque, resembles what Vandycke gives to many of his family pictures.

The legend —

SIR WILLIAM WOOD

appears beneath the first portrait; and —

WITH ABUNDANCE
OF LOVE

an expression he often used — beneath the second.

For years previous to the establishment of the Toxophilites, there were very few Finsbury Archers remaining, Mr. Constable being the oldest. He became a Toxophilite, and presented these valuable relics to his new associates, in whose possession they have since continued.

The gift of an annual prize by his Majesty entitled the members of this society to make the addition to their original title usual with bodies patronised by the monarch; so they are at present known as THE ROYAL TOXOPHILITES. In various challenges from contemporary societies, to which their reputation has subjected them, I know of but one instance where they have not come off triumphant. On the 5th of August, 1834, a match took place between eleven of the West Berks Archery Club, and the same number of Toxophilites; the former being victorious by a small number of hits. At the great meeting of British Archers before described, they had the honour of carrying away the gold medal; and when the second meeting on Dulwich Common, gave a prize to be shot for by five selected members of any society, who were to excel in number of hits during the whole days' shooting, the challenge was accepted by the Toxophilites, and they came off victorious by a majority of one hundred and ninety shots. In September, 1792, when a select party shot a match of archery in the Flemish style, at Mr. Anderson's grounds, near Highgate, Dr. Howarth, of the Toxophilites, received a medal given for the greatest number of prizes. The elder Mr. Waring, already known as the founder of the society, has been seen to put twenty successive arrows, shooting two at each end, into a four-foot target, at the distance of one hundred yards. In the space of one minute, he has likewise shot twelve arrows into a mark two feet square, at forty-six yards.* Mr. Crunden, now the father of the Toxophilites, aiming the same number of arrows at a sheet of paper eight inches square, put in ten successive shots at thirty yards. On another occasion, he drove fifty-two arrows out of a hundred into a four-foot target, distant one hundred yards. † And, lastly, two other Toxophilites, Messrs. Froward and Green, clapt each two arrows, at the same end, into a six inch square paper, six score yards off. ‡ This is admirable shooting, from which we may estimate the degree of excellence to which those archers would have arrived, had they undergone the severe drillings familiar to their forefathers. One meets occasionally with game-keepers who, by early practice with the fowling-piece, not only succeed in killing every thing which runs or flies, but flatten their lead ten times successively against a halfpenny thrown into the air. Among gentlemen, how many are there who, at the distance of sixteen paces, can snuff a candle, and hit a wafer, with a pistol ball, or split it upon the edge of a table knife. Exactly the same degree of adroitness would certainly be the result of a proportionate devotion of our time to the exercise of archery.

Reasoning from my own tastes, I do not think the reader will be displeased at these little digressions. I will therefore cite an instance or two of what is done by nations who undergo a course of discipline similar to that of the old English bowmen, and whose acquirements are of course exceedingly parallel. In a curious French work, entitled Voyages au Nord, the author speaking of the archery of the Samoiedes remarks that they shot excellently well with the bow. Two of these savages, brought

* Roberts. † Ibid. ‡ Ibid.

to Moscow by order of the Czar*, being commanded to exhibit a specimen of their art, aimed their arrows with such extraordinary dexterity as to excite the admiration of the spectators, one of them placed a very small dernier † against the trunk of a tree, and retiring to such a distance that the mark was scarcely visible, he repeatedly struck it with his arrow.‡ Dumont, an early French traveller, tells an anecdote respecting the accuracy of aim exhibited by the Turkish archers of Constantinople. He observes that there are two ancient columns in that city, known as the Burnt and the Historical Columns. Adjoining these, he saw a large court appointed for the use of such as chose to exercise themselves, in archery. The master of the sport presented him with a bow, and he had the pleasure of shooting some arrows at the mark. It was fastened against a wall, and contained several lesser marks, gradually decreasing, so that the last was not bigger than a Dutch skilling ; yet he saw many persons hit it at every shot, though they stood one hundred paces off. §

Thus much for Turkish archery : and quitting Constantinople, we will once more transport ourselves to the Regent's Park, where, in the pleasantest portion of one of the most delightful suburban scenes ever created by the taste and industry of man, the Royal Toxophilite Society have established their present quarters. The ground, on account of the plantations, is not visible from the road, except on the days of meeting, when the targets, glittering with crimson and gold, are just discernible through the masses of foliage that encircle the spot. Three pairs of earthen butts, surmounted according to ancient usage, with urns of the same material, are ranged on its green closely shaven turf, at the usual distances. An elegant iron railing

---

* The Russians levy a tax of two copecs on every Samoiede who can draw the bow.
† A coin about the size of a sixpence.   ‡ Vol. i. p. 136.
§ Dumont's Levant, p. 195.

and gravelled path encloses the whole area, which, except in the space between the targets, is tastefully dotted with clumps of trees and flowering shrubs. The remainder forms a beautiful parterre, embellished with a profusion of flowers; and the whole management reflects much credit on the taste of the Hon. D. Finch, the secretary, under whose direction it was planned, and whose judgment in ornamental gardening appears no way inferior to his skill as an archer.

The banquetting-hall, where the Toxophilites dine, is erected in the genuine old English style of architecture, thus harmonising with an amusement all whose associations are connected with the fashions of a by-gone age.

The interior is fitted up with elegant simplicity. In the centre of the apartment stands a range of oak dining tables, sufficient to accommodate the members on their occasional festivals. To the left on entering, is a lofty antique chimney-piece of oak, with a dial in the centre. The windows, opening on a broad veranda, which encircles the whole edifice, are of richly stained glass, proudly decorated with the heraldic bearings of its founder; his Majesty, the patron; and the Earl of Aylesford, president. They bear in addition the following inscriptions:—

First Window.

Toxophilite Society.　　Sir Ashton Lever,
A. D. 1781.　　　　　　　Knight,
　　　　　　　　　　　　Founder.

Second Window.

His Majesty William IV.
Patron.

Third Window.

Earl of Aylesford,
President.

Massive shields of carved oak, emblazoned with devices emblematical of archery, adorn the ceilings of this interesting apartment; and around its walls are placed a range of Aschams*, ornamanted with crest and coronet, as well as the colours and pattern of each archer's arrow-mark. The badge and painting already described, with a portrait of the elder Mr. Waring, are also preserved at the banquetting-hall.

The Toxophilite Society possesses many valuable prizes †, of which the Queen will annually present one. In 1795, Mr. Palmer, a member, bestowed an elegant silver gilt arrow, on condition that it should be shot for during four successive years. At the expiration of that period, his crest and cipher were engraved on it, and the four archers who had been already successful, again contested its final possession.

The Toxophilite costume, in Sir Ashton Lever's time, was a single-breasted coat, of grass green, with an arrow engraved on the buttons; buff kerseymere waistcoat and small clothes; Hessian boots, hat turned up on the right side, with black feather; belt, bracer, and shooting-glove.

We will now bid them farewell, and transport ourselves to the sunny greensward of Meriden Heath, where

> All clad in Lincoln green,

beneath their trysting tree, our presence is anxiously awaited by —

THE WOODMEN OF THE FOREST OF ARDEN.

Oliver. Where will the old Duke live?
Charles. They say he is already in the FOREST OF ARDEN, and a many

---

* For explanation of this term, see p. 360.

† The Prince's bugle, contested at three lengths; viz., 60, 80, and 100 yards.

July 1836.— King's cup, won by Captain Norton; silver cup, by Mr. Haddes. *Present*—The Prince of Orange; and the King of Oude's ambassador.

merry men with him; and there they live like the old Robin Hood of England; and fleet the time carelessly as they did in the golden world.*

> We are warriors gallant and true,
> But our triumphs are not stained with tears;
> For our only war cry is the huntsman's halloo,
> And the blood that we shed is the deer's:
> > And the green wood tree
> > Is our armoury,
> And of broad oak leaves our garlands be.
>
> We sleep not the sun's light away,
> Nor shame with our revels the moon;
> But we chase the fleet deer at the break of day,
> And we feast on his haunches at noon;
> > While the green wood tree
> > Waves over us free,
> And of broad oak leaves our garlands be.
>
> We drink not the blood-red wine,
> But our nut-brown ale is good.
> For the song and the dance of the great we ne'er prize;
> While the rough wind, our chorister rude,
> > Through the green wood tree
> > Whistles jollily,
> And the broad oak leaves dance to our minstrelsy.
>
> To the forest then, merry men all;
> Our triumphs are ne'er stained with tears;
> For our only war cry is the huntsman's call,
> And the blood that we shed is the deer's;
> > And the green wood tree
> > Is our armoury,
> And of broad oak leaves our garlands be. †

* It was not lawless "minions of the moon," as Falstaff termed his rogueish associates, who resorted to these places of sylvan rendezvous for the distribution of their booty; archers, as well as lovers, had their places of assignation beneath the forest bough. Rangers and woodsmen of the royal hunting grounds

---

* SHAKESPEARE.— *As you like it.* † NEALE.

also pitched upon a conspicuous oak, growing in some central situation, as a kind of head-quarters. Thither each forester, after his evening perambulation, bent his steps; there he sat down to await his comrades' arrival, and discuss the events which had occurred in reference to their guardianship "of the green hue and hunting." An old comedy, called "The Merry Devil of Edmonton," contains this brief but very pleasant allusion to the foresters' trysting tree: —

> *Enter* BRIAN *and his man, with a hound.*
>
> *Brian.* Ralph, heard'st thou any stirring?
> *Ralph.* I heard one speak here hard bye, in the bottom. Peace, Master! speake lowe; nownes if I didn't hear a bow go off, and the buck bray, I never heard deer in my life.
> *Brian.* When went your fellowes to their walkes?
> *Ralph.* An hour agoe.
> *Brian.* Life! are there stealers abroad, and we cannot have them? Where the devil are my men to night? Sirrah, goe up the wind * toward Buckley's lodge. I'll cast about the bottom with my hounde, and then meet thee under Coney's Oak.

This ancient forest of Arden once covered nearly the whole of Warwickshire, Worcestershire, and the neighbouring county of Stafford. Thus Drayton: —

> Muse, first of Arden tell, whose footsteps yet are found
> In her ‡ rough woodlands more than any other ground
> That mighty Arden held, even in her height of pride;
> Her one hand touching Trent, the other Severn's side.

The Woodmen assemble within a few miles of Coventry; and exercising a nominal, as their predecessors did a real, authority over vert and venison, their officers receive appropriate designations. Of these, the lord warden is chief. They have

---

* To prevent footsteps, or other accidental sounds, from discovering his approach. In hunting, this precaution was observed, because a buck can by his scent, discover the hunters at a considerable distance.

† The county of Warwick.

likewise master-foresters, verderers *, and most probably a bow-bearer, whose name indicates his duties, and who, in some districts, anciently ranked next to the lord warden, he being the monarch's most favoured attendant during his hunting parades. In the first lieutenant's absence, likewise, his oath of office obliged him to attach every one found trespassing on the timber or the deer, often styled in sylvan parlance, " the green hue and hunting."

George III. was the last of our monarchs who required the performance of this ancient service. When he visited Lyndhurst in state, the Rev. Sir Charles Hill, Bart., attended him as bow-bearer, leading a brace of milk-white greyhounds.† Such I have here attempted to describe, appears to have been the

---

* The foresters took care of the venison; the verderers, of the vert or timber.

† One very usual tenure by which men held their estates during the middle ages, were military or personal services connected with archery. The presentation of a barbed arrow at certain seasons, was, in a hundred instances, the only acknowledgment required for large grants of land; and by the office of bow-bearer to the king, when he came to hunt in particular districts, several ancient families, besides that just mentioned, originally acquired possession of the broad and fertile manors they at present enjoy.

Sibertoft, county of Northampton. — This manor was held by Nicholas le Archer, by the service of carrying the king's bow through all the forests in England.

Upton, county of Gloucester. — Geoffroy de la Grave holds one yard of land in Upton, in the county of Gloucester, by sergeantry of following our lord the king, in his army in England, with a bow and arrows at his own cost for forty days; and afterwards at the cost of our lord the king.

Molesey county of Surrey.— Walter de Molesey holds his land in Molesey of our lord the king by the sergeantry of his being his crossbowman (balistar) in his army for forty days at his own costs; and if he should stay longer, at the cost of the king.

Waterhall county of Bucks. — Reginald de Gray holds the manor of Waterhall, in the county of Bucks, of our lord the king by the service of finding one man upon a horse without a saddle, of the price of fifteen pence, and one bow without a string, and one arrow without a head, when the king shall command him for his service for the said manor to be in his army.

U

ancient vocation of a forester. We will now contemplate him under his more modern guise.

The meetings of the Woodmen, appropriately styled " grand annual wardmotes," are accompanied by all the pride, pomp, and circumstance of archery. The fine band of the Warwickshire militia attends upon the ground, exhilarating the already buoyant spirit by strains of martial music. A bugle call announces the opening of the targets, and summonses the archers to the contest; while the united clangor of trumpet and kettle-

---

PETITES SERGEANTRIES.

Aston Cantlou, county of Warwick. — The manor of Aston Cantlou (so called from the family called Cantiloup) was, by inquisition, after the death of Lawrence Hastings, Earl of Pembroke, returned to be held in this form; viz., that that manor is held by itself of our lord the king in capite, by the service of finding a foot soldier, with a bow without a string (arcu sine corda), with a helmet or cap, for forty days, at the proper charges of the lord of that manor, as often as there should be war in Wales.

Chittington, county of Salap. — Roger Corbet holds the manor of Chittington, in the county of Salop, of the king in capite, by the service of finding one footman in time of war, in the king's army in Wales, with one bow and there arrows, and one pale *, and carrying with him one bacon or salted hog; and when he comes to the army, delivering to the king's marshal a moiety of the bacon; and thence the marshal was to deliver to him daily some of that moiety for his dinner, so long as he stayed in the army; and he was to follow the army so long as that half of the bacon should last.

Brineston, county of Chester. — The manor of Brineston, in the county of Chester, is held of the king in capite, by the service of finding a man in the army of our lord the king going into the parts of Scotland barefoot, clothed with a waistcoat and breeches, having in one hand a bow without a string, and in the other an arrow unfeathered.

Bryanstone, county of Dorset. — Ralph de Stopham holds the manor of Bryanston, in the county of Dorset, by the sergeantry of finding for our lord the king, as often as he should lead his English army into Wales, a boy carrying a bow without a string, and an arrow unfeathered (buzonem sine pennis), at his own proper costs, for forty days.

---

* Pale — a stake shod at both ends with iron, carried into the field by each archer, and planted obliquely on the ground before him, on the approach of cavalry.

drum proclaims the victor's triumph. Their prizes are various and beautiful, among which, "the bugle horn of Arden" appears to be a special favourite, and always excites more than ordinary emulation.* The distance for this prize varies from nine to twelve score yards, which exempts the Woodmen from the operation of a statute alluded to elsewhere.

There are also —

THE MASTER FOERSTER'S GOLD MEDAL, claimed by the first shot in the gold.†

THE VERDERER'S SILVER MEDAL,‡ — by the second shot in the gold.

SILVER ARROW, § — nine score yards.

DIGBEAN GOLD MEDAL, ‖ —OPTIME MERENTI.

DIGBEAN SILVER MEDAL, ¶ — BENE MERENTI.

This society was originally established by the Marquis of Aylesford, father to the present lord warden. His Lordship's strength of arm, and the consequent low range of his arrow, has been often a subject of remark; and his vigorous shooting has descended like a heirloom to his successor.

I will now give a list of all, or most, of the original members, commencing with the officers, who gain their rank by a display of superior skill:

Lord Aylesford	Lord Warden.
R. York, Esq.	Master Forester.
—— Digby, Esq.	Secretary.
W. Dilke, Esq.	Senior Verderer.

---

* Wardmote of August, 1832, won very dexterously by the Hon. and Rev. Charles Finch, who gained three successive ends.

† Lieut. Colonel Stewart, first shot in the gold.

‡ Hon. and Rev. Charles Finch, second shot in the gold.

§ By the present secretary, Rev. Thomas Coker Adams.

‖ By the same Woodman, 45 hits. The possessor of this prize ranks as Captain of Numbers.

¶ By the Hon. and Rev. Charles Finch, 42 hits. The silver medal confers the Lieutenancy of Numbers.

Rev. W. Bree
E. Finch, Esq.
Cradock Hartopp, Esq.
—— Palmer, Esq.
} Verderers.

In 1786 there were about thirty-six woodmen, besides the these officers; viz. —

Lord Lewisham.	—— Lewit, Esq.
Lord Walgrave.	—— Adderly, Esq.
Lord Warrick.	—— Dilke, Esq.
Sir Robert Lawley.	—— Lawley, Esq.
Sir George Shuckburgh.*	—— Okeover, Esq.
Sir John Sheffield.	Frank Mills, Esq.
Rev. —— Reynolds.	W. Mills, Esq.
Rev. J. Dilke.	—— Moland, Esq.
Charles Greville.	Ralph Adderly, Esq.
William Finch.	—— Bateman, Esq.
Featherstone Dilke.	—— Wright, Esq.
—— Palmer, Esq.	—— Boultbee, Esqs. (two).
—— Gresley, Esqs. (two).	—— Malloy, Esq.
—— Sadler, Esq.	—— Frod, Esq.
—— Croxall, Esq.	&c. &c.
—— Reppington, Esq.	

Their uniform was a plain frock of Kendal green, with gold buttons bearing an arrow, on which is inscribed the word "ARDEN"; white waistcoat; round hat, and black feather.

* The following anecdote has relation to an illustrious ancestor of this gentleman. As King Charles I. marched to Edgecott, near Banbury, on 22d Oct. 1642, he saw Richard Shuckburgh, Esq. hunting in the fields, not far from Shuckburgh, with a very good pack of hounds. Upon which, it is reported, he fetched a deep sigh, and asked who the gentleman was, who hunted so merrily that morning, when he was on the way to fight for his crown and dignity. And being told it was this Richard Shuckburgh, he was ordered to be called, and was by him very graciously received. Upon which he immediately went home, armed all his tenants, and the next day attended the king on the field, where he was knighted, and was present at the battle of Coghill. After the taking of Banbury Castle, and his Majesty's retreat from those parts, he went to his own seat, and fortified himself on the top of Shuckburgh Hill, where being attacked by some of the Parliamentary forces, he defended himself till he fell, with most of his tenants about him. Being picked up, however, and life appearing in him, he was taken to Kenilworth Castle, and there forced to purchase his liberty at a dear rate. — DUGDALE.

A mutual exchange of honours soon ensued between the Royal Toxophilites and the Woodmen of Arden. The former conferred the freedom of their society, with permission to shoot on their ground, &c., by a diploma, elegantly emblazoned, and enclosed in a box of yew. That by which the Woodmen returned the compliment, was received in a box made of the heart of oak, the growth of the forest whence they derive their name.

The following is a chronological list of the archers who have been victorious at their grand annual wardmotes, during a nearly consecutive series of years.

Date	Prize	Score yards	Winner
Sept. 1792.	Silver arrow,	9	Rev. J. Dilke.
	Bugle horn,	9½	J. Featherstone, Esq.
	Annual target gold and silver medals,		W. Palmer, Esq.
Sept. 1795.	Silver arrow,*	9	Rev. J. Dilke.
	Bugle horn,	12	Lord Aylesford.
	Master Forester,		Rev. W. Bree.
	Senior Verderer,		Wriothesley Digby, Esq.
	Captaincy of Numbers,		Thomas Anderson, Esq.
	Lieutenancy of Numbers,		Thomas Palmer, Esq.
Aug. 1796,	Bugle horn,	11	Thomas Featherstone, Esq.
	Silver arrow,	9	Rev. J. Dilke.
	Gold medal, and Master Forester		R. York, Esq.
	Silver medal, and Senior Verderer,		W. Dilke, Esq.

* Given by the Countess of Aylesford.

		Score yards.	
Sept. 1797.	Silver arrow,	9	Richard Gresley, Esq.
	Bugle horn,	10	Henry Grimes, Esq.
	Gold medal,		Rev. — Bree.
	Silver medal,		R. York, Esq.
Aug. 1798.	Silver arrow,	9	Gilbert Beresford, Esq.
	Bugle horn,	10	Rev. J. Dilke.
	Gold medal,		W. Holbeache, Esq.
	Silver medal,		R. York, Esq.
Aug. 1799.	Gold medal,		Rev. Gilbert Beresford.
	Silver medal,		Earl of Aylesford.
	Silver bugle,	12	Rev. G. Beresford.
	Silver arrow,	9	Thomas Palmer, Esq.
Sept. 1800.	Gold medal, and Captaincy of Numbers,		Lord Aylesford.
	Lieutenancy of Numbers,		Thomas Palmer, Esq.
	Silver medal,		Rev. J. Wilkie.
	Silver arrow,	9	Rev. J. Dilke.
	Silver bugle,	10½	T. Featherstone, Esq.
Aug. 1801.	Gold medal,		C. Reppington, Esq.
	Silver medal, and Captaincy of Numbers,		T. Palmer, Esq.
	Silver arrow,	9	T. Featherstone, Esq.
	Silver bugle,	10	T. Palmer, Esq.
Aug. 1802.	Silver arrow,	9	William Palmer, Esq.
	Silver bugle,		Rev. J. Dilke.
	Captaincy of Numbers,		Earl of Aylesford.

SOCIETIES OF MODERN ARCHERS. 295

                      Score yards.

	Lieutenancy of Target,	W. Palmer, Esq.
	Silver arrow,	Rev. J. Dilke.
Aug. 1803.	Gold medal,	Lord Aylesford.
	Silver medal.	Edward Croxhall, Esq.
	Captaincy of Numbers,	Earl of Aylesford.
	Lieutenancy of Numbers,	F. Barker, Esq.*
	Silver arrow,	Earl of Aylesford.
Sept. 1804.	Captaincy of Target,	T. Palmer, Esq.
	Lieutenancy of Target,	Rev. Gilbert Beresford.
	Silver arrow,	T. Featherstone, Esq.
	Silver bugle,	Rev. J. Dilke.
Sept. 1805.	Gold medal,	Rev. J. Dilke.
	Silver medal,	J. Boultbee, Esq.
	Silver arrow,	T. Palmer, Esq.
	Silver bugle,	12 T. Featherstone, Esq.
Sept. 1806.	Gold medal,	Earl of Aylesford.
	Silver medal,	Sir Grey Skipworth.
	Silver arrow,	T. Palmer, Esq.
	Silver bugle,	10½ Rev. J Dilke.
Aug. 1807.	Gold medal,	Rev J. Dilke.
	Silver medal,	Ed. Reppington, Esq.
	Silver arrow,	Charles Hudson, Esq.
	Silver bugle,	Rev. J. Dilke.
Aug. 1809.	Gold medal,	Lord Guernsey
	Silver medal,	W. Palmer, Esq.

* One of the Royal Toxophilites.

Score yards.

	Silver arrow,		Rev. J. Cattel.
	Silver bugle,		W. Willoughby.
Aug. 1810.	Captaincy of Numbers,		Earl of Aylesford.
	Lieutenancy of Numbers,		Lord Guernsey.
	Gold medal,		T. Featherstone, Esq.
	Silver medal,		Joseph Boultbee, Esq.
	Silver arrow,		Lord Guernsey.
	Silver bugle,	9½	Hon. Henry Verney.
Aug. 1811.	Captaincy of Target.		W. Palmer, Esq.
	Lieutenancy of Target,		Rev. T. L. Freer.
	Gold medal,		—— Verney, Esq.
	Silver medal,		—— Breton, Esq.
	Silver arrow,		Rev. Egerton Bagot.
Aug. 1812.	Gold medal,		Rev. Coker Adams.
	Silver medal,		W. Palmer, Esq.
	Silver arrow,		R. Willoughby, Esq.
Aug. 1815.	Gold medal,		Rev. J. Cattel.
	Silver medal,		H. C. Adams, Esq.
	Silver arrow,		Rev. C. Palmer.
Aug. 1816.	Gold medal,		J. E. Eardley Wilmot, Esq.
	Silver medal,		Rev. Charles Palmer.
	Silver arrow and forest bugle,		Earl of Aylesford.
	Lieutenancy of Target,		R. Willoughby, Esq.
	Captaincy of Numbers,		Earl of Aylesford.

		Score yards.	
	Lieutenancy of Numbers,		H. C. Adams, Esq.
Aug. 1818.	Gold medal,		C. G. Reppington, Esq.
	Silver medal,		Rev. T. C. Adams.
	Silver arrow,		Earl of Aylesford.
	Silver bow,		Hon. and Rev. E. Finch.
Aug. 1832.	Master Forester's gold medal,		Lieutenant Colonel T. E. Steward.
	Senior Verderer, silver medal,		Hon. and Rev. C. Finch.
	Lieutenancy of Target,		John Drinkwater, Esq.
	Silver arrow,		Rev. Coker Adams.*
	Bugle horn of Arden,	10½	Hon. and Rev. C. Finch.
	Digbean gold medal.		Rev. Coker Adams.
	Digbean silver medal,		Hon. and Rev. C. Finch.

HEREFORDSHIRE BOWMEN.

ARCHERS OF ARCHINFIELD.

This society was formerly distinguished by the splendid character of its public archery breakfasts, given at Archinfield House, near Hereford, invitation cards being sometimes issued to between two and three hundred individuals.

The Herefordshire bowmen occasionally hold their meetings at Moccas Court, near Bradwardine, the seat of Sir George Cornewall, Bart. It is worthy of remark, that an ancestor of this gentleman led a band of ninety archers, his own tenants, to the field of Agincourt†, obeying the King's summons, in com-

---

* Secretary.   † Sloane MS. Rymer's Fœdera.

pany with his friend Sir Roger Vaughan of Bradwardine; who, with David Gam and Watkin Llwyd, were knighted by Henry in death.* When Henry was preparing to force the passage of the Somme, he first sent over this Knight and Sir Gilbert Homphreyville, with a strong detachment of bowmen, to take possession of the opposite bank. Sir J. Cornewall had the good fortune on that memorable day to make the Count of Vendosme his prisoner†; but as he appeared unable to command the necessary ransom, his captor nobly set him at liberty on parole. The memory and date of the Count's arrival in England has been handed down by vulgar tradition, associated with other remarkable events of the period, in the following quaint lines : —

> The third of November, the Duke of Vendosme passed the water;
> The fourth of November, the queen had a daughter;
> The fifth of November, we escaped a great slaughter;
> And the sixth of November was the day after!‡

Another ancestor died by an arrow shot at the siege of Berwick. " Edward got to Berwick. At this place was Sir John Cornewall, a noble Englishman, slain by one George Fleming, shooting a quarrel out of the Red Haill."§

Lady Cornewall was a recent patroness of this society. Sir George Cornewall, Canon Russel, Mr. Arthur Clive, and the Rev. J. Hill Lowe, are adroit bowmen.

The Richmond Archers, Yorkshire,

Have selected for their target-ground a beautiful spot on the banks of the Swale, opposite the venerable ruins of St. Agatha's Abbey. The silver arrow, and captaincy of the target recently became the prize of a gentleman bearing the con-

---

* See Welsh Archery.

† Johannes Cornwall cepit Ludovicum de Bourbon Comitem Vendosme, apud bellum de Agincourt; cui Johanni, Rex dedit dictum comitem financiam suam. See Sir N. H. Nicholas; also Rolls of Parliament, vol. iv. p. 30.

‡ Ray's proverbs. § Leland's Collectanea.

genial appellation of " Bowman." Lieutenant of the target, J. Fisher, Esq. C. Croft, Esq. obtained the captaincy of numbers, after winning more prizes than ever fell to the lot of the same individual at Richmond. Silver cup, and lieutenantcy of numbers, G. Croft, Esq.*

STAFFORDSHIRE BOWMEN.
E. C. Pole, Esq., President.
C. Arkwright, Esq.

CARISBROOK ARCHERS†, CARISBROOK CASTLE.
Thomas Hastings, Esq.; Captain Campbell; — Hastings, junior, Esq.

STOKE LEIGH CAMP ARCHERS, SOMERSETSHIRE.
William Gibbons, T. Danson, Henry Goldwyer, John Norton, Henry Vizer, and — Harford, Esqs.

MERSEY BOWMEN, LIVERPOOL.
Colonel Nicholson, &c. &c.

HARLEY BUSH BOWMEN.
Captain Phillips; D. Somerville, Esq.

SOUTH SAXON ARCHERS.
Lord Gage; Sir G. Shiffner, Bart.; — Farlie, — Warburton, — Davies, Esqs.

NEWTON VILLA ARCHERS.
Walter Ray, and Christopher Bennet, Esqs.

WEST BERKSHIRE UNITED ARCHERY CLUB.‡
On the 29th of October, 1834, a fine display of Archery took place between this society and the Royal Toxophilites, for two

* In this list of the different societies, only one or two names from each are selected, as having chiefly distinguished themselves.

† This very pleasant society owes its origin to Thomas Hastings, Esq., of East Cowes Cottage, Isle of Wight, a good archer, and author of a good book, " The British Bowman." The Carisbrooks recently issued a challenge to all England.

‡ A pleasant handicap match for a subscription plate, given by W. Merry, Esq., honorary secretary to the East Berks Club, took place at Benham Park,

valuable pieces of plate. The first prize, a claret vase and stand, was won by Edwin Meyrick, Esq., who scored 203 for fifty-five hits. The second prize, a silver inkstand, became the property of the Rev. E. Scott, for the best arrow in the gold.

ROYAL SHERWOOD FORESTERS.

W. W. Pelham Claye, and Bennet Martin, Esqs., recent presidents, Colonel Wildman; and J. B. Warwick, Esq.

MELKSHAM FORESTERS (WILTSHIRE).

H. Mereweather, and — Estcott, Esqs.

SELWOOD FORESTERS, SOMERSETSHIRE.

E. Hobhouse, and C. Plunket, Esqs.

WEST SOMERSET ARCHERS.

Established by — Carew, Esq. of Crowcombe Court.

ALBION ARCHERS, STOCKWELL PARK, SURREY.

Evans, Guibard, and Langton, Esqs. Prizes, — medals, foreign bows, &c. &c.

BRIXTON ARCHERS.

WELLSBURNE ARCHERS.

CLAPTON ARCHERS.

WINDSOR FORESTERS.

---

in the autumn of 1835, between the Royal Toxophilites, the East and West Berkshire Clubs, the Windsor Foresters, and the Wellbourne and Clapton Archers distance 100 yards; seventy ends; three arrows each.

They scored as follows : —

— Marsh, Esq., Clapton	- -	286	- 70 hits.
— Moore, Esq., West Berks	-	285	- 75 hits.

— Peters, Esq. Royal Toxophilites, and — Meyrick, Esq. West Berks, scored very near the above.

The prize given by Mr. Hughes for the actual numerical superiority of hits, was gained by Mr. Moore. Contribution gold prize — Atwood, Esq., West Berks.

The Benham handicap is open to every archery society of England.

SOCIETIES OF MODERN ARCHERS.

ARCHERY AT BEULAH SPA*, Norwood, near London.

There are continual exhibitions of shooting within these pleasant grounds during the summer season. In one of recent date, got up under the superintendence of Mr. Betty, who shoots extremely well, they scored as follows, with the disadvantages of a high wind:—

Watts	253
Forsyth	182
Betty	154
Calvert	104
Edgington	92

ROYAL EDINBURGH ARCHERS.

THE KING'S BODY GUARD FOR SCOTLAND.

> The Douglas drew a bow of might,
> His first shaft entered in the white;
> And when in turn he shot again,
> The second split the first in twain.
> *Lady of the Lake.*

> So an arrow with a golden head,
> And shaft of silver white,
> Each man that day did bear away,
> For his own proper right.
> *Old Ballad.*

The Highlanders, or red shanked men of Scotland, be exceeding good archers. — *Taylor, the Water Poet.*

Among the bowmen of Great Britain, none have displayed more taste in the selection of the appellations by which they choose to be distinguished, than the Woodmen of the Forest of

---

* For the names of other societies, see p. 285.; where particular description is omitted, the author was unable to obtain the necessary details.

Arden, and the Royal Edinburgh Archers, the King's body guard for Scotland.*

The latter company which I am now about to describe, existed as early as the reign of James I.; and in 1677, during the reign of his grandson, was recognised by an act of the Privy Council, when they obtained a piece of plate to be shot for at their weapon shawings; all which rights and privileges were held by feudal tenure, in fee, by the annual service of presenting to the sovereign a pair of barbed arrows. During the early portion of the last century, the archers took a prominent and distinguished part in the stormy politics of a disputed succession, and devotedly attached to the exiled family, they omitted no opportunity of its public manifestation. The approaching death of Queen Anne, in 1714, infusing new vigour into their party, then it was that the laws were first splendidly engrossed upon vellum, adorned with thistles in festoons, and subscribed by the members. "This subscription," says Maitland, in his "History of Edinburgh," is divided into five columns of names, filled up to the length of fourteen feet and a half; and they did not hesitate to enter upon their minute-book, in terms which could not be misunderstood, that they remembered on his birthday the health of an exiled prince. On the 14th of June following, the Earl of Cromartie, their Captain General, although then upwards of eighty years of age, and the Earl of Wemyss, as Lieutenant General, marched at the head of above fifty noblemen and gentlemen, clothed in uniform, equipped in military array, and distinguished by their proper standards, from the Parliament Square to the palace of Holyrood House, thence to Leith, and shot for the silver arrow given by the city of Edinburgh. They returned in similar parade,

* A very curious volume has recently been printed by — Dunlop, Esq., for private circulation only, containing a history of the Scottish archer guard described in "Quinten Durward," which for ages served in France, and was retained about the person of its monarchs. These, however, were quite distinct from the body guard of which I am speaking.

having received from the different guards which they passed the same military honours which are paid to the King's forces."

After the rebellion, in 1715, the archers made no display for nine years; but the Duke of Hamilton being chosen their Captain General, they marched through Musselborough, A. D. 1714, and met occasionally the nine succeeding years. But after the second rising, in 1748, the English ministry looked upon this society with so jealous an eye, that they actually appointed spies to watch their conduct and frequent their assemblies.

The archer guard consists, at present, of upwards of a thousand members, among whom they reckon some of the principal nobility, gentry, and chief professional men of Scotland. Their affairs are managed by a president, secretary, and six councillors, who meet weekly for the despatch of business. His Grace the Duke of Buccleugh is their present Captain-General, an appointment previously held by the late venerable Earl of Hopetoun, who died in 1823. An ancestor of his grace of Hamilton held the same honourable office upwards of a century ago; whose installation was celebrated in a poem, from which the following is an extract:—

> Again the year returns, the day
> That's dedicate to joy and play,
>   To bonnets, bows, and wine.
> Let all who wear a sullen face
> This day, meet with a due disgrace,
>   And in their sourness pine:
>
> Be shunn'd like serpents, that would stang
>   The hand that gies them food.
> Sic we debar from lasting sang,
>   And all their grumbling brood.
>
> While to gain sport and halesome air,
> The blithesome spirit draps dull care,
>   And starts from business free.
> Now to the fields the archers bend,
> With friendly mind the day to spend,
>   In manly game and glee.

First striving who shall win the bowl,
    And then gar 't flow with wine.
Sic manly sport refresh'd the soul
    Of stalwort men lang syne.

   *   *   *   *

Come view the men thou lik'st to ruse ;
    To Bruntsfield Links let 's hie,
And see the Royal Bowmen strive,
Who far the feather'd arrows drive,
    All soughing through the sky ;

Ilk etting with his utmost skill,
    With artful draft and stark,
Extending newes with hearty skill,
    In hopes to hit the mark.

See Hamilton, who moves with grace,
Chief of the Caledonian race
    Of peers ; to whom is due
All honours and a fair renown ;
Who lays aside his ducal crown
    Sometimes, to shade his brow

Beneath St. Andrew's bonnet blue,
    And joins to gain the prize ;
Which shows the merit match'd by few,
    Great, affable, and wise.

This day, with universal voice,
The archers him their chieftain chose :
    Consenting powers divine
Have blest the day with general joy,
By giving him a princely boy,
    To beautify his line. —&c. &c.

The same collection contains another short poem, addressed to the Duke, on the remarkable occasion of his having shot an arrow through the neck of an eel whilst swimming : —

As from his bow, a fatal flame,
Train'd by Apollo from the plain,
    In water pierced an eel :
So may the patriot's powers and art
Sic fate to souple rogues impart,
    That drumble much the common weal :

> Though they as any eels are slid,
>   And through what's vile can scud,
> A bolt may reach them, though deep hid
>   They sculk beneath the mud.

The Edinburgh Archers lay claim by Royal charter to the curious and honourable privilege of acting as the King's body guard, whenever he approaches within five miles of their metropolis. Accordingly, when George IV. visited his Scottish dominions, they immediately put in their claim, and his Majesty's well-known predilection for every thing connected with the usages of chivalry and romance, added to his having been himself a member of the Royal Kentish Bowmen whilst Prince of Wales, renders it scarcely necessary to state, that their application was good-humouredly acceded to. The occasion, the season of the year, the state of the weather, combined to render the whole spectacle one of the most splendid and imposing in its kind seen in this island for a considerable period. On the occasion just referred to, and for ages before, their costume was a modification of the "garb of old Gaul," at once manly and elegant. It consisted of tartan, lined with white, and trimmed with white and green fringes; white sash, with green tassels; and blue bonnet, ornamented with St. Andrew's cross and feathers.* Their chief place of public rendezvous is the Meadows, or Hope Park, a spot deriving its name from Sir Thomas Hope, who drained and converted it into what it now is, an elegant and well frequented promenade.

In their public progresses through Edinburgh, to shoot for their numerous and valuable prizes, an officer precedes them, bearing — instead of a mace, the ordinary badge of corporate bodies — a bow of vast dimensions, from which is suspended his Majesty's purse, &c. &c.

The following may be considered as a list of the chief prizes annually shot for by the Royal Edinburgh Archers: —

* Their dress has recently undergone some considerable modification.

Prize I. A SILVER ARROW, presented by the town of Musselburg, A. D. 1603. In 1793, this curious antique relic was encircled with 116 medals, and ten years afterwards, when they amounted to 118, varying in size and shape, one or two being also of gold, its weight was 160 ounces.

Medal 1. is that of Johnstone of Elphinstone, 1603. It bears his arms, and also his motto, " Guide there." Reverse, a man drawing an arrow, surmounted by initials between two roses; besides which there are those of, —

Medal 63. Sir Alexander Macdonald; 1st August, 1733. Motto, — Nec tempore nec fato. On the reverse, an archer in the dress of the Royal Company, wearing the St. Andrew's cross in his bonnet; a bent bow in his left hand, and four barbed arrows in his right; surrounded by a tablet, inscribed, — Nul se s'y frotte.

The Musselburgh arrow was also won three times successively by George Drummond, merchant, Edinburgh. On the shield bearing his arms and motto there are also, I believe, the following quaint lines : —

>When Androse was a man,
>   He could not be pealed;
>At the old sport he wan,
>   When Androse was a man.
>But now he neither may nor can;
>   Alas, he's fail 'd.
>When Androse was a man,
>   He could not be peal'd.

Three other remarkable inscriptions run thus, —

Robert Biggar, merchant, Edinburgh, did win this arrow for the third time, August, 1745; and on the opposite side,

Robert Biggar, whilst victor of this arrow, did win both the prizes belonging to the Royal Company of Archers, in the year 1747; and which prizes were never in the hands of any archer before, at one time.

John Henderson, Esq., architect, won this arrow by three successive shots, at Musselburgh, A. D. 1783.

As the Musselburgh arrow, like that of Peebles and Edinburgh, with many other prizes belonging to the Royal Company, does not become the actual property of the winner, it must be considered as merely an honorary distinction. In order to afford each member an opportunity of gaining these prizes, the successful archer, after one year's possession, returns them to the company, with a medal attached, bearing his arms, motto, and an inscription setting forth the day and year of the contest, as in the previous and following instances:—

Prize II. THE EDINBURGH SILVER ARROW.

The first seven pieces are of silver, all the rest are gold.

Medal 1. Drummond, Esq., advocate, 1709.

Medal 8. The Right Honourable John Earl of Wigtown gained this arrow at Leith, 11th July, 1726, in the presence of 144 members of the Royal Company of Archers. Reverse, arms, and motto,—Let the deed shaw.

Medal 29. Robert Biggar, merchant, Edinburgh, did win this arrow by three successive shots, April 13th, 1747. Again,

N.B. Robert Biggar did win this year both prizes belonging to the Royal Company of Archers; being likewise victor of the Musselborough arrow, which was never done by one archer before.

Medal 37. John Sinclair, writer, Edinburgh, gained this arrow, the 14th July, 1755; and the same year, the other public prizes, the Royal Company's bowl, and Musselborough arrow. Reverse, arms; motto, — Vincula temno.

Medal 52. J. C. Ramsay, advocate, son of W. Ramsay of Temple Hall, victor, 9th July, 1770, by three successive shots. Accidit in puncto, quod non speratur in anno.* Reverse, arms; motto, Nil time.

---

* "That come to pass in an instant, which is not expected in a year," in allusion to the successful arrow.

Medal 54. John Macpherson, teacher of music, gained the Edinburgh arrow, 12th July, 1792. Reverse, motto, Touch not the cat, but with a glove.

Medal 55. Charles Macdonald, Esq., of Largee, 12th July, 1773. Reverse, a man standing in the habit of an archer, with a bent bow in his left hand, in the graceful attitude of shooting an arrow, which is seen sticking in the distant clout; motto, It must fall somewhere.

Prize III. THE ARCHER'S BOWL.

This magnificent piece of plate, composed of genuine Scottish silver, and sufficiently capacious to hold two bottles of rum converted into punch, is valued at about three hundred guineas. Like the silver arrows, it is encircled with rows of gold medals, bearing the arms and inscriptions of the victorious archers. These, in the year 1793, amounted to seventy-three. The bowl therefore, like the rest, must be considered as merely a nominal prize, although I believe the original intention was, that the individual who gained it for three consecutive years, should retain permanent possession. An instance of such good fortune did actually occur; but the victor*, considering it would better grace the sideboard of " Archers' Hall," than that of a private residence, and unwilling also to deprive his brother bowmen of the pleasures of a contest, generously restored the bowl, on the express condition that the above-mentioned privilege should be for ever abolished. It is, consequently, now the common property of the company, and graces their table at all convivial meetings held in Archers' Hall, above mentioned.

Medal 1. James, Earl of Weemyss, 1720.

Medal 8. Robert Lows, M. D. gained this prize a second time the 26th of August, 1727.

Medal 28. Robert Biggar, merchant, in Edinburgh, did win this bowl for the third time on the 19th of September, 1747.

* I believe this gentleman to have been Dr. T. C. Hope, brother to James Hope, Esq., W. S., whose name is inscribed on the seventy-seventh medal.

Medal 75. Dr. Thomas Speirs, July 1. 1793. Reverse, crest, with motto, Si Deus, quis contra.

Medal 30. August 1727, finishes the first tire, which are all oval medals of gold; most of the others being round.

The first medal of the second tire, is that of George Lockhart of Carnwaith, President of Council, and Major General of the Scotch Archers, June 11th, 1750. Reverse, a Scotch thistle, with a royal crown, encircled with this motto, Grata superveniet quæ non sperabitur hora.

Medal 36. J. Sinclair, writer, Edinburgh, 26th July, 1755. The same year he also gained the Musselburgh and Edinburgh arrows.

Prize IV. His Majesty's Purse of Twenty Guineas. The contest of the Royal gift excites an unusual degree of emulation among the Body Guard, and the utmost impartiality attends its award; an observation applicable, indeed, to the distribution of all their prizes. "To gain the purse," is regarded as a very distinguished honour. The winner purchases a piece of plate, of whatever fashion he pleases, of the same value as the purse. The insignia of archery must form its chief ornaments, and on producing it to the treasurer, the twenty guineas are paid.

Prize V. A second Bowl, formed of East India pagodas, the gift of a gentleman of high rank in the Company's service.

Prize VI. A Silver Bugle, presented by Sir William Jardine.

Prize VII. Another Bugle, the gift of the Body Guard.

Prize VIII. St. Andrew's Cross, given by Sir George Makensie, Bart., of Coul.

These prizes are shot for at *Rovers*, the marks being placed 180, and sometimes 185, yards apart. Few things in Edinburgh furnish more amusement to a stranger than these archery parades.

Besides the picturesque dress of the Body Guard, they number in their ranks some of the tallest and finest men of Scotland, who use bows of proportionate size and strength. A writer, signing himself λ, in Dr. Brewster's Encyclopædia, modestly asserts, that among the Archer Guard there is a considerable number of gentlemen whose dexterity probably equals, if it does not surpass, whatever has been exhibited in Scotland during the most warlike times. He might have gone further, and stated, with great propriety, that the stout Archer Body Guard of England, whom the homely muse of Taylor celebrated nearly three centuries ago, would have rejoiced to enlist them within their ranks.

A singular match was decided on 6th of June, 1827, between a portion of the married and unmarried members, at 180 yards; the Benedicts of the company, who reckoned thirteen points more than their adversaries, carrying away the prize, of course.

It is curious, that what is called " goose-shooting," now and anciently a favourite amusement among Flemish archers, should have been early practised in Scotland. It probably might have been once a favourite pastime among their southern neighbours likewise; for the Hon. Daines Barrington, in his paper on archery, describes it thus: " A living goose was enclosed in a turf butt, having its head alone exposed to view; and the archer who first hit the goose's head, was entitled to the goose as his reward. But this custom, on account of its barbarity, has long been laid aside; a mark, about an inch in diameter, being fixed upon each butt; and the archer who first hits this mark is captain of the butt-shooters for a year."

The Flemings still practise the game with all its original cruelty, and the devoted bird is suspended by its wings from a cord stretched across the shooting-ground. Anciently the Edinburgh archers covered the animal's body with hay, allowing the head only to appear. But though the game of goose-shooting annually takes place, the bird is, with a commendable humanity, first submitted to the cook's hands, who returns the head as a mark for the archers, and dresses the goose itself as part of their dinner. They stand 100 yards off; and as it is a rule that the company do not dine until an arrow has pierced the mark, the shooting sometimes continues by torch-light. About October, 1798 or 1799, Dr. Speirs, one of the Body Guard, being unwell, grew exceedingly fatigued during a protracted contest of this sort. He therefore called for a chair, and, sitting down, drew his bow, and immediately drove his arrow through the head.

There is in many respects a great similarity between archery as practised in Scotland, and the same amusement as it is pursued by the inhabitants of Flanders. In both countries the butts are formed of straw placed endways, closely pressed, and afterwards cut smooth. The popinjay game is also not unknown to Scotch archers, who differ only slightly from the Flemings in their mode of fixing up the mark. Like the Greeks, who exhibited their dexterity at those funereal games celebrated on the death of Hector, the latter aim at a bird perched upon the summit of a tall mast.* The Scotch, on the contrary, who, I believe, do or did annually practise this game at Kilwinning, affix their popinjay to a piece of wood or iron, projecting from the church steeple, the archer placing his left foot against the base of the tower, and, of course, discharges his arrow perpendicularly. The mark is not solid, like that used by the Flemings, but consists of three distinct portions, the body and the two wings, united by iron spikes; and, unless his arrow strikes close to one of these, the archer cannot displace them.

The Royal Company of Scottish Archers have attracted a very large portion of the public notice from the period of their first institution. As early as the year 1725 there appeared a volume of complimentary poems, in English and Latin, ad-

* There is this distinction, however, between the Greek and the Flemish mode: Merrion, Teucer, and Pandanus shot at a living dove; the Flemish archers use a small wooden figure, about the size of a sparrow. See a future portion of this work.

dressed to them; and among its contributors we have the name of the well-known Allen Ramsay. In a previous paragraph, I have quoted a few verses addressed to the Duke of Hamilton, and other skilful archers of that period; the following lines commemorate the achievements of Mr. D. Drummond, who gained the Edinburgh arrow at Leith, 24th June, 1719: —

> Hail, veteran in victory grey!
> Whose arrow oft has borne away
> The conquest of a glorious day.
> Old Caledon does know thy fame;
> Each archer field reveres thy name,
> Who came, saw, conquer'd when you came.
> No higher can your glory rise.
> Through many a tough contested prize
> You've won Olympus by degrees.
> Now, at the post of Jove's great son,
> Lay your strong bow and arrows down,
> Mellow with age and with renown.

Again:

> To Mr. DAVID DRUMMOND,
> President of the Royal Company of Archers,
> 1725;
>
> By Sir WILLIAM BLANE.
>
> Could Fergus raise his lofty head,
>   He'd smile on this propitious day;
> Pleas'd with the ancient arms and weed,
>   Would bless his sons in this array,
> Whom oft he led in days of yore
>   To triumph o'er the vanquish'd foe;
> Then, bearded shafts drank hostile gore,
>   Or fixed the panting stag and doe:
> Now, harmless arrows pierce the sky;
>   Unfrighted dames do view the show;
> Till Phœbus hears some virgin's cry,
>   And glory crowns her lover's brow.
> Thus keep your brawny nerves in ply,
>   That should your country's cause invite,
> You, ready, could your aid supply,
>   And do that injur'd country right.

THE ARCHER'S MARCH.

Sound the music sound it,
Let hills and dales rebound it,
Let hills and dales rebound it,
   In praise of archery.

The origin divine is,
The practice brave and fine is,
Which generously inclines us
   To guard our liberty.

The deity of Parnassus,
The god of soft caresses,
Diana and her lasses,
   Delight in archery.

See! See! yon bow extended,
'Tis Jove himself that bends it;
   O'er clouds on high it glows.

All nations, Turks and Parthians,
The Tartars and the Scythians,
The Arabs, Moors, and Indians,
   With bravery draw their bow.

Our own true records tell us,
That none could e'er excel us,
That none could e'er excel us,
   In martial archery.

With shafts our sires engaging,
Opposed to Romans raging,
Defeat the fierce Norwegian,
   And spar'd few Danes to flee.

Witness the Largs and Loncartre,
Dunkeld and Aberlemno,
Dunkeld and Aberlemno,
   Rosline and Bannockburn;

The Cheviots, all the borders,
Were bowmen in brave order;
Told enemies, if further
   They moved, they'd ne'er return.

> Sound, sound! the music! sound it;
> Let hills and dales rebound it,
> Let hills and dales rebound it,
> > In praise of archery.
>
> Used as a game, it pleases;
> The mind to joy it raises,
> And throws off all diseases
> > Of lazy luxury.
>
> Now, now our care beguiling,
> When all the year looks smiling,
> When all the year looks smiling,
> > With healthful harmony;
>
> The sun in glory glowing,
> With morning dew bestowing
> Sweet fragrance, life in growing,
> > To flow'rs and every tree;
>
> 'Tis now the Archers Royal,
> A hearty band and loyal,
> A hearty band and loyal,
> > That in just thoughts agree,
>
> Appear in ancient bravery,
> Dispising all base knavery,
> Which tends to bring in slavery
> > Souls worthy to be free.
>
> Sound the music! sound it;
> Fill up the glass, and round w' it,
> Fill up the glass, and round w' it,
> > Health and prosperity.

In the summer of 1832, the Body Guard received his Majesty's gift of a pair of splendid colours, through the Duke of Buccleugh. Their ancient standards were two: the first having on one side, figures of Mars and Cupid, encircled with a thistle wreath, and the motto, IN PEACE, IN WAR; on the other, a yew tree, and two archers in full costume, surrounded with the same garland, and the words, DAT GLORIA VIRES. The second standard displays on one side a lion rampant gules, on a field encircled with a wreath, surmounted by a thistle and arrow; motto, NEMO ME IMPUNE LACESSIT. The other side has St. Andrew's cross on a field argent; a crown, and the legend, DULCE PRO PATRIA PERICULUM. So much for archery in reference to its practice in the Caledonian metropolis. There are other societies in Scotland; particularly one of modern date, at Glasgow; and, in former ages, the men of Perth had the reputation of being extremely dexterous in the use of the bow. "Archery," says a note inserted in the 'Muses' Thernodie,' "of which the gentlemen of Perth are great masters, was made an indispensable branch of education from the days of James I. That prince passed an act forbidding the favourite diversion of football, substituting in its place the shooting with bows and arrows; so that every boy, when he reached the age of thirteen, was obliged to use archery at certain bow marks. There is a piece of ground without the north port, on the left hand of the road leading to Huntingtower, called the Bow-butt, where this exercise was occasionally practised. But the strong archers had their's on the South Inch. Near the south end of this inch, there lately stood a stone, which tradition assigned as the southern mark. The northern was near the north-west side of the ditch surrounding the moat, and stood on a rising ground, called the Scholars' Knowl. The distance between these marks is above five hundred fathoms; so they must have been very strong and expert archers who could shoot an arrow betwixt them."

Strong, indeed! Five hundred fathoms are one thousand yards; between twice and thrice the greatest range possessed by those strong war bows used at Cressy and Agincourt; tradition, therefore, has erred in assigning to these objects the honour of being the ancient bow-butts of Perth. But whatever was their extent, the Scottish archers made very good use of them, and occasionally proved successful rivals of their southern neighbours, as the following anecdote from old Pitscottie will show: —

"In this year there came an ambassador out of England, named Lord William Howard, and a bishop with him, with many other gentlemen, to the number of three score horse, which were all the able men and waled men for all kind of games and pastimes, shooting, louping, running, wrestling, and casting of the stone; but they were well sayed ere they past out of Scotland, and that by their own provocation: but ever they tint: till at last, the Queen of Scotland, the King's mother, favoured the Englishmen, because she was the King of England's sister: and therefore she took an enterprise of archery upon the Englishmen's hands, contrary to her son the King, and any six in Scotland that he would wale (pick), either gentlemen or yeomen, that the Englishmen should shoot against them, either at pricks, revers, or butts, as the Scots pleased. The King hearing this of his mother, was content, and gart her pawn a hundred crowns, and a tun of wine, upon the Englishmen's hands; and he incontinent laid down as much for the Scottish men. The field and ground were chosen in St. Andrew's, and three landed men and three yeomen chosen to shoot against the Englishmen; to wit, David Wemyss of that ilk, David Arnot of that ilk, and Mr. John Wedderburn, vicar of Dundee; the yeomen, John Thompson, in Leith, Steven Taburnea, with a piper called Alexander Bailie. They shot very near, and worsted the Englishmen of the enterprise, and wan the hundred crowns and the tun of wine, which made the King very merry that his men wan the victory."

So late as the reign of William III., the grenadiers of Highland regiments carried bows and arrows when recruiting. Their bow was shorter than that used by the ancient English and modern Scotch archers; the arrow heads were barbed, and unusually long. Specimens of both are preserved in the armory at Abbotsford, the well-known residence of the late Sir Walter Scott.

One very singular circumstance connected with the history of Scotch archery is mentioned in Home's " History of the Rebellion." He tells us a clergyman performed divine service during the civil wars with a long bow in his hand, and a sheaf of arrows tucked into a silken sash, fastened round his waist! Every Sabbath did he march to the church, himself carrying the good weapon, while his servant came after with his case of arrows, and a claymore in a black silk belt. Peace be to thy ashes! simple, single hearted old soldier of the church militant! for the shafts of a stronger archer has laid thee prostrate in the grave this many a long year. No doubt, you considered that to be truly genuine, practical piety, which thus armed you, " PRO ARIS ET FOCIS," and prompted the brandishing of your carnal weapon in the pulpit. Out of it, there is good reason to suspect you could handle your tackle " righte yeomanlike." No one would be likely to select such weapons, unless confident of ability to use them to some purpose.

And now, having pretty well exhausted my knowledge of Lowland archery, with the reader's permission we change the scene, and, in imagination, transport ourselves to the lonely shores of some Highland lake, where, amid congenial scenery, we'll listen while a plaided shepherd, in language simple and homely as his garb, tells his tale of the renowned Scottish archer Calum Dhu.

No braver warrior than Calum Dhu followed the banners of the chief of Colquhoun; and with them, the powerful M'Gregors were at inveterate feud. His cottage stood at the base of a steep fenny hill, within a sequestered glen, that lay beneath the lofty Ben Lomond. Thus retired from the rest of the clan, he nourished deadly hatred towards the M'Gregors, and was ever foremost in danger when they joined in red unyielding battle. For skilful archery, Calum Dhu never knew a rival; in wielding the claymore too, he had few equals; but the bow was the weapon of his heart.

The son of the chief of the M'Gregors, with two of his clansmen, were at the chase. Their game being wide, they wandered far, and found themselves, a little after mid-day, on the hill top, just above Calum Dhu's cottage.

"Come," said the young chief, "let us go down, and try the strength of Calum Dhu's bow, which men say none but he can bend. You and I, Evan, are reputed the best archers of our clan, and it will go hard with us if we cannot show him that the M'Gregors have thews and sinews equal to the task. Hast thou forgotten how often he has stained his arrows with the heart's blood of our bravest warriors, piercing them through and through, as if they had been straw butts set up for holiday sport? On, I say! he knows us not. Should he, we are three to one, and I owe him somewhat," he continued, with eye of fire, and voice quivering from subdued passion, "since our last affray, when he drove an arrow through my uncle's gallant bosom. Follow then!"

The will of a Highland chieftain was ever law to his clansmen.

"We will go down, if a score of his best claymores were with him," cried Evan fiercely.

"Nay, be not rash; we'll first bend and break his bow," replied the chief; "and then, then for my uncle's blood."

"They say he is good at the sword," remarked the third M'Gregor, who had hitherto been silent; "but this," drawing his dirk, "shall stretch him on the sward."

"Strike not behind," rejoined his lord; "hew him down in front; he deserves honourable wounds, for he is brave, though an enemy."

A rising knoll had hitherto concealed the cottage, which they now reached, knocking loudly at the door, after some delay, a little, thick-set, grey-eyed, oldish looking man came forth.

Threads and thrums hung from his black bushy head, as if he had been employed in weaving the coarse linen of the country and the time. Though the most incurious observer could not have failed to remark the disproportionate length of his arms in comparison with his stature, in all other respects, the man before them had none of the muscular symptoms of prodigious strength, which Calum Dhu was reported to possess, and which had often proved so fatal to the M'Gregor clan. To a querulous demand of what they might want, uttered in the impatient tone of one interrupted in some engrossing worldly employment, they replied, by inquiring if Calum Dhu was at home?

" Na, na, he's gone to the fishing. But an ye ha ony message for our chief (Heaven guard him), about the coming of the red M'Gregors, and will trust me with it, Calum will get it frae me. Ye may as well tell me as him. He stays long when he gaes out, for he's a keen fisher."

" We were only wanting to try the bending of his bow, which report says no man can do, save himself."

" Hoo gin that's all, ye might have tell'd it at first, and no keepit me sa lang frae my loom. But stop."—Thus saying, the old fellow paused, and gave his shoulders an impatient shrug, as it appeared to his visitants ; to a keen observer, however, the action might have expressed satisfaction, triumph, and determination. Then, re-entering the house, he quickly brought out a sheaf of arrows, and a bow of the dark red yew, so tall and stout, that the young men were persuaded the Colquhoun chieftain was quite another sort of person from the dwarfish being with whom they were then conversing. He threw the arrows carelessly on the ground, and said, " Ye will be trying your strength at a flight? Like a glance of lightning, I hae seen Calum send a shaft over the highest point of that hill ; and once, when the M'Gregors came raging up the glen, like red deevils as they are, mony of their best warriors fell at the farthest entry o' the pass, every man o' them wi' a hole in his breast, and its fellow at his back."

Whilst thus speaking, he had taken the longest arrow out of the sheaf, and stood playing it in his hand, seemingly ready to give it to the first of his visitors who should bend the bow. The three M'Gregors were tall, muscular, and in the prime of manhood. The young chief first took up the bow, and, after examining its unbending strength, laid all his might into it. He strained till the blood rushed to his face, and his temples throbbed almost to bursting, but in vain; the string remained slack as at first. Evan and his associate were alike unsuccessful; as well might they have striven to root up the gnarled oak of their native mountains.

"There's not a man," exclaimed the chief of the M'Gregors, chagrined at the absence of the man he sought, and his own and his clansmen's vain efforts — "there's not a man in your clan can bend that bow; and if Calum Dhu were here, he should not long ——" Biting his lip, he suppressed the rest of the sentence, for the third M'Gregor gave him a glance of caution.

"Ha!" said the old man, still playing with the long arrow, without seeming to observe the latter part of this speech; "if Calum was here, he would bend it as easily as ye wad bend that rush; and gin ony of the M'Gregors were in sight, he wad drive this lang arrow through them as easily as ye wad drive your dirk through my old plaid. More, I say; the feather wad come out at the other side, wet with their hearts' bluid; and sometimes even the man behind is wounded, if they are any way thick in their battle. I once saw a pair of them stretched on the heather, pinned together with one of Calum's yard-long shafts."

This was spoken with the apparent simplicity and composure of one talking to friends, and careless of foes. Still, closer attention would have discerned a chequered shade of pleasure and triumph cross his countenance as M'Gregor's lip quivered, and the scowl of anger descended upon his brow, at the tale of his kinsmen's destruction by the aim of their direst foe.

" He must be a brave warrior," at length observed the young chief, compressing his breath, and looking with anger and astonishment at the cool tenacious old man. " I should like to see this Calum Dhu."

" Ye may, soon enough ; and, gin ye were a M'Gregor, feel him too. But why is the man glunching and gloaming thus? Gin ye were Black John himsel, ye could na look mair deevilish like. And what are *ye* fidging at, man?" he continued, addressing the third M'Gregor, who had marked the anger of his lord, and gradually moved nearer the old tormentor, with his right hand below the left breast of his plaid, probably grasping his dirk, ready for the signal of vengeance. The faith of the Gael is deeper than, " to hear is to obey," the slavish obedience of the East; his, is to anticipate and perform. To know and to accomplish, or to die, is the stern devotedness of the North.

The old man kept his keen grey eye fixed upon him, whilst he continued in the same unsuspecting tone. " But is there ony word of the M'Gregors coming over the hills? Calum wad like to try a shot at Black John, their chief; he wonders could he pass an arrow through his great hardy bulk, as readily as he sends them through his clansmen's silly bodies. John has a son, too, he wad like to try his craft on, who has the name of a brave warrior. I forget his name. Calum likes to strike at noble deer, though he is forced sometimes to kill that which is little worth. But I'm fearful he o'er-rates his own strength. I think his arrow would only stick weel in Black John; but ——"

" Dotard, peace !" roared the M'Gregor till the glen re-echoed with his voice; his brow darkening like midnight. " Peace ! or I'll cut that sacrilegious tongue out of your head, and, nailing it to yon door, shew Calum Dhu you have had visiters in his absence, and make him bless his stars he saw them not."

A dark flash of suspicion crossed his mind, as he gazed at the individual he was addressing, who quailed not at his frowns. But it vanished as the imperturbable old man resumed his discourse.

"Ha, oh! ye are no a M'Gregor; and tho' ye were, ye surely wadna mind the like of me! But anent bending this bow," striking it with the long arrow which he still held in his hand, "there's just a knack in it; and your young, untaught strength is useless, as ye dinna ken the gait o't. I learned it frae Calum, but I'm sworn never to tell it to a stranger, and there is mony a man in the clan I ken naething about. But as ye seem anxious to see this bow bent, I'll no disappoint ye. Rin up to yon grey stone — stand there; it will no be as if ye were near me when I'm doing it, but it will be just the same to you, for ye can see weel enough. When the string is on the bow, ye may come down, an ye like it, and try a flight. It's a capital bow, and that ye'll fin."

A promise is sacred with the Gael. As the Colquhoun was under one, they did not insist on his exhibiting his art while they were by; nevertheless, curious to see the sturdy bow bent — a feat of which the best warrior of their clan would have been proud — and perhaps thinking Calum Dhu would arrive in the interval, they walked away in the direction pointed out. Unsuspicious of treachery, as the old man appeared ignorant of their names, and could not be supposed capable of sending an arrow so far, the M'Gregors thought not of looking back, until close to the grey rock. Then turning round, they saw him suddenly bend the stubborn yew, and fix an arrow upon the string. In an instant he drew strongly to his very ear, and the feathered shaft of a cloth yard length was fiercely launched in air.

"Mac Alp—hooch!" exclaimed the dying youth, instinctively endeavouring to raise the M'Gregor war cry, and clapping his hand on his breast as he fell.

"Ha!" cried Calum Dhu, for it was he himself, " clap your hand behin; the arm shot, which never sent arrow that came out where it went in,"—a rhyme he used in battle, when his foes fell fast as he could nock arrows upon the bowstring.

The first impulse of two remaining M'Gregors, was to rush down and cut to atoms the slayer of their beloved young chief; but seeing him fix another arrow to that bow, the terrible powers of which they had just witnessed, and fearing they might be prevented from carrying to the old chieftain the news of his son's death, they started over the hill like roes. Still, flight availed not; a speedy messenger was after them, for a second arrow sent by the same powerful and unerring arm transfixed Evan's shoulder, just as he descended out of sight. To catch him, it must have grazed the bent that grew on the hill top, as nought but his shoulder could be seen from where Calum Dhu stood.

On flew the other M'Gregor, with little abatement of speed, till he reached his chieftain with the bloody tidings of his son's death.

"Raise the clan! dearly shall they rue it," burst from the lips of Black John; and a party, breathing all the vengeance of mountain warriors, were soon far on the way of fierce retaliation. Calum Dhu in the meantime had not remained inactive. Knowing, from the escape of one of his three foes, a battle must quickly ensue, he collected as many clansmen as he could, and with his terrible bow, calmly awaited the onset. The M'Gregors concealed not their coming. Loudly and fiercely their pipes flung their notes of warlike defiance on the gale, and, far and wide, mountain, cliff, and glen, echoed to the martial strains. The foes met; and long and desperate was the conflict which ensued. No warriors of that age could withstand the hurricane onset of the bold M'Gregors, the tide of battle flowed full in their favour, while Black John raving through the field like a chafed lion, shouted in a voice of thunder, heard far above the clash, groans, and yells of the unyielding combatants, for the murderer of his son. None defied him — to none was afforded time, for he cut down in his headlong rage every foeman he encountered; until but few remained on whom he could wreak his vengeance, or exercise his great strength. Gazing round the field, he at length spied an old man seated on a fern bank, while his hands grasped the bloody stump of his leg which had been stricken off. He beckoned the grim chief to come nearer, and Black John rushed forward, brandishing his bloody sword, and still crying in a voice which startled the yet remaining birds from the mountain cliffs, "Where was his son's murderer?"

"Shake the leg out of that brogue," said the old man, speaking with difficulty, and squeezing his bloody stump with both hands in all the energy of pain. "Go, bring me a drink of water frae yon burn, and I'll show you Calum Dhu, for he is yet in the field, and lives: rin, for my heart burns and faints."

The M'Gregor, without uttering a word, shook the leg out of the brogue, and hastened to do his foeman's bidding. But whilst he stooped to dip in the blood-stained brogue, "Mac Alp — hooch!" faintly broke from his lips, and he splashed lifeless into the stream, which in a moment ran thick with his blood.

"Ha!" cried Calum Dhu, for it was he again, "Clap your hand behin! that's the last arrow shot by the arm which ne'er sent those which came out where they went in."

Callum Dhu.

SECTION VIII.

OF YEW TREES, YEW BOWS, &c. &c.

> Make glad chere, said Little John,
> And frese * our bowes of ewe,
> And loke your hearts be seker and sad; †
> Your strynges trusty and trewe.
>
> Good sooth! it was a gallant sight
> To see them all of a rowe;
> With every man a keen broad sword,
> And eke a stout ewe bowe.
> *Old Ballad.*

Des Arcs, qui en voudroit savoir, qu'il aylle en Angleterre, car c'est leur droiet mestier.— *Les Chasses de Gaston Phebus, Comte de Foix,* 1470.

THOSE honours decreed the oak, the forest monarch, since Englishmen first made ocean's bosom the theatre of their greatest triumph, were once assigned to the yew. Among poets, it became synonymous with the weapon manufactured from it; and thus we read of the "twanging yew;" "the yew obedient to the the shooter's will." "Son of Luth," says Ossian, "bring the bows of our fathers; let our three warriors bend the ewe." Pope's translation of the Iliad ventures still further, and by the violent application of a well-known rhetorical figure, writes "forceful yew," when speaking not of a wooden but a horn bow.

The growth of yew is now altogether neglected, except where it canopies the humble graves of some village church-yard, or, dark and sombre, creates an agreeable contrast among the gay tints of summer foliage in lawn and shrubbery. In many situ-

---

* Prepare.   † Firm and resolute.

ations it is considered a nuisance, especially when growing in the hedgerows of pasture and meadow lands. Vegetation languishes and dies under the influence of its noxious shade; and, though poisonous to horses, these animals feed greedily on its berries and tender branches. Hence, where landlords make no opposition, the farmer generally extirpates the yew, once, like the falcon, so highly esteemed, that to cut down the one for any purpose except the legitimate uses of the bowyer, or to destroy the other's eyrie, even in a man's own grounds, was punished with fine and imprisonment. But in the progress of human taste and ingenuity, they have experienced a nearly similar fate. The falcon, from being guarded by laws which esteemed her destruction a far more heinous offence than manslaughter, from being the constant companion of kings and nobles, is now regarded as vermin, and nailed, like a felon, to the kennel-door. The yew, when preserved from rotting on the spot where it fell, rarely aspires to uses more honourable than the repair of a gate-post, or as a serviceable log to cheer the rustic group assembled around its owner's Christmas fire. Occasionally, however, trees having an unusually fine butt are hauled home, and converted into planks; but instead of cleaving these into bow-staves, as did his ancestors, the Vandal fabricates them into some vulgar article of domestic furniture. *Verbum satis sapienti:* the materials for many a fine self bow may be rescued from destruction by keeping on fair terms with the village joiner, where yew grows abundantly; a hint not thrown away on those acquainted with the value and extreme rarity of good bow wood.

Although yew abounds not around London, and what little does exist is severely guarded against the bowyer's fell inroads, there are several parts of this kingdom absolutely overrun with it. Of these, certain districts in North and South Wales, with the lovely woodlands of Hereford and Monmouth, may be stated as the principal.

> In summer time when shaws be sheene,
>   And leaves are large and longe,
> And 'tis merry walking in fair forest
>   To hear the fowlys song;
> To see the deere drawe to the lea,
>   And leaves their hillis hee;
> And shadow them in the leaves green
>   Beneath the broad oake tree, —

its appearance among the extensive copses of that portion of England produces a charming contrast when viewed in connection with the paler, more delicate, foliage of oak, alder, hazel, and mountain ash. In that dreary season, too, when storm and tempest —

> Breathe a browner horror o'er the woods,

its dark green verdure, uniting with the varnished holly, the fir, and those few other evergreens indigenous to our soil, throws an air of cheerfulness over the scene, and the mind feels a consciousness that Nature, like Lazarus in the tomb, "is not dead, but sleepeth."

Notwithstanding the extensive demand for yew during the ages of military archery, there is no reason for believing it was propagated otherwise than by chance. In the thirteenth and fourteenth centuries, England abounded with vast forests. To clear these, not to extend them, was the care of the ancient husbandman, who thought as little of planting any species of timber as modern backwoodsmen of Canada.

All persons familiar with rural sights and scenes, have noticed the frequent recurrence of yew trees in village churchyards, and are aware that the motives which induced our ancestors to foster them there has been variously stated. The archer, always an enthusiast, always anxious to magnify the importance of his favourite hobby, stoutly maintains, at all times and in all places, that the extensive application of yew to making bows, at the period when most of our county churches were erected, renders any further explanation unnecessary.

Thy wish is father, Harry, to the thought.

Unluckily, however, for the stability of this pleasant hypothesis, not a single argument can be adduced in its support; while half a score may be speedily collected to effect its demolition. First then, if the trees were originally planted for that purpose, our forefathers afterwards changed their minds, since they remain *in statu quo*, even unto the present hour. It may be answered that those we now see are possibly the fifth generation left standing when archery gradually gave place to fire-arms. The nature of the tree itself disproves this; for our sepulchral yews are, in a majority of instances, of equal and superior antiquity to the churches they shelter and adorn. Many were never planted by the hand of man; but having been found growing on the spot destined to receive the sacred edifice, they were suffered to remain for ornament, and the purposes hereafter stated.*

Secondly. In certain districts of England, from some cause

---

* Persons acquainted with forest matters know, that on cutting through a yew tree, the number of concentric rings visible on the surface of the wood indicates its age. Mr. Jesse, whose unaffected love of nature entitles him to rank as the worthy successor of White of Selbourne, has made some very interesting remarks respecting the growth and age of these trees, of which I regret being unable to extract more than a fragment: — " That there are yew trees in England as old or older than the introduction of Christianity into our island, no doubt can exist. The yew appears to me of all European trees, that which attains the greatest age. I have measured the deposits of one of 70 years, and Veillard measured one of 280. These two measurements agree in proving that the yew grows a little more than one ligne annually, in the first 150 years, and less than a ligne from 150 to 250.

" Those of Fotheringay, in 1770, had a diameter of 2558 lignes, consequently we must reckon them at from twenty-five to twenty-six centuries. Those of Brabourne churchyard in Kent had, in 1660, a diameter of 2810 lignes; and, if still living, must have attained a period of three thousand years!"— *See the whole paper in* " *Gentleman's Magazine*" *for June* 1836.

or other, yew trees, in a state of nature, are almost unknown. Here, then, plantations would have been most appropriate, in order to supply the deficiency, had our ancestors designed them for the bowyer's use. Yet the churchyards, in such situations, are as destitute of yew as the open country; its place being supplied by lime, elm, chesnut, and occasionally by oak. The mere presence, then, of some sort of foliage, and not the cultivation of one species of timber, for any specific purpose, was the object of our fathers in thus planting their sepulchres. In certain parts of Monmouthshire, on the other hand, the *Taxus baccata* * is seen starting from every cranny, cleft, or " coin of vantage " of its mountainous and rocky surface; where, even at the present day, bowstaves might be procured within the circuit of a few miles, sufficient to equip a thousand archers. I say with all this profusion of wild yew, yet is there scarcely a village burying-ground unoccupied by some gigantic patriarch of the species. Is it not absurd to suppose men would plant, within these contracted bounds, a single tree of such slow growth that, in the space of a century, its height and substance are scarcely sufficient to furnish half a dozen bow staves, while numbers were courting the woodman's axe on every hill side?

Thirdly. The piety, or, as some men may choose to style it, the superstition, of our ancestors would have been decidedly opposed to the application of wood reared within consecrated ground to any such use.†

Fourthly. Instead of the fine clean growth, indispensable in

* The Linnæan name for yew.

† Not within consecrated ground only, but even the domains of the clergy. When Harry V. issued his commission to Nicholas Frost, the royal bowyer, to enter upon the lands of private individuals, and cut down yew and other wood for the public service, he expressly forbids his trespassing on estates belonging to any religious order.— *Sir N. H. Nicholas.*

Ne rector prosternet arbores in cemeterio, — is one of the stipulations of Magna Charta.

trees intended for the bowyer, they in most cases present gnarled, knotty, crooked trunks, with branches springing close to their roots, — of all objections to me the most conclusive.

Fifthly. Every yew tree growing within the united church-yards of England and Wales, admitting they could be renewed five times in the course of a century, would not have produced one fiftieth part of the bows required for the military supplies. The reader will more clearly perceive the force of this objection, by perusing the following extract from an original MS., once in the possession of Dr. Leith, entitled, " A complete List of the Royal Navy of England, in the year 1599." Be it also recollected that archery was then rapidly on the decline.

At the Tower of London.

Bowes, with cccliijvi. decaied	- 8185
Bowstaves	- 6091
Slurbowes	- 15
Crossbowes	- 180

On perusing this document, the archer will marvel likewise what became of these bows, since arms of every other kind have been scrupulously preserved there from a much earlier period. I regret being unable to throw any light upon this subject; but since it is certain no bows have been seen at the Tower within the memory of man, most probably they were used as firewood.

I have thus endeavoured to show what our ancestors did not intend, when they planted their village cemeteries with this species of evergreen. It is now incumbent on me to acquaint the reader with the real purposes for which they were designed. That the existence of a yew tree of extraordinary size and beauty within the district where a church was to be erected, often determined its exact position, is a very rational surmise. The prodigious antiquity of many now growing in Herefordshire, when compared with the date of the building, renders it quite apparent they must have attained considerable bulk before the foundation stones were laid. The utility of masses of dense foliage, in shielding the church from the rude blasts of the north wind, is alluded to in the second statute passed in the thirty-fifth of Edward I. The yew afforded this protection in winter, the time it was most needed, and when deciduous trees present no barrier against the fury of the tempest. Here we have one good and sufficient reason: another was, its continual verdure, which rendered it a fitting emblem of the immortality enjoyed by those whose bodies mouldered beneath its ample shadow. A tree of baneful influence, observes Sir Thomas Browne, yet its perpetual verdure was an emblem of the resurrection of that eternal vigour which the soul enjoys after death. It may be added that, previous to the Reformation, slips of yew were substituted by the Roman Catholic priesthood on Palm Sunday, for the exotic plant, from which the festival derives its name.

In many of the little green inclosures, forming the burial grounds of this sequestered corner of Britain, there are yews truly gigantic, whose enormous arms, thrust out on every side, cover not the gravestones only, but sometimes a portion of the church-roof besides.* What a venerable and magnificent

* Village churches in Wales have rarely either spire or tower. Many of these simple structures owe their origin to the early British Christians. They generally stand in the midst of fields, and on the banks of rivers, embowered in trees, at a distance from human habitations. The body of the church, and occasionally the tower, are whitened. In some instances the tower is uncoloured, and in others the battlements only are whitewashed, for the natives of the Principality evince a great fondness for the lime brush. Not only are their cottages whitened inside and out, but should a fragment of rock or stone stile lie within their fields, it is sure to receive a coating of lime, which they frequently renew. The practice is of remote antiquity; their earliest bards, and I believe some Roman authors, allude to the snow-white cottages of the Britons. At one season of the year, generally Easter, the villagers place slips of yew, intermingled with every variety of wild and garden flower, around the edges of their family grave mounds. The bard

tree stands in the centre of Llanelly village churchyard! *
Many a time and oft have I loitered there, admiring its prodigious trunk, around which the small green hillocks cluster, as if exulting in the protection of some guardian genius of the place; and in Aberdwy churchyard, Glamorganshire, are two uncommon yews, under the branches of which sixty rustic couples have danced at the annual feast.

From my earliest initiation into the mysteries of bolt and butt-shaft, — and it was somewhat betimes, — to me this tree has ever been an object of singular interest; but whether decorating the romantic slopes and woody dingles of Piercefield Park, overshadowing the rustic bench of some road-side inn, or waving from the rocky precipices of the stupendous Wyndecliffe, still the *cui bono* alone possesses the archer's imagination. Insensible then to all the charms of the picturesque, to him it appears interesting only when levelled by the woodman's axe, and after being, like Falstaff, " sawed into quantities," reposing upon the shelves of some bowyer's workshop.

The general inferiority of English yew has been rather too much insisted on, since, as I have just stated, there is much excellent wood growing in most parts of Hereford and Monmouth. I think it was before the porch of a little inn in the former county, bearing the singular appellation of the " Kite's

---

Davyth ap Gwilym, in describing the beauty and fertility of Glamorganshire, pathetically alludes to the practice here described: —

> And thus, 'mid all thy radiant flowers,
> Thy thick'ning leaves and glossy bowers,
>   The poet's task shall be to glean
> Roses and flowers that softly bloom,
> The jewels of the forest gloom!
>   With trefoils wove in pavement green,
> With sad humility to grace
> His golden Ivor's resting-place.

* Monmouthshire.

Nest," that I once noticed several noble trees of this species. They are specially recommended to the attention of Mr. Waring.

Much fine bow-wood grows in the vicinity of Chepstow. Above 100 trees might be selected in that neighbourhood, from twelve to twenty inches in diameter, straight as the mainmast of a Seventy-four, and rising to the height of seven feet without branch, knot, or wind-gall. Even the woods of Italy, Castile, Tyre, and Crete, the grand nursery whence our English bowyers drew their supplies, could hardly produce any thing superior.

The yew tree appears to be a native of almost every temperate climate of the old and new world. It abounds in Canada; is in many parts of Germany, Switzerland, Norway, Sweden, Russia, and Poland; Italy as well as Spain had anciently the reputation of abounding with extraordinary fine timber of this species; and the forests of Castile, in the latter country, once supplied England with highly prized bow-staves, —

All made of Spanish yew, their bows were wond'rous strong.*

But subsequent to the invasion of Edward the Black Prince, the Castilians decreed that, not only should all yew trees then existing be destroyed, but their increase be put a stop to for ever afterwards. And little wonder either; for if at any time the Spaniards tasted the sharpness of our arrows, it was then. France does not possess much; it is very rare in the Netherlands; but European Tartary grows, on the other hand, a prodigious quantity, enough to have supplied not England only but all Europe, ere musketry banished the bow.

Switzerland also has yew in abundance; its rocky mountainous surface being well adapted to its nature; and along the banks of the beautiful Orbe, flowing beneath the Jura, through a valley of the same name, we find enough of these trees. The

* Drayton.

inhabitants of the Pays de Vaud are also fond of archery, and Vevay, Geneva, and Lausanne, have their bow-meetings. Yet, with such an abundance of fine yew, they prefer the *Cytise*, or Laburnum, which also grows plentifully on their mountain-slopes. Bows of the latter wood have certainly a very pretty appearance, the back being white, like those of its rival the yew, and the belly of a rich dark brown. They are durable, elastic, and take a very high polish.*

Previous to dismissing the subject of *Dendrology*, I will indulge in a remark or two upon another interesting tree. If the yew be so essential to the complete equipment of the English bowman, the lordly oak likewise shines conspicuous in real and fictitious records of his art; and the assembly of archers under their " trysting tree," † is frequently alluded to by the early poets and ballad writers. Thither the bands of outlaws, who roamed through the vast forests by which England was formerly overrun, came together through secret approaches known only to themselves; and there, after sharing the booty, they feasted upon the king's deer, slaughtered with their arrows. Secure from pursuit in these impenetrable fastnesses, these outlawed Saxons sallied forth in the broad day, plundering indiscriminately the travelling merchant, the lordly bishop, and the belted earl. Even the lion-hearted king Richard fared no better than his subjects. Travelling, on one occasion, under the disguise of a churchman, he encountered a party of these marauders, who after obliging him to " stand and deliver," bore him off to

---

* I take this opportunity to copy the card of one very excellent Swiss bowmaker: —

BOURGOGNE,
Fabricant d'arcs et de Flesches,
Place St. Laurent, No. 14,
Lausanne.

† A rendezvous, or appointed place of meeting.

feast upon his own venison, and witness a display of their archery beneath the oaks of merry Sherwood.

> The king came to Nottingham,
>   With knyghtes in great arraye,
> For to take that gentle knight,
>   And Robin Hood, if he may.
>
> All the pass of Lancashire,
>   He went both farre and neare,
> Till he came to Plompton park
>   He fayled many of his deare.
>
> Where our kynge was wont to see
>   Herdes many a one;
> He coud not fynde one dere
>   That bare ony good horne.
>
> The kynge was wonder wroth with all,
>   And swore by the trynyte,
> I wolde I had Robyn Hode,
>   With eyen I myght hym see;
>
> And he that wolde smyte of the knyghtes head,
>   And brynge it to me,
> He shall have the knyghtes londes,
>   Syr Rycharde at the Le;
>
> I give it him with my charter,
>   And sele it with my honde,
> To have and holde for ever more,
>   In all mery Englonde.
>
> Half a yere dwelled our comly kinge,
>   In Nottingham, and well more,
> Coude he not here of Robyn Hode,
>   In what countré that he were; —
>
> But alway went good Robyn,
>   By halke and eke by hill;
> And alway slewe the kinges dere,
>   And wilt them at his will.
>
> Than bespake a proud forèstere,
>   That stode by our kinges kné,
> If ye will se good Robyn,
>   Ye must do after me;

Take five of the best knightes
   That be in your lede,
And walk downe by yon Abbay
   And gete you monkes wede.

*   *   *   *

Full hastly our kinge was dight,
   So were his knightes five,
Everich of them in monkes wede,
   And hasted them thither blithe.

Our kinge was grete above his cole,
   A brode hat on his crowne;
Right as he were abbot like,
   They rode up into the towne.

Stiff botes our kinge had on,
   Forsooth as I you say,
He rode singinge to grene wode,
   The convent was clothed in graye.

There they met with good Robyn,
   Stondinge on the waye,
And so dide many a bolde archere.
   For sooth as I you say,

Robyn toke the kinges horse,
   Hastely in that stide,
And said, Sir Abbot, by your leve,
   A while ye must abide.

We be yeomen of this foreste,
   Under the grene wode tre,
We live by our kinges dere,
   Other shyft have not we;

And ye have chirches and rentes both,
   And gold full grate plenté;
Give us some of your spendinge
   For saynt Charité.

Then bespake our cumly kinge,
   Anone then said he,
I brought no more to grene wode,
   But forty pounde with me;

Robyn toke the forty pounde,
   And parted it in two partye;
Halfendell he gave his merry men,
   And bad them mery to be.

Full curteysly Robyn gan say,
  Syr, have this for your spendinge;—
We shall mete another day,
  Gramercy, than said our kinge.

Robyn toke a full grete horne,
  And loud he gan blowe;
Seven score of wight younge men,
  Came redy on a rowe.

All, they kneeled on their knee,
  Full faire before Robyn.
The kinge said himselfe untyll,
  And swore by saint Austyn,

Here is a wonder semely sight,
  Me thinketh, by Godde his pyne;
His men are more at his biddinge,
  Then my men be at myne.

Full hastly was their dyner dyght,
  And thereto are they gone,
They served our kinge with al their might,
  Both Robyn and Lytell Johan.

Anone before our kinge was set
  The fatte venyson,
The good whyte brede, the good red wyne,
  And thereto the fyne ale browne,

Make good chere, said Robyn,
  Abbot, for charyté:
And for this same tidinge,
  Blyssed mote thou be, &c. &c.

Within the still extensive, and once royal forest of Wentwood[*], on the left hand side of the road that leads from Llanvoir castle, is a little detached clump of trees springing from an undulating surface of bright green velvet turf. Two of these woodland patriarchs, remarkable beyond their fellows for magnitude and antiquity, have long been familiar to the neighbouring rustics by the appellation of "Foresters' Oaks."

[*] Monmouthshire.

You will easily recognise by their form; for the growth and storms of centuries have given a most giant-like, fantastic air to the limbs of the first; and above the finely arched summit of the second, a huge blasted leafless bough, resembling the antlers of some colossal stag, shoots up from a mass of brilliant foliage, so dense that, like another Boscobel oak, it might securely shelter a fugitive monarch within its impenetrable recesses. Even at the present day, I believe a meeting of the forest tenants sometimes assembles there.* There, also, the woodmen of Worcester's great marquis were wont to halt, and ease their shoulders of the red deer venison which once roamed within the chase of Wentwood. Other scenes, too, of a more sombre character have occasionally been enacted there. Brief examination and a speedy fate awaited the luckless Saxon, who loving a buck's haunch more than he feared the penalties of forest law, was detected under any suspicious circumstance, set forth in cabalistic verse: —

>   Dog draw,
>   Stable stand,
>   Back berond,
>   Bloody hand. †

Their trysting oak afforded a ready gallows ‡ : his own bowstring the halter by which they strangled him like a hound.

* In the records of a Speech Court, held under "Foresters' Oaks," Wentwood, in the year 1688, it is said that Sir William Bandmele claimed to have houseboote and hayboote at his house at Oditton, from the Conquest, &c. — WILLET.

† These are the four evidences by which, according to the old feudal laws, a man was convicted of deer stealing. The first relates to an offender detected in a forest, drawing after a deer with hound in leash; the second, to him caught with bent bow ready to shoot; the third, to bearing away the venison on his shoulders, and the fourth, to him merely found with hands stained with blood of the game. Edward the Confessor's Red Book contains the following caution: — "Omnis homo abstineat a venariis meis, super pœnam vitæ."—"Let every man refrain from my hunting grounds on pain of death."

‡ In Wales, poetically styled Dialbren, "The Tree of Vengeance."

Beneath the branches of these stately trees, also, the oath of fidelity was administered to candidates for the forester's vocation in the following quaint doggerel: —

> You shall true liegeman be
> To the king's majestie;
> Unto the beasts of the forest you shall not misdo,
> Nor to any thing that doth belong thereto.
> The offences of others you shall not conceal,
> But to the utmost of your power you shall them reveal
> Unto the officers of the forest,
> And to them that may see them redress'd.
> All these things you shall see done,
> So help you God at his holy doom.

Among the extraordinary oaks found in Monmouthshire and South Wales, is that between Old and New Radnor, measuring twenty-seven feet in girth. Another remarkable tree extends its branches over a large fish pool near St. Arvan's, on the Piercefield estate. At Newcastle, a village some distance from Monmouth, a huge oak upwards of nine yards in circumference, stands on the left side of the road. Its pendant matted branches have a most fantastic appearance; and when one of the largest was recently severed by a storm of wind, it yielded full fifteen cart loads of fire wood.

Here terminates my stock of knowledge respecting the birth, parentage, and education of yew tree and oak. I will next con over a chapter, *de arcubus*, of bows.

Previously to the battles of Cressy and Agincourt, so famed in the annals of archery, and for centuries afterwards, our countrymen were accustomed to no other sort of bow than that now styled *self*, or formed of a single piece. When summoned on domestic military service, the archers, those living upon Crown lands excepted, came armed into the field; but, if engaged on foreign expeditions, the necessary equipments were provided at the public cost. A comparatively small number of their bows then consisted of English yew, its grain being often so knotty and defective that no part could be relied on, except the portion of the heart protected by its exterior stratum of sapwood. Yet, the entire butt of a clean tree, inside as well as outside, is available for self-bows, provided the staves are not sawn, but cleft from the plank, and in that case only; and a passage in Ascham will decide that such was the ancient practice. " The best *color* of a bow," says he, " is when the back and belly in working are much alike; for, oftentimes in wearing, it proves like virgin wax or gold."* In bows cut from the outside of yew, those parts can never resemble each other; the heart of the tree, which forms " the belly," being red or reddish brown; while the outside stratum, through which the sap flows, and which forms the back, is perfectly white.

England alone, being unable to supply the prodigious demand of its ancient armaments, imported great numbers of bow staves, and the government hit upon a clever expedient for rendering them as inexpensive as possible. Since all timber possesses a harder texture and finer grain when grown in a warm climate, than when reared in one less genial †, the Lombard merchants were compelled to deliver a certain quantity of foreign yew with every cask of Greek and Italian wine admitted into the London custom-house. Edward IV., with whom this law originated, fixed the number of bow staves at four; Richard III., his successor, increased them to ten for each butt. ‡ The merchants, or supercargoes, therefore bribed the country people to fell and convey to the ports where they traded a number of yew trees ready lopped and trimmed. From these he selected as many as, by a rough guess, seemed equal to the wine on board, and made them useful as dunnage among

---

* That is, becomes silky, smooth, and takes a fine polish.

† As you approach the tropics, this characteristic becomes more and more obvious. The Demerara Indian bows have a beautifully fine grain; several in my possession are without flaw or blemish from nock to nock.

‡ 1 Richard III. chap. ii.

the casks, like large bamboo canes in the hold of a modern East Indiaman.

About the period when Stowe composed his Survey of London, the London bowmakers presented a memorial to the Privy Council, complaining that these foreigners had discontinued their supply of yew. The rejoinder of the merchants was curious. They stated that the Turks being in possession of the Levant countries, whence they formerly obtained it, they no longer durst show their beards within fifty leagues of their old haunts; and to this cause, and the consequent adoption of fire-arms, we may attribute the decay of military archery towards the end of the seventeenth century, none of the tropical woods, at present worked up into bows, being then known. When, therefore, the foreign supply ceased, the bowyers in most parts of the country found it impracticable to meet even the limited demand arising from archery used as a recreation only; and, seeing their occupation thus rapidly on the decline, they bethought themselves of a modified construction of the Lapland and Oriental bow. They accordingly glued a thin slip of ash, elm, hickory, or other very tough wood upon yew taken from the brittle plank; and by thus forming an artificial back to save the bow, it was in less danger of breaking when drawn up. By the success of this experiment, the heart of trees previously condemned for firewood was brought into use, and the *Backed Bow*, so well known to the votaries of modern archery, quickly became a ruling favourite with shooters of every degree. It is remarkable this improvement should have been first adopted in Lancashire, where the yew tree never grew plentifully, while the distance of that county from the metropolis must have rendered a foreign supply uncertain and difficult.*

---

* Liverpool was at that period a paltry village, inhabited by a few fishermen.

Had archery retained its ancient warlike reputation, after the date of this improvement, it is probable bows on the new principle would have been adopted in the army, as well as at the butts. In a clever little tract, of the sixteenth century, elsewhere more fully noticed, the author directs a squadron of mounted archers to be thus equipped: "Let their bows be of good yeugh, long, and well nocked and backed." Still, such a bow seems not well adapted for military service; since a few hours' rain, or a night's lodging on the damp ground, would be very likely to put it *hors de combat*, by softening the glue, and causing the back and belly to part company.

But, after all, English bowyers cannot claim the merit of having first availed themselves of this imitation of the Lapland and Tartar bow: it has been well known to the French and Flemings for nearly three centuries. In the twenty-first article of the rules and regulations agreed to by the master gun-makers and bowyers of Paris, A. D. 1575, it is declared that the members of this craft shall make and sell bows formed of several pieces, which were to be carefully fitted together, and glued with good glue well and sufficiently.*

Notwithstanding the little communication subsisting between distant nations at the beginning of the sixteenth century, it can easily be shown, that our countrymen were familiar with the construction of many sorts of foreign bows and arrows. In the catalogue of rarities, preserved in the museum of the celebrated John Tradescant, at South Lambeth, are mentioned, " Bowes, 12; arrows, 20; quivers, 12: from India, China, Canada, Virginia, Guinea, Turkey and Persia."† In Chaucer's Canterbury Tales, the attendants of a knight are represented bearing after him his warlike accoutrements, among which we have the Oriental bow.

* Vide laws and regulations of the Guild of Paris armourers.
† Museum Tradescantium, A.D. 1580.

> And eke upon these steeds great and white,
>   There satten folk of which some bare his shield,
> The third bare with him two bows Turkeis,
>   Another his speare up in his hondes held;
> Of brent gold was the case and the harneis.*

So, in the Romance of the Rose, Love is said to have " deux arcs Turquois."†

While Sir John Shirley resided in Persia as ambassador from the British Court, he received a splendid present from the Shah. There were sword blades of Damascus steel, China bowls, and pelisses of costly silks and furs; but, like a true English soldier, nothing pleased him so much as " nine beautiful bows, and an equal number of quivers filled with arrows," which he brought home to England.‡ " Of the South American bowes and arrowes," says Huighen Van Linschoten, " there needeth no great description, because so many of them are brought into these countries.§ It is unnecessary to cite additional authorities, for the purpose of showing that Englishmen in the fifteenth and sixteenth centuries were familiar with the construction of foreign implements of archery.

Hazel, elm, ash, and wych bows, are enumerated in our old statutes, to be sold at a very low rate. ‖ A law of Queen Elizabeth enumerates auburne and arbour: the former possibly means La Cytise, or Laburnum, a species of dark brown wood, preferred to yew by the Swiss archers, although they have plenty of the latter. Matthiolus mentions that tree as being used for making the best kind of bows; but Mr. Waring, who made some unsatisfactory experiments on fir, also tried the laburnum, but with no better success.¶ Perhaps the auburne

---

* Knight's Tale, line 289. † V. 924.
‡ Relation d'un Voyage en Perse, A. D. 1598, par un Gentilhomme de la Suite du Seigneur Shirley, Ambassadeur du Roi d'Angleterre.
§ Travels, vol. i. p. 253.
‖ 33 Henry VIII., c. 9.
¶ English Bowman, p. 131., note.

and arbour are synonymous; if not, the latter may be walnut tree, also much used on the Continent, and which certainly makes no despicable weapon. By the Indians of North America it is highly esteemed. " The toughest wood in that country," says an old writer, "is the walnut tree; and therefore made use of for hoops and bowes, there being no yews there growing. In England, they make the bowes of wild hazel, ash, and elm, the best of outlandish yew; but the Indians make them of walnut." * For butt practice, and other sportive exercises, these " heavy sluggs," as Barnes styles them, do well enough, but except on emergencies, such as a *levy en masse*, they were rarely used in war. Admiral Frobisher, speaking of the archery of the people of the Jesso Isles, says their bows were of aulne — the alder tree. This species of wood grows plentifully on the margin of most English rivers and brooks; but its qualities are as yet unknown to the bowyers. In the preface to " Gesta Dei per Francos," the excellency of a wood called nassus, growing in the island of Corsica, is greatly enlarged upon. A certificate of Decayes of Castle, Towne, and Citadell of Carlisle, by Walter Strickland, 1569, enumerates seventy bows of *elm* not serviceable †; but such entries do not often occur.

In selecting a bow, whether backed or *self*, the modern archer has little occasion to exercise critical acumen, except in deciding upon the power he chooses it shall possess. Mr. Waring of Bedford Square, the only London maker of whom I have any experience, furnishes us with bows so excellent in material, proportion, and finish, that the juvenile may safely forego his own choice, and leave to him the care of equipping him suitably. If altogether unacquainted with archery, begin with a self-bow; and when familiar with its use, try your hand with one that is backed;

* Jossleyn's Voyage to New England, A. D. 1644.
† Sir S. R. Meyrick's Armour; also MSS. Brit. Mus. Titus XIII. folio 220.

but the former will safely admit of liberties, which would prove fatal to its more elegant and complicated rival. Still, should the latter's showy appearance induce a preference, avail yourself of some veteran archer's instructions; for the principle on which these backed bows are made admits not of their being trifled with.

Ascham speaks as if he were acquainted with the self-bow only, at least he makes no allusion to any other kind. As it is probable not one archer in five score possesses, or has ever seen, the " Toxophilus," I will present the reader with a specimen of his style, making a comment or two as we proceed.

" The Ethiopians had bows of palm trees, but we have no experience of them."

Not in your time, friend Roger, but our experience of such matters has been somewhat enlarged since those glorious days, when you dunned our Royal Bess into the mysteries of " propria quæ Maribus," and " As in presenti." Mr. Waring will furnish a very good looking serviceable bow of this same palm, or " Cocoswood," — its more modern and fashionable name. But let us get on with the text.

" The Indians had their bows of great strength, which were of reed. In Alexander's life, it says those bows were of so great strength that no harness* or buckler, though ever so strong, could stand a shaft from them. The length of the bow was as high as the user."

I have had many bows of this kind in my own possession, but none were of the prodigious strength mentioned by Ascham. What he calls a reed is the male bamboo; and a species growing upon the mountains of Thibet, from its superior closeness of grain, is well adapted for bows. They form them of two exterior pieces, the inner sides of which, after being well smoothed and fitted, are united together by many strong bands. The Lama Gyap, who spent the greater part of

---

* Armour.

his time in the amusement of archery, put one of these cane bows into the hands of Mr. Turner, envoy from the Indian government to Thibet. The Englishman, however, was unable to stir the string, when taking it himself, he shot the arrow against a mark upon the opposite hill, a distance, according to Mr. Turner, of between five and six hundred yards. Such bows might riddle the armour of Alexander's co-mates, although the arrows shot were only light hollow reeds; indeed, the rapidity and force with which a shaft of this description will strike an object is truly astonishing. Zenophon corroborates the account here given by Ascham, and says, in reference to the Carducians, another nation of bowmen, that they drove their arrows with prodigious force, piercing through the shields and corslets of his men; and as these arrows were extremely large, the Greeks used them for javelins. The long reed arrows of the Indians of another hemisphere appear to have worked effects equally destructive upon the Spaniards in their attempts to subdue the Floridas; and Garcilasco de Vega describes an encounter between two cavaliers of that nation completely armed and a single naked Indian warrior.

One morning, whilst the troops were halting to refresh themselves, two Indians, splendidly accoutred, after the fashion of their country, approached to within three hundred paces of the camp. They there commenced parading up and down beneath a large walnut tree, one on one side, and the other on the other, in order to guard against any sudden surprise. When the Spanish general was informed of this, he ordered all the soldiers to their quarters, calling the Indians "fools and madmen, only worthy of contempt." In obedience to this command, they were allowed to continue unmolested, until the return of a detachment of horse, who had been all day abroad on a foraging party. Perceiving the Indians near their quarters, they inquired of their comrades who they were, and learned the orders of the general. All obeyed except Juan Paez, who fiercely exclaimed, "Since these barbarians are fools and madmen, it is proper that a greater fool should chastise their folly;" and thereupon spurred towards the tree. The Indian stationed on the side by which the cavalier was approaching, advanced boldly to meet him, whilst his companion retired still further beneath the branches, thus intimating that the combat was to be man to man. In the mean time, Paez had galloped to within a short distance, when the Indian discharged an arrow so adroitly, that it pierced the fleshy part of his adversary's arm, penetrating through both sides of a coat of mail*, and remaining crossed in the wound, so that

---

* What will modest Mr. Humphrey Barwick[1], the self-styled "gentleman soldier, captain, et encor plus oultre," say to this?

So much for the "disabilities of the long bow," when used against armour of Spanish steel; but we'll go further, and meet this veracious champion of the musket on his own ground, who scruples not to affirm, that an English steel-headed shaft, far from inflicting wounds through a military buff coat, would scarcely penetrate ordinary broad cloth.

Now this is very audacious in one who had repeatedly witnessed the effects of archery on the field of battle; but the whole book is beneath contempt. Nevertheless, I will cite an instance or two in disproof of his assertions, merely because the narrative itself is too amusing to be omitted in a work of this sort. First, then, for "the broad cloth."

"Drawing near to the landing-place," says the author of "Proceedings in New England, A.D. 1638," "the number of Indians that rose from behind the barricado amounted to between fifty and sixty fighting men; straight as arrows, very tall, and of active bodies. Having their arrows nocked, they drew near to the water-side, and let fly at the soldiers as though they meant to have made an end of us all in a moment. They shot a young gentleman in the neck, through *a collar, for stiffness, as if it had been an oaken board*, and entered his flesh a good depth. Myself received an arrow through my coat sleeve; a second against my helmet on the forehead; so, if God, in his providence, had not moved the heart of my wife, to persuade me to carry it along with me, which I was unwilling to do, I had been slain. Let no man, therefore, despise the council of his wife, though she be a woman."

A little further on, the same author enables us to deal with the buff-coat after a similar fashion.

---

[1] Author of a work entitled, "Disabilities of the Long Bow, in comparison with Weapons of Fire," &c.

the bridle reins dropped from his hand, and he remained powerless over horse and weapon. His companions immediately galloped

---

"Having given fire we approached near to the entrance, which they had stopped full with arms of trees or stakes. Myself, approaching the entrance, found the work too heavy for me, to draw out all those that were strongly forced in. We therefore gave orders to Master Hedge and some other soldiers to pull out those stakes. Having thus done, and laid them between me and the entrance, they proceeded of themselves, without order, to the south end of the fort. But it was remarkable to many of us, that men who run before they are sent most commonly have an ill reward. With our carbines, in our left hands and our swords in our right, we approached the fort. Master Hedge was shot through both arms. Captain Mason and myself, entering into the wigwams, he was shot at, and received many arrows against his head-piece, but God preserved him from any wounds. Myself received an arrow through the left hip, *through* a sufficient *buff-coat*, that, if I had not been supplied with such a garment, would have pierced me through and through. Another I received through neck and shoulders, hanging in the linen of my head-piece; others of our soldiers were shot, some through the shoulders, some in the face, some in the head, some in the legs, Captain Mason and myself each losing a man. I had twenty wounded."

An Indian chief, named Carrara, requested permission to examine the sword of a Portuguese officer, with whom he was in company. The owner having observed that this weapon would pierce through a double buff-coat, our Indian friend immediately requested to see it done. This the Portuguese performed, but sorely bruised his hand with the pomel of the sword, the coat being placed across the back of a chair. When the Indian saw the effects of the sword, he asked for his bow, and, adding a third fold to the leathern garment, made so furious a shot that he pierced it through and through. All present stood astonished at the power of what they had previously considered an insignificant weapon.

The facts here adduced receive additional corroboration from the following return of killed and wounded in a battle with archers. This statement, which is interesting from its rarity, was published by Mons. de la Fueillard, at the siege of Candia, A.D. 1667.

De Torci, of the brigade of St. Paul, before the town; dead.
M. Ourq, wounded by an arrow in the thigh; since dead.
De la Roque, by an arrow in the shoulder.
De Milieu, an arrow-shot in the kidneys.
De Hougre, by an arrow in the head, of which he died.
De Charmon, an arrow-shot in the arm.

after the Indians, who fled hastily on seeing themselves pursued by so many enemies; but the Spaniards came up with them ere they could reach the forest, and, unmindful of the gallantry which is said to be characteristic of their nation in all matters connected with the laws of chivalry, they lanced them to death.

Revenons a nos moutons. Let us again hear Roger Ascham, who next informs us that the Romans entertained a predilection for the yew; and, tell it not in Gath! attempts to confirm his assertion by a blundering quotation from Virgil. This dweller in academic halls, who, in his preface, seems to regret that he had not composed the "Toxophilus" in Greek or Latin[*], is convicted of a classical mistake by the author of the "English Bowman."[†]

Taxi torquentur in arcus,

writes this ancient pedant, quoting the Georgics, 2d Book, line 44.

Ityræos taxi torquentur in arcus,

says Roberts, and he says rightly. However, "fair play is a jewel all the world over," according to a venerable adage; and candour demands we should notice an error of which, oddly enough, Roberts himself is guilty in his note on this same passage. "Vegetius," says he, "speaks of the wooden bow, with a preference in comparison of other bows, as follows:—' Prope tertia vel quarta pars juniorum quæ aptior potuerit reperiri, arcubus ligneis sagittis que lusoriis, ad illos semper exercenda palos.'"[‡]

De la Coste, by an arrow in the head.
Le Chevalier de Vausel, by an arrow in the arm.
Le Capitaine la Forest, by an arrow-shot in the belly, of which he immediately died.
Le Sergeant Major Pini, by a stone in the shoulder, and an arrow-shot in the belly; dead.

[*] The reader will probably consider that "the force of pedantry could no farther go."
[†] Page 130. note.
[‡] Page 131.

Now the Roman expresses no such partiality, as every one will readily see. He merely asserts that wooden bows and plaything arrows will do well enough for the butt practice of an awkward squad of boys.

But *Jocosè hæc.* Roberts was, nay perhaps is, a right good archer, and his book the best among our slender stock of toxophilite literature.

" A good bow," continues Ascham, " is known by the proof. If you come to a shop and see one that is small, long, heavy, and strong; lying straight, and not winding or marred with knots, buy that bow on my warrant. The short grained bow is for the most part brittle." He here compares yew with itself, of which the heaviest kind makes the best bows; a stave taken from the bole of a tree considerably outweighing one of the same dimensions from its branches.

" Every bow is made of the bough or plant of a tree. The former is commonly very knotty, small, weak, and will soon follow the string.* The latter proveth many times well, if it be of a good clean growth; and, if the pith is good, it will ply and bend before it breaks. Let the staves be good and even chosen, and afterwards wrought as the grain of the wood leadeth a man, or else the bow must break, and that soon, in shivers. This must be considered in the rough wood. You must not stick for a groat or two more than another man would give for a good bow; for such an one twice paid for is better than an ill one once broken. Thus a shooter must begin, not at the making of his bow like a bowyer, but at the buying of his bow like an archer. Before he trust his bow, let him take it into the fields, and shoot with dead heavy shafts. Look where it cometh most, and provide for that place, lest it pinch and so frete. Thus, when you have shot him, and perceive good wood

---

* This rule has its exceptions. I once made a beautiful self-bow from a large branch of yew, which was amputated, *after* two valuable coach-horses had been poisoned by feeding on its leaves.

in him, you must have him to a good workman, which shall cut him shorter, and dress him fitter, make him come round compass every where."

The following inference may be drawn from the above passage. A new bow was anciently kept in an unfinished state until the purchaser made his selection, and ascertained by trial its merits or demerits, for the course here recommended by Ascham would ruin, instead of improving one of Waring's highly finished productions. Roberts thinks the passage, "make him come round compass every where," implies that a self-bow was thus formed in the back as well as in the belly; but I would suggest "every where" must be interpreted to mean from nock to nock; a precaution of course not accurately attended to in the rough unfinished article. In Ascham's time, as at present, they made the back nearly, though not quite, flat, and such was the form of a bow about three centuries old, which I had once an opportunity of inspecting. This curious relic of our forefathers' archery, measuring exactly six feet in length, probably possessed a power of seventy pounds: I say probably, for we did not attempt to bend it. It was yew of course, and the fine silky fibres, which might be distinctly traced from horn to horn, left little doubt of its foreign growth. The horn tips were split by age, and, owing to decay of the glue, had nearly separated from the wood. Its handle of purple velvet was elegantly braided with silver lace, so that the original possessor seems to have been some person above the common rank. There were indeed some small knots or pins scattered over its surface; for a bow-stave entirely free from them is of very rare occurrence. These, conformable to the plan recommended by Ascham, were all carefully "raised." Not, however, in little smooth wart-like excrescences such as we sometimes remark upon Waring's best bows, but large square lumps, which gave the weapon a most singular appearance. It had also another peculiarity. Besides that prominence in the centre, without which no bow can be considered perfect, there was a gentle swelling at the back for about four inches above and below the handle, and I consider this formation to have been universal in the ancient self-bow, although neglected at the present day. In Dr. Grew's "Rareties of Gresham College" are mentioned, among other foreign implements of savage warfare, "A West Indian bow, arrows, and quiver." "This bow," says Dr. Grew, "is made of ash*, near two yards long: in the middle, not an inch broad, but *highbacked and bellied;* viz. above an inch, *as our bows:* between the middle and ends of a far different shape; viz. above an inch and a half broad, and not above half an inch thick."

It is rather curious that a bow, once in my possession, and decidedly the best I ever handled, should have been distinguished by this peculiarity in a very remarkable degree. It was procured, together with a bundle of reed arrows nearly the same length, from a Demerara Indian chief. Jet black and glossy, like the complexion of its original master, the wood resembled ebony, thickly marked with veins of deep crimson. For any mark within seven score, a better certainly never drove arrow into target.

Every one who has spent an hour in looking over the "Toxophilus" must be aware it is a sort of archer's catechism, carried on between a master of the art and his pupil. One writer only, however, has succeeded in this mode of conveying instruction; and certainly a more delightful treatise than his, upon a most delightful art, never proceeded from mortal pen; I mean the CONTEMPLATIVE MAN'S RECREATION, by amiable old Isaac Walton. But Walton's mind was imbued with the true spirit of poetry, and an unaffected love for the whole range of external nature: in this the great charm of his book consists. Ascham, on the contrary, who evidently had not one poetical feeling in

---

* This must be a mistake of the learned doctor. Ash does not grow in that climate, and if it did, the Indians possess too many varieties of excellent wood to resort to one so inferior.

his composition, writes like a dry, unimaginative pedant. Walton pours forth his simple melodies, seated among the wild thyme, on the banks of his favourite trout stream. The branches of some spreading oak wave over him, while, to use his own expression, "the clouds rain May butter," and the storm-thrush whistles her shrill, long-drawn notes above his head: —

> The woodwele sang and would not cease,
> Sitting upon a spray.

"With the making of a bow," says Ascham, "I will not meddle much, lest I may be thought to enter into another man's occupation." Without troubling myself whose peculiar vocation it might be, I confess to having made, first and last, a great many; and for the benefit of archers who reside at a distance from the metropolis, in a country abounding with yew, and who know the use of a carpenter's tool-chest, I shall give the result of my experience, at the risk of being considered a most irregular practitioner by the Worshipful Company of Bowyers. The habit, nay almost necessity, of making my own fly-rods, in this land of trout fishing*, led to the other; and both have proved a most agreeable resource on many a wet and dreary winter's day.

Besides the pleasure of knowing he is laying up a stock against that season returns, when meads are damasked o'er with daisies, and

> The jocund merle perched on the highest spray,
> Sings his love forth, to see the pleasant May,

the archer has the advantage of being able to construct bows of great strength, and to work up yew plants of singular and eccentric growth, many of which will catch his eye during a woodland ramble; and they often turn out bows as excellent in shooting as their form is picturesque. In the selection of wood,

---

* The greater portion of this work was written in a mountainous district of Wales.

the principal thing to be looked to is the getting it clean, and free from knots: a tree not entirely bare of branches to the height of six feet from the ground will assuredly have a pin at the place where each branch is lopped off. Perambulate, therefore, the woods and copses of your neighbourhood with a hawk's eye, and, for a private mark, put a deep notch in the bark of such saplings as please you. Good archer's yew has generally a fine smooth bark, of a reddish grey hue; and the freer it is from excrescences, the more safely may you build expectations upon it;—I say expectations, because no wood promises so fairly and turns out more deceptive when cut open. There are also other external defects, by being aware of which the amateur bow-maker will save himself much disappointment and waste of labour. Hollows in the bark, filled with black decayed matter, indicate unsoundness within. Rough cankerous swellings, or windgalls, as the wood-cutters term them, are equally suspicious. Choose something as clear as possible from these blemishes, and where they are inevitable, cut your wood so that the part destined to form the back, be as free from knots, &c. as it will allow. Let all or most of the defects be in the belly of the bow; on the good wholesome principle of keeping your enemies always in the front.

Never fell yew or any other wood in the summer season, but only during November, December, and the two following months, whilst the sap is down. Summer timber, besides being subject to the dry rot, will be much longer in seasoning.

For a self-bow, it is of little moment if the tree incline naturally in the direction which the bow will follow when strung, provided it is not at the same time cast, or twisted to the right or left. Should the wood be green, strip off the bark, and then get a muster roll of all the old wives in your village, who, "fruges consumere natæ," purpose heating their ovens during the ensuing fortnight. Make your bow stave circulate among each of these successively, and when the loaves are removed, and the warmth has considerably abated, let it occupy their place until "all is cold."

Having thus given it what Ascham calls the "requisite heatings," defer his "plenty of tillerings," until a fairer opportunity. Saw off from either side as much as will reduce it in breadth to nearly the substance you intend your bow shall possess at the centre of the handle. Should the yew be already seasoned, the above-mentioned process must be dispensed with, as well as what follows; if not, let it lie, thus reduced in quantity, upon the bacon-rack within the influence of a kitchen fire, in amicable confraternity with hams, bacon, chines, walking staves, hunting poles, fowling pieces, hedging bills, seed pods, angling rods, and other "miscellaneous items," as George Robins would style them, which usually crowd that indispensable fixture of a rural mansion. There let it remain six months at least, before the work is farther proceeded in.*

After sawing off two pieces from the sides, you will observe the heart to be of a reddish purple colour, the outside being protected by a stratum of pure white wood. A portion of this sap must be left for the back of your bow. Where the tree measures full four inches in diameter, with a stem straight and upright as a butt shaft, carefully split it down the centre by means of wedges. You may thus get two self-bows out of it; but when grown in a wavy or serpentine form,—and such pieces sometimes make very beautiful looking bows,— this is not so practicable. If the stave be perfectly straight, you are at liberty to select, from the two opposite sides of white wood, the one which presents the cleanest and smoothest surface, as well as the most regular thickness throughout. If, on the contrary, it

* All wood is best seasoned by exposure to the weather, care being taken to protect it from the sun, which would make it *shaky*, as the woodmen term it, that is, full of cracks. As this process will occupy eighteen months at least, I have recommended the other, lest the archer's patience should evaporate.

have the natural curve alluded to above, the convex side only will serve, how inferior soever it be to that you are compelled to cut away.

I omitted to mention, until now, that the smallest collection of tools requisite for this work, consists of a large and small saw, a long plane, a smoothing double-ironed ditto, one fine and one coarse rasp, and a steel scraper. You must also have a glue-pot, suspended in a hot-water kettle, and filled with a mixture composed of isinglass, spirits, and common glue. A small carpenter's bench, about seven feet long, but not more than fourteen inches in width, and provided with a wooden screw or vice, will give great facilities to every stage in the process of bow-making. Having screwed your stave to the bench with the back uppermost, work that with your file, then with the scraper, and lastly with sand-paper, until it is rendered as level as the growth of the piece will admit. Measure and mark the exact centre with a pencil line, then, having reversed its position in the screw, turn up the belly, and proceed to work upon *the handle*, the top of which must be fixed about an inch above the middle mark, towards the upper horn. Be very careful how you execute this part of the business; for should you cut away too much, the whole is marred beyond redemption. According to the intended power of the bow, leave plenty of wood in the handle, which should be rounded in the belly part only, and fall away with a gradual slope towards either arm.

Having proceeded to your own satisfaction thus far, lay the bow upon the bench on its side, and make a slight notch in the centre of each extremity, and two others at equal distances from it, to mark the proper width of the part destined to receive the horn tips. Plane away with an almost imperceptible slope, until the ends are reduced to about half the width of the centre. If it be perfectly straight, the belly may be rounded and sloped off, with a smoothing plane; should it bend and wind, that tool will be useless, and the business must be patiently executed with coarse and fine files. When the wood has been of the latter description, I found the operation much facilitated by cutting into the belly with a hand-saw at intervals of about two inches, and then striking out the pieces thus separated with a chisel and mallet. But this must also be executed with care and judgment.

Lastly, procure a piece of any kind of common timber about four feet long, six inches broad, and three deep. Cut a large notch in its upper end, sufficient to receive the whole of the bow handle, and about eight and twenty inches below (the usual length of an arrow) make a smaller one, similar to that in the stock of a child's cross-bow. This instrument is the "tiller" alluded to by Ascham, and is used to ascertain if the bow bend equally in both its arms. You should leave the stave a little longer than it is ultimately intended to be, that the two notches made for the tillering cord may be cut away, before putting on the horns. Brace the bow, fix the handle in that part prepared for it, and draw down the string to the notch, until the whole resembles a huge cross-bow ready charged. Whilst in that state, you can judge of the defects, and remedy them accordingly, until, after repeated trials, the bow being found to " come round compass," you put the last polish to it with coarse and fine glass-paper. The village butcher will supply the horn tips, which should be chosen of a jet black colour; and, by the help of a vice and files, you may be indebted to your own ingenuity for a very elegant ornament to the ends of your bow. When bored with a centre bit, and roughly modelled into the intended shape, soak them in boiling water, which, by softening the horn, makes it adhere more closely to the wood, and then glue them on. It is best to polish them after they are fixed.

The choice of the material for the handle is a matter of fancy. Green or red worsted lace, velvet, damask silk, plush, leather, are all used for this purpose, and all answer well. However, I think the first has the neatest appearance. A breadth of four inches and a half is amply sufficient, and the bow should be first strongly whipped with twine. If green or red lace be preferred, it is proper to bind in about half an inch with the twine at the commencement, which will secure one end; and, having first well moistened the surface of the handle with hot glue, wind on the remainder closely and evenly, securing the last inch of the lace, by drawing it underneath the three last turns with a noose of string, and confine it, until the glue is set.

The bowyers may laugh, as I have already observed; but, follow my directions in the main, and you will have a very respectable self-bow.

It is unnecessary to describe the formation of a backed one. With only one or two exceptions, I never knew anything satisfactory result from this sort of handicraft; so the archer's best plan will be to purchase from a respectable maker. I never saw any two-piece bows which could rival Waring's; but Wrigsley of Manchester, if he be still living; Ainsworth of Walton le Dale, Lancashire; and an individual at Wrexham, — his name I forget; but, in allusion to his two-fold vocation, he, like Caleb Quotem, may justly sing or say

> I'm parish clerk and *bowyer* here, —

all deserve the archer's patronage.

Various kinds of hard and elastic timber, the production of the East and West Indies, South America, and Africa, known by the several names of topaz, lancewood, cocos, ruby, tulip, fastic, &c., make excellent backed bows. The Islands of St. Vincent and Tobago, with the British settlement of Demerara, have several species of trees, which, when cut up, afford wood of a deep red and black colour. The best proof of its fitness for the purpose is, that the natives themselves make their bows from it; and whoever has the good fortune to be master of one of these Indian snake-like weapons, will join me in commending their quickness of cast, and fine form, considering the makers possess only the rudest implements, or rather, as we should say, no implements at all.

Bois de lettre, as the French settlers term it, is the heart of the Dolcabolla tree, a wood highly esteemed by the tawny archer of Guiana. The black spots which appear thickly scattered over its rich ruby-coloured ground appear rather as a painted imitation, than the work of Nature's hands; and when carefully polished, these bows have a very elegant appearance, but owing to its great scarcity — a small portion only being procurable from each tree — they are rarely seen, except in a chieftain's hands. Superior courage and bodily strength form, among the red men of the forest, the sole qualifications of a leader, where that office is not hereditary; and, truly, all specimens of the Dolcabolla bow, which I have seen, must have belonged to men well entitled to the distinction, for they were full ninety pounds' power, and measured seven feet, at least, between the nocks. They have, besides, iron-wood, red and black; the netergo, of a dark purple colour when newly cut; snake-wood, copic-wood, guiapariba, a Brazilian tree, called by the Portuguese pao d'arco, or bow-wood, &c. &c.; but none of these have yet been tried by the archers of England. It may be useful to know that when, from the increased power of his drawing arm, a Demerara Indian bow is no longer equal to its owner's strength, an artificial back will render it again serviceable.

In Hindostan and its dependencies, there are the tabulghu, teak, and janlot, an excellent wood, much used by the Cingalees of Ceylon. They have likewise the lontar, or ton of Western India, a species of palm, dark, hard, and tough; the nibung, or true mountain cabbage tree, possessing similar properties; the jack or nunghu of a yellow tint; lastly, the timaka, capable, like the jack, of receiving an exquisite polish.

Apropos of polishing; I will say a word or two on the most approved method of keeping a bow in good case. Your thorough-bred archer is not merely ambitious of being a marks-

man; the perfect condition of every part of his shooting tackle*
will occupy a reasonable portion of his time. Ascham recommends a bow to be frequently rubbed with a waxed woollen cloth (a care never to be omitted after shooting) till it shines and glitters; which, in time, forms such a hard slippery polish, that the weather will not injure, nor any fret or pinch be able to affect it." Sir John Smith's receipt for the same purpose — viz., a mixture of tallow, wax, and rosin — is a very excellent one. But that solution of gums in spirits of wine, generally known by the name of French Polish, proves, I think, far superior, being thoroughly water-proof, and, as the mode of applying it is somewhat peculiar, a word or two of instruction may not be superfluous. If the bow has been previously rubbed with a wax cloth, cleanse the surface by washing it with spirits of turpentine; this done, wipe with a morsel of sponge, or flannel dipped in oil; enclose a small quantity of cotton wool in a bit of flannel, and dip its surface, first in oil, and then in the polish, previously poured out in some small shallow vessel; rub it upon the wood, until nearly dry, and continually renew the oil and polish, until a fine clear lustre appears on the surface of your bow. This operation may be continued as often as you think proper; three or four times, however, are generally found sufficient. Remember that the *wood* need not be oiled more than once.

Every archer keeps his bows in bags of green baize, sometimes enclosed in additional tin cases. Many have also a wooden cupboard, called an ASCHAM, in honour of the learned individual whose name it bears. The common height of this contrivance is about eight feet; its breadth and depth two. A board pierced with round holes, sufficient to receive a few dozen arrows, occupies the lower part in front, forming a kind of quiver, which

---

* Archers are not, perhaps, aware that the Welsh word *tackl* literally means "an arrow." By extension, it is properly applied to the whole shooting apparatus.

extends, however, only half the depth of the Ascham, so as to leave sufficient room for the bows, which are placed behind. A drawer, three inches deep, occupies the top, to hold strings, with sewing silk, and wax for whipping their centre; white kid or chamois leather to bind the eyes and nooses; scarlet or green riband for tying the string to the upper bow horn; spare arrow piles*, horns, and all the other little nicknacks of an archer's gear. Suspended around the sides within, on a number of small brass hooks, are the belt, brace, shooting glove, and several pairs of six inch pasteboard butt marks painted and gilt. The whole is, of course, secured by a door, which should always be kept locked. When of a rich green colour, and emblazoned with the owner's armorial bearings, and the pattern of a riband corresponding to his arrow-mark, the Ascham is a rather ornamental piece of furniture in an archer's hall: where numbers appear ranged on either side of the apartment, proudly surmounted by shields, banners, and trophies, all tinged with the glories of a western sun, they are pre-eminently so. Truly, I pity the man who retires from such a spectacle, uninfluenced by the magic of the scene, or unshackled by a vow to invoke Waring's assistance, ere the lapse of another day. Insensible to every romantic impulse, he can be estimated but as a " clod of the valley;" or, like the unmusical savage denounced by Shakspeare, as one whom Nature has expressly destined for deeds of

Treason, stratagem, and spoil.

---

* Steel heads.

SECTION IX.

OF THE POWER OF MODERN BOWS.

> Still then stoode that prowde potter,
>   Thus then sayde he,
> An I had a bowe, then by the wode,
>   One shot should you see.
>
> Thou shalt have a bowe, sayde the sheriffe,
>   The beste that thou wilt choose of three;
> Thou seem'st a stalward and a stronge,
>   Assayed shalt thou be.
>
> The sheriffe commanded a yeoman thereby
>   Straight some bowes to bringe,
> The best bowe that the yeoman brought,
>   Robin set on a stringe.
>
> Now shall I knowe if thou be good,
>   And poul it uppe to the ear.
> So God me help, sayde the prowde potter,
>   This is righte weak gear.
>   *Old Ballad.*

Most of my brethren are aware of the existence of an act of parliament [*], forbidding any man under the age of twenty-four years, "to shoot at standing pricks, except they be rovers [†], whereat he shall change at every shoot his mark, upon pain to forfeit for every shoot doing the contrary, four-pence. And that no person above the said age of twenty-four years, shall shoot at any mark of eleven score yards or under, with *any* prick shaft or flight, under the pain to forfeit for every shoot, six shillings and eight-pence."

[*] 33 Henry VIII. c. 9.
[†] An accidental mark, in contradistinction to butts and targets: trees, bushes, posts, mounds of earth, landmarks, stones, &c., are roving marks.

The object of this enactment is probably not quite apparent to all my readers. The archers of the sixteenth century, degenerating from the vigour of their predecessors, showed an inclination to discontinue the ancient long distances at which the military archers had been accustomed to "bend the yew," adopting weaker bows and a lighter arrow, which was the first symptom of the decline of archery; eleven and twelve score yards being once no uncommon range for the heaviest, and twenty score, or four hundred yards, for the lightest, shaft. Thus the archers were not only interdicted from practising at short lengths, but the six-and-eight-penny fine compelled them to shoot with a bow strong enough to cast either description of arrow at these respective distances.

This law, certainly a good one, remains still unrepealed. Verbum sat sapienti. May some patriotic informer take advantage of the hint. Reader, conceive the panic a paragraph like what follows, running the round of the newspapers, would create among all and every the bow-meetings of Great Britain.

"INFORMATION EXTRAORDINARY—CAUTION TO ARCHERS —MARYLEBONE OFFICE. Yesterday morning a considerable degree of curiosity was excited in this neighbourhood, by the appearance at the office of the whole Company of Royal T——ilites, whose elegant shooting grounds form one of the most distinguished ornaments of the metropolis. The appearance of the archers in our streets reminded us of descriptions we have frequently met with in some of the olden writers, touching the 'splendid shows and shootings,' common to days of chivalry and romance. They were gallantly attired in the full costume of their society; viz., black hat and feather, with doublet of the Lincoln green; and had marched through Portland Place, on their way to this office, with 'drums beating, colours flying, trumpets sounding,' as the old military phraseology has it, though not with 'matches lighted at both ends, and bullets in their mouths*,' for it is sufficiently well known their peculiar weapons require none of these. Each archer, on the contrary, came bow in hand, and wore his bracer, shooting-glove, and belt, within which appeared the gallant grey goose wing. Summonses had been issued against them severally. The charges were founded upon an ancient, but unrepealed, statute, which, as far as we understand it, for we don't pretend to be very deep in the pages of Roger Ascham, prohibits the practising at any marks placed within a certain distance, with what are termed flight, or very light arrows. On referring to the act in question, it appeared the shortest length allowed was two hundred and twenty yards. The informer swore, and his evidence was corroborated by the oaths of two witnesses, that he had repeatedly observed defendants' targets fixed on earthen butts, between which not half that space intervened; and the archers, being unable to refute this part of the charge, were severally mulcted by the worthy magistrate in the sum of 4*d.* each. To prove the infringement of the second clause, the informer produced a very beautiful arrow, which he stated he had picked up. On its being submitted to the examination of a celebrated bowyer, then present, he reluctantly pronounced it to be a mere butt shaft, precisely the sort of arrow prohibited by the act in question. The informer here underwent a very severe examination by the defendants' solicitor, as to how he was enabled to swear the arrow then produced came from the defendants' shooting ground. It appeared that, for a long period, he had despaired of being able to substantiate this part of the accusation, as, during the two hours he was engaged in watching their proceedings, not one shaft in twenty failed of the butt. Towards sunset, however, and after the party returned from the refreshment of a few glasses of champagne, a stout, good-looking, middle-aged gentleman, whose dexterity had been eminently

---

* See Heath's Surrender of Ragland Castle.

conspicuous during the day, prepared to lead the game. Perhaps he mistook the broad disk of a summer's sun for the target's golden centre: perhaps he merely raised his bow-hand a little higher than ordinary; however this be, instead of alighting in its accustomed place, the arrow went "soughing through the sky," until it ploughed up the gravel at witness's feet.

Magistrate. Sou—sou—soughing,—what's that, what's that?

Witness. It means a whistling, or whizzing, your Worship.

Magistrate. What countryman are you?

Witness. Please your Worship, I'm a Scotchman.

The worthy magistrate then declared the charge to be completely established, and adjudged each of the defendants to pay an additional fine of 6s. 8d. intimating at the same time his fixed determination of rigorously enforcing the existing laws relative to archery, in all cases brought under his future cognisance."

But, jocosè hæc; for England still boasts within its merry woodlands more than one corps of archers, whose practice in both respects is in strict accordance with the ordinances of their ancestors.

Every man is not profoundly versed in the theory of projectiles, and I am probably not the only one who, whilst shooting in public, has amused himself by exciting the wonder of the uninitiated after the following most approved fashion. Set up your targets only eighty or one hundred yards apart, and not one of the spectators but fancies every arrow which drives into the turf beneath, or a few yards beyond the mark, has reached its goal, in other words, that your bow will shoot only between mark and mark. As they thus stand watching the sport, exert yourself to place a single arrow in the centre of the target, just to inspire them with a becoming respect for the archer's skill. Pass a second exactly over its upper edge, so that it may lodge in the ground about half a dozen yards beyond. Then, drawing the third from your belt, fix your eyes steadfastly upon the first vagrant rook which

> Wings his way unto the rocky wood,

across the bottom of the target ground, and in my country, half a score might be espied in about as many seconds; — elevate your bow hand to an angle of 45°, and launch the arrow at the bird, already distant thrice the space betwixt target and target. Reader, if blest with a taste for falconry, an ancient and a kindred sport, thou art not oblivious of that mad and desperate lurch, by which a heron seeks to evade the fell and simultaneous swoop of a cast of falcons' peregrine wheeling within three paces of her neck, with eyes of fire, and talons distended, in the hope of blood. Even so the rook. Among the astutest of the feathered tribes, he likes not the aspect of the grey winged messenger which flies to meet him, and dashes off at a tangent also. And though nought, except, indeed, one of the demon shafts, for which those who tampered with the art " men may not name*" are said to have sometimes bartered their immortal part, could reach a flying mark full three hundred paces off, yet in the eyes of the spectators it appears so to do. As regards them, therefore, the triumph of archery will be complete. The noble attitude necessarily assumed by the shooter; an attitude

> * His father was a clerk of fame,
> Of Bethune's line in Picardie:
> He learned the art men may not name,
> In Padua, far beyond the sea.
> *Lay of the Last Minstrel.*

At Malling, in Kent, one of Queen Marie's Justices, upon the complaint of many *wise men* and a few foolish boys, laid a poor, but very skilful, archer by the heels, because he shot so near the white at butts; for he was informed and persuaded, that the poor man played with a fly, otherwise called a devil or familiar; and because he was certified that the archer aforesaid shot better than the common shooting which he before had heard of or seen, he conceived it could not be in God's name, but by enchantment; whereby this archer, as he supposed, abusing the Queen's liege people, won, one day with another, two or three shillings, to the detriment of the commonwealth and to his own enriching. And therefore the archer was severely punished, to the great *encouragement* of archers, and to the *wise example* of justices; but specially to the overthrow of witchcraft !— *Reg. Scot's Discovery*, p. 35. edit. 1665.

which even the most awkward can but little degrade; the extraordinary flight of the arrow; the all but apparent death stroke to the bird; these will excite the spectators' mind to admiration for a weapon, of whose powers they had previously formed a very inadequate idea.

Shooting in public, at distances of sixty yards and under, is certainly injudicious, since it tends to disparage the noble exercise of archery in vulgar eyes; indeed, all bow meetings should be held in the most sequestered situations, until the majority have attained a certain degree of proficiency. On witnessing the abortive efforts of some weak-armed, inexpert, slovenly bowman, to lay his arrow in a mark within range of dust shot from a paltry fowling-piece, our sensations are nearly allied to contempt for the shooter and his amusement. Bow, arrows, belt, bracer, and shooting glove, originally the best of their kind, in his hands, too, have become wretchedly dilapidated; for a certain *gaucherie* and bad taste appears to be the birth-right of some persons. Mark now, on the other hand, how the loiterer's admiring eye is rivetted upon him who next steps in front of the target. His air and demeanour are alone sufficient to proclaim him a master of the game. A plume snatched from the eagle's wing, decorates his dark velvet bonnet, and the rest of his neat and appropriate costume is green as the grass he treads on. His stout and polished yew bow, glistening like a mirror, o'ertops its master's height full half a cubit. The well waxed string, unfrayed even in a single fibre, is carefully whipped at the centre, with silk of black and crimson; at its eye and noose, with the finest chamois leather. Buckled beneath a richly worked belt of russet-coloured buffalo's hide are his burnished shafts. The painted pattern of some elegant riband serves to distinguish them from those of his associates; and their snowy feathers, still pure and unruffled as in the hour they fell from the wild bird's wing, reveal to the archer's eye, that their place is oftener in the target than beneath it. Confident of skill, the reward of unremitted practice, he stands prepared to challenge even the distant rifle to a trial of superiority. His arrow is already in the string; the mark reclines its broad circlets of crimson and gold, nothing short of two hundred paces off, on yonder green hill-side. Firmly setting his feet upon the turf, he grasps his trusty bow with the strength and steadiness of a vice. His eyes, lost to every thing besides, are immoveably fixed on the object of his distant aim, whilst he draws manfully, until the thumb of his shaft hand grazing his right ear, warns him of the precise moment when to loose.

<blockquote>
The string let fly,
Sounds shrill and sharp, like the swift swallow's cry.
</blockquote>

As the glancing meteor or falcon's flight, the arrow whistles through the sky, for no human ken can mark its trackless course. Thus, like the statue of Apollo Belvedere, our gallant archer remains rivetted to the spot, with look of pride, and arm still extended. But the pause is momentary; the music of that short sharp sound,

<blockquote>So familiar to his ear,</blockquote>

announces the arrow's entrance into the target, and justifies the expectations to which his gallant bearing had given rise.

In thus advocating strong bows and distant shooting, let it not be understood that the archer is to injure himself by overstraining his muscles, or mar his success at the target by using bows beyond his management. The degree of power proper for ladies' and youths' bows I have already explained; but no man, having reached his full strength, and not an invalid, can run the slightest risk from beginning with one of fifty pounds. At the same time let me observe, that every archer risks an imputation on his manhood, who finally settles down to any thing short of a seventy-five, which commands all lengths within four hundred yards. The strength of the drawing arm rapidly accommodates itself to the increased power of the bow, for nothing tends more to fortify and invigorate the muscles of that, and indeed every other portion of the human frame, than archery. We have all seen a bow somewhat above the shooter's strength during his first season, entirely under command by the ensuing summer, if in constant use. Ten pounds additional weight should be added to every new bow. Let the archer, however, " wrestle with his gear," as Ascham terms it, and achieve these conquests in private; for no bow should be taken to a shooting match, which the owner cannot use with perfect facility, since the struggle consequent on an attempt to draw up the arrow, when a man is *over-bowed*, will so disorder his aim, that by chance only can he hope, under such disadvantages, to meet with the target. " It makes some men," writes the author just quoted, " to overshoot the mark, some to shoot far wide, and perchance to hurt a by-stander." " I had my bows," says Bishop Latimer in one of his sermons, " bought for me according to my age and strength, and as I increased in them, so my bows were made heavier and stronger." Τοξαρια δε έκαστον κατα τ' ιδιαν ισχυν και ουχ υπερ αυτην, μαλλον δε και απαλωτερα. Let the bow of every archer be proportioned to his strength, that is, not above, but rather beneath the power of the shooter, says Leo in his tactics; and the observation proves him to have been well acquainted with the subject on which he wrote.

SECTION X.

OF THE SHAFT,

ANCIENT AND MODERN.

> The Winchester and Taylor's goose * I see
> Are all too heavy and too hot for me.
> I will retain the honor, to emblaze
> Of the grey goose, that on the green doth graze.
> Throughout the world the trumph of fame loud rings,
> To spread the glory of the goose's wings.
> The Huns, the Goths, the Vandals, and the Gauls,
> With arrows made great Rome their several thralls;
> Yea all the nations the whole world around,
> The grey goose wing hath honored and renown'd.
> *Prayer of the Grey Goose Wing*, 1627.

A shaft hath three principal parts, the stele, the feather, and the head; each of which *must* be severally spoken of.
TOXOPHILUS.

TRES-BIEN, fair sir! your high behest shall be obeyed: it would ill become me to gainsay the commands of so venerable a Toxophilite. Yet, before I enter upon my description of these component parts of the arrow, permit us, friend Roger, to have a word respecting its ancient dimensions, on which you are most unaccountably silent. That so erudite a classic as yourself,

---

* The late meeting of the Kendal archers was well attended, and afforded much sport. The populace, however, crowded so near the targets, that a tanner and two tailors received shots not intended for them. The tanner's hide was proof against the keenest shafts: one of the tailors was happily preserved from danger, by the glancing of the arrow against his goose, and he received merely a flesh wound. The other is thought to be in some danger principally arising from fright. *World*, Oct. 7. 1791. *Bankes's MSS.*

fortified by the wisdom of past ages, should not have foreseen the dire consequences of thus casting the apple of discord among your descendants*, is wholly incomprehensible. How much reason have we to regret you were not born with the gossiping propensities of amiable old Isaac Walton; with more *bonhommie* and less learning. A treatise on archery, written in the style and with the minuteness of detail which characterises the " Contemplative Angler," would at this day be purchased, as was a certain black letter tome now in safe keeping of the Roxburgh Club, with guineas in one scale, and your book in the other. We should then have been informed of a thousand facts and incidents, whose interest, not at all limited to the votaries of archery, would throw important light on the domestic habits of your contemporaries. We should have ascertained who was London's WARING in the merry days of Queen Bess; whether the Kelsals of Lancashire had then the reputation of making the best bows in England, as they are said to have done a century later. You would have given us the dimensions of every shaft in your own quiver; nay, you would have done still better; privileged by your right of access to your royal mistress's residence, you would have been a frequent visiter at the court of guard at Greenwich palace, and told us of the arrows borne by the tallest archer who lounged within its precincts.

At the cost of a morning's visit to the Tower, you might have inspected many thousand noble bows and goodly shafts, lying rotting† there; most of them, be it remembered, as old as the

* The real length of the ancient war arrow has been much contested.

† Extract from an original MS. in the possession of Dr. Leith, entitled " A Complete List of the Royal Navy of England, in the year 1599.
At the Tower of London.
Bowes with ccciiijvi decaied, 8185. Wreckes of Bowstaves, 983.
Arrowes, viz.
Livery arrowes, 14,125 shafts, whereof 731 shafts to be repayred, and 30 shafts decaied. Crosbowe arrowes, decaied, 500. Muskett arrowes, with 56 To be new feathered, 892. Longbowe arrowes with firewoorkes, 98 shefe decaied, &c. &c.

period, when, it is reported, the archers of our fifth Harry drew every man a yard.

And then, what delightful anecdotes of individual skill, recorded from your own personal experience; yet of these, the Toxophilus is barren as a Caermarthenshire heath. Not one allusion to the various drillings you necessarily witnessed among the Queen's yeomen; or the marvellous flight shots made by individuals in Finsbury and Tutthill fields; and lastly, not a single name recorded of all the London 'prentices " proper and tall," whose reputation for archery stood high among the graver citizens. By the rood! friend Roger, the truth seems to be, that with abundant materials you know not the art of making a pleasant book.

Mark now, how cheerfully old Walton enters into all the minutiæ of his art. After his own delightful gossiping fashion, we learn that the best tackle of all kinds came in his day from Yorkshire. The length and strength of his favourite rod; the wood of which it was fashioned; how it was spliced and bound together with silk; its singular lightness and elasticity; are made as familiar to me as the merits and material of my own specimen of Kelly's* unrivalled handicraft. The tyers of the most killing flies, and the names of many an old friend, once skilful in the use of them, but, "now with God," are likewise chronicled with equal minuteness, by this simple-hearted piscatory enthusiast of nearly two centuries ago. Nor are we even left to guess the number and weight of trouts killed by a fisherman of that age, on what might be called an angler's red letter day: all is set forth to us with the most amusing, amiable garrulity. Details such as these would have been invaluable to the archer; yet we have them not; and excepting one story of an old bow, spoiled by being left strung all night, I do not recollect an anecdote in the whole work.

An amusing instance of the zeal with which the old English arrow's length is debated by men of the bow and quiver, once

---

* A famous Dublin fishing-tackle maker.

occurred to me, during an excursion in the western counties. As I stood at an inn-door, to await the arrival of the stage-coach, a gentleman, observing some bows among my luggage, fell into conversation upon the topics they naturally suggested, but more particularly on the subject of the present chapter. I quickly perceived he was no tyro, and although our arrangements did not allow of any discussion whilst the carriage was in motion, at every occasional stoppage, the subject was commenced *de novo* in the posthouses.

"And so, Sir," observed my interlocutor, "you do not conceive I am exactly correct in believing that our English yeomen, those, for instance, who fought with the gallant Harry of Monmouth at Agincourt, drew every man his cloth yard shaft."

"There is no question, but that such arrows were in use among the archers of Agincourt and other ancient military expeditions: it is their universal adoption by the whole army, which I dispute."

"Let us hear your reasons: but first allow me to remind you of a passage in Paulus Jovius, a traveller who visited this country about the middle of the sixteenth century, and whose opinion as a foreigner and eye-witness is certainly deserving attention. 'Eas minimo digito crassiores*,' he repeated in a triumphant tone, chastened, however, by innate good breeding; at the same time grasping the little finger of his left hand, with the thumb and fore finger of the right, in illustration of his author. Then again suiting the action to the word, he touched his elbow and middle finger alternately, as he went on; '*Bicubitales que*†, et hamato præfixas ferro, ingentibus ligneis arcubus intorquent.'"

---

* I interpret my friend's Latin for the ladies' sake: Eas minimo digito, crassiores; bicubitales que et hamato præfixas ferro, ingentibus ligneis intorquent: they (the English) shoot arrows, somewhat thicker than a man's little finger, *two cubits* (36 inches) long, and headed with barbed steel points. from wooden bows of extraordinary size and strength.

† Bicubitales que— two cubits long.

" True, Sir : I well remember the spirited picture which the historian has sketched of the arms and discipline of our tall English bowmen. That there were tens of thousands of arrows in the gallant band to which you have just alluded, I readily allow. But there were a still larger proportion, the dimensions of which no ways exceeded those sold by our modern fletchers. My enthusiasm for all that relates to a favourite hobby, led me at an early age, to the scene of that extraordinary victory. Whilst traversing the field of Agincourt, a peasant brought me the head of an arrow, unquestionably English, and specially adapted for piercing armour; indeed, there can be no doubt it belonged to that 'iron sleet of arrowy shower,' which rained destruction upon the steel clad chivalry of France. The ferule by which the head was originally attached to the wood, is still very perfect; but its diameter proves the shaft could not have measured more than eight and twenty, or at the furthest, thirty inches. I have repeatedly compared it with ———."

" Shorten that 'ere off leader's bearing rein a hole or two ; " with " Now if you please, gennelmen ; " here broke from the hoarse voice of our red-faced, bottle-nosed Jehu, as he received his whip from the horsekeeper, and gathered up the *ribands* in his left hand. A naval captain on the quarter deck of his frigate, and a stage coachman on his box, are held to be equally omnipotent. Silently, therefore, we resumed our respective places ; and our disputation,

> Like the story of the bear and fiddle,
> Begun, but broke off in the middle,

immortalised by Hudibras, was doomed to the procrastination of another stage. I could not but be gratified with the pertinacity of argument displayed by my opponent. His wish was evidently father to the thought ; and *that* originated in anxiety to uphold the honour of the English long bow. At length we arrived where our further progress in the same vehicle was to cease; when advancing towards me in the coach-office, he resumed the conversation; but like many similar conversations, it only tended to illustrate a venerable adage —

> He that's convinced against his will,
> Is of the same opinion still.

Thus we parted; my short-lived acquaintance laughingly observing as he bade me good bye, that, in the words of the Spectator, " a good deal might be yet said on both sides."

Of the nature of our concluding desultory arguments, and whether they were couched in poetry or prose, the reader will be informed, since their substance is detailed in the remaining pages of the present chapter.

That the arrow was of remarkable length, even so late as the age of Queen Elizabeth, may be inferred from a passage in the Discourse on Weapons. " Our English bows, arrows, and archers do exceed and excel all other bows used by foreign nations, not only in thickness and strength, but also in the length and size of the arrows."

It is sufficient for my purpose that their dimensions generally were thought worthy of notice by Sir J. Smith, although he errs in the latter part of his assertion. I have here by me an iron wood Guiana bow, nearly eight feet high, though disproportionately slender, and the arrows imported with it, which are about five feet long.

In the reign of Edward the Third, the woollen manufacture, from the exquisite fineness of our native fleeces*, had already become an important branch of the national industry. To foster, encourage, and regulate this, in common with other branches of commerce, an act was passed called the Statute of the Staple,

* It is known, but not very generally, that the celebrated Merino, and other breeds of Spanish sheep, repurchased by our graziers at enormous prices, were originally derived from English stock. A small parcel of choice rams and ewes, reared on the Gloucestershire Cotswold hills, was sent as a present to the Spanish monarch, whose battles Edward's heroic son had so successfully fought.

declaratory that there shall be but one weight, measure, and yard throughout the realm.

Among the Cotton collection of MSS.* is a very ancient act of parliament, in which the following sentence occurs : — " Tres pedes faciunt ulnam." Three feet make an ell. Though this is neither the Flemish nor the English measure laid down by Cocker, it establishes its identity with the clothiers' yard at one most glorious period in the history of ancient archery, and on no other supposition can we reconcile the indiscriminate use of " yard and ell " by historians and poets when speaking of the arrow. The Flemish measure of twenty-seven inches was too inconsiderable to have elicited any extravagant praise. The modern English ell of forty-five inches no one could manage with effect, except such men as Earl Strongbow, whose arms, as tradition reports, reached to his knee-joints.

Thus have we arrived at something like a satisfactory conclusion respecting what constituted the integral parts of these two ancient English measures. I will next endeavour to show in what respect my fellow-traveller and his ancient friend Paulus Jovius, had rightly considered the question at issue.

> Draw me a clothier's yard,

exclaims poor old crazed Lear, when raving on the attitude and equipments of his bowmen. Another authority, still more ancient than Shakspeare or the Latin historian, gives similar dimensions to the English shaft, when describing, in a highly popular and pathetic ballad, how the gallant Percy was avenged.

> An English archer then perceived
> The noble earl was slain.
> He had a bow bent in his hand,
> Made of a trusty tree;
> An arrow of a cloth yard long,
> Unto the head drew he.

---

* Claudius, D. 2.

> Against Sir Hugh Montgomery,
>   Aright the shaft was set:
> The grey goose wing that was thereon,
>   In his heart's blood was wet.

In Drayton's picturesque sketches of the Sherwood Rovers it is said,

> All made of Spanish yew, their bows were wondrous strong,
> They not an arrow drew, but 'twas a cloth yard long;

and "The Lyttel Geste" of Robin Hode also describes the equipments of a hundred tall yeomen, attendants on Sir Richard of the Lea, when journeying to redeem his patrimony from St. Mary's Abbot, to the same effect.

> He purveyed him a hundred bowes,
>   The stringes were well y dighte;
> An hundred sheafe of arrowes goode,
>   The heads burnyshed full bryghte.
>
> And every arrowe an elle longe,
>   With peacock well y dighte;
> Innocked all with white silver,
>   It was a seemly syghte.

So far we are indebted to "the irritabile genus vatum," for unravelling this Gordian knot; let us next apply ourselves to the ancient chroniclers in prose. It is remarked by Clement Edmonds, "that in the reign of Henry the Fifth, the English bowmen did shoot an arrow of a yard long besides the head." "To give you some taste of the skill of the Cornish archers' sufficiency," says Carew, "for long shooting, their shaft was a cloth yard; their pricks twenty-four score: for strength, they would pierce any ordinary armour." Mr. Kempe, a frequent correspondent of the Gentleman's Magazine on various interesting subjects, thus speaks of the arrow's length, in a letter addressed to that periodical. Quoting Hall, he observes that "at the battle of Blackheath, fought in the year 1496, the Cornish archers of the rebel party, who defended the high road at Deptford Bridge, by which the main body of the King's army was to pass to the assault, shot arrows in length a full yard. I have a memorandum by me," he continues, " that I saw, in 1825, at the ancient mansion of Cothele, upon the Cornish side of the Tamar, some arrows which I conceived to be old English, three feet two inches in length ; and it is a rather remarkable coincidence with the chronicler above mentioned, that these long arrows should be extant in Cornwall. The heads were not barbed, they were solid pyramidal pieces of steel.* The shafts, made of beech or some light wood, had no feathers, and the nocks were not guarded with horn." There is no doubt but Mr. Kempe is perfectly correct. Only one kind of foreign arrows will at all answer this description, — I mean those brought from Chinese Tartary, which so closely resemble the old English arrow in their general appearance that I was once deceived in them myself. But that any such should be found in an ancient mansion on the banks of the Tamar, seems so improbable that I unhesitatingly subscribe to this writer's opinion.

We now come to the most conclusive testimony of all, in favour of the ell and cloth yard shaft. It is an extract from a MS. in the Cotton collection; headed, " Affairs from the Public Records, — ninth year of the reign of Edward the Third."

" The king commanded the mayor and sheriffs of the county to purvey three hundred good and sufficient bows, with strings proportionable to them; and also four chests† of arrows of the length of one ell, made of good well seasoned wood; the heads of the said arrows to be duly sharpened, and the flukes or barbs of a large size, &c. &c.

* The Agincourt arrow in my possession agrees exactly with this description. In the list of curiosities preserved at Don Saltero's coffee house, Chelsea, are mentioned, two ancient broad-headed arrows, once belonging to Robin Hood.

† " I and another boy went from York towards Scotland, with a horse whereupon we carried a chest of arrows, for the use of the king's army, which afterwards won the fight of Flodden."—*Life of old Parr.*

It is unnecessary to adduce any further evidence to support the "bicubitalesque," of Paulus Jovius. The truth of his assertion has, no doubt, long ere this, been apparent to the reader's mind. Those, however, who do battle for the inviolability — if I may so express myself — of the cloth yard arrow, and assert that our present measure of twenty-seven inches is a modern innovation, the result of modern degeneracy, err in the other extreme. Like the prejudiced travellers, described in the fable,

They all are right and all are wrong;

It requires but a very brief argument to prove them so; a crowd of witnesses being at hand, to show that the arrow's length varied continually, and was confined to no arbitrary standard.

The reader who feels his curiosity at all interested in the question is referred to 5th of Edward IV., chapter 4. He will there find " every Englishman, and Irishman dwelling with Englishmen, and speaking English, being between sixteen and sixty years of age, is commanded to provide himself with an English bow of his own length, and one fistmele at least, between the nocks, with twelve shafts of the length of three quarters of the standard. Old fashioned phrases like fistmele, are better understood in the country than elsewhere. It is a pure Saxon word, meaning the measure of the clenched hand with the thumb extended. You would smile to witness how accurately the old woodmen, " in leathern guise," ascertain the dimensions of a fallen tree, unassisted by the carpenter's, or any other rule except this fistmele of his forefathers. He cuts a hazel rod from the copse, and commencing at one end, grasps it six times with his alternate hands, cuts off the remainder, and lo! a very accurate three foot measure.

The arrow then, nearly four centuries ago, during the contests of the Roses, one of the most warlike periods of English history, was exactly the length adhered to by Waring for those of modern archers. Yet all this involves no contradiction. We can readily understand that in remote districts of the kingdom, like North Wales, Gwentland, Yorkshire, and Cornwall, a large proportion of archers made their own bows, just as anglers there at the present day, manufacture fishing rods. Poverty and necessity are the parents of invention. Some of my readers may possibly have encountered one of those grey coated, blue stockinged, weather beaten old fishermen, who haunt the silver ripples of Uske or Tave; Teivi or Maes y pandy, with the constancy of a river god. In that section of a walnut shell, which he calls a coracle*, see him glide down the foaming torrent as if on a voyage to the ocean of eternity. Innumerable flies coiled round the crown of his ragged, battered, shapeless hat, dance in the evening breeze; in his hand he brandishes a rod formed of a couple of hazel sticks rudely bound together; and his line is nothing more than the tribute of half a dozen cows' tails. A cockney would doubtless laugh at such primitive looking equipments, until his visage resembled Falstaff's " wet cloak, ill laid up." No matter. The spring and play of that ill-shapen wand; and the colour of those coarse looking flies, are worth the whole contents of Chevalier's shop.

Of equally unprepossessing exterior, but similar intrinsic excellence, was the bow of our English rustic; for like this mountain patriarch of the rod, he was frequently too poor or too distant from any market to purchase of the regular bowyers.

* A singular kind of boat formed of basket work, at the present day covered with painted sailcloth, but anciently with skins. They are so light that the fisherman when he wishes to cross to another stream, or avoid the trouble of threading the serpentine mazes so characteristic of Welsh rivers, takes his coracle upon his head bottom upwards, and thus, like a snail in his shell, journeys along. These boats are as old, and older than Cæsar's invasion of Britain, and it is stated that when the Romans withdrew from the island, the Picts and Scots began to infest its inhabitants, by crossing over the friths and forths, " in little wicker boats covered with leather."

To the wooded glens and rocks surrounding his native village, he resorted for the proper material, and always kept a number of yew plants seasoning upon the beams and rafters of his cottage. Master Nicholas Frost, Harry V.'s bowyer, might have laughed also: though I fancy his master owed somewhat, to no inconsiderable number of these home-made bows, on St. Crispin's day, A. D. 1415.*

According to his strength and height, the archer equipped himself. The tall and muscular rustic of six feet and upwards, found a powerful bow of seven feet best suited to his purposes; and his arrows were a cloth yard besides the head. His neighbour, to whom nature had been less bountiful, would be satisfied when the former was less than six feet, and the latter only "three quarters," to which he reduced them if originally of the full standard. It appears, indeed, that it was quite usual for the ancient archer to obtain loose arrow heads, and fix them on the shaft himself. I find many statements of persons possessing a number of the former, without any of the latter to correspond; one being a perishable, the other an imperishable material; thus, in an Herefordshire Muster Roll of the reign of Queen Elizabeth, is an entry as follows: —

"John Hughes. An arrow case and heads for a sheaf thereof, but no bow or arrows." †

At the battle of Agincourt, says Ascham, the army of Henry V. consisted of such archers that most of them drew a yard. "In my time," observes the author of the "Discourse on Weapons," "it was the usual practice for soldiers to choose their first sheaf of arrows, and cut those shorter which they found too long for their use." Among that splendid collection of ancient arms and armour, preserved at Goodrich Court, there is a unique specimen of the ancient English arrow. Some of its wooden stele or shaft, yet remains, particularly the

* The date of the Battle of Agincourt.
† Grimaldi's Origines Genealogicæ.

lower part, and from its substance, I judge the shaft to have been no more than twenty-seven inches, and only a few years back, I recollect meeting with an iron arrow, probably five centuries old, of exactly the same length. The *jet* of the argument, may therefore be enclosed in a nutshell. All our ancient armies had numerous bodies of tall picked men, answering to the grenadier companies of modern regiments, whose strength and length of arm enabled them to draw the cloth yard shaft. Of this class were the archers described by Paulus Jovius. The other soldiers accommodated the size of theirs to convenience, or inferior stature. I trust the reader is satisfied: if not, let him hear one, who to a knowledge of ancient weapons offensive and defensive, beyond that of any other man in Europe, adds considerable experience in practical archery; I allude to Sir Samuel Rush Meyrick, author of the valuable history of ancient arms and armour. " With respect to the size of the bow," he observes; " the string ought to be the height of the man, and the arrow half the length of the string. Now, as from *that*, to the top of the middle finger, is equal to half his whole height, it must be equal also to the length of his arrow; and the left hand, therefore, being clenched round the bow, will leave just room for the arrow head beyond it; from this it will appear, that a man six feet high, must shoot with a cloth yard arrow, and vice versâ."

The following is a list of the several kinds of wood made use of by ancient fletchers.

Alder.	Black Thorn.	Sugar Chest.
Asp.	Elder.	Service Tree.
Ash.	Fustic.	Sallow.
Brazil.*	Horn Beam.	Turkey Wood.
Birch.	Oak.	

* There is no necessity for supposing this word a misprint for *hazel*, as Roberts thinks. Ascham mentions it again in connection with Fustic, Turkey, and Sugar Chest, all foreign woods, from warm climates.

To these should be added, deal, or the wood of our British fir-tree, though unnoticed by Roger Ascham. An old English traveller in the Levant, describing the amusements of the Turks, observes, "they were admirable archers; and that he saw, among other trophies, at the gate of Belgrade, a head piece, which they held to be petronel* proof. It was nevertheless shot clean through on both sides, and, as they asserted, head and all, with one of their bows. The arrow, he tells us, was still sticking in this helmet, and resembled, "as all theirs do, one of those little red ones, which our children use."† I have seen many Turkish arrows; they were all of red deal. In an apartment of the Castle of Cauca, in Crete, still or very recently a portion of the Turkish empire, arrows lie strewed in scores upon the floor. The good natured Turkish centinel will allow you to carry off any number for the consideration of a handful of paras, perhaps about one shilling sterling.

Brazil, sugar-chest, and fustic, are West India woods not now used. The black-thorn and elder grow in every hedge; and I think the former would make nice arrows, if procured of a proper thickness to be sawn into lengths. Respecting the latter, Ascham does not mean the hollow shoots filled with pith, of which school-boys make their pop-guns, but those immense butts, of half a century's growth, which are entirely solid. Elder possesses the qualities of lightness, toughness, and elasticity in a very remarkable degree. I make exquisite fly rods from it; and, generally speaking, all wood suitable for that purpose is equally well adapted for arrows, nearly the same requisites being indispensable in both. Hornbeam grows plentifully in our copses. The service tree bears a species of fruit much eaten in the country; but though all these woods are now likewise obsolete, let the archier campagnard amuse himself by making occasional experiments with them. A piece of well

---

* A kind of large pistol.
† Voyage into the Levant, by H. B. 1637.

seasoned, unbarked hazel, easily procured perfectly straight, makes an exceedingly good and strong arrow for rough usage. In shooting rovers, over a country much covered with thickets and brambles, arrows are frequently lost. Those of home manufacture will not be so much regretted, and can easily be replaced. Remove the bark with a file, just where the feathers are to be glued, and head them with small iron ferules.

The woods used for modern arrows are lance-wood, lime, asp, deal, and poplar. Of the last the French and Flemings make theirs, and call it arbêle. Lance and lime are confined to roving shafts. Of deal, the fletcher chooses the lintels, doors, and wainscotting of old houses, in preference to new timber. I once saw some very beautiful arrows, which Waring sent into the country, with a note, stating they were made from deal upwards of a century old; yet the white wood he commonly manufactures is so truly excellent, that it leaves nothing for the archer to desire.

In early ages they seem to have preferred asp for making war arrows. The poet Spencer, when enumerating the different kinds of trees indigenous to the British Isles, and the uses to which their timber was applied in his time, speaks of

> The sailing fir, the cypress death to plaine,
> The shooter eugh, the aspe for shaftes so faine.

The vast consumption, indeed monopoly, which the public service thus created, was productive of a very droll contest between the fletchers[*] and another class of men, of a somewhat less romantic calling, viz., the "poure patyn makers of London." In the early part of Henry V's reign, the former presented a memorial, praying that these patten makers might be altogether prevented from using asp, which it appears, they had gradually been substituting for willow, alder, &c.; and, in consequence, aspwood was become so scarce that sufficient could

---
[*] Arrow makers.

not be procured for arrows, which had been greatly increasing in price.* Independently of its fairness, a request of this nature might be expected to awaken the fullest sympathy in the breast of the warlike Henry. Little more than a twelvemonth had elapsed, since, at the head of his yeomen archers, he

Cropped the fleurs-de-lis of France,

and made its monarch a tributary of the British crown. The fletchers were, therefore, protected, by a penalty of 100s. on every pair of clogs thenceforward manufactured of asp-wood; but as this regulation was very severely felt by the traders in these articles, which, it would appear, the miry condition of London streets in the fifteenth century rendered indispensable to both sexes, the " poure patyn makers" got up a counter petition, in which their grievances are thus pathetically enlarged upon: —

" Mekely beseechen unto your noble wisdomes, the pouere felship of the crafte of patymakers, piteously complayninge of the grevous hurtes and losses that other persons, sometyme of this oure crafte, now dede, and alsoe your beseechers have of long tyme borne and sustained. It is soe, righte worshippfull sirs, that the sayde tymbre of aspe is the best and lightest tymbre to make patyns and clogges, and most easiest for the wear of all estate gentils, and all other, the king's people, of any tymbre that groweth. And there is much tymbre of aspe that will in no wise serve the fletchers to make arrowes of, which is as sufficient, able, and accordinge to make into patyns and cloggs, as is the remnant of the said tymbre to make arrowes."

The privy council contrived to keep the peace between

* " Item supplient les communes, pour profit du roy et du roiaume, que comme les flèchiers of the city of London and elsewhere, within the said kingdom, have in all time heretofore used and do use to make all manner of arrowes and 'autre archerie' of the material called aspe, and of no other material,—les ditz patyn-makers," &c. &c.—*Rolls of Parliament, temp. Henry V.*

both litigants. They issued an order, allowing their petitioners the use of all such asp-wood as, from its length, knottiness, or cross grain, was rejected by the rival craftsmen.

Though piecing the stele seems to have originated in the wish to preserve a favourite arrow, which had been broken, in Ascham's time it was done for the sake of ornament also. Modern fletchers frequently foot arrows with dark, heavy wood; but they are not so durable as those made from one piece; for the earth's moisture, dew, &c., will inevitably destroy the glue. I never could discover the qualities of an arrow to be at all improved by this process, though our ancient archers were much in favour of it.

> Their arrows finely paired, for timber and for feather,
> With birch and brazil *pieced*, to fly in any weather.*

Roberts misunderstood the following directions of Ascham on this subject. "In piecing," says he, "two points are sufficient to prevent the moistness of the earth from penetrating into the piecing, and so loosening the glue." "Two points," observes his commentator, "must be taken to signify the length of two piles or arrow-heads." Not so: he is alluding to the shape of the joints only; and many modern fletchers cut them into four points, as Ascham describes, "for gainess;" so that the union of the dark and light woods, may form a regular indentation all round the arrow. Ascham recommends a joint of one single deep notch, like the insertion of the fore-finger of one hand between the two first fingers of the other.

The bard Gwilym, who has, I trust, already found favour with my readers, alludes in one of his poems to

> An arrow of quarter'd birch,

using the remarkable Welsh phrase, pedr-yollt, "four split," which has, I think, clearly a reference to the fashion above described. I may add, that his countrymen seem to have been

* Drayton's Polyolbion, song 26.

fond of shafts made wholly of this sort of timber. David Ranmor, in his ode to Rydderch ab Jevan Llwyd of Gogerddan, speaks of a sheaf of birchen arrows, observing that "out of his handful, not one broke into fragments."

I shall here close my remarks on the stele, by observing, that for very long flight shafts, those curious unjointed canes, of which Guiana Indian arrows are made, answer beautifully. The original nock, which is of hard wood, very neatly inserted, will serve when a little deepened; but their extreme lightness requires a proper counterpoise at the head. I may add, that our adventurous countrymen became acquainted with these weapons at an early period. An emigrant to the New World, upwards of two centuries ago, in describing an attack upon his little party by a band of Indian archers, says, "We picked up eighteen of their arrows, which we have sent to England by Master Jones, some whereof are headed with brass, others with hartshorn, and others with eagle's claws. Many more, no doubt, were shot, for these we found almost covered with leaves; yet, by the especial providence of God, none of them either hit or hurt us, though many came close by, and on one side; and some coats which hung up in our barricade were shot through and through.*

The nock† of English arrows, for a century past, has been a piece of taper horn glued into the wood. When Ascham wrote, it was merely a notch in the stele, left rather large and round there, as we see in Persian and Chinese arrows. That curious relic preserved at Goodrich Court, furnishes an interesting specimen of the old English nock. The difference of size between European and Turkish arrow nocks did not escape the attention of a shrewd old soldier named De Broquière, who wrote an account of his adventures, "to animate all noble gen-

* Journal of Plantation, &c. 1620.
† Synonymous with *notch*; but always spelt and pronounced as above.

tlemen to see the world."* He evidently traversed the Turkish empire with no other motive than that of "spying into the nakedness of the land;" for on his return, he very gravely set about calculating the number of troops and peculiar weapons necessary for reducing it under the dominion of his master. "I would have," says he, "first, from France, gens d'armes, archers and cross-bowmen, in as great a number as possible; second, from England, 1000 men-at-arms, and 10,000 archers; and from Germany, as many as possible of gentlemen and their mounted bowmen (crennequériers). Assemble together from these three nations, about 25,000 or 30,000 men, and having first invoked the blessing of God, I'll answer for leading them from Belgrade to Constantinople. I shall add, that, in case of need, our archers could make use of the Turkish arrows; but they *cannot use ours*, because the nock is not sufficiently large, and the cords of their bows are a great deal shorter than ours, being made of sinews."

The feather, a very important part of the arrow, next presents itself to our attention. "Unfledged arrows," says Roberts, "cannot fly far, and are greatly affected by the wind." The latter part of this assertion is correct; the former, experience disproves; but although I can shoot an unfeathered shaft eight-score paces, beyond ten or twelve, it flies off at a tangent. But among various savage tribes, whom necessity instructs in every practicable degree of skill, this distance has been greatly surpassed, as the following anecdote will show. Mr. Gore, who accompanied Captain Cook in his voyage round the world, was

* " To animate and influence the hearts of all noble gentlemen who desire to see the world, and by order and command of the most high, most puissant, and most redoubtable Lord Philip, by the grace of God, Duke of Burgundy, Lorraine, Brabant, and Limburg, Count of Flanders, &c., I, Bertrand de la Broquière, native of the duchy of Guienne, Lord of Vieux Château, Councillor, and first Squire tranchant of the said most redoubtable Lord, Seigneur, have been induced to write the little journey that I made."—*De Broquière's Travels, A.D.* 1432. *King's Lib. Paris.*

considered a very dexterous archer, and whilst the ships lay at one of the South Sea islands, he challenged Tabourai Tamaide, a distinguished warrior, to a shooting match. The chief, accordingly brought his bow and arrows down to the fort, supposing it to be a trial which could cast an arrow furthest, as he does not appear to have valued himself on being a marksman. Mr. Gore, on the contrary, did not greatly affect flight shooting, so that no exhibition of skill took place between them. Tabouri Tamaide, however, to gratify those present, drew his bow and shot an unfledged arrow to the distance of two hundred and seventy-four yards, which is something less than the sixth part of a mile.*

"Neither wood, horn, metal, parchment, paper, nor cloth, but only a feather, is fit for a shaft," says Ascham: the latter being sufficiently plentiful every where, we are not compelled to resort to any of the former. Paper and cloth I should not greatly affect; parchment might serve; that horn, wood, and even leather, were once used for winging cross-bow bolts, is proved by a better authority than his; I mean the collection of ancient quarrils† preserved in the armoury of Goodrich Court.

We form a prodigious idea of the ancient consumption of goose feathers‡, on reflecting that at least twenty thousand sheaves of arrows, requiring nearly a million and a half of feathers, went to the equipment of one inconsiderable armament.

---

* Cook's Voyages, vol. ii. p. 147.

† Cross-bow arrows are so named. The word is derived from *quarrè*, square; in allusion to the form of the head

‡ A gentleman of Berkshire being asked counsel of a certain burgess in the same shire, what he thought expedient and worthy to be proposed in parliament on his first taking his seat there, said, that it was a matter of importance, the killing of so many goslings and *grean geas*, and that for special reasons; the first for that the force and mighte of England was consisting in such artillery as bowes and arrowes, which required the wings of well grown geas. — *MS. Common Place Book, belonging to the eldest son of George Fox, the historian, A.D.* 1635.

The fact that the "grey goose quill" was in small request, save for the feathering of a shaft, ought, indeed, to be placed as a set off against this calculation. If men in those merry days rarely steeped its point in the inky fluid, we well know they often dyed its feather in the heart's blood of their country's foes.

>   And every arrow an ell long,
>   With peacock well y dyght.

Ascham notices the use of this feather, only to condemn it. "And certainly," says he, "at short butt, which some are accustomed to, the peacock feather doth seldom keep up the shaft either straight or level, it is so rough and heavy: so that men who have taken them up for their gay appearance, laid them down again for the sake of utility." The expressions, "gainess and roughness" lead one to conclude he means the beautiful eye of the peacock's tail feather. Yet, as it could never be applied to an arrow, I suspect he had never seen one fledged with peacock's feathers, and entirely mistook the kind used by fletchers. The Flemings still use the *wings* of that bird with great success. They are of a fine reddish brown, but neither very rough, nor very gay; and I prefer them to the goose feather. In the reign of Edward II. arrows thus winged were worth one penny each, as appears by the following entry in that prince's Wardrobe Account: —

Pro duodecim flechiis, cum pennis de pavore, emptis pro rege 12 den.

"For twelve arrows with peacock's feathers, purchased for the king, 12*d*." *

Turkeys' wings are also in much request with the Belgian archers, either in the natural state, or dyed scarlet, blue, green, or yellow. The tints are very skilfully applied, and much enhance the beauty of these feathers.

* MS. Cott. Nero, C. viii.

The natives of the Jesso Isles rear a species of bird of prey, called sima fokoro, for winging arrows*; and the Turkish city of Babadagy derives no trifling advantage from trading in eagles' wings, as that bird frequents a neighbouring mountain in vast numbers. "The bow-makers throughout Turkey and Tartary are all supplied from thence, although they use only the twelve tail feathers, which are commonly sold for a Leonine. They are esteemed superior to all others for winging arrows, and a skilful archer does not care to use any other. If a man has several shafts in his quiver, with other feathers, and but one among them fledged with an eagle's quill, that one, remaining untouched, will eat all the rest to the wood." † This property certainly savours a little of the marvellous; yet Saxo Grammaticus, who belonged to a very different age and nation, also ascribes a corrosive property to the plumage of this

King of all that beat the air with wings. ‡

The term cock-feather is applied to the one standing perpendicularly, when the arrow is properly nocked upon the string. It was formerly, and at the present time is, often black or grey, to distinguish it from the rest.

Old English archers carried into the field a sheaf of twenty-four barbed arrows, buckled within their girdles. A portion of these, about six or eight, were longer, lighter, and winged with narrower feathers than the rest. With these flight shafts, as they are termed, they could do execution further than with the remaining heavy sheaf arrows. The advantages occasionally derivable from this superiority of range, when directed by a skilful leader, have led to very important results, of which the

---

* Oriental Collections.
† Demetrius Cantimir, p. 319. note.
‡ "Eagles' feathers joined to other feathers in quivers of arrows, &c. will devour them, especially goose feathers."

reader has seen a remarkable instance at the commencement of this work.*

The ancient fletchers frequently sheared their shafts somewhat convex, and round at the broad end, nearest the nock. In almost every painting and print I have met with, on the subject of archery, particularly in a very beautiful family portrait, the size of life, representing a gentleman charging his arquebuse with a fire shaft, the wings are exactly of this form. Ascham makes favourable mention of the triangular fashion, and gives several ingenious reasons why it should be adopted.

A few hints respecting the mode of setting on this important part of the arrow will be prized by archers. My ingenuity has been sadly taxed, at times, to repair a favourite shaft when injured by moths, a blow against the target stand, or other contingency, and I invented all sorts of complicated, perhaps some of them were ingenious, instruments, for holding on the feather, until the glue became dry. However, after witnessing the process in the workshop of a Brussels fletcher, my own laboured contrivances, and its simplicity, formed an amusing contrast.

Split the quill down its stem, which must be cut to a proper length, and pared until of the requisite thickness, with a sharp and thin-bladed knife. A flat piece of iron is afterwards to be moderately heated, over which the stem of the feather, so cut and dressed, should be passed rapidly, till all its inequalities being charred off, it is rendered smooth and dry to receive the cement. For this, take equal parts of isinglass and the best common glue, dissolved in brandy, which is of a proper consistency, if when heated, it will barely drop from the point of a slip of wood. The stele of the arrow being ready prepared, or, where only a single feather is to be set on, after all the old glue has been removed with sand paper or a fine rasp, you may commence operations. Dip a cloth in hot water; squeeze it,

---

* Note, page 7.

and lay the feathers therein, until quite limp and soft. Take out a single one, and with a morsel of wood apply the glue, the heat of which will cause the feather to curl round. Place the *centre* of this convexity upon the centre of that part of the stele usually occupied by the feather, and if your glue be thick enough, it will closely adhere there. Then, with finger and thumb, immediately press down and settle the remainder straight and even. Arrange the other feathers in a similar manner, and lay your arrow to dry, in a warm situation somewhere near the fireside, but do not attempt to shear it, until all is firm. In this, as in every other manual operation, much depends on practice; for a regular fletcher can wing many arrows in a very short space of time; Mr. Waring having the reputation of being able to finish a dozen per minute. It is unnecessary to describe the piles of modern arrows. Our ancestors, even when shooting for pastime, used them much heavier than we do. One of their high-crested silver spoon-shouldered heads, to which Ascham alludes, probably outweighed three of the present time. For military purposes they were still larger, since my Agincourt arrow is equal to even thrice that number. Specimens of ancient war heads are to be seen in many collections: they generally weigh from half an ounce to one ounce and a quarter, and measure an inch in breadth, from barb to barb; it is worthy of notice that the mark set upon government stores, &c. should be a " broad arrow," to which it has some resemblance. I am not aware of the existence of any ancient butt or roving piles; yet it is possible such may be found at Goodrich Court. Brown Willis's MS. account of the parish of Bletchley*, mentions an ancient cross on the village green, and two large butts or hillocks for the bowmen, which stood near it. At their base—for this Goth dug them down for the sake of their earth, when building his seat of

* Bodleian Library.

Waterhall, in 1711—were discovered many steel arrow heads, which, being shot deep into the earth, came off, and were never drawn out again.

Modern archers paint their arrows with the pattern of some riband immediately above the feathering. I have seen in the British Museum a small thick duodecimo volume, pasted full of exquisite patterns of this sort, once belonging to Miss Bankes, the daughter of Sir Joseph, and collected from the elder Mr. Waring, about the year 1790. By the by, they prove an absolute decay in the riband manufactory; since nothing comparable to them could be purchased at the present day.

The American Indian warriors carefully mark every arrow of their quivers, whether designed for war or the chase. As the amount of enemies slain decides their pretensions to military merit, each combatant is thus enabled to ascertain with exactness the number which has fallen victims to his prowess; and in the chase, whilst the plain is strewed with the carcasses of bisons and moose deer, disputes about the possession of any particular piece of game are avoided, because each takes quiet possession of the animals transfixed by the arrow bearing his own mark.

The barbed arrow is a truly inhuman weapon; and how feelingly the torture it inflicts has been alluded to by some of the older writers: the effects of some ten thousand alighting among a large body of cavalry, is painted with no fancied exaggeration, by our poet Drayton:—

> Upon the horses, as in chase they fly,
> Arrows so thick in such abundance light,
> That their broad buttocks men like butts might see,
> Whereat, for pastime, bowmen shooting be.

Again, he compares the anguish inflicted upon these poor animals to the stings of envenomed insects.*

* To the honour of the English be it spoken, they never, like the Spaniards, resorted to the hateful expedient of using poisoned arrows. Yet,

And in their flanks like cruel hornets hung.

The Lord de Joinville dwells with much enthusiasm upon the impetuous valour displayed by the French monarch in his

---

as some information on this subject may be acceptable to the reader, I will insert a description of the mode of preparing those deadly weapons, common to the red warriors of Guiana and other portions of the South American continent.

When the Indian intends to chase the paccari, surprise the deer, or rouse the tapir from his marshy retreat, he carries his bows and arrows instead of the blow-pipe.

The bow, which is generally about six or seven feet long, is strung with a cord spun from the silk grass. The forests of Guiana furnish many species of hard, tough, and elastic wood, out of which beautiful and excellent bows are formed.

The arrows are from four to five feet in length, made of a yellow reed, without a knot or joint, which is found in great plenty up and down throughout Guiana. A piece of hard wood, about nine inches long, is inserted into the end of the reed, and fastened with cotton well waxed. A square hole, an inch deep, is then made in the end of this piece of hard wood, done tight round with cotton to keep it from splitting. Into this the Indian inserts a spike of poisoned coucourite wood, which may be kept there or taken out at pleasure. A joint of bamboo, about as thick as your finger, is fitted over the poisoned spike, to prevent accidents, and defend it from the rain, and is taken off when the arrow is about to be used. Lastly, two feathers are fastened on the other end of the reed to steady it in its flight. Besides his bow and arrows, the Indian carries a little box, made of bamboo, which holds a dozen or fifteen poisoned spikes, six inches long, and prepared in the following manner: — A small piece of wood having been dipped in the poison, with this they give the spike a first coat, and expose it to the sun or fire. When dry, it receives another coat, and a second drying; then a third, and sometimes even a fourth, taking great care to put the poison on thicker at the middle than at the sides, by which means the spike retains the shape of a two-edged sword. It being rather a tedious operation to make one of these arrows complete, and the Indian not being famed for industry, except when pressed by hunger, he has hit upon a plan for preserving his arrows which deserves notice. About a quarter of an inch above the part where the coucourite spike is fixed into the square hole, he cuts it half through; and thus, when it has entered the animal, the weight causing the arrow to break off there, it falls uninjured to the ground, so that should he have no other arrow with him, and a second shot immediately occur, he has only to take another

encounters with the Saracens. On one occasion, news was brought him that his brother lay in the greatest peril. Nothing

poisoned spike out of the little bamboo box, fit it on his arrow, and send it to its destination. Thus armed with deadly poison, and hungry as the hyena, he ranges through the forest, in quest of the wild beasts' track. No hound can act a surer part. Without clothes to fetter him, or shoes to bind his feet, he observes the footsteps of the game, where an European eye could not discern the smallest vestige. He pursues it through all its turnings and windings, with astonishing perseverance, and success generally crowns his efforts. The animal, after receiving the poisoned arrow, seldom retreats two hundred paces before it drops.

The Indians of the settlement of Macoushia seem to depend more on the wourali poison for killing their game than any thing else. Their blow-pipes hung from the roof of the hut, carefully suspended by a silk grass cord; and on taking a nearer view of them, no dust seemed to have settled there, nor had the spider spun the smallest web on them, which showed they were in constant use. The quivers were close by them, with the jaw-bone of the fish pirai, tied by a string to their brim, and a small wicker basket of wild cotton, which hung down to the centre: they were nearly full of poisoned arrows. It was with difficulty these Indians could be persuaded to part with any of the wourali poison, though a good price was offered for it. They gave us to understand it was powder and shot to them, and very difficult to be procured.

In passing over land from Essequibo to the Demerara, we fell in with a herd of wild hogs. Though encumbered with baggage, and fatigued with a hard day's walk, an Indian got his bow ready, and let fly a poisoned arrow at one of them. It entered the cheek-bone and broke off. The wild hog was found dead about one hundred and seventy paces from the place where he had been shot, and afforded us an excellent and wholesome supper.

One day, while we were eating a red monkey, erroneously called the baboon in Demerara, an Arowack Indian told an affecting story of what happened to a comrade of his. He was present at his death. As it did not interest this Indian in any point to tell a falsehood, it is very probable his account is a true one. If so, there appears no certain antidote for the wourali poison, or at least no antidote that could be resorted to in a case of urgent need; for the Indian gave up all thoughts of life as soon as he was wounded.

The hunter just alluded to, said that, about four years ago, whilst he and his companion were ranging the forest in quest of game, the latter discharged a poisoned arrow at a red monkey in a tree above him. It was nearly a perpendicular shot. The arrow missed the monkey, and in its descent struck

could check his ardour. He would wait for no one, but striking spurs into his horse, galloped into the midst of the battle. He suffered many hard blows; and the enemy shot barbed arrows at him, until they covered his horse's rump and tail with Greek fires.

In another passage, he affords a curious illustration of the prodigious quantity of these missiles expended in a single engagement. "The Saracens vigorously attacking the Templars, defeated them in a short time. It is certain that, in the rear of the Christians, there was about an acre of ground so covered with bolts, darts, and arrows, that you could not see the earth beneath them, such showers had been discharged against the Templars by the Saracens. The commander of our battalion had lost an eye in the preceding battle of Shrove Tuesday, and this time he received an arrow shot in the other, and was slain: God have mercy on his soul!"*

When Zisca lay encamped before the town of Rubi, he rode out to view a portion of the works where he intended an assault. Being observed by the besieged, an arrow shot from the wall struck him in the eye. The wound proving exceedingly dangerous, the army surgeons proposed his being carried to Prague, where the arrow was extracted; but being barbed, it tore out the eye along with it.

Whilst leading a furious charge against the enemy at the head of his Saxon billmen, our English King Harold fell among heaps of slain, pierced to the brain by two Norman shafts;

---

his arm, a little above the elbow. He was convinced it was all over with him. 'I shall never,' said he in a faltering voice, and looking at his bow, as he uttered the words, 'I shall never bend this bow again.' And with that, he took off his little bamboo poison box, which hung across his shoulder, and putting it, with his bow and arrows, on the ground, laid himself down close by them, bade his companion farewell, and never spoke more."—*Waterton's Wanderings in South America.*

* Joinville, vol. ii. page 152.

and his gallant brethren, fighting valiantly in front of their respective battalions, shared the same fate. With day dawn on the morrow, some monks of Waltham, (a religious establishment founded by the sons of Godwin,) were seen slowly pacing over the field of slaughter, towards the conqueror's tent. Entering, they bent humbly before this stern soldier, presented him ten marks of gold, and obtained leave to search for, and carry away to decent burial, the corpse of their benefactor. They withdrew; and, hurrying to the spot where death seemed to have been busiest, examined the heap of bodies one after the other, but in vain, the trampling of the iron heels of horses and men, together with the wounds of which he died, had so disfigured the king's person, that they failed to recognise him. Despairing to succeed in further search, alone, they applied to a female called Edith, poetically named, in Saxon, Swanes Hals, or Swan's Neck, once beloved by Harold, and entreated her to assist them. She joined in the melancholy procession; and by the instinct of affection was not long in discovering the remains of him to whom she was devoted even in death.

Even the unbarbed arrow has been found to inflict wounds far more painful and difficult to heal than the stroke of a musket ball. Whilst Mariner resided at the Tonga islands, he frequently accompanied their warriors on hostile expeditions against the surrounding insular tribes. In one of these affairs, he received an arrow in his foot, which passed through the broadest part. Luckily it was not a bearded arrow; but the wound, nevertheless, proved a very bad one, and he was disabled by it for several months. On another occasion, the follower of a chief named Timon had made himself a sort of breast-plate of an earthen strainer, such as is placed at the bottom of dishes when fish appears at table. The man had procured this unique piece of armour at Port au Prince; but unluckily it happened that an arrow pierced him directly through the hole which is commonly in the middle of such utensils. This wound laid him

Edith discovering the dead body of Harold.

up eight months, and he was never afterwards, in Mariner's time, able to hold himself perfectly erect.*

That jolly Dominican, Fray Juan de Gallegos, who accompanied Hernando de Soto in his expedition to the Floridas, was rather more fortunate, although his armour was of a nature still more extraordinary than that of the poor South Sea islander. In a very sanguinary battle, which took place between the Indians of Florida and their Spanish invaders, a gentleman named Baltazer de Gallegos greatly distinguished himself; for he was ever foremost in the hottest of the mêlée, and fought on foot. The peril to which he thus became exposed was anxiously observed by his brother, the portly friar just alluded to. Our ghostly father, therefore, rode forth in his sacerdotal habit, with the intention of resigning his ambling palfrey to the soldier; but influenced by that wholesome maxim, which terms discretion the better part of valour, he kept himself warily on the outskirts of the field. There he vainly continued hallooing and making the most energetic signals; for Gallegos, who loved glory as a passion, resolutely maintained his rank, and refused the proferred steed. In the mean time, his cries and gesticulations were observed by an Indian, who, imagining him to be one of the Spanish generals encouraging his men, let fly an arrow, which struck the fat monk just between his brawny shoulders. The wound proved trivial, because he wore a double hood with a large hat of felt, which being secured by a string, had fallen backwards, and hung like a shield upon his back. It was, however, enough; and the wandering savage saw the man, whom he looked upon as the bulwark of the Christian army, turn his bridle, and make an inglorious, hasty retreat in the direction of the Spanish camp.

The Inca Garcilasco de Vega, in his amusing history of Hernando de Soto's expedition against the Floridans, relates a

* Vol. i. page 96.

singular instance of suicide perpetrated by means of a barbed arrow.

Orders had been issued by the Spanish general, that Juan de Anasco, with thirty of his comrades, should descend along the banks of the river Cofaciqui, to a spot at some distance from the native villages, where it was expected the princess of the country lay concealed, whom they were commissioned to bring with all gentleness to the camp. Anasco accordingly set out with his companions, taking with them an Indian youth of high rank, whom the queen-mother had appointed for their guide. This Indian, who was accompanied by several domestics, had been ordered to press onwards when he arrived near their destination, give notice of the Spaniards' approach, and conjure his mistress, in the name of her daughter and the inhabitants generally, to set out for the camp where preparations had been made for giving her an honourable reception, and where she would be received with affectionate joy. The lady of Cofaciqui had despatched this young noble, because, having been brought up by her mother, he was tenderly beloved by her, and on which account, she imagined she might more favourably entertain the Spaniards' request; besides, he possessed all those external advantages which are calculated for materially assisting the success of such a design, since to an address at once noble and prepossessing, he added a lofty stature, and handsome countenance. His step was light and active, like the rest of his countrymen; his head was gaily adorned with a majestic plume of different coloured feathers; a beautiful mantle of deer skin hung from his shoulders; he carried in his hand a glittering painted bow, and a quiver filled with arrows was suspended at his back. Thus, with a gallant bearing, worthy of his distinguished rank, this young Indian preceded the Spaniards, every word and look expressive of the gratification he derived from being instrumental in promoting their desires. When Anasco and his associates had journeyed about three leagues, they halted beneath the shelter of a large tree, to repose themselves during the noontide heat. Then it happened, that the young chieftain, who was seated in the centre of the band, which he had been hitherto delighting with descriptions of his native province and the surrounding districts, suddenly became moody and thoughtful, and at length falling into a deep reverie, leaned his head disconsolately on his shoulder, and uttered loud and repeated sighs. Every one noticed his dejection, but from a fear of increasing it, they forbore to inquire the cause. At length his sighs became interrupted for a short period, during which he unslung his quiver, and drew forth, one after another, nearly the whole of its contents. These arrows were singularly remarkable for the beauty of their workmanship, and the Spaniards passed them successively from hand to hand around the group, pointing out to each other the exquisite delicacy of their form, for a Floridan of rank greatly prides himself on the perfection of this kind of arm. As the reader, also, will doubtless derive satisfaction from knowing how they are made, I will as briefly as possible describe those carried by this young Indian noble. They were formed of reeds, winged with the feathers of birds of the most gaudy plumage, each arrow having something peculiar in its construction, which distinguished it from the rest. Some were headed with deer's horn, or the pointed bone of a fish; others with palm wood, carefully pointed and indented at the sides with an elegance and uniformity, which our best artists in steel could hardly hope to rival. Whilst the Spaniards were thus busily employed, the Indian, watching an opportunity when he fancied himself to be unobserved, gently drew out of the quiver an arrow headed with flint, long, and resembling a dagger blade, and stabbed himself desperately in the throat. He immediately fell dead; when his friends, astonished at the catastrophe, and shocked that they were unable to prevent it, called together the native attendants, eagerly inquiring what motive could have hurried their master to this act of desperation. With tearful eyes they answered he had destroyed himself from a fear that his errand, and above all the services he was rendering the Christians, would draw upon him the displeasure of her who had been the guide and protectress of his youth. That, as she had not come when first requested, they believed her to be offended; and their young chieftain, doubtless, considered the course he was pursuing, an unbefitting return for the care bestowed upon his nurture, and the love she had vouchsafed him. The poor attached slaves added, that a failure in his mission would, on the other hand, draw upon him the displeasure of the younger princess, and thus harassed between love towards one and duty to the other, he had chosen to die, as the best proof of his loyalty and devotion to both.

The book of " Messire Ambroise Paré, Concilleur et Premier Chirurgeon du Roy Frances I.," who followed the armies of that monarch, treats extensively of the wounds peculiar to military men, especially those inflicted by arrows. In order that his professional brethren might more fully comprehend the method of cure, the precautions to be adopted, the incisions they might venture upon, and the use of the necessary instruments, he has delineated these, as well as many different kinds of arrows in use in his time, and particularly the form of their heads, on a proper acquaintance with which, the cure of such wounds much depended. Thus, in exerting himself to promote a knowledge of surgery, he also performed unconsciously a very signal service to the antiquarian.* Among the arrows he

* He was a Huguenot, or Protestant, and, with one other individual, alone escaped the dreadful massacre of St. Bartholomew, of which he was an eye-witness. He tells us that he was called in to dress the wounds of Admiral Coligny, after the first unsuccessful attempt to assassinate that great and virtuous individual on the same memorable occasion. He also gives a very *naïve*, interesting narrative of his campaigning adventures, from which it appears that he underwent much suffering and personal inconvenience, and was unable to confine his practice wholly within professional bounds. Speaking of a " Sergeant of Chastellat," one of his patients, he says, " I per-

has introduced, I remark several where the stele* enters into the head, while in others the head is inserted into the stele; so that in either case, the point remained behind in the flesh and rendered the wound extremely dangerous. He does not pretend to give the forms of every arrow used in his age, but of those only which he himself had at various times extracted. Paré thus describes his mode of removing an arrow from fleshy parts of the body:—

"Si le fer estoit barblé ainsi, qui souvent est les *flèches Angloises*, et estoit à l'endroit d'un os, ou inséré dedans, ce qui souvent advient au profond des muscles de la cuisse, des bras, des jambes, ou d'autres parties des-quelles y auroit grande distance, lors ne le convient pousser, mais plustôt dilater la playe, en évitant les nerfs et grands vaisseaux, ainsi que fait le bon et expert chirurgien anatomique. Aussi faut appliquer un dilatatoire, cavé en sa partie intérieure, et faire en sorte, que l'on puisse prendre les deux ailes du fer, puis avec le bec de Grüe le tenir ferme, et tirer les trois ensemble."

It would appear that arrows having their heads poisoned were used by certain European nations of the fifteenth and sixteenth centuries; for Paré enters largely into the mode of

---

formed towards him the office of physician, surgeon, apothecary, and cook," dressing his dinner as well as his wounds until the time that he was completely cured. "Le Dieu le guerisse toujours," adds the doctor, so that we may infer his patient's gratitude, for these accumulated benefits, did not evaporate with the causes which had elicited them; a source of complaint very familiar to the medical experience of modern times. Our curiosity respecting the amount of remuneration given to professional men in the sixteenth century, is afterwards gratified by the following statement:—" The men at arms attached to Messire de Rohan's company gave me each a crown, and the archers half-a-crown." He then adds, " I protest to God that three different times I was on the point of being starved to death, not from any want of money, but because we could obtain no provisions, except by force; the base peasants having deserted their farms, and taken refuge, with all their cattle and effects, in castles or walled towns, as if we were church robbers, or something worse."

* Stele — the wooden shaft of an arrow.

extracting the venom from wounds arising therefrom. In my dissertation on the cross-bow, I have stated that the Spaniards frequently shot at game with poisoned quarrils, and the general sanguinary character of that people leads us to suspect they availed themselves of the same deadly expedient in the battle-field. Such wounds, says Paré, are to be detected by the great and poignant agony they cause to the patient, exactly as if he were stung by a swarm of bees. He recommends deep and immediate scarification of the part, and that it should be carefully sucked by a person, holding in his mouth a small quantity of sweet oil, to attract and dilute the venom, and being particularly cautious that he has himself no ulcer on the gums or lips to be injured thereby.

One John Morstede appears to have been our surgeon-general in the reign of Henry V., who authorised him to press into the army, as many of his brethren as were considered necessary for the expedition against France.* Yet one only, the same John Morstede landed there; and though he afterwards selected fifteen assistants, three of them served as archers under Sir Thomas Erpingham at Agincourt instead of dressing the wounded! Probably all did military duty of some kind, and consequently were in like manner exposed to a soldier's fate. The wounded, therefore, had no assistance beyond nature and their own exertions. On the English side, they were certainly few; while those of the enemy, as we learn from the details of the battle, perished without the slightest efforts being made for their relief.†

So much for the ancient treatment of arrow-wounds received in the field of Mars. Instances of their voluntary infliction in that of Venus, the reader may glean from "Lady Mary Wortley Montague's" amusing gossip. She informs us that Turkish lovers manifest

The pangs they endure for the fair,

---

* Sir N. H. Nicholas.   † Ibid.

by enacting Cupid in their own persons, and pierced with barbed arrows, present themselves torn and bleeding before their inexorable mistresses. Among the savage tribes of North and South America, these weapons are used to preserve life as well as to destroy it. After Lionel Wafer quitted the buccaneering vessel to which he had acted as surgeon, he was detained captive, somewhere about the Isthmus of Darien, by an Indian chief named Lacenta. It so happened that Lacenta's wife, a woman of great beauty, being taken ill, they wished to bleed her, an operation there performed by seating the patient upon a large stone in the middle of some shallow stream, and with a small bow shooting little arrows up and down her body, not missing any part. The arrows being gagged, did not penetrate further than we usually thrust our lancets; and when the operators chanced to hit a vein, so that the blood spirted out ever so little, the Indians leaped and skipped about, making many antic gestures of triumph. Wafer, who witnessed this exhibition of primitive phlebotomy, now told Lacenta that he would show him a method far less tormenting to the lady. "Let me see," quoth the great man. Our Englishman accordingly bound up her arm with strips of bark, and drawing forth his case of lancets which he had preserved, instantly breathed a vein. But the attempt had nearly cost him his life, for when the chief saw a stream of blood, which before came only drop by drop, following the wound of the polished and formidable-looking steel, he started up, and laying hold of a lance, swore by his " tooth, that if she did otherwise than well, he would have his heart's blood." The squaw recovered health, and Wafer liberty, as the recompense of his skill. I observe the following entry in a catalogue of the museum at Don Saltero's coffee-house, a place of entertainment well known to the visiters of Chelsea during the past age: —

"Indian arrows for bleeding; Glass Case, No. 11."

SECTION XI.

ROVING, OR RURAL ARCHERY.

> *Lingua riseth in her sleep.*
> *Common Sense.* How's this? is she asleep? have you seen her walk thus before?
> *Memory.* It is a very common thing. I have seen many sick of a peripatetic disease.
> *Anamnestes.* By the same token, my lord, I knew one that went abroad in his sleep, bent his bow, shot at a magpie, killed her, fetched his arrow, came home, locked the doors, and went to bed again.
> *Common Sense.* What should be the reason of it?
> *Lingua, or a Combat of the Tongue.* 1658.

THE author of the comedy probably witnessed this case of somnambulism, certainly a very extraordinary instance of *roving*.

Though constant practice at unvarying marks may enable you to exhibit advantageously on a prize day, it never makes a scientific bowman. So, by diligent attendance at Battersea-fields and Chalk Farm, with the consumption of a proportionate quantity of ammunition, a man acquires the reputation of a first-rate shot, among persons knowing little of the matter. He *is* so at the pigeon trap, when aware of the precise moment at which the game will spring; and you may then securely back his gun for ten shots out of twelve. Beware, however, how you do so, when he attempts to range the open country in search of wild game.

Thus it is with the archer. He must not content himself simply to "read my book," and frequent the target-ground only. Let him labour from "morn till dewy eve," *out* of the target-ground, in acquiring a facility of deciding at a glance upon the relative distances of different objects. The trunk of some distant oak, a hillock, or a thorn-bush, barely within the range of his lightest flight-shaft; with the mole hill and the thistle top, distant, on the contrary, only a score of paces, must alternately be the objects of his aim. Birds and rabbits afford a delightful variety in these rustic rambles. Rooks, when they congregate in numbers upon the tall ancestral oaks, which shelter the

Ancient homes of England,

afford pleasant sport. Whether my archer chooses to lie in wait for the family gentlemen, winging their way homewards from the broad fallows, or dispatches his feathered deaths towards the *branchers**, perched upon the topmost boughs, a bolt is his only weapon. The Flemings use such for popinjay shooting; and the best I ever had were purchased at Ostend.†

Reader, in thy lone piscatory rambles, by the rocky margin of the Doithëa‡, or the vast stretches of gravel which border the glittering streams of Wye, hast thou ever encountered a heron? His maw shall hold more trout, and of the best, in one morning's fishing, than occupies thy basket in three. How gladly in such a moment would Chevalier be exchanged for Waring; thy angling rod for yew and bird bolt. Mark, how like a fragment of the grey rock he appears, whilst standing with his spindle shanks half concealed in the rippling current. As to head and neck, they match his lower extremities well, but you can't see them; they, as well as his long sharp beak, being almost buried in the plumage of his breast, ready to pounce down upon the scaly prey. There! he has him; a lamprey. In vain the slimy little monster writhes his supple body round the chaps that holds his like a pincers, until, with a shake and a gobble,

---

* Young rooks.   † See French Archery.

‡ Carmarthenshire; an excellent fly-fishing stream, that flows not far from Tom Shawn Catti's Cave.

he is sent to join his fellows in that capacious maw; but now he hops ashore, meditative of flight. That's your time, if you have a bow; if not, I'll show you how to use one on some other opportunity. Don't be hasty, treat him like a sportsman; fair *law*, forty yards at least. Wait till he's well balanced upon his long flagging wings; draw then to your ear, and bringing eyes and mind to bear simultaneously on that dark feathered spot, close beneath his pinion, loose sharply The world has not a fairer mark; and, unless you are a bungler, both fish and fowl shall furnish out your supper; the first will eat as well from master heron's craw, as from your own basket; and the plumed poacher himself is not only eatable, but a rare delicacy. *Experto crede me Roberto.*

The blunt-headed bolt, herein-before described, will be hardly sufficient to bring down so large a bird. Barbed and double-headed arrows were once used at this sport. "In shooting at birds upon houses, trees, or butts, with the longbow or arc à jallet*," says the author of La Maison Rustique†, "the sportsman should be furnished with a peculiar description of arrow. For geese or other large birds, they should be double-forked, sharp, and strong, to cut a wing or a neck clean off. The blow from a common shaft rarely inflicts a wound sufficient to bring down the game at once: notwithstanding she be hurt or shot through, she will fly off and die in another place." Nor does even the barbed arrow constantly prove effectual, where a bird is covered with very thick and strong plumage; for Martyn, in his "Account of the Scottish Western Isles," mentions that the steward of St. Kilda had found an arrow, besides other strange items in a Solan goose's nest; the former doubtless had fallen from her wounded body: and I recollect, some few years ago, noticing an account of a stork being shot in Germany, with a barbed shaft sticking in its

---

* Stone bow. † Liebault, A. D. 1620.

body. A small portion of the stele, which was of jointed cane, remained attached to the head, whence it was pronounced, by a competent judge, to be one of those used by the natives of Interior Africa, where the bird must have received its hurt.

The chase of rabbits with the longbow is also a delightful species of roving. Of course, certain situations are better adapted to this kind of shooting than others; for, unlike the sportsman with a gun, our archer, ere he makes a shot, must reflect whether his missile may be lost or injured by it.*

All the world has probably seen or heard of Britton Ferry, a magnificent sea-view near Swansea, on the shores of Glamorganshire. The road thence to the Ferry passes over about four miles of beautiful velvet turf, called the "Burrows;" and although patches of yellow blossoming gorse are scattered here and there, in general, it is a plain, bare and level as a bowling-green. Thousands of rabbits inhabit this charming spot; and a better situation for an archer to acquire dexterity I do not believe exists. It will greatly enhance the pleasure of this sport, if the archer provide himself with a brace of dwarf spaniels, or beagles of the smallest size, which must be broken especially to the bow, just as a falconer trains the setter for his peculiar sport. In a very short time, these dogs will recognise, and testify as much pleasure on seeing the apparatus of archery, as they commonly do at the sight of a gun.

When brought to hunt within twenty or thirty yards of the archer's feet, they may be considered sufficiently under command. If a rabbit gets up and runs in direct line from the shooter, he should aim somewhat before its head: the same allowance holds good for a cross shot; but for all this I cannot lay down any precise rules, because the distance varies, according to the power of the bow, which, for flying or running shots, should be rather below the shooter's strength; as is set forth in the

---

* See Shakspeare, at page 79, 80. of this work.

Book of King Modus. Let not the thoroughbred sportsman entertain any qualms about indulging in my French style of hunting. Our most ancient game laws expressly permitted the hare or the roebuck to be killed by an arrow, even whilst the hounds were in full cry.*

Perhaps the suggestions here thrown out will appear like novelties in the practice of modern archery; so much the better. But, in sober truth, they are merely drafts on the "wisdom of our forefathers;" they knew by experiment that a correct knowledge of distance, so essential to the military archer, was only to be acquired by this desultory mode of shooting, and wisely made laws to discourage that at ordinary butts or targets.

With the exception of the poorest classes, every Englishman provided himself with a couple of bows. One of these served him in war, the other, weak and slender, was used for field sports. "Bring hither my birding bow," exclaims either Master Ford or Master Fenton, I forget which, when preparing for some rural excursion.† A Sloane MS.‡, asserts that "ille sicarius famosus, Robertus Hood," became an exile to avoid the consequences of killing a king's forester, who had insulted him. "One of his first exploits was the going abroad and bearing with him a bowe of exceeding strength. It fortuned that he got in company with certayne rangers or woodmen, who fell to quarrel with him, as making show to use such a bowe as no man was able to shoot withal. Whereto Robin replied, he had two better at Lockesley, only he bare that with him now, as a binding bowe," &c. &c.

The fragment of a romance called Wylliam and the Werwolf §, written towards the close of the fourteenth century, speaks of killing game with the long bow.

* See Welsh Archery, page 168.
† Merry Wives of Windsor.
‡ No. 1715.
§ Preserved in the library of King's College, Cambridge.

> A bow, also, the bold bairn* got him that time,
> And so to shoot under the shaws, sharplie he learned,
> That birdes and small beastes with his bow he quells
> So plenteously in his play, that soothlie to tell,
> When he went home each night with his drove of kine,
> He came himself charged with coneys and hares,
> With pheasants and fieldfares, and other fowls great;
> That the hind and his wife, and all his whole meyne,
> The bold bairn with his bowe at that time fed.

But of all modes of roving with which I am familiar, none are entitled to compete with the scientific rat shooting exploits of a Tonga island chief; but I will first describe another of their rural sports connected with archery, in which considerable ingenuity is displayed.

There is a particular kind of bird bred in the South Sea Islands, termed "Calai," a word signifying *trained for sport*. These are forbidden to all except the king and chiefs of high distinction; indeed, the expense and trouble of keeping and training them, renders the amusement of Fauna Calai beyond the means of ordinary men. Like our European falcon, the Calai is considered a present worthy the acceptance of a prince; and, as was usual also in our superior hawking establishments, one man is solely occupied in taking care of a single pair of birds. They teach them to utter a peculiar kind of call, by which the wild ones of the same species are attracted within bowshot, where the sportsman has concealed himself within a large wicker cage disguised with green branches. On the roof of this cage, the male Calai is secured by his leg, and the hen occupies a smaller receptacle hard by. No sooner do the decoy birds commence their treacherous manœuvres, than numbers of the wild species, male and female, flock towards them. Whilst these are hovering in the air, or sit perched on the branches of surrounding trees, the sportsman has ample leisure to transfix them with his arrows.

* Child.

This and what follows are solitary instances of archery being used merely as a pastime, by any people essentially barbarous. The care in most cases requisite for providing their daily sustenance, with its attendant fatigue, leave these children of the wilderness neither leisure nor inclination to exercise their skill unproductively. The advantages of soil and climate possessed by the South Sea islanders may account for their forming an exception to a rule so general; but let me no longer detain the reader from his interview with our accomplished rat shooters. These vermin of the Antipodes are smaller than the European rat, being somewhat between that and a mouse; and, subsisting chiefly on vegetable substances, such as sugarcane and bread-fruit, are accounted good food by the poorer class of natives. The privilege of indulging in the game of fauna gooma, or shooting them, belongs to their chiefs, mataboots, and mooas. All unqualified persons, therefore, who venture to trespass on the rat preserves of these dignitaries, are considered poachers, and punished with even more severity than falls to the lot of the same class of audacious marauders in England.

I will now endeavour to enlighten my readers respecting the laws and regulations of fauna gooma. It will be seen that no more elaborate and arbitrary ones were ever promulgated for the use and behoof of the frequenters of the Finsbury roving marks, by those pains-taking individuals Messrs. Shotterel and D'Urfey.

When a party of chiefs signify it is their pleasure to go rat-shooting, the attendants incontinently busy themselves in the preparation of a supply of roasted cocoa nut. The scene of action is the high road, and when these bait distributors have ascertained what ground the archers intend sporting over, they walk slowly along, chewing the roasted nut very finely, and spitting, or rather blowing some fragments with considerable force on the road as they proceed. The skill of the bait men consists in scattering the particles sufficiently thick to attract the attention of the rat, and in pieces small enough to tempt him to stop and eat, instead of seizing and racing off to his hole with the prize. Should this novel hunting ground be intersected by cross-ways, a reed is stuck upright, just where the latter unite with the main road, as a *taboo*, or mark of prohibition, warning all passengers to avoid the baited road, that the rats may not be driven off; and by a tacit understanding among these people, none will violate the taboo. A petty chief or man of the lower orders, would do so at the peril of his life, and even when a chief of the highest dignity becomes aware of this prohibition, he halts and remains quietly at some distance, out of respect and politeness to his peers.

Being arrived at the appointed termination of their labours, the attendants sit down to prepare cava or refreshments, orders having been previously issued in the names of the chiefs, that a supply of pork, fowls, yams, and ripe plaintains, should be sent from the neighbouring plantations. In the mean time, we are to suppose the princely rat shooters to have commenced the work of slaughter; for having divided themselves into two parties, they set off equipped with their bows and arrows, about ten minutes after the boohi or distributors of bait. They do not separate, however, but proceed in Indian file[*], along the middle of the road. The most illustrious chief goes foremost; behind him comes an antagonist, then follows one of his own party, and so on alternately.

And now for the rules of the game. As soon as each archer has made his shot, hit or miss, he changes place with the man behind him. Thus all the shooters continually vary their position in the rank; the first being sometimes last, and the last first. If a rat *shows* some distance in advance of the whole party, no one may shoot except he who then happens to be the leader; but as regards those which get up either behind or abreast

---

[*] A single line.

of any individual bowman, there is no restriction. Though rats form the chief object of their pursuit, the archer is not restricted to any particular mark, so that it be a living one; should he espy a bird fairly within range, he may shoot; if the arrow kill it he reckons one, and changes place with the man behind him. Occasionally, they halt to perform a squeaking concert, in imitation of the noise uttered by the animal they are in chase of. Practice has rendered their old hands marvellously expert at this; they actually tempt the rats out of the bushes, and whilst seated upright on their haunches in the act of listening, the hunter transfixes them to the earth.

Ten's the game; and the party first triumphantly exhibiting that number of long tails, carries off the prize.

On passing each taboo the reed is pulled up, that no unnecessary hinderance may be given to passengers; and when they arrive where the attendants have made ready their repast, the jovial rat shooters cast themselves on the green turf, shadowed by some umbrageous plaintain tree. There, with bows and arrows beside them, they "taste the good the gods provide," with all the hilarity of a knot of English sportsmen, reposing about noon on a warm September day.

They usually bait the roads for about a quarter of a mile; and should there be abundance of rats, they often agree to play three or four successive games; in which case, the boohi are sent forwards to renew their former occupation. The war arrows used by the natives of the Tonga islands, measure a cloth yard only. Those appropriated to the game of fauna gooma are nearly six feet long. Their great length appears to assist the steadiness of their flight, and is advantageous in taking aim through a thick bush; they have no feathers, and are headed with a splinter of ironwood. Each bowman carries a pair of arrows only, for no sooner has one been discharged, than it is immediately fetched by the attendants. I have a bundle of these rat arrows by me; and the bow originally belonging to them is also longer than that borne in battle, being of the same dimensions as the arrow. Four feet and a half is the ordinary size of the war bow. Nor are they nearly so difficult to bend, as ought ever to be the case, where this weapon is used for the purpose of killing very small game.*

It only remains for me to notice one other exercise connected with rural archery. I allude to the popinjay, a game familiar to the ancients, and forming a division of the funereal sports described by Homer and Virgil.

> Those who in skilful archery contend,
> He next invites the twanging bow to bend.
> The mast which late a first-rate galley bore
> The hero fixes on the sandy shore;
> To the tall top, a milk-white dove they tie,
> The trembling mark at which their arrows fly.
> Whose weapon strikes yon trembling bird, shall bear
> These two-edged axes, terrible in war;
> The single, he whose shaft divides the chord.
> He said: experienced Merion took the word
> And skilful Teucer: in the helm they threw
> The lots inscribed, and forth the latter flew.
> Swift from the string the sounding arrow flies,
> But flies unblest: no grateful sacrifice,
> No firstling lambs, unheedful didst thou vow
> To Phœbus, patron of the shaft and bow.
> For this, thy well aim'd arrow turn'd aside,
> Err'd from the dove, yet cut the chord that ty'd;
> Adown the mainmast fell the parting string,
> And the free bird to Heaven displays her wing.
> Seas, shores, and skies with loud applause resound,
> And Merion, eager, meditates the wound:
> He takes the bow, directs the shaft above,
> And follows with his eye the soaring dove,
> Implores the god to speed it through the skies,
> With vows of firstling lambs and grateful sacrifice.
> The dove in airy circles as she wheels,
> Amid the clouds the piercing arrow feels,

---

* The Lichfield Museum, among other rarities, possessed a very ancient bow and arrows for "killing rats and mice."

> Quite through and through the point its passage found,
> And at his feet fell bloody to the ground.
> The wounded bird, ere yet she breathed her last,
> With flagging wings alighted on the mast,
> A moment hung, and spread her pinions there,
> Then sudden dropt, and left her life in air.
>
> *Iliad.*

"The mast which late a first-rate galley bore" will be unnecessary. Some lofty elm in the centre of a large grass field, or growing isolated in a park, will answer better. You need only employ the best climber of the village, and every parish boasts some hero of this description, to ascend as high as is practicable, dragging after him a straight pole about six yards in length. Let him take a hammer and nails in his pocket to secure it to some bough of proportionate thickness; the popinjay itself being of course previously attached to its extremity. A wooden bird, small flag, or ox bladder stuffed with wool, will serve for this purpose.

The ingenious archer who wishes to vary his shooting as much as possible, may carry up his mark by means of a common paper kite. The advantage of such a contrivance is, that it can be elevated or depressed at pleasure.

The popinjay game was practised in London during the last century, by a party which met at Mr. Anderson's shooting ground, near Highgate.

The sport usually began by shooting at the Flemish blazon, or square target, the face of which is divided into fifty small squares, each marked as a blank or prize, the latter progressively increasing in value from one to twenty-six.

At the meeting in September, 1792, which consisted of parties of the Toxophilites, Robin Hood's Bowmen, and Woodmen of Arden, the shooting lasted three hours, when J. Palmer, Esq. of the Woodmen of Arden, won the medal for the central shot, and Dr. Howarth, a Toxophilite, that for the greatest number of prizes.

The figure of an eagle fixed on a perch 140 feet high, was also shot at for about an hour; and this sport afforded much entertainment from its novelty. At the expiration of that time,—— Paecock, Esq., of Robin Hood's Bowmen, shot it off the perch, and thereby won a gold medal.

After dining with his friends in the lodge, Mr. Anderson amused them with fireworks emblematical of the archery of the day.

Ayme for Finsburie Archers.*

ROVING MARKS.

From	To	Scores.	Yards.
Castle	Gardstone	9	5
Gardstone	Absoly	9	15
	Arnold	10	0
	Castle	9	5
Bloody House Bridge	Arnold	7	14

* " Ayme for Finsbury Archers; or, an alphabetical table of the names of every mark within the same fields, with their true distances, both by the map and dimensuration with the line, published for the ease of the skilful, and behoof of the younger beginners in the famed exercise of Archerie, by T. J. and C. B. London, 1594. 16mo.

To be sold at the sign of the Swan in Grub Street, by F. Sargeant.

I imagine it was originally drawn out to illustrate one of the little guides for archers, which was arranged in the manner of the modern books of hackney coach fares, and passed through several editions, varying as the marks were changed."— From a pamphlet by A. Kempe, F. S. A., printed for private circulation only. This gentleman has communicated some very intelligent papers on archery to the Gents.' Magazine.

Before the " genus irritabile vatum," as Horace christened his brother poets, had invaded Grub Street, that locality was possessed by the bowyer and fletcher caste. Charles Cotton thus sarcastically writes of some one: —

And arrow loosed from Grub Street bow
In Finsburie, to him is slow.

Sir W. Davenant likewise, in a mock heroic poem, entitled " The Long Vacation," describes the idle attorneys and proctors making archery matches in the Finsbury fields: —

With loynes in canvas bow case tied,
Where arrows stick with mickle pride,
Like ghosts of Adam Bell or Clymme,
Sol sets, — for fear they'll shoot at him.

THE BOOK OF ARCHERY.

From	To	Scores.	Yards.
Arnold	Turkswhale	8	4
	Absoly	9	1
	Gardstone	10	0
Absoly	Daysdeed	9	11
	Turkswhale	13	5
	Arnold	9	1
	Gardstone	9	15
Turkswhale	Arnold	8	4
	Absoly	13	5
	Daysdeed	9	12
	Lambeth	3	13
	Dial or Monument	10	3
Daysdeed	Lambeth	8	14
	Turkswhale	9	12
	Absoly	9	11
Lambeth	Turkswhale	3	13
	Daysdeed	8	14
	Old Speering	10	8
	Dial or Monument	6	10
	Westminster Hall	11	7
Dial or Monument	Blackwell Hall	10	16
	Star or Dial	9	19
	Westminster Hall	8	4
	Lambeth	6	10
	Turkswhale	10	3
Westminster Hall	Lambeth	11	7
	Dial or Monument	8	4
	Star or Dial	8	8
	Whitehall	11	2
Whitehall	Pitfield	7	17
	Edward Gold	12	2
	Scarlet Lion	12	2
	Star or Dial	7	0
	Westminster Hall	11	2
Old Speering	Blackwell Hall	6	9
	Star or Dial	9	16
	Lambeth	10	8
Star or Dial	Whitehall	7	0
	Scarlet Lion	9	14
	Blackwell Hall	9	5
	Old Speering	9	16
	Dial or Monument	9	19
	Westminster Hall	8	8
Blackwell Hall	Old Gawthan or Jehu	9	18
	Scarlet Lion	9	6
	Star or Dial	9	5
	Dial or Monument	10	16
	Old Speering	6	9

ROVING, OR RURAL ARCHERY.

From	To	Scores	Yards
Old Gawthan or Jehu	Old Absoly	8	17
	Edward Gold	9	9
	Scarlet Lion	4	2
	Blackwell Hall	9	18
Scarlet Lion	Old Gawthan or Jehu	4	2
	Old Absoly	9	11
	Edward Gold	7	2
	Pitfield	11	3
	Whitehall	12	2
	Star or Dial	9	14
	Blackwell Hall	9	6
Edward Gold	Old Gawthan or Jehu	9	9
	Scarlet Lion	7	2
	Whitehall	12	2
	Pitfield	6	11
Pitfield	Whitehall	7	17
	Scarlet Lion	11	3
	Edward Gold	6	11
	Old Absoly	10	16
	Bob Peek	11	3
Old Absoly	Bob Peek	8	12
	Pitfield	10	16
	Scarlet Lion	9	11
	Old Gawthan or Jehu	8	17
Bob Peek	Old Absoly	8	12
	Pitfield	11	3
Rosemary Branch	Pitfield	9	17
Levant	Welsh Hall	8	18
Welsh Hall	Egg Pye	10	10
	First Butt	11	11
Butt	Butt	6	18
	Short Butts	2	9

"We know from history," says Mr. Kempe in the pamphlet already quoted, "how jealous the London youth were of keeping the fields round the city of London open for the practice of archery; and that on one occasion of their being obstructed in the reign of Henry VIII., a tanner under that license for mad pranks in ancient days, a disard's or clown's coat, ran through the city, shouting 'Shovels and spades! Shovels and spades!' The cry was readily understood; and as the author of Nigel quotes, —

> Uprose the 'prentices one and all,
> Living in London, proper and tall.

They rushed forwards with resistless prowess, and in a few hours levelled all the dykes, hedges, and inclosures, which the spirit of exclusive appropriation had erected, to obstruct the manly votaries of the English long-bow.

This good old national cause was aided by James I. in a more legal way. He directed his letters patent in 1605, to the Lord Mayor, the Lord Chancellor and others, as commissioners, commanding them to cause the fields about the city, in which archery had been practised from time immemorial, to be cleared of all obstructions to that exercise, for the space of two miles.

Another similar commission was issued by Charles I. in 1632; and the contest was doubtless continual, until at length, the great march of bricks and mortar was triumphant. Some of the last skirmishes which took place about fifty years ago, are thus described in Highmore's History of the Artillery Company, from the Records of that Society.

On the company's march to Baunes, on the accession in 1762, they found the gate of a large field, in which stood one of their stone marks, named Ball's Pond, both locked and chained, and four men placed to prevent their entrance. The adjutant ordered it to be forced, after which they marched across, and opened another gate.

In 1784, a committee was appointed to ascertain the situation of the butts, &c., and to report thereon.

In October of the same year, the company marched to Finsbury Fields, to view their several marks, beginning at the Pretend Mead, where the castle stone stood, and thence extending to Baune's Fields, and Islington Common, they removed several obstructions, &c.

In July, 1786, considerable encroachments having been made on the ancient marks belonging to the company, the court ordered notice to be given to all occupiers of lands in Baune's and Finsbury Fields, between Peerless Pool south, Baune's Pond north, Hoxton east, and Islington west, wherein any of their marks were placed, to remove all obstructions to the company's rights.

On the 12th of August following, the company on its march over Baune's Fields pulled down by the pioneers several parts of the fence of a piece of ground enclosed, about two years since, by Mr. Samuel Pitts for gardens and summer houses. Through these breaches, the company marched from the marks of Gardstone, to Arnold; and from Arnold to Absoly. Being come to a field lately enclosed with a brick wall by Messrs. Walker, Ward, and Co. the proprietors of a lead-mill, between the marks of Bob Peake and the Levant, the company were induced to desist from pulling down or making a breach in the wall, by the representations and assurances of one of the partners, that at the time of forming this enclosure, he was ignorant of the company's right in those fields. He added, they were willing to enter into any reasonable terms of accommodation with the company for what they had done. One of the archer's division was then ordered to shoot an arrow on the wall, as an assertion of the company's right, after which the battalion proceeded on its march to several of the other marks.

Lastly, in 1791, when the long butts on Islington Common were destroyed, by digging gravel, a detachment marched to the spot, pursuant to a previous notice to the occupiers and commissioners of the roads, to remove every obstruction and to replace the mark : these objects were attained.

The distance from mark to mark in the " Aime for Finsbury archers," is very much varied, and thus as I have observed, excellent practice for archery at roving distance was afforded. The greatest length seen in the plan for 1737 is thirteen score, five yards. In the dimensurations of 1628, the great length of nineteen score is laid down, the shortest distance is nine score.

The eminence called Shooter's Hill probably obtained that appellation from the archers constantly seen practising at rovers there. John Haywood has a quaint epigram, tending to show this etymology to be correct.

OF AN ARCHER ROVING.

Q. What a shaft shoots he?
A.   With a roving arrow.
Still he hits his mark, be it wide or narrow.
Q. Where shooteth this sharpshooter, Will?
A. He shooteth most at rovers, on Shooter's Hill.

SECTION XII.

GREEK AND ROMAN ARCHERY.

Ξυνίημι καὶ τοῦ Ἀπόλλωνος, τοξότης ὁ θεὸς καὶ μουσικὸς, καὶ φιλῶ μὲν τὴν ἁρμονίαν αὐτοῦ, φοβοῦμαι δὲ τὴν τοξείαν.

I acknowledge Apollo also, the musical and the archer god, and I love his harmony, but fear his arrows.—*Maximus Tyrius*, xxix.

> He that grasps
> The skilful-aiming bow, hath in his hand
> One thing that much avails him, whence he sends
> A thousand arrows 'gainst the breasts of others,
> Himself from death defending; and his stand
> Held distant, pours his vengeance on his foes.
> *Euripides.*

Pudor est nescire sagittas.
It is a reproach to be ignorant of archery.
Statius.

The same fine taste which guided the armourer of antiquity when fabricating the helmet, buckler, sword, or the cuirass, and gave these accoutrements of the Grecian warrior forms the most exquisite of which they are susceptible, appears eminently conspicuous in the fashion of his bow.

Its figure exhibits a perfect combination of symmetry and strength. How graceful the curve, with which either horn recedes from the centre-piece or grip, occupied by the archer's hand; how imperceptibly they taper towards their extremities, where the extended jaws of a serpent receives the bow-string. How elegant the contrast between "the beaten gold," adorning those points, and the glossy jet black material of which the whole weapon was constructed. Those who are but imperfectly acquainted with the nature of the materials employed by our modern bowyers, must doubtless be surprised they have never attempted to work upon a model so faultless as this.* For ladies' bows, especially, it appears most desirable; although, in reality, a bow fashioned thus of wood, the only substance used in England, would not retain its shape during a single day's, perhaps not an hour's, shooting.

"Of what, then, was the Grecian bow composed?" pettishly inquires some fair Toxophilite, a *leetle* chagrined at being unable to figure as the buskined goddess of the chace.

Homer, madam, shall answer you, by describing the bow of Pandarus. He, like our own Shakspeare, seems to have possessed an almost intuitive knowledge of every art common to the age in which he flourished. The passage is distinguished by perfect accuracy of description, clothed in the most harmonious verse: —

> He heard, and madly at the motion pleased,
> His polish'd bow with hasty rashness seized.
> 'Twas form'd of horn, and smooth'd with artful toil;
> A mountain goat resign'd the shining spoil,
> Who pierced long since, beneath his arrows bled.
> The stately quarry on the cliffs lay dead,
> And sixteen palms his brows large honours spread.
> The workmen join'd and shaped the bended horns,
> And beaten gold each taper point adorns.

Though Homer has not said so, we may conclude that the Greek had an eye principally to those "brows large honours." Like a true archer, he probably thought less of the venison than of the splendid bow which its spoils promised to supply.

* I once possessed a very ancient German steel bow, which, in outline, exactly resembled that usually given by sculptors to Cupid. The length was four feet, and, although as difficult to draw as an ordinary wooden bow of sixty pounds, it never shot even the lightest flight beyond one hundred and fifty yards. Its defects are wholly attributable to the sluggishness of the metal, and in no respect to its form.

Several modern Oriental bows of horn are suspended round the apartment where I am writing. How little has the bowyer's art varied in the East during a period of some thousand years! Those I refer to are such as we usually find in the armouries of Rajpoot and other Hindostanee chiefs. Some are formed of buffalo, others of goats' horns, curving exactly alike, and united in the centre. In one or two specimens there is a wooden tip to receive the string, beautifully painted, gilded, and varnished. The custom of ornamenting the bow with gold leaf and pigments, like other Oriental practices, is very ancient. It will explain the "beaten gold," which adorned the bow of Pandarus, and the "golden bows," frequently alluded to by other poets besides Homer; for gold, in itself, possesses no elasticity whatever. Steel is the only metal convertible into a bow; and even that, as before noted, proves inferior to many kinds of wood.

Among a host of writers, who have favoured the world with disquisitions upon the works of the Grecian Bard, in vain do we look for any critical notice of those splendid pictures of archery with which his works pre-eminently abound. One of these commentators charges Homer with grossly exaggerating the length of the horns, in the passage above quoted. If our ideas of the goat be confined to that species seen in large flocks, cropping the heathblossoms, or reposing among the thymy verdure of the chases and heaths of Monmouthshire, those dimensions certainly appear somewhat fabulous. But Homer speaks of the Asiatic goat, whose "brows large honours" often attain; nay, even exceed the length of sixteen palms; and archers who feel interested in the question, may satisfy themselves by visiting the British Museum, where they will see many specimens of the species to which Homer alludes.

Ad interim, perhaps they would like to hear what Mr. Pashley, our latest traveller in Crete, says on this subject. " The meal furnished by the hospitality of my Samariste guide consisted chiefly of the flesh of a wild goat, killed by him on an expedition from which he had just returned. I obtained from him three pairs of the animal's horns; they are all nearly of the same size, viz., on the outer edge, 2 feet 7½ inches, and on the inner edge, 2 feet 1½ inches. The wild goat is alluded to by the epithet ξαλος, bestowed on it by Homer; and the length of the horns, which I obtained at Samaria, is very nearly that assigned in the well-known description of the bow of Pandarus."* The palm is four inches; making, therefore, due allowance for a certain portion necessarily consumed in joining the horns under its handle, the bow of Pandarus must have measured nearly five feet. In northern Asia, where this animal sports very extraordinary horns, they manufacture bows of similar dimensions at the present time.

When Mr. Turner, one of the East India Company's officers, visited Thibet, he was received with great kindness and courtesy by the Teshoo Lama. This personage, who delighted in archery, presented his guest with many exquisite arrows, having characteristic names inscribed upon each, indicative of remote and steady flight; together with a beautiful horn bow, nearly five feet long.† It may here be observed, that the dry, bracing atmosphere of northern Asia, like that of Greece, is peculiarly favourable to the perfection of these weapons; but India, where, especially during the rainy season, the air is extremely humid, they fall out of shape, and become nearly useless. So the bow in question, when removed from Thibet to Madras, soon lost the fine symmetry which Mr. Turner tells us had originally distinguished it. The cold of our English climate proves even more prejudicial. Here they frequently fly into pieces as you string them, of which I once witnessed the following instance.

* Vol. ii. p. 271.　　　　　† Asiatic Researches.

Whilst strolling through the bazaar at Calcutta, a gentleman observed a native with three or four bows and several sheaves of arrows for sale. Struck with the beauty of one in particular, which was of horn, black and glossy, like polished marble, he inquired the price; that was reasonable enough, especially as a bundle of reed arrows formed part of the bargain. Previously to paying for it, however, the purchaser, by signs, expressed some doubts of its enduring the violent strain produced by arrows nearly two thirds its own length. The Indian bowyer, a wild savage-looking hillsman, smiled grimly in reply as he beckoned his customer out of the bazaar, and prepared for an indisputable proof of the bow's elasticity, and his own extraordinary address. Placing the snake-like weapon between his legs, he strung it up with that graceful motion elsewhere described; and ran with an arrow from the bundle which lay at his feet, with monkey-like agility towards a neighbouring mud wall, where he whipped off his slipper, and stuck it heel upwards in a chink; then skipping away to the distance of about fifty or sixty paces, he drew his arrow to the head, without an instant's pause, and the admiring Englishman saw it launched against and quivering in this novel target, the heel of which it had firmly nailed to the wall. No more satisfactory proof of the excellence of his ware could be required, and you may be sure the bargain was immediately concluded. Yet, on merely attempting to string the same bow some time afterwards in England, I saw it break into several pieces, to the great peril of sundry fragile articles suspended around the apartment where the experiment was made; so completely had change of climate destroyed its original toughness and elasticity. In Shea's Mirhonda, the hero complains he never could cast his arrow ten paces during the wet season; and the name of Chaeh, a famous bowyer, has been immortalised by the Persians, because his bows were rarely affected either by heat or damp.

But to return. In describing the bow of Pandarus, Homer

says, the two horns were artificially united by a centre piece, which served for the archer's grasp. The old Greek bowyers practised another ingenious contrivance. Without separating the animal's horns from its skull, they sawed off a portion of the *os frontis* to serve for the handle, and then, by means of heat and mechanical appliances familiar to artizans, modelled the whole into its requisite shape. But as no bow can shoot with force unless the centre piece or fulcrum be considerably stronger than either arm, the workman must have provided for this, by the addition of wood, or some similar material. A covering of gilded scrollwork and painted flowers probably completed the work, justifying the epithet "golden," and producing, by its contrast with the glossy jet black horn, an exquisitely beautiful effect. But if the ancient Greek bow had little resemblance to that common to the northern nations of Europe, their mode of shooting was equally dissimilar. Like the modern Turks, Persians, Tartars, and many other Orientals, they drew the bowstring with the thumb, the arrow being retained in its place by the forefinger.

Many sculptures extant in public and private collections, especially those splendid casts from the island of Egina, now in the Bristol Philosophical and Literary Institution, represent several archers drawing the bowstring as I have described.

The modern practice differs also from that of antiquity in another respect. Our English archer pulls the bowstring always to his ear. The Greek, on the contrary, raised his shaft hand only to the breast. The Roman soldier did the same for a considerable period. Latterly, however, they adopted the other method. I think it is the Emperor Leo[*], who observes that drawing to the ear, instead of to the breast, was a great improvement in the archery of his age.

" Doth it become thee," exclaims a very ancient Persian

---

[*] Tactics.

poet, apostrophising his mistress, "doth it become thee to draw thy bow even to thine ear, that the shaft aimed at my bosom may inflict a deeper wound?"*

Procopius also expresses an opinion, that men drew stronger and longer by the former method than by the latter. There is no doubt of it. Let any one, wishing to make the experiment, take up a yew bow of seventy pounds, and try by which of them he can more easily draw a thirty inch arrow to its head.† The statue of the Apollo Belvidere affords one a satisfactory example of the Grecian mode of shooting, and Homer's vivid description places this matter entirely beyond dispute.

> Then by the Greeks unseen, the warrior bends;
> Screen'd by the shields of his surrounding friends:
> There meditates his mark, and crouching low,
> Fits the sharp arrow to the well-strung bow.
> One, from a hundred feathered deaths he chose,
> Fated to wound, and cause of future woes.
> Then offers vows with hecatombs to crown
> Apollo's altar in his native town.
> Now with full force the yielding horn he bends,
> Drawn to an arch, and joins the doubling ends.
> *Close to his breast* he strains the nerve below,
> Till the barb'd point approach the circling bow.
> The impatient weapon whizzes on the wing,
> Sounds the tough horn, and twangs the quivering string.

---

* Persian MS.

† In the last century, a man named Topham exhibited surprising feats of strength at the London theatres, and other places of public resort. Happening to fall in with a party of archers at some tavern near Islington, he seemed inclined to treat the English bow as a toy beneath his attention. One of them, who possessed a tolerably strong bow, forthwith laid him a wager that, notwithstanding his boasted muscular powers, he could not draw an arrow to its head. Confident of success, the giant immediately commenced his trial; but, being ignorant of the positions, drew according to the Grecian, instead of the English, fashion. Of course, the result was, he reluctantly gave in, with the additional mortification of paying the wager. But had he pulled the arrow to his ear, a slight exertion of such strength as his, would have bent the bow till the horns met, or, what is more probable, until it flew into splinters.

The extreme tension here given to the bow, was rendered necessary by the length of the arrow, and could not be safely practised except with one formed of very tough materials. The Tartar horn bows, measuring about four feet in length, admit the use of arrows, which if drawn to the head in an English wooden bow of even six feet, would inevitably shiver it into fragments.

Whilst perusing the above passage, the reader, whether he be or be not an archer, feels enraptured with the fitness and beauty of those epithets by which it is adorned. How truly natural seems the phrase " feathered deaths," when applied to the arrows of an unerring marksman. With no less felicity is the shaft styled " impatient," both from the strain felt in the archer's drawing hand, and the velocity with which, when loosed, it flies towards its destined mark.

The rich resources of Homer's genius are further displayed in that art, with which he varies the circumstances, when describing this action in another part of his poem.

——The string let fly
Sounds shrill and sharp, like the swift swallow's cry,

recalls to our remembrance that enthusiastic burst of the Roman historian *, when he exclaims, " Methinks I see the attitudes of the archer. I hear the twang of his bow!"

Though the Iliad has frequent allusions to this subject, Homer's most finished picture of Grecian archery occurs in the Odyssey. With that exception, however, I believe no trace exists in any very early writer, whereby we may judge of the discipline pursued in training the bowmen of antiquity; nor are we at all familiar with the details of those sportive contests in which also they sometimes engaged.

The return of Ulysses to his native soil, despised and unknown, and the plan devised by Penelope for extricating herself

* Gibbon.

from the dissolute band by whom she was assailed, furnishes all we know on the subject of an ancient Greek archery match. That the trial consisted in a challenge, first, to bend, and then employ her husband's bow, in a feat requiring consummate skill, every schoolboy knows full well. It was a shrewd and happy device; for those abandoned nobles, enervated by luxury, had become so utterly inexpert in manly exercises, that their failure might be securely anticipated. Unconscious, however, of this, they clamorously demanded a trial. It is then the poet indulges in one of those simple and affecting touches of nature peculiar to no age, time, nor individual, since they belong to the unchangeable and noblest impulses of the human heart. Having reached the costly chamber where the weapon was deposited, she lingers in melancholy fondness over this sole relic of her absent lord. Unwilling to part with it hitherto, even for a moment, her heart now upbraids her with an act of profanation, in thus resigning it to the lawless crew whose clamorous orgies still resound within her ear.

> The prudent Queen the lofty stair ascends,
> At distance due, a virgin train attends.
> A brazen key she held, the handle turn'd,
> With steel and polish'd elephant adorn'd;
> Swift to the inmost room she bent her way,
> Where safe reposed the royal treasure lay.
> * * * *
> She moves majestic through the wealthy room,
> Where treasured garments cast a rich perfume.
> Then from the column, where aloft it hung,
> Reach'd in its splendid case*, the bow unstrung.
> Across her knees she laid the well known bow,
> And pensive sate, and tears began to flow.

---

* The bow-cases of modern Orientals form, perhaps, the most costly portion of their military equipments. I have seen something of this sort, so richly adorned with "barbaric gold and pearl," that the value of the former alone was estimated at thirty guineas. The Life of Bayadur˙ Khan has a

As Telemachus could not dig a trench in the marble pavement of a palace court, the contest must have been decided somewhere out of doors, yet near the entrance, on account of the resistance its gate offered to the arrows.

> A trench he opened, in a line he placed
> The level axes, and the points made fast.

None of the critics notice that, when the marks are produced, they prove to be axes, not rings. The ordinary hatchet has no point whereby it could be "made fast." If the rings were poised upon the ends of the handles, while the iron-heads rested upon the ground, a more clumsy, awkward contrivance can hardly be imagined. An equal number of pointed stakes would have done better. Homer, therefore, probably meant the battle or pole-axe, which has always a spear projecting from the head, and not unfrequently a ring at the extremity of the handle. Probably also, they were intended to be carried off by the victor as an additional reward; for at the funereal games in honour of Hector, axes are distributed as prizes.

> Whose weapon strikes yon trembling bird, shall bear
> These two-edged axes, terrible in war.

Although no hint is given us of the precise distance shot, it must have been unquestionably within point blank range, about fifty yards*, otherwise the arrow would have gradually

---

little anecdote about these bow-cases.[1] When Mohammed Sooltan and Hodsun Sooltan were mingled in the forward battle, the former, unconscious that his bow-case had been torn from his hip, passed onwards, sabre in hand. Hodsun, who had seen the bow fall, and between whom and Mohammed there existed a generous rivalry, picked up the weapon and restored it to the warlike Khan, who exclaimed, "Brother, that which thou hast this day performed to me shall be the seal of an eternal friendship between us;" and he remained true to his vow.

* The extreme range of Ulysses' bow may be set down at between four and five hundred yards, when the arrow was elevated to an angle of 45°, the highest point that can extend the flight of a projectile.

---

[1] Vie de Bayadur Khan, p. 118.

descended to the ground, after passing through the first and second ring. I think Plutarch alludes to the sport of driving an arrow through several consecutive rings. The modern Turks frequently amuse themselves with aiming arrows at the circlet used for javelin exercise.* When the Duke of Holstein sent an ambassador to Persia, the shah entertained him with an exhibition of archery, though, as he observed, being past the meridian of life, he had lost much of his youthful dexterity. Still, willing to show the Frank that even "an old man could do somewhat," he suspended by a single horse-hair, one of those thumb rings which the Persians use to bend their bows. Then, placing the youth who held it at the distance of six paces, he cut the hair twice successively with his arrows.† The ring itself is a common mark in that country; but the emperor chose to depart from the ordinary practice, that his guest might be enabled to judge of the accomplishments of his youth, by the feats he was still able to perform at the age of forty-five.

> And now his well-known bow the master bore,
> Turn'd on all sides, and view'd it o'er and o'er,
> Lest time or worms had done the weapon wrong;
> Its owner absent, and untried so long.

But we are approaching the final catastrophe of this domestic drama, which commences with a splendid simile, unparalleled even in the works of a poet, distinguished above all others for the appropriate introduction of that species of illustration.

> Then, as some heavenly minstrel taught to sing
> High notes responsive to the trembling string,
> To some new strain, when he adapts the lyre,
> Or the dumb lute refits with vocal wire,

---

* "The third archer shot through the ring, at which the Albanians had been previously exercising with the lance." — *Vertomannus's Travels in the East.*

† *Ambassador's Travels.*

> Relaxes, strains, and draws them to and fro;
> So the great master drew the mighty bow.
> One hand aloft displayed the bended horns,
> And one the string assay'd.

The son of Laertes, once more feeling the trusty companion of his youthful sports within his grasp, forthwith prepares for a fatal manifestation that his arm still retains its pristine vigour; and the insulters of his honour, and the despoilers of his household, have held their latest revel.

> Then sitting as he was, the chord he drew,
> Through ev'ry ringlet, levelling his view;
> Then notched the shaft, released, and gave it wing,
> The whizzing arrow vanished from the string,
> Sung on direct, and threaded every ring.
> The solid gate its fury scarcely bounds,
> Pierced through and through, the solid gate resounds.

Pope has somewhat obscured the sense of this noble passage. Ulysses appears to draw the bowstring before he applies the arrow to it; equally absurd as if we were to talk of firing off an uncharged fowling piece. Under correction, I conceive the poet's meaning may be thus judiciously paraphrased. After the King of Ithaca had strung his bow, he placed himself opposite the mark, and regarded the circlets through which his arrow was to pass, with a firm and steady look; repeatedly drawing and loosing the bow string as he did so. When his eyes were thus in some degree familiarised with objects to which they had long been strangers, he nocked an arrow on the string, and bringing his arms to the requisite elevation, without an instant's pause, launched it against the mark.

The position in which Homer places Ulysses during the performance of his extraordinary feat, is not unworthy of notice. From the nature of the objects at which he aimed, and their trifling elevation, a sitting posture was certainly the most convenient he could have chosen. A little experiment easily made, will show that a very tall man would be able to command a

Ulysses destroying his Wife's Suitors.

bow five feet six inches, while seated on the ground. This style of shooting has prevailed in Turkey from the earliest period; but whether they copied it from the men whose country they have usurped, I leave for antiquarians to determine. Two travellers of the seventeenth century, Busbequius and our own Sandys, have the following pertinent remarks; for unlike their touring brethren of modern times, they appear to have considered every thing connected with national habits and customs worthy attentive illustration. The former, though a Frenchman, was fond of archery; and he tells us he regularly joined the Turks in their after dinner shooting parties, for the purpose of assisting his digestion.* As the latter lived in an age when every gentleman received a military education, and before the bow had entirely ceased to be a weapon of war, he naturally makes some observations on its use.

"The Turks of Constantinople do constantly exercise themselves in the noble game of archery, sitting cross-legged on carpets spread upon the ground. In divers streets and crossways of Constantinople, there are also places, where, not only children and young men, but even the graver sort, do exercise. There is one that takes care of the butt, who waters it every day, otherwise it would be so dry, that the Turks' arrows, being always blunt, would not well stick therein; and he that oversees the mark is very particular to draw out and cleanse the arrows, and throw them back to the archers; and he hath a stipend from them, sufficient to maintain him. The front of the butt bears some similarity to a little door; whence perhaps was derived the Greek proverb, that when a man missed the mark, he is said to shoot extra januam, 'beside the door;' for I suppose *the Greeks used this way of butting*, and that the Turks borrowed it from them." So far the learned Busbequius. The following are Sandys's remarks: — "Their bows are for form and length not

* "After dinner I exercised myself with the Turkish bow."—*Third Letter.*

unlike the lath of a large cross-bow*, made of the horn of buffaloes, mixed with sinews; of admirable workmanship, and some of them exquisitely gilded. So slothful they be, that they never walk up and down for recreation, nor use any other exercise than shooting. Therein they take as little pains as may be, sitting on cushions in the shadow, and sending their slaves for their arrows. They also shoot against earthern walls ever kept moist in shops and private houses for that purpose, standing not above six paces from the mark, and that with such violence, that the arrow often passes through and through."

Those unacquainted with the prodigious violence with which an arrow is propelled from a strong bow, may perhaps regard the force ascribed to that of Ulysses as a mere poetical exaggeration. An authority or two drawn from the author last quoted, and from the writings of the grave historians of our own country, must remove their scepticism. "I have seen," says Sandys, "their (Turkish) arrows shot by our ambassador through targets of steel, pieces of brass two inches thick, and through wood, with an arrow headed with wood, of eight inches." So stands the original; yet the words "two inches thick," must be a mistransposition, and the sentence should stand thus: "through pieces of wood two inches thick." Even then, with such arrows, I confess, it still appears to me a marvel; however, Lord Bacon asserts the same, and Greaves's Pyramidographia and Barclay's Icon Animorum, have something very like it.

"It happened during a siege," writes Geraldus Cambrensis, "that two soldiers running in haste towards a tower situated at a little distance from them, were attacked with a number of arrows from the Welsh; which being discharged with prodigious violence, some penetrated through the oak doors of a portal, although they were of the breadth of four fingers in thickness."

* Lath, the steel bow. The modern Turkish bows have exactly this form when strung.

In the MS. diary of Edward IV. is a memorandum that on a certain day, a hundred archers of his guard, shot in his presence, twice each, at an inch board of well-seasoned timber. Some of the arrows pierced quite through it; others penetrated that, and also another board placed behind. As deal was then unknown, we may conclude the target to have been made of good solid oak.

Whilst Athens continued free, the citizens maintained a numerous body of archers as a kind of municipal police.* Its wise and polished citizens, showed an excellent discrimination in their choice of these mercenaries, who were Scythians, a nation skilled in the management of the bow †, beyond every other of antiquity. Uninfluenced by the splendour and refinement which every where presented itself, these barbarians retained unaltered, the simple habits which had accompanied them from their native deserts. They lived together in tents, encamped in the most public parts of the city, wore garments formed of skins, and adored the same uncouth images as their countrymen did in the Steppes of Tartary. Altogether, their appearance and mode of living must have presented a singular contrast to the luxury and polished manners of their masters. It was civilisation and barbarism in juxtaposition.

* A work recently announced under the title of "Athens and Sparta, by Mr. J. A. St. John," will probably contain some curious information upon the Greek bow.

† Le dos de la sigma imite, à certain point, la forme de l'arc qu'on voit sur nombre de monumens et de médailles: c'est l'arc Sythe, qui se faisoit du bois léger, mais dont la fibre étoit très liée. On faisoit une roinure en queue d'aronde[1] tout le long du dos, et on y faisoit entrer de force, une verge de corne amollié à la fumée de l'eau bouillante. On sent que cet arc un fois sec, et tendu par des gens tels que les Scythés, devoit fouetter un trait avec une force extrême. Tel étoit le " cydonium cornu," si vanté dans les poètes. — *Athenæus*, 4. 161. *Villebrune.*

[1] Roinure en queue d'aronde — signifies that sort of joint called a dovetail, by carpenters.

By the by, Herodotus narrates a very remarkable instance of sanguinary revenge perpetrated by a tribe of these wandering bowmen, who, revolting from the body of the nation to which they belonged, had taken refuge in Media, during the reign of Cyaxares son of Phraortes. The shah at first received them with open arms, as suppliants, treated them with great hospitality, and entrusted to their care a number of his children to be taught the Tartar language, and the use of the bow. It was the custom of these Scythians to go forth constantly to the chase, but when they returned empty-handed, Cyaxares, a man of ungovernable passions, behaved towards them rudely and contumeliously. Indignant at this, the Scythians soon came to a resolution not to endure it, and, in revenge, to slay one of the children whom they were instructing, and serve his flesh up to the king as game, and both Cyaxares and his courtiers eat of this horrid mess. They then fled to the court of Alyattes, king of Lydia, who, refusing to give them up to the Median monarch, a war ensued, which ultimately terminated in the ruin of the Lydian empire.

Julius Africanus, of whose writings some fragments only have survived to the present time, is one of the few authors of antiquity that treats specifically upon archery. He lived in the reign of the Emperor Severus, to whom, as Eusebius states, he dedicated a portion of his work. In the nine books entitled ΚΕΣΤΟΙ Cestis, he discusses an infinite diversity of subjects, following sometimes his own ideas, sometimes supplying extracts from other authors. His last book has the following curious calculation.* If an arrow were to continue its flight with equal swiftness, and uninterruptedly, for twenty-four hours, it would traverse the distance of twenty thousand stadia, or two thousand five hundred miles. He says the experiment was once made in his presence, in the following manner: Ten men stationed

---

* I here give a translation.

themselves one hundred feet apart, each provided with a strung bow, and an arrow ready nocked. At the instant the first arrow passed over the second archer's head, he also shot; the third did the same, and so on through the whole number. Afterwards, on multiplying the space by the time, it was found that the arrows would be one hour in traversing a thousand stadia, and consequently twenty-four stadia in twenty-four hours. The author deducts four thousand stadia for the time occupied in drawing up, loosing the arrow, &c., thus reducing the calculation, in round numbers, to twenty thousand. This mode of deciding the experiment does not appear very exact; but he cites in confirmation of it, the authority of one Smyrnus a Scythian, and Bardisanes the Parthian, the most famous archer of his time. They made a similar calculation; so that if nothing else, the names of two distinguished men in their way are rescued from oblivion. Julius Africanus then relates anecdotes of several persons of his acquaintance, who had excelled in the art of drawing the bow. He begins by exalting the extraordinary dexterity of a certain King Enanearus and his son Manneres, of whose history, however, like that of our friend King Modus, nothing is at present known. One day when the author accompanied them to the chase, suddenly an enormous boar rushed out of his lair, and furiously attacked the hunter band. While all sought safety in flight, Manneres called on them to fear nothing, and having rapidly discharged two arrows, he pierced the eyes of the animal, so accurately, that being blinded, and no longer formidable to any one, it was despatched without resistance. He next alludes to the singular address of the Parthian Bardisanes above mentioned. This unrivalled archer, once placed a young man armed with a buckler at a certain distance, and aimed with so much precision, that he sketched the outline of a human face with the indentations caused by the points of his arrows. Lastly, he eulogises the exploits of another dexterous bowman, the Syrmus aforesaid, of whose expertness he also states he was himself a frequent spectator. This man exposed his body as a butt to the arrows of another archer, without taking even the precaution of putting on his coat of mail. Depending on his exquisite skill, he aimed with such address, that he never failed to arrest the flight of his antagonist's arrow midway, by striking it with his own. As he used bolts or broad-headed arrows, whilst those of his opponent were pointed, it invariably happened that by the violence of the concussion, the one penetrated the other, and both fell firmly united to the ground.*

Chapters 50, 51, 52. of Africanus's book also relate to archery. Its ancient professors required three qualifications in a well trained bowman, viz. to aim correctly, to shoot with force, and with rapidity. In this division of his work, he treats each acquirement separately. The superiority possessed by the archers of one nation over those of another, says he, is best exhibited when two hostile armies, drawn up in opposition, discharge many successive flights of arrows without changing their ground. It is otherwise when one party remains stationary, and the other is in motion; when both sides shoot as they advance; when one attacks, as the other retreats; or when one side pursues while the enemy, Parthian-like, discharge their arrows as they fly.

The power of shooting with extraordinary force, says Julius, depends on the strength of the bow, and the length of the arrow, as well as on the vigorous arm which practice and continual exercise has fortified. Constant assiduity is likewise requisite to enable archers to discharge the arrow with rapidity. A considerable number were exercised together at the same

* These feats of archery are certainly extraordinary, but I speak advisedly in saying there is nothing of the marvellous in them. Whoever has seen the Bashkir Tartars divide a single horse hair many times successively with an arrow, or recollects the rapidity with which the Indian of Demerara brings down a small bird on the wing, will cease to think them so.

target; each bowman having his arrows differently marked, and when the shooting terminated, the most successful archers received a gratuity in proportion to their adroitness.

It was considered eligible also that the soldiers' training-ground should contain a series of butts, at which the men were exercised, running one after the other, at full speed. All these different branches of archery were subjected to certain rules and to particular discipline. The author then treats of the manner of handling the bow; with how many fingers the string should be drawn, and if it be better to draw to the ear or to the breast; giving an opinion that the archer has greater command over his bow by the former than by the latter method. Lastly, he recommends the shooter to practise assiduously at an elevated, and rarely at a point blank, mark.

Foremost among those Romans, whose adroitness has been thought worthy of record, appear the Emperors Gratian, Commodus, and Domitian. The skill acquired by the former in the management of a horse, the dexterity with which he could dart a javelin, and draw a bow, had inspired him with an ardent passion for the chase. Large parks were enclosed for the imperial pleasure, and plentifully stocked with every species of wild beast. A body of Alana were received into the domestic and military service of the emperor; and the admirable skill they had been accustomed to display in the unbounded plains of Scythia, was exercised in the parks and enclosures of Gaul. In admiration of the talents and customs of these favourite guards, the emperor assumed the fur dress, the bow, and the quiver of a Scythian warrior.*

Many persons living in the reign of Domitian, have seen that emperor slaughter a hundred wild beasts in a single day, at his seat at Alba, where he drew the bow with such dexterity, that, at two successive discharges, he could fix a pair of arrows like horns, upon the heads of the affrighted objects of his aim.

* Gibbon.

Though last in the catalogue of archers royal, not least in reputation is Commodus. Herodian asserts that he never failed of his mark, either with the bow or the lance, and that the most veteran Parthian archers yielded to him the palm of dexterity. The amphitheatre at Rome was the public scene of his exploits, where he slaughtered with his arrows immense numbers of every description of wild animals to gratify his vanity, and increase the accuracy of his aim. But when thus engaged, he preferred showing his art rather than his courage, as he secured himself in a position considerably elevated beyond the reach of any attack. Lions, panthers, stags, and every other species of game fell in vast quanties by his hand, nor was a second arrow necessary, for each wound proved mortal. He could pierce an animal at any particular point he chose with the greatest accuracy, in the head, or in the heart. Occasionally a panther would be set upon a criminal in the Circus; but no sooner was the animal crouching for its fatal spring, than the imperial bowman discharged an arrow, which saved the culprit, and laid his enemy lifeless upon the sand. A hundred lions, and the same number of bears, were introduced at once upon the arena, and with a hundred shafts he laid them prostrate. With arrows having heads of a semicircular form, he frequently amputated the neck of an ostrich when running at full speed; and Herodian further observes, that when the emperor severed the neck of one of these animals, the stroke was so instantaneous that the body sometimes proceeded several paces as if still living: the motion not being immediately checked.

But Cambyses, the son of Cyrus, another celebrated tyrant of antiquity, and equally adroit in the use of this weapon, did not always confine the objects of his aim to inferior animals. Towards the close of his life, he perpetrated several acts which savoured strongly of madness; and among others, the following, which may be considered as the most tragical of all. In the list of his principal courtiers was one Prexaspes, whose son he had promoted to be his cup-bearer, an office esteemed honourable in Persia, as elsewhere. Addressing himself one day to this nobleman, "Tell me, Prexaspes," said he, "in what estimation am I held among the Persians? And what generally do they say of me?"

"My Lord," replied the honest courtier, "they are loud in your praises; but yet think you are somewhat too much addicted to wine."

At this the indignation of Cambyses was kindled, and he exclaimed: "So, then, they imagine me a wine-bibber, and devoid of reason? But thou shalt now be thyself judge whether madness belong to them or to me. For if I shoot thy son, who stands in the door-way yonder, right through the heart, it will be evident that they wrong me; but, if I miss, there will appear to be truth in their accusation." And with the words he bent his bow and shot the youth; and when he dropped, the king commanded his breast to be opened, and the arrow having been found upon examination to have penetrated the heart, he rejoiced and laughed exceedingly, and turning to the father, "you see," said he, "that it is the Persians who are mad, not I. For tell me, whom hast thou ever known who could have shot so true."

Perceiving that the man was mad, and fearing for his own life, Prexaspes replied, "Even the god * could not have taken a surer aim." †

---

* Apollo.

† Herodotus. This anecdote was made the subject of a drama, by one Thomas Preston, about the year 1566, now extremely rare, the title of which runs thus:—" A lamentable Tragedie, mixed full of pleasant Mirth, containing the Life of Cambises King of Persia;" and in truth, it is a very bombastic, fustian sort of production; not, however, entirely destitute of merit as the following lines will testify. To it, Falstaff alludes, when, at the Boar's Head in Eastcheap, he proposes to counterfeit the king, and examine Prince Hal upon the particulars of his wayward life. "I must speak in passion," says he, "and I will do it in King Cambyses' vein."

I shall close this chapter with an anecdote of a celebrated Greek archer, named Aster, who, whilst King Philip was be-

---

Prexaspes addressing Cambyses.

The Persians much do praise of our grace, but one thing discommend,
In that to wine, subject you be, wherein you do offend.
Sith that the might of wine's effect, doth oft subdue your brain,
My council is, to please their hearts, from it you would refrain.

King.

—— Prexaspes, tell me why,
That to my mouth in such a sort, thou should'st announce a lie?
Of drunkenness me thus to charge, but thou with speed shall see,
Whether that I a sober king, or else a drunkard be.
I know thou hast a blissful babe wherein thou dost delight;
Me to revenge of these thy words, I will go wreke this spite.
When I the most have tasted wine, my bow it shall be bent,
At heart of him even then to shoot, is now my whole intent;
And if that I his heart can hit, the king no drunkard is;
If heart of his I do not kill, I yield to thee in this.
Therefore, Prexaspes, fetch to me thy youngest son with speed,
There is no way, I tell thee plain, but I will do this deed.

Prexaspes.

Redoubted prince, spare my sweet child, he is mine only joy;
I trust your grace to infant's heart no such thing will employ.
If that his mother hear of this, she is so nigh her flight,
In clay her corps will soon be shrined, to pass from world's delight.

King.

For fear of my displeasure great, goe fetch him unto me.
Is he gone? Now by the gods, I will do as I say;
My lord, therefore fill me some wine, I heartily you pray,
For I must drink to make my brain somewhat intoxicate.
When that the wine is in my head, O! trimly I can prate.

Lord.

Here is the cup with filled wine, thereof to take repast.

King.

Give it me to drink it off, and see no wine be waste;
Once again enlarge this cup, for I must taste it still.
By the gods, I think of pleasant wine, I cannot take my fill.

sieging a certain city, solicited to be received among his troops. It would seem, the Macedonian monarch estimated this soldier's

---

Now drink is in, give me my bow, and arrows from Sir Knight,
At heart of child I mean to shoot, hoping to cleave it right.

KNIGHT.

Behold, O King, where he doth come, his infant son in hand.

PREXASPES.

O mighty king, your grace's behest with sorrow I have scann'd,
And brought my child fro mother's knee, before you to appear,
And she thereof no whit doth know, that he in place is here.

KING.

Set him up my mark to be, I will shoot at his heart.

PREXASPES.

I beseech your grace not so to do, set this design apart.—
Farewel, my dear and loving babe, come kiss thy father dear.
A grievous sight to me it is, to see thee slain even here.
Is this the gain now from the king for giving counsel good,
Before my face, with such despite, to spill my son's heart's blood?
A heavy day to me this is, and mother in like case.

YOUNG CHILD.

O father, father, wipe your face,
  I see the tears run from your eye.
My mother is at home sewing of a band.
  Alas! dear father, cease you thus to cry.

KING.

Before me as a mark now let him stand,
I will shoot at him my mind to fulfil.

YOUNG CHILD.

Alas, alas! father, will you me kill?
Good master king, don't shoot at me, my mother loves me best of all.

CAMBYSES SHOOTS.

See, I have despatched him! down doth he fall;

military qualifications at the same ignoble rate as Lycus did those of Alcmena's son.

>   ——— He with no merit held
> The fame of daring courage;
> His left hand never knew to raise the shield,
> Never advanced his right the spear, but held
> The bow, a coward's weapon; and to flight
> Was always prompt: no proof of manhood, none
> Of daring courage, is the bow.

Be this as it may, he rejected his application, and the disappointed archer took an early opportunity of rejoining the besieged. One day, whilst stationed on the walls, he espied Philip within bowshot. Hastily inscribing on an arrow, "To Philip's right eye, Aster sends the king a deadly messenger," he drew, and the shot took effect. Then Philip retaliated by ordering an arrow to be discharged among the besieged, labelled thus:

As right as line his heart I've hit.
Nay! thou shalt see, Prexaspes, stranger news yet,
Ho, knight! with speed his heart cut out, and give it unto me.

KNIGHT.

It shall be done, O mighty king, with all celerity.

LORD.

My Lord Prexaspes, this had not been, but your tongue must be walking:
To the king of correction you must needs be talking.

KNIGHT.

Here is the heart, according to your grace's behest.

KING.

Behold, Prexaspes, thy son's own heart:
Oh! how well the same was hit:
After this wine to do this deed, I thought it very fit.
Esteem thou may'st right well thereby, no drunkard is the king,
That, in the midst of all his cups, could do this valiant thing.
My lord and knight, on me attend, to palace we will go,
And leave him here to take his son, when we are gone him fro.

"When Philip takes the city he will hang up Aster." And he was enabled to execute his threat.

Here, gentle archers, reluctantly bidding ye adieu, I abandon my pen, which, although no longer, as of old, a tribute from the grey goose wing, still resembles a good arrow in its well tempered steel-point. Many of the older writers with whom I have recently been on familiar terms — and men say, we become personally acquainted with an author through his works — conclude their labours with this classical motto, FINIS CORONAT OPUS. In humble imitation of this example, allow me to subjoin a plain English one, — MAY SUCCESS CROWN MINE. Yet a few anxious weeks, and all expectations on this point will be set at rest. *En attendant,* let us cheer our hearts by joining in a congenial, old-fashioned roundelay.

> Bright Phœbus, the patron of poets below,
>   Assist me of archers to sing;
> For thou art accounted the god of the *bow,*
>   As well as the god of the *string.*
>
> The practice of shooting 't was you that began,
>   When you launched forth your beams from the skies;
> Young Cupid was first in adopting the plan,
>   Next, the goddesses shot with — their eyes.
>
> On beautiful Iris, Apollo bestow'd
>   A bow of unparalleled hue;
> The herald of peace — and as on it she rode,
>   Like a swiftly winged arrow she flew.
>
> Diana, who slaughter'd the brutes with her darts,
>   Ne'er pierced but one lover or so,
> For Venus excelled her in shooting at hearts,
>   And had always more strings to her bow.
>
> To earth came the craft of the archer at last,
>   And 't was followed with eager pursuit;
> Still, the sons of Apollo all others surpassed,
>   With such monstrous long bows did they shoot.

Ulysses the hero, was known long ago,
  In wisdom and strength to excel; —
So he left in his house an inflexible *bow*,
  And a still more inflexible *belle*.

The Parthians were archers of old, and their pride
  Lay in shooting and scampering too;
But Britons thought better their sports to divide,
  So they shot, — and their *enemies* flew!

Then a health to all true British bowmen be crown'd;
  May their glory ne'er set in the dark,
May their bows e'er prove strong, their strings ever sound,
  And their arrows drive straight at the mark.

THE END.

LONDON:
Printed by A. SPOTTISWOODE,
New-Street-Square.

OUTLINE ILLUSTRATIONS,

SELECTED, ARRANGED, AND ENGRAVED ON STEEL,

BY

W. H. BROOKE, F.S.A.

THE following series of Illustrative Etchings, relative to the use and management of the Bow from the earliest authentic period of antiquity, are from the pencil of W. H. Brooke, F.S.A., to whom this portion of the embellishments was allotted. The subjects, in consequence, have been carefully selected from the most correct and valuable authorities, redrawn and etched on steel by himself, and chronologically arranged from the Egyptian age, through the different nations of the world down to the present period; thus affording the young Toxophilite an opportunity of judging, at a single view, of the actual form, dimensions, and usage of each variety of the bow and arrow throughout the globe.

DESCRIPTION

OF

THE OUTLINE ILLUSTRATIONS.

PLATE I.
EGYPTIAN AND GRECIAN IMPLEMENTS.

1. Egyptian quiver for arrows. 2. Egyptian quiver. 3. Egyptian arrow. 4. Græco-Egyptian quiver. 5. Quiver for arrows with cover. 6. Etruscan bow. 7. Phrygian quiver and bow-case. 8. Grecian bow. 9. Grecian arrow. 10. Phrygian quiver;— Sir Samuel Meyrick on Ancient Armour.

PLATE II.
EARLY EGYPTIAN ARCHERS.

1. Rameses III. returning triumphant in his chariot;— from the sculptured walls at Thebes. — Denon. 2. Sesostris slaying his enemies with arrows; —from the sculptured walls at Ipsambul. — Champollion.

PLATE III.

1. Amenophis the vanquisher, and his army of archers. 2. Egyptian archer shooting with a bird-bolt. 3. Egyptian in the act of stringing his bow — Rosselini's coloured work of Egyptian sculpture.

PLATE IV.
GRECIAN AND ORIENTAL IMPLEMENTS.

1. Theban bow-case and quiver. 2. Roman quiver of arrows. 3. Grecian arrow. 4. Theban Greek bow. 5. Theban Greek bow in ornamented

case. 6. Calcutta bow. 7. Hindostanee bow. 8. Four varieties of Indian arrows. 9. Indian bow of antelope's horn, covered with fish skin. 10. Ancient Turkish bow-case and arrows;—Sir Samuel Meyrick; Columnâ Trajana, and No. 6. and 7. from bows in the possession of the author.

PLATE V.

GRECIAN AND PERSEPOLITAN.

1. Greek and Trojan archers contending for the dead body of Patroclus;—from "Gallerie Mythologique." 2. Darius Hystaspes hunting;—from a sulphur cast taken from a small cylinder or signet found in the ruins of Persepolis.

PLATE VI.

MACEDONIAN AND PARTHIAN.

1. Battle of Alexander the Great against Darius;—from mosaic pavement discovered at Pompeii. 2. Parthian archers. 3. Macedonian archers;—from Columnâ Trajana et Antonina.

PLATE VII.

ROMAN.

1. Roman cavalry;—from the bas-reliefs of "Triumphus Sigismundi." 2. Roman foot archers in scale armour. 3. Roman pedestrian archers in iron belt armour;—Columnâ Trajana.

PLATE VIII.

ORIENTAL IMPLEMENTS.

1. Persian bow. 2, 3, 4, Ancient Persian arrow heads of steel. 5. Polygar Indian quiver. 6. Japanese bow-case of leather, gilt and ornamented. 7. Chinese quiver of arrows. 8. Chinese bow, and ornamented bow-case. 9. Persian thumb ring of agate. 10. Vambrace (Bracci) of the Tartar tribes. 11. Tartar bow; form of the Ancient Scythian bow;—Alexander's Costume of China, and Meyrick's Armour.

PLATE IX.

PERSIAN.

1. Persian prince slaying a dragon;—from the Shah Namah, a highly illuminated Persian MS. supposed of the 10th century. 2. Modern Persian archers shooting on horseback.

PLATE X.

CHINESE AND TARTAR.

4. Chinese military bowman. 2. Mandarin of war. 3. Tartar dragoon. 1. Yakouti Tartar;—from Alexander's China, and Müller's Costume of Russia.

PLATE XI.

AMERICAN AND AFRICAN IMPLEMENTS.

1. Bow of whalebone and wood; from N. W. Coast of America. 2. Bow made from root of the vine; from New Hebrides. 3. Wooden bow strengthened with string. 4. Reed arrows with flint heads; from N. American Indians. 5. Bow from Asiatic coast of N. Pacific Ocean. 6. Bows of wood from the Tschutski. 7. Ornamented quiver from Tongataboo. 8. Bamboo quiver from Otaheite. 9. Bow of the Gambian Africans. 10. Multibarbe arrow from S. Africa. 11. Hottentot arrow. 12. Quiver of arrows of African Bushmen. 13. Quiver of arrows of Gambian Africans. 14. Bow of cane from Central Africa;—Sir Samuel Meyrick's Collection of ancient Armour at Goodrich Court, engraved by Skelton.

PLATE XII.

AFRICAN.

1. Mounted Mameluke archers of 1800; from Denon's folio work on Egypt. 2. Ethiopian prince. 3. Hottentot Bushman;—Vienne's Caravanne, and Habitus Variarum.

PLATE XIII.

ORIENTAL.

1. East Indian natives in 1650. 2. Malabar Indians. 3. Circassians. 4. Turkish Spahi;—Vienne's Caravanne, and Col. Todd's India.

DESCRIPTION OF THE

PLATE XIV.
NORTHERN ASIA.

1. Tungoose. 2. Kamschatdale. 3. Samoyed hunter. 4. Kirghi Russians;—from Sir Robert Ker Porter's Travels in Russia; Müller's work on Russia, and Voyage en Siberie.

PLATE XV.
SOUTH AND NORTH AMERICA.

1. Monte Video Indian. 2. Mexican Indian. 3. Ottawa N. American, 4. Cherokee Indian;—Recueil des Habillements des différentes Nations, and Harper's N. American Indians.

PLATE XVI.
GRECIAN AND BRITISH IMPLEMENTS.

1. 3. Grecian arrow heads found on the Plains of Marathon. 2. Ancient British arrow heads of flint. 4. Grecian bronze arrow head found at Persepolis. 5. Ornamented ivory bracer, temp. Eliz. 6, 7. British arrow heads. 8. Ornamented case for bird-bolts, temp. Eliz. 9, 10, 11, 12, 13, 14, 15. Arbalist, quarrils, bird-bolts, verrous, &c., for hunting. 16, 17, 18, 19, 20, 21, 22, 23, Ancient arrow heads of various forms;—Grose's Military Antiquities. Meyrick's Inquiry on Ancient Armour; Skelton's Illustrations of Armour at Goodrich Court.

PLATE XVII.
EARLY ENGLISH.

1. Saxon archer of the year 730. 2. Saxon hunter. 3. Norman archers, A. D. 1066, in flat ringed armour. 4. Norman archer in leathern vest; same date. 5. English archer of 1250, with the " Spicula Ignita," or arrow headed with Greek fire;—Meyrick's Armour, and Strutt's Military Antiquities.

PLATE XVIII.
THE ARBALIST OR CROSSBOW.

1. Arbalist, date 1579, exquisitely carved in black oak. 2. The Sphynx. 3. Steel bow. 4. Lock. 5. The bridge. 6. The arrow. 7. Large stir-

ruped crossbow with moulinet pulleys and two movable handles. 8. Richly ornamented crossbow at Goodrich Court. 9. Quarril formed of bone, found at the Danish earth works, Danbury. 10. Arbalist, or Arcus Balistanus ; — Sir Samuel Meyrick on Ancient Armour; the Mirror, vol. xix., and Grose's Military Antiquities.

PLATE XIX.

EARLY ENGLISH ARCHERY.

1. Archer shooting at a mark. 2. Female archer hunting a buck. 3. Archers practising with the crossbow ;—from Illuminated MS. Brit. Mus. 2 B vii. temp. 1320 and 1330.

PLATE XX.

ENGLISH ARCHERY, 11th and 12th CENTURIES.

1. Mounted archer with hauberk, surcoat, and conical helmet. 2. Foot archer similarly equipped, drawing his bow. 3. Foot archer in hauberk, surcoat, &c., stringing his bow ; these three archers are temp. Edward II., 1312. 4. Norman cross-bowman, A.D. 1259. 5. English cross-bowman at battle of Cressy, with stirruped arbalist, moulinet, and pulleys, 1356 ;— Sir John Froissart's Chronicles ; Sir Samuel Meyrick's Inquiry into Ancient Armour.

PLATE XXI.

ENGLISH AND SWISS ARCHERS.

1. English cross-bowman and pavisiers of 1380. 2. Italian cross-bowman, 1472. 3. William Tell. 4. Swiss archer, costume of 1450 ;—Hamilton Smith's Ancient Costume of England. Swiss Costume by Hans Holbein. Ancient wood-cut by Ulric Hahn, printed at Verona.

PLATE XXII.

FRENCH AND ENGLISH.

1. French archers of 1442. 2. French cross-bowman of 1460. 3. Archer of the Scottish Guard in the service of Louis XI. of France, 1471 (vide Sir Walter Scott). 4. English bowmen temp. Edward IV. 1482 ;— Montfaucon's Monarque Française Attaque de la Bastille de Dieppe ; Hamilton Smith's Ancient Costume of England.

PLATE XXIII.
ENGLISH ARCHERY, 14th, 15th, and 16th CENTURIES.

1. Brigandine archer, 1554. 2. Archer in brigandine armour stringing his bow, 1590. 3. King Charles I. as an archer, 1625. 4. Costume of English bowmen in 1780;—Skelton's Outlines of Armour at Goodrich Court; Markham's Book of Archerie.

PLATE XXIV.
MODERN ARCHERY.

1. Scottish archers of the King's Royal Body Guard practising in 1745. 2. Meeting of Royal British bowmen at Erthig, Denbighshire, the seat of Simon York, Esq.;—original drawing by one of the members.

EGYPTIAN AND GRECIAN IMPLEMENTS.

I.

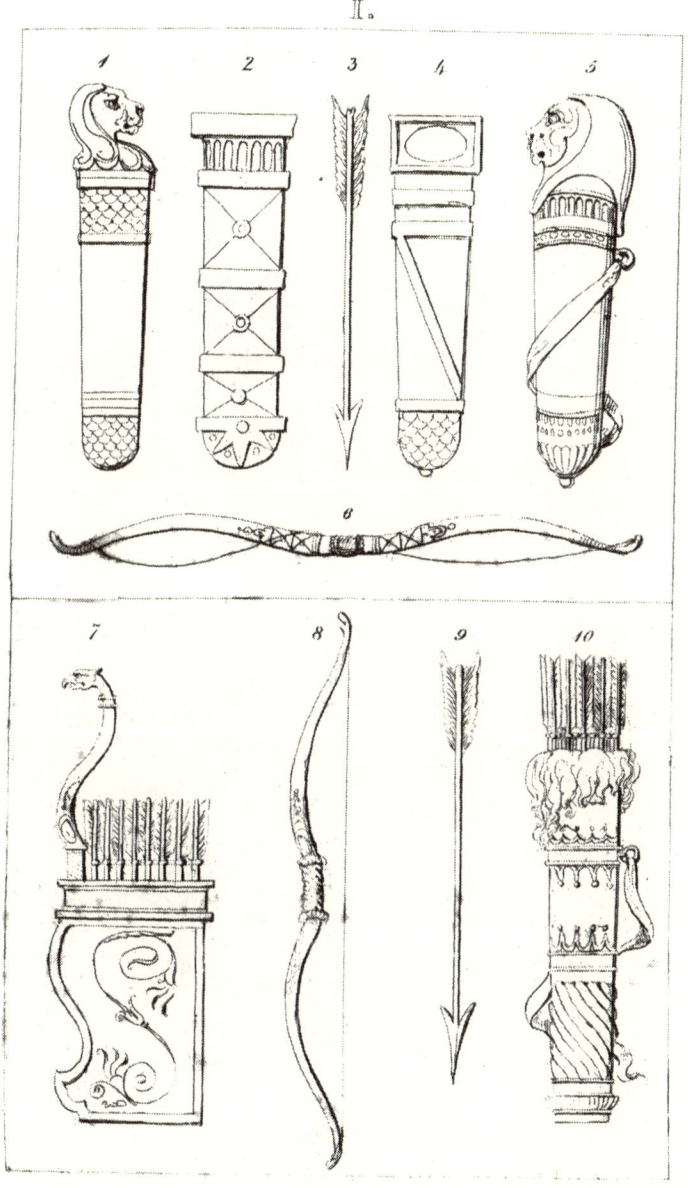

EARLY EGYPTIAN ARCHERS.

II.

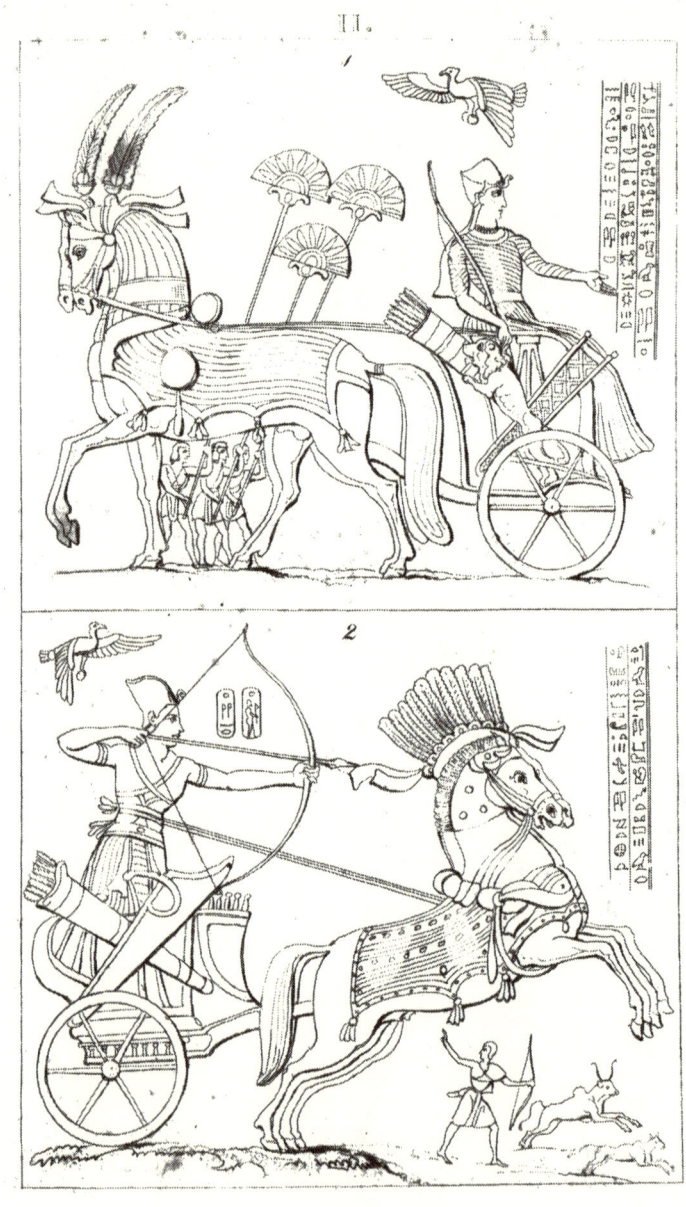

EARLY EGYPTIAN.

III.

GRECIAN AND ORIENTAL.

IV.

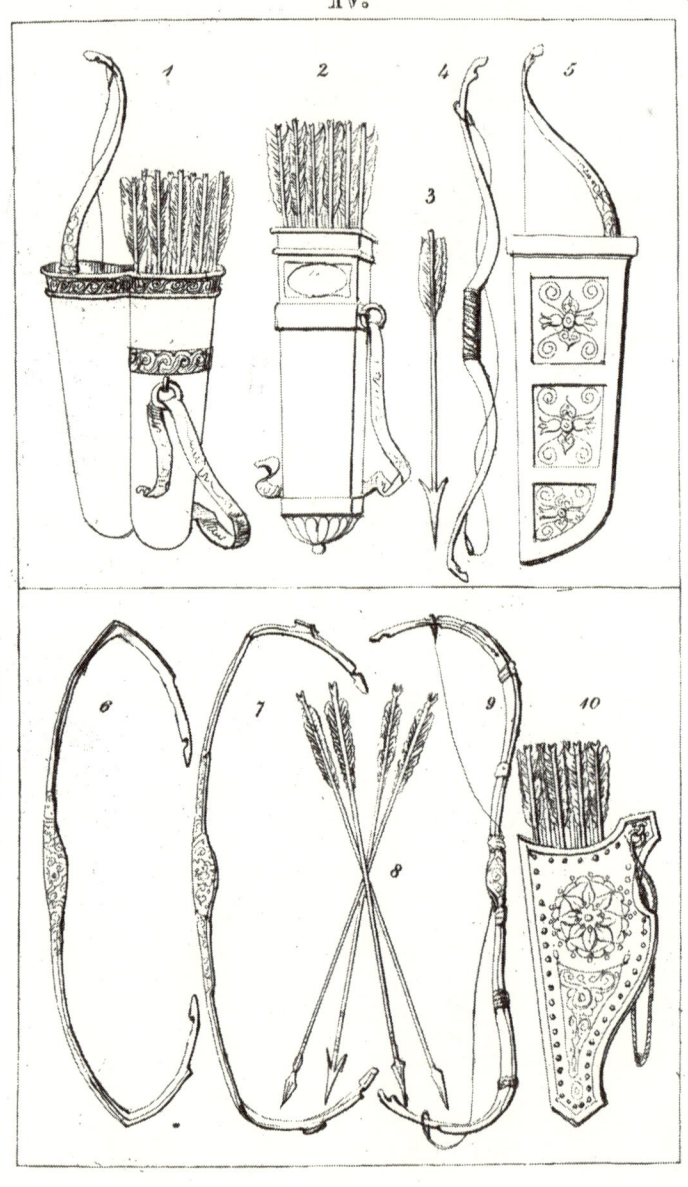

GRECIAN AND PERSEPOLITAN.

V.

1

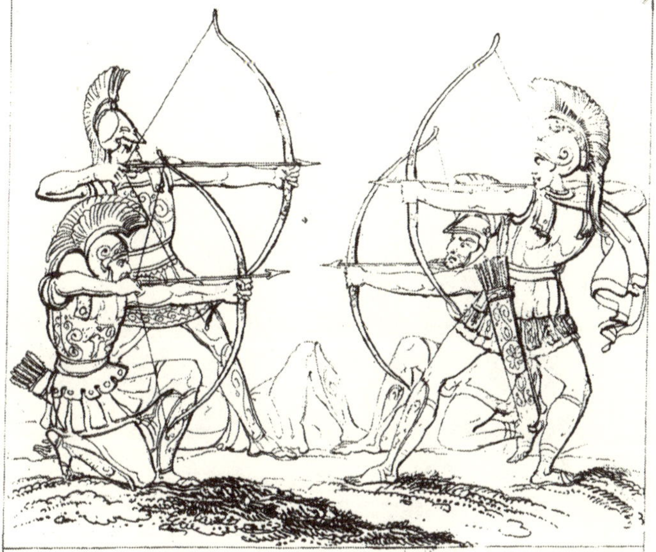

2

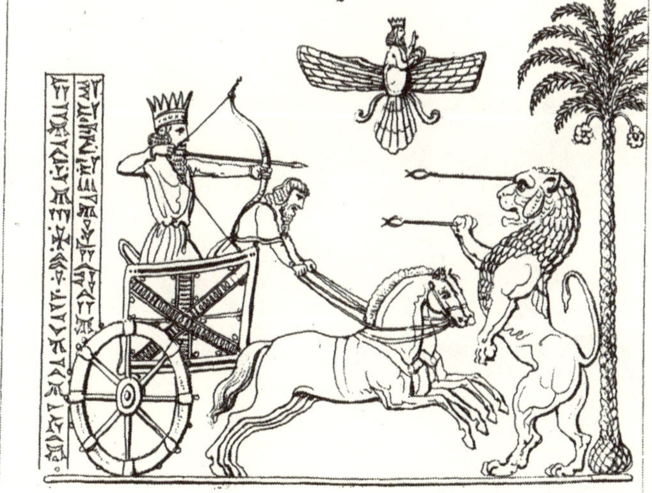

MACEDONIAN AND PARTHIAN.
VI.

ROMAN ARCHERS.
VII.

ORIENTAL IMPLEMENTS.

VIII.

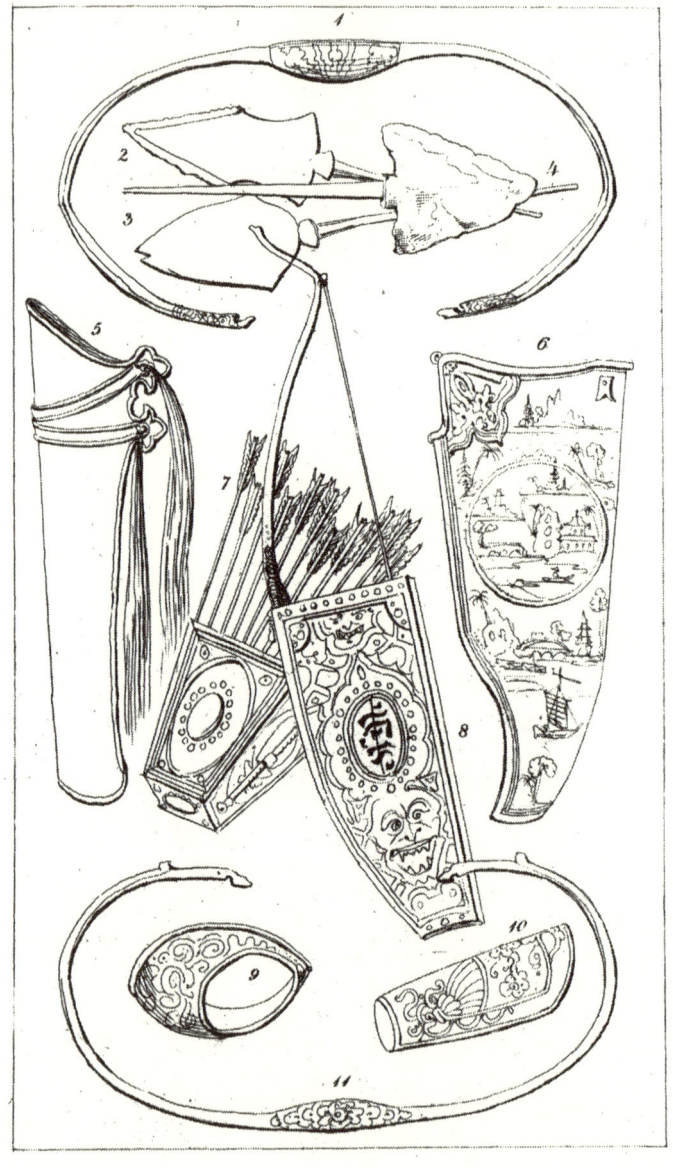

PERSIAN ARCHERY.
IX.

CHINESE AND TARTAR.

X.

AMERICAN AND AFRICAN.
XI.

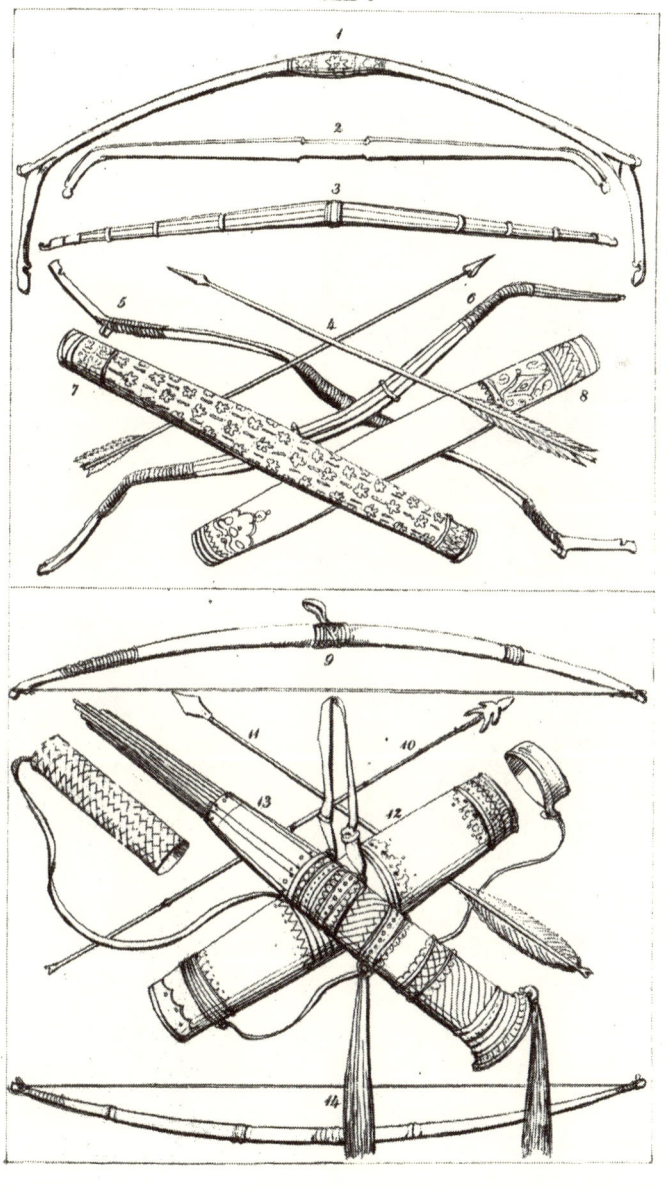

AFRICAN ARCHERS.

XII.

ORIENTAL ARCHERY.
XIII.

NORTHERN ASIA.
XIV.

SOUTH AND NORTH AMERICAN.
XV.

GRECIAN AND BRITISH.
XVI.

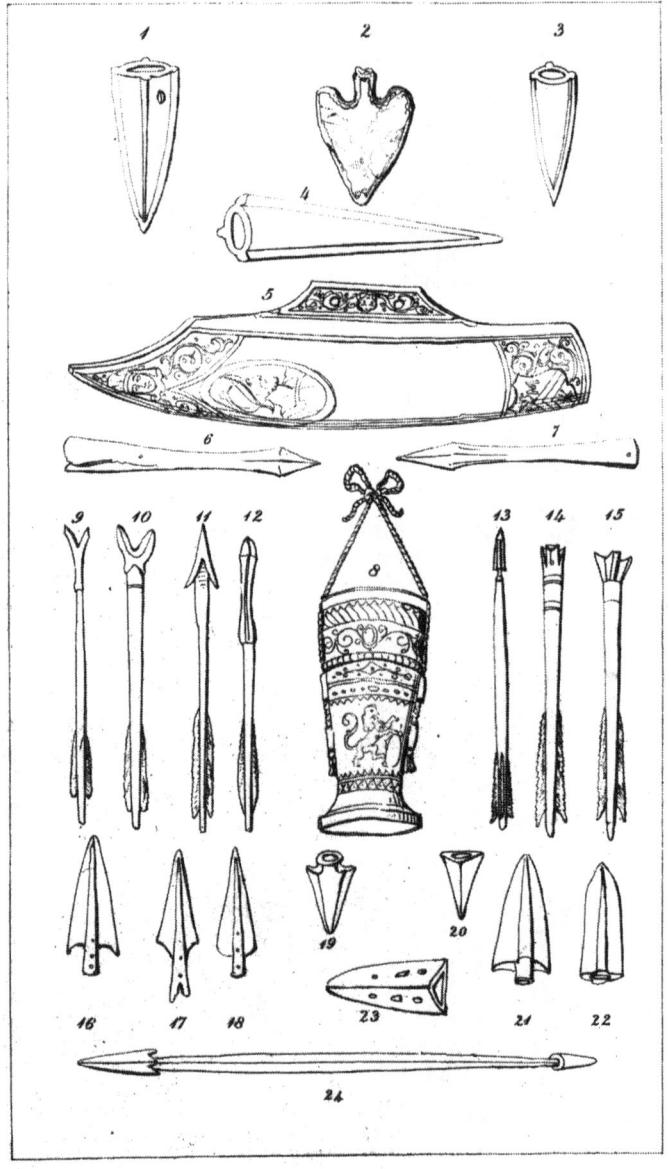

SAXON AND NORMAN.
XVII.

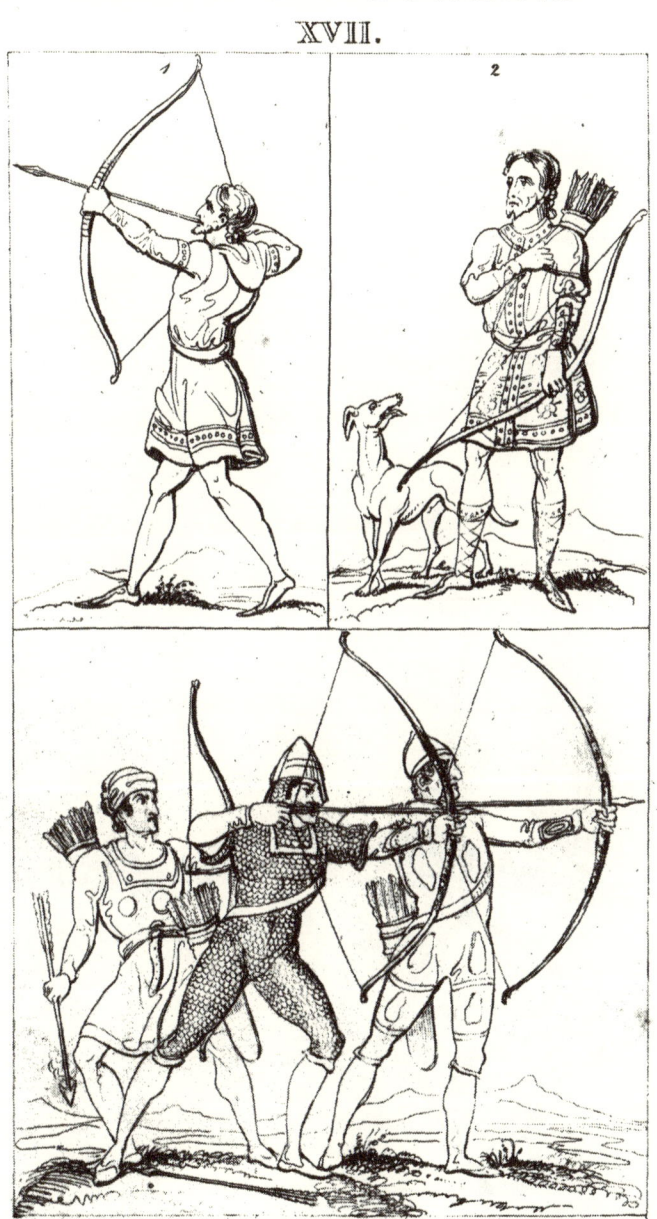

ARBALIST OR CROSS-BOW.
XVIII.

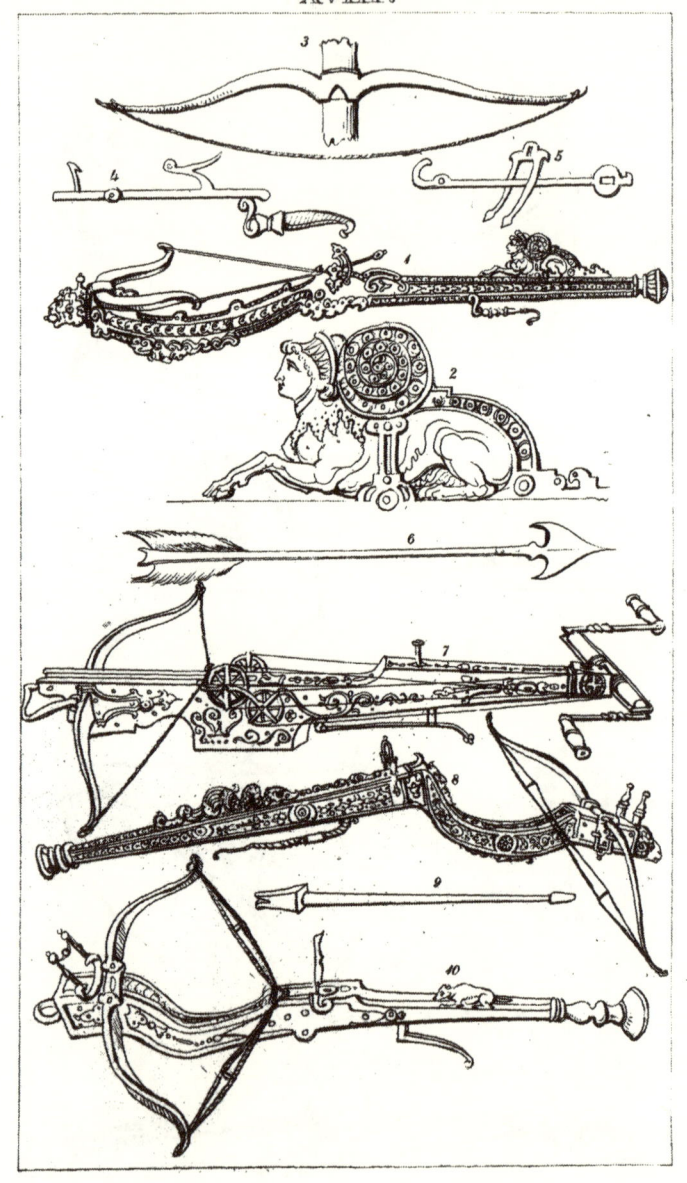

EARLY ENGLISH.
XIX.

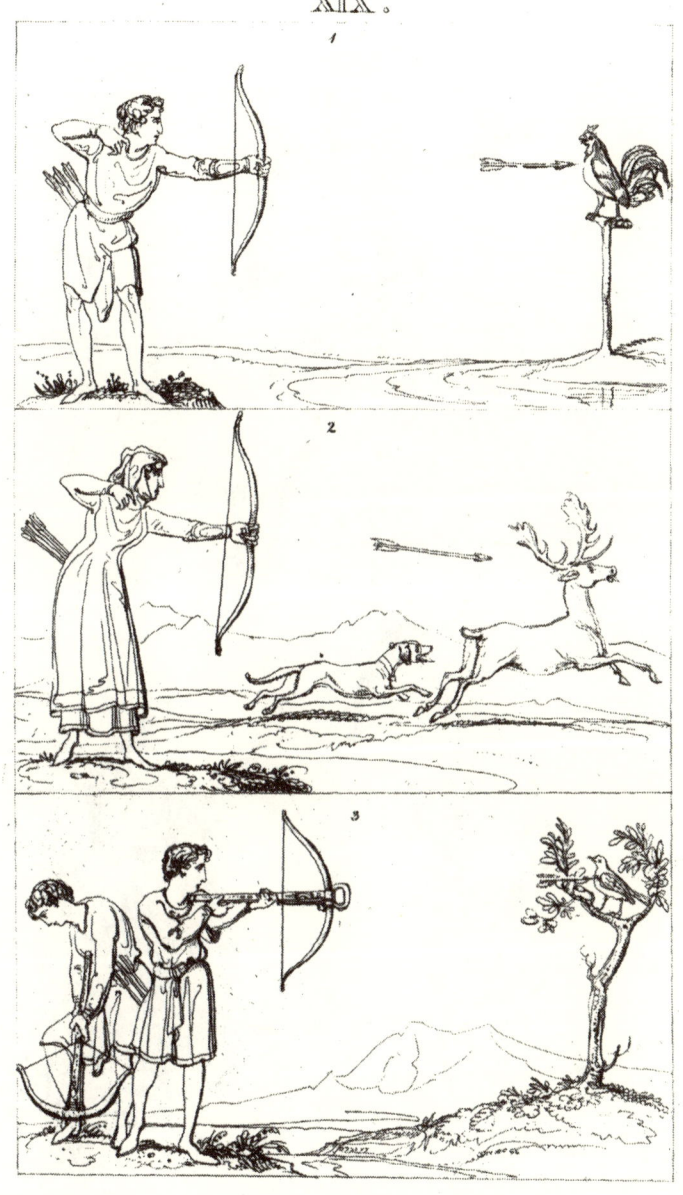

EARLY ENGLISH.
XX.

ENGLISH AND SWISS.
XXI.

FRENCH and ENGLISH.
XXII.

XXIV.

www.ingramcontent.com/pod-product-compliance
Lightning Source LLC
Chambersburg PA
CBHW030409100426
42812CB00028B/2882/J